# STARVE
# THE
# BEAST!

## HOW TO SAVE AMERICA

# DAVE DOUGHERTY

## A must read for everyone!

At a time when Congress and the United States Supreme Court have abandoned their constitutional responsibilities to check the power of the presidency, and when every new bill emanating from Congress ladles on more spending, more debt, and more regulations to the American economy and more restrictions on personal liberty, what can a citizen do?

Dave Dougherty has some answers and offers a detailed strategic plan for taking on the federal government in a much different way—by denying it the money it needs to grow. He doesn't expect this to be painless or without sacrifice, and to his credit Dougherty lays out every response a citizen will meet, and soberly walks the reader through each cost. In the end, it will be up to individual Americans to decide it they can, and will, stop the out-of-control monster we call the federal government… before it's too late.

Larry Schweikart, best-selling author of *A Patriot's History of the United States*.

By making the historic link to tactics successfully employed by the Founders against British tyranny, *Starve the Beast!* provides a pathway for today's patriots desiring liberty from an ever-increasingly oppressive government.

Richard C. Fischer, Publisher; *White River Current*

## AUTHOR BIO:

Dave Dougherty is the author of a Civil War history book, as well as co-author of three books with Larry Schweikart, and a producer with Rockin' the Wall Studios. Formerly a professor of management and computer science at Cleveland State University and the University of Texas at El Paso, Dougherty also has had an extensive career in private industry, both as an executive and an entrepreneur. An ex-intelligence case officer, Dougherty specializes in intelligence history as well as military history. He has an extensive regional political following in Arkansas and Missouri, has hosted his own radio show, and makes numerous civic and political speeches in the region. It was through his efforts that the Secretary of Interior was forced to withdraw his designation of the White River watershed as a National Blueway in 2013. In spite of his academic, technical, and business accomplishments, Dougherty is relatively unknown nationally.

# Table of Contents

# Introduction

As of this moment, the United States is still head and shoulders above all other nations, and we still are functioning, or at least many of us are, under the principles of American Exceptionalism and its four great pillars, a Protestant Christian culture, Common Law, the sanctity of private property, and free-market capitalism. Unfortunately, all four of these elements, the basic foundation of our culture that has made us great, are under heavy assault by the forces of Progressivism. Whether the United States will survive as the land of the free and the home of the brave, indeed, will survive at all, is absolutely in doubt.

The same questions keep coming up. "How can our downfall be stopped?" "What will it take?" "What can I do?"

One must look back at 1774, when the first Continental Congress was formed, and at the Articles of Association it produced on October 20th. Although not a constitution, that document put the American Revolution into motion and ensured that patriot energy and commitment to combat England's tyranny would be sufficient to achieve independence. It has particular relevance for grass roots Tea Partiers. Their movement to restore liberty and fiscal sanity in the United States has weakened over time without institutional recognition, a national organization, and most of all, funding. They also lacked new Articles of Association.

In June of 1774 the Boston Port Act went into effect and one newspaper opined, "Every act, however injurious to freedom, loses its horror by repetition. Thus by progressive steps, and the pleading of precedents, we may expect shortly to see all of our most valuable privileges taken from us, without so much as feeling their loss, till their restoration is irremediable."[1]

What was true in 1774 is true today: what the steady drumbeat of

Progressive changes is wreaking on American liberties *is* losing its horror by repetition. The trend is ***only*** in one direction—the loss of individual freedom and the establishment of big government tyranny. The evidence is there for all to see. What cabinet department has ever been eliminated? Only the Navy Department, but it actually grew larger when integrated into the Department of Defense. The Departments of Energy and Education have utterly failed to accomplish their missions, yet every year they grow. And every year they fail more grievously. Even when a lower-level organization is abolished through a sunset provision like the Interstate Commerce Commission, its functions and employees are absorbed by other departments. Only wartime agencies seem vulnerable to elimination, but, even then, there is often a relatively straight line to successor organizations. For example, the Office of Strategic Services in World War II was abolished in 1945, but soon resurrected through intermediate agencies as the Central Intelligence Agency in 1947.

Only very rarely are cases of government overreach, outright errors in judgment, or legislative mistakes corrected in the passage of time. Only a single constitutional amendment has ever been repealed: the 18th, dealing with the manufacture, sale, and transportation of intoxicating liquors. Although some of the original articles have been modified, such as the mechanism for electing senators, more often, amendments subsequent to the Bill of Rights extended Federal powers. The "equal protection" and "due process" clauses in the 14th Amendment have been interpreted to give the Federal Government extraordinary powers in addition to those specified in the articles, and the $16^{th}$ Amendment, giving the Federal Government the power to tax incomes, established a solid financial base for unlimited government expansion.

The concept of American Exceptionalism has been around in various forms since Alexis de Tocqueville wrote about the exceptional nature of Americans and their political system in his *Democracy in America* in 1835, but until recently, there has been little agreement on a definition, or indeed, what the term means at all. Many people apparently believe it refers to the nation's geographical advantages, various appealing aspects of its political system or its people, or the national identity as demonstrated by individual Americans.

Charles Murray, in his work *American Exceptionalism*, discovered the term was first coined by Joseph Stalin when he denounced the "heresy of American exceptionalism" in 1929.[2] Murray identified several features of the concept, including the stress on limited government and individual liberties, industriousness, egalitarianism, religiosity, and civic involvement. But these are attitudes and behaviors of the people, not elements of a system under which people live. Other writers have made equally tortuous definitions, some to dispel, ridicule, or mythologize American Exceptionalism in an attempt to reduce the United States to just another country, no better or worse than any other state.[3] Perhaps the ultimate dismissal of American Exceptionalism was made by President Barack Obama in 2009, "I believe in American exceptionalism, just as I suspect that the Brits believe in British exceptionalism and the Greeks believe in Greek exceptionalism."[4] This was the view of someone who was not, culturally, an American, and lacked a grasp of what his constituents believed.

The definition used in this work is that developed by historians Larry Schweikart and Dave Dougherty and first published in 2012 in their " *A Patriot's History of the Modern World.*"[5] In their work, American Exceptionalism was defined as having four basic pillars upon which the culture of America and the characteristics of its people rested: Christianity (especially Protestant Christianity), Common Law, the sanctity of private property, and free-market capitalism.

*Christianity—particularly Protestant Christianity.* From that comes latitudinarianism, associations, civic participation, morality, charity, and virtue. Latitudinarianism is defined as tolerance of various doctrines and beliefs, and at the secular, policy-making level, it is the idea that no single religion is the one true religion and all others heresies or abominations, but instead, all religions can be right for their believers. It is what allows competing religions to peacefully co-exist, and was a standard feature of the religions in the thirteen colonies at the time of America's founding.

In 1795, even Roman Catholics under Bishop John Carroll accepted this idea, and, in its spirit, Carroll did everything is his power to develop common ground with Protestantism. But the importance of religion for American Exceptionalism lies not in being tolerant, but in establishing a basis for universal virtue in the citizenry. A representative democracy can only function if a majority of the voting citizens are virtuous. Virtue requires morality, enforced through believing in a higher power than oneself, and that requires religion. For example, because

3

most Americans are virtuous, we pay taxes voluntarily—a concept virtually unknown in the vast majority of other nations.

*Common Law*. This is law that comes from God—a Judeo-Christian God—directly to the people. The people then put the law into effect through religious adherence and common practice, and elect or appoint representatives to codify and administer that law. In almost all other nations in the world, some type of Civil Law reigns—law that is made by an emperor, high religious authority, dictator, king, or cabal of elites, and descends on the people to obey as subjects.

*Sanctity of Private Property*. People can own and use their property as they see fit.—It is not awarded by government to favored individuals, but is based on a system of deeds and ownership documents, maintained by the state, open to all, and clearly establishing and maintaining ownership rights. In the vast majority of nations today such a system does not exist. People are forced to bribe government officials to own or retain property, and ownership is always tenuous. Without proof of property ownership, people cannot pledge their assets as collateral on loans, thus rendering capitalism nearly stillborn in most nations to a very large degree. In the case of intellectual property, most nations do not protect such ownership except for people or corporations with influence.

*Free market capitalism*. Our Founding Fathers bequeathed to American citizens a system in which anyone and everyone could start a business or means of earning a living as he saw fit. Whether the individual prospered or not was dependent upon his ability, knowledge, and industry, not on government favors or assistance. Government did not set prices and control production, and with everyone free to compete, heretofore unimaginable innovation and productivity took place. Public infrastructure was built by entrepreneurs themselves: roads, ferries, bridges, railroads, electric lighting systems, and even airports. Free-market capitalism allowed every individual to select his own place of residence, career, religion, life style, and political orientation. In the U.S., no one had to de-register and re-register with the police when moving from one city to another (a common practice in Europe), and until the late 20th century, few occupations were licensed and controlled by the government.

These four pillars of American Exceptionalism—that no other country possesses anywhere close to the degree found in the U.S.—define the United States and make its Government unique. The President does not lead the people—he leads the Government. The Government's function is to enable the people to take care of themselves. Only in wartime does the President lead the nation as commander-in-chief, but even in Revolutionary times, it was not the Government that caused the Revolution or fought at Lexington, Concord, or Bunker Hill.

At Bunker Hill the leadership was comprised of citizen volunteers—and the Patriots would have won if they hadn't run out of ammunition. In the United States, the Government was not constructed to lead its virtuous citizenry, but to follow citizen inputs and directions as made through legislative representatives to the best of its ability.

All four of the pillars of American Exceptionalism are under assault today by the Progressive Federal Government and those who wish only to "go along to get along." With respect to Protestant Christianity, main-line Protestant denominations are in drastic decline throughout the U.S. Over 2.7 million Christian church attendees in North America and Europe cease to be Christians each year, a loss of over 7,600 per day.[6] Much of this is due to liberalization in main-line denominations. Conservative evangelical churches, on the other hand, have mushroomed. The trend is clear—if a church moves to humanism and Progressivism, it loses its members. But all churches in the U.S. are under government attack. The 1st Amendment has been altered from protecting religion from Government to protecting Government from religion.

The landmark case for this change was adjudicated in 1947, *Everson v. the Board of Education*. The majority opinion, written by New Dealer Progressive Justice Hugo Black, reflected the Court's Progressive agenda and rationalized its ruling with false historiography.

Since then, ***every Supreme Court ruling dealing with religion has utilized Everson as its defining precedent and gone against Christianity***. Added to all this is the unceasing attack on Christians as being inferior beings because of their beliefs. Even sociologist and political scientist, Charles Murray, an icon among Libertarians and author of the seminal work, *Coming Apart*, presented this opinion in 2013: "Intelligent people gave up the superstitions of religion long ago. Europe, which is, effectively, a secular continent except for Muslim immigrants, is more advanced than America in this regard. The continuing vitality of religion in America is a force for reactionary policies, not a force for good."[7] It is difficult to avoid concluding that this anti-Christian bias is the norm among American elites.

With respect to America's legal system of Common Law, the majority of the American Bar Association already prefers changing to Civil Law to make the system more efficient. Trial by jury has come under increasing criticism, and the European system of one- or three-judge panels and tribunals is used wherever possible. So much for law by, of, and for the people.

The third pillar, that of private property, has been eaten away by tax policies and Supreme Court decisions such as the one in *Kelo v. New London* in 2005. Private property can now be taken by any government entity so long as it shows some public purpose to the taking,—such as making the land available to private, well-connected developers who will augment the town's tax base. Prior to that decision, the property had to be taken for public "use" not "purpose," as for a bridge, road, or public building. In addition, the idea of property taxes originated to force owners to make their property productive so money would be generated to pay taxes. But homes, securities, vehicles, and other non-productive assets are now taxed. Property taxes have become a tax on wealth. In a very large sense, real estate is no longer owned by individuals and corporations. By being subject to seizure and sale for non-payment of taxes, real property has effectively become leased from the government with the annual property tax being the lease payment.

Lastly, free-market capitalism is under siege. The vast majority of university professors are Progressives with lifetime guaranteed employment, and they routinely use their classrooms to spread socialist/Progressive ideology and promote far-left political positions. In K-12 schools, the teachers' unions rule, and students are often taught little more than socialist and Progressive propaganda. Children, whose brains are not fully developed until about age twenty-five, readily believe what those in authority teach, unless those classroom dictates are countered with information, context, and a healthy dose of skepticism from their parents.

The Progressive war on capitalism is not limited to the classroom. President Roosevelt's National Industrial Recovery Act failed during the New Deal because it set prices and wages, and it regulated commerce to an extreme, but such policies were re-instituted during World War II, and further promoted under President Truman. They continue to be expanded today, particularly in agriculture and minimum wage legislation, and federal regulations have driven manufacturing and industrial production, the lifeblood of an economy, out of the United States. In its already partially successful program to fundamentally transform the United States into a European-style failed socialist state, the Government has increasingly inserted itself into the daily lives of its citizens. In 1950 less than one American occupation in seven required a license, but by 2014 the ratio was nearly one in two.

Many observers have noted that, starting with the Progressive Age introduced by Teddy Roosevelt, the idea that the Government is God has made steady gains throughout the nation. FDR, in his 1944 State of the Union speech, presented a second Bill of Rights, consisting of human rights to be granted by the Federal Government.

Roosevelt claimed these rights had already been accepted by the people in concept, and included the *right* to a useful and remunerative job, thereby allowing a citizen to earn enough to provide adequate food, clothing, and recreation while employed. But Roosevelt's list was not limited to a government-managed economy for the good of all citizens; it also included the *right* to a decent home, adequate medical care, a good education, and no economic fears in old age or sickness.[8] From that time forward, the concept that the Federal Government instead of God creates human rights became almost a platform plank for the Democrat Party. The notion became official when the Speaker of the House, Representative Nancy Pelosi, announced after the Patient Protection and Affordable Care Act was passed in 2010 that Congress had created a new human right—a right to health care, even though the act truly dealt only with health insurance. Having assumed the mantle of God, the Democrats were ready to take the small step remaining to marginalize Christianity. At the 2012 Democrat Party Convention, a majority of the delegates opposed any mention of God in their party's platform.

Since Woodrow Wilson took office in 1913, many political scientists have characterized all Democrat presidents as being European-style social democrats, and, as that same term is used to identify those in favor of the nanny state variation of socialism, it is

7

certainly a defensible label. All Republican Presidents since Coolidge, with the exception of Ronald Reagan, governed from the center, but were still Progressives much like their European counterparts. President Reagan was clearly not personally a Progressive, but his administration contained many Progressive elements and individuals that maintained the growth rate of the Federal Government and increased its social programs.

Today's conservatives might look to the Republican Party as a vehicle to halt the downwards spiral into Progressivism and totalitarianism, but there has been little evidence the Party wishes to reverse the general course of politics in the country. Since Reagan, all Republican candidates for president have been from the moderate or left wing of the party (the Republican Establishment), following party wisdom that only a candidate who can attract moderate Democrats and Independents can win. Few Republicans in Congress talk about rolling back government or entitlements, and almost no one talks about eliminating dysfunctional or failed departments.

In many respects, it seems that both parties increasingly look to the Federal Government for programs to address every little problem that comes up, and the Republican Party is often described as "Democrat-lite." Instead of halting the growth of government or reducing it, the Republicans strive to slow the *rate* of growth. It is indicative that when representatives from both parties speak of making budget cuts, these are cuts to the rate of growth, not cuts from the current level. Budgeting itself, when it occurs at all, is done following a procedure called "baseline budgeting." That is Congress starts with the current year's budget as the baseline, and makes increases from there. The normal method used by citizens' households, "zero-based budgeting," is simply not felt to be applicable. In its case, the budget for all items starts at zero, and each item is assessed with respect to its value and priority, and considering the available funds.

Worst of all for the Republicans is that the entitlement society has caught on with young people, not the least because that is what they have been taught in school. In 2012, President Obama won the under-thirty-years-old voter by a whopping sixty percent, and the common statement by those voters was that they considered the Republican Party to be run by anti-abortion, anti-gay, anti-women, and anti-Hispanic religious nuts. Obviously, reality was substantially different, but as so often said in politics, "perception is reality." The Democrat/Progressives have been extremely effective in controlling the debate and manipulating the American citizenry.

Nor can the Republican Party contest elections by claiming fraud. In 1981, during the gubernatorial election in New Jersey, a lawsuit, *Democratic National Committee v Republican National Committee, Case No. 09-4615*, was brought by the Democratic National Committee and others against the Republican National Committee (RNC) and others, accusing them of violating the Voting Rights Act of 1965 (VRA), 42 U.S.C. §§ 1971, 1973, and the 14th and 15th Amendments to the Constitution of the United States.

It alleged, among other things, that the RNC created a voter challenge list by mailing sample ballots to individuals in precincts with a high percentage of racial or ethnic minority-registered voters, and later put the names of individuals whose postcards were returned as "undeliverable" on a list of voters to challenge at the polls.

To settle the lawsuit, the RNC entered into an agreement—or Consent Decree—in 1982 that was national in scope and limited the RNC's ability to engage or assist in voter fraud prevention. The RNC agreed it would, among other activities, refrain from "...undertaking any ballot security activities in polling places or election districts where the racial or ethnic composition of such districts is a factor..."

In 1987, the Consent Decree was modified and "ballot security activities" was re-defined to mean "ballot integrity, ballot security, or other efforts to prevent or remedy voter fraud."

In 2010, the RNC unsuccessfully appealed to vacate or modify the Consent Decree. This appeal was heard by Obama appointee, Judge Joseph Greenway of the U.S. Court of Appeals for the Third Circuit. Judge Greenway noted the Decree limited the RNC's ability to engage or assist in voter fraud prevention, but affirmed the district court's judgment by tortuous logic. The playing field was left heavily tilted in favor of the Democrat Party.

Since that time many allegations have been made concerning massive voter fraud and stolen elections, including Obama's re-election in 2012 and the election of Minnesota Senator, Al Franken, in 2008 where recounts in heavily Democrat districts subsequently discovered large numbers of "uncounted ballots" that reversed the

9

election's outcome. The Republican Party was prohibited from challenging those outcomes. Under the Consent Decree, Republicans are left without recourse and marginalized as a political force.

So if conservatives can't count on the Republican Party or the younger generations, who can they count on? The answer seen by this author is, "only themselves."

This, therefore, is the premise of this work: if the United States is to be saved as an exceptional nation, the Patriot must take action now, counting only on himself and whatever like-minded people might be around him. The first step is to become informed on the issues. The second is to become trained in how to handle professional facilitators that are used by Progressives to control meetings and debates whenever confrontations arise. And the third is to take effective action.

The first chapter of this book is meant to inform the reader of the Progressive agenda and outline the staggering number of defeats suffered by American Exceptionalism and personal liberty since the beginning of the Progressive Era. The second presents the mechanism used by the Patriots to form an effective opposition and strategy to Great Britain in 1774. This background is necessary to give the reader an understanding of what is required to overthrow tyranny. The third chapter discusses Progressive programs and initiatives that can and should be defeated by citizen activists and political action, although, such correction will not prevent the general collapse of the U.S. and the end of the American experiment in democracy. At best, it can only slow down the Progressive drive into a brave new totalitarian world.

Chapter Four presents the current state of Christianity in the U.S., the pressing need for a new Great Awakening, and how this fits into an overall strategy to restore liberty in the U.S. The fifth chapter presents the heart of the action plan by individual citizens and citizen groups to reign in federal and state spending and force a re-evaluation of federal programs. This plan with all its elements, probably will not prevent an economic collapse, but is intended to give American citizens a fighting chance at survival as something other than serfs. The plan also presents possible mechanisms to expose Progressivism to the heavily propagandized American public as the train wreck it is, and prevent the formation of an autocratic leftist dictatorship from arising when the collapse occurs.

In order to promote ready recognition of the real enemy of democracy and the American Republic, Chapter Six presents the insidious side of Progressivism and its true nature. The Progressive is clearly identified, both by ideology and actions. Chapter Seven discusses the actions that will probably be taken by Progressives and a Progressive federal government when confronted with citizen non-violent and lawful resistance to their policies and actions. The inherent risks of this work's action plan are outlined in Chapter Eight, but the reward may well be the creation of a successor state or states that will take America's rightful place in the world with respect to individual liberty. Chapter Nine warns the reader of "doing nothing" as a practical strategy, as there will be no escaping the long arm of Government if Progressivism continues to be supported by the nation's elites and tacitly condoned by the people. The conclusion and a call for action are contained in Chapter Ten, and if the reader is not won over by then, the U.S. is doomed. The hour is late, and options are few.

As Ayn Rand stated, "You can ignore reality, but you cannot ignore the consequences of ignoring reality."

**Notes on Capitalization:**

The words "Progressive" and "Progressivism" are capitalized when referring to the ideology of Progressivism and individuals who espouse Progressivism and to eliminate all confusion with "progressive," meaning, "to move forward." The capitalized "Patriots" refers only to Americans who supported the establishment of the United States of America as an independent nation. When "Government" is capitalized, it refers to the U.S. Federal Government.

**Disclaimer:**

This work is not intended to, in any way, incite, promote, or support harmful, treasonous or seditious actions or activities that are, or potentially could be, inimical to the health and prosperity of the United States, its government on any level, or to the people. This is meant as a basis for discussion, much in the sense of *Atlas Shrugged*, but in a non-fiction format rather than a novel. Any action, opinion, or thought on the part of any individual while or after reading this work is understood by the reader to be strictly his own, and for which he alone bears full responsibility. All readers, by reading any part of this work, implicitly indemnify the writers and publishers of this work from any action or statement made by such readers or any claim that this work has inspired said readers to any particular action, without limit.

# Chapter 1
## How We Got Here

The sentiments contained in the Declaration of Independence were noble and without precedent in the world, far ahead of their time, and representing a convergence of minds the world had never before experienced at one time and in one place. Not all of the Founding Fathers were present that June and July of 1776, but the signers of any one of the documents that initially defined the United States were deserving of being considered great. The Declaration of Independence, Articles of Confederation, Constitution, Articles of Association, and Bill of Rights, provided the nascent country with an extraordinary blueprint for an exceptional nation. Only the intractable problem of slavery marred the founding, and that would wait seventy years for resolution, and another hundred before the descendants of slaves realized a substantial measure of equality. It was as if God burdened the new nation with an on-going problem to be solved at a later date as a reminder of the fallibility of man compared to the greatness of God.

Other documents and defining speeches would follow the Founders, none perhaps more meaningful to the present day than the inaugural speech by John F. Kennedy in January of 1961. He understood that a nation's people, their beliefs, culture, and resolve made it great,—nothing else. He said,

"…The world is very different now. And yet the same revolutionary beliefs for which our forebears fought are still at issue around the globe—the belief that the rights of man come not from the generosity of the state, but from the hand of God…We dare not forget that we are the heirs of that first revolution. Let the word go forth from this time and place, to friend and foe alike, that the torch has

13

been passed to a new generation of Americans—tempered by war, disciplined by a hard and bitter peace, proud of our ancient heritage—and unwilling to witness or permit the slow undoing of those human rights to which this Nation has always been committed, and to which we are committed today at home and around the world...Let every nation know, whether it wishes us well or ill, that we shall pay any price, bear any burden, meet any hardship, oppose any foe, in order to assure the survival and the success of liberty..."[9]

These were fine words, and although his performance as president hardly measured up to such a standard, the speech turned out to be applicable through the ages as almost no other speech since Washington left office in 1797. But Kennedy was not true to his words, and during his time as president, he introduced the New Frontier, a Progressive program challenging the New Deal, and he avidly replaced God with the Federal Government. The Progressive federal bureaucracy that had been established under FDR's New Deal, aided by a Progressive media and educational establishment, continued to grow enormously under Kennedy and successive Progressive Presidents and Congresses. By the twenty-first century, it had created rules and regulations covering almost all aspects of a citizen's life.

Throughout the life of the American nation, the American citizenry has been unable to control the power and growth of the Federal Government. Simply put, federal officeholders have only one lever to pull in addressing presumed problems confronting the nation: expand government by creating a program or other mechanism within the government, thereby expanding the role and size of government. This growth has always diminished individual liberty and self-determination, replacing individual freedom of action and voluntary action with government strictures, rules, regulations, and laws, often purposely made incomprehensible to the average citizen by Congress and Executive Branch bureaucrats.

The first great transfer of power to the Federal Government came over the issue of slavery which had shown that embedded self-interest at the state and local levels could prevent America from realizing the great promise of its founding. The 14th Amendment, proposed in 1866 and ratified in 1868, was meant to secure the blessings of liberty for every individual in the United States, but it could be—and later was interpreted to set—legal principles never conceived by the Congress that passed the amendment or the state legislatures that ratified it.

The second great transfer of power came about under the avalanche of immigration from Eastern and Southern Europe that irreversibly changed the demographics of the nation. These immigrants, coming through Ellis Island which opened in 1892, introduced unions, socialism, communism, and, as noted in other works, became the driving force behind Progressivism.[10] They were escaping economic deprivation and autocratic governments, and were often already radicalized by communism and socialism. They had no idea how America worked, little understanding of American culture, no understanding of American Exceptionalism, and saw no difference between an autocratic monarch such as a tsar of Russia and an American president.

Eagerly taking advantage of their new rights, in particular the right to assembly and the right of free speech, they formed unions, joined the socialist party, created communist cells, and began seeking power. It was lying around, waiting to be picked up, and men such as David Dubinsky were able to make the most of their opportunity—in his case by seizing control of the garment workers union, composed almost exclusively of women, but run by Dubinsky and a couple of henchmen.

Under Progressivism the Federal Government assumed for itself the power to determine rights at all levels: the individual citizen, families, communities, counties, cities, states, regions, the nation, and even the world. The original balances between the powers and rights of the Federal Government and those of the states, to say nothing of those reserved to local jurisdictions and the people, were destroyed, and the 10th Amendment became null and void, along with the intent of holding universal sovereignty in the people. The Constitution was irrevocably altered through relentless Progressive interpretations and applications of Progressive ideology from the time of Teddy Roosevelt to the present day. Unable to defend themselves and their culture from Progressive forces, Americans are currently facing the imminent destruction of the four pillars of American Exceptionalism.

As the country grew, various challenges were increasingly met through the expansion of the Federal Government to implement solutions that, formerly, would have been solved locally by the citizenry without government intervention. The consistent rationale for the Federal Government's unrelenting assumption of power was always some putative necessity of using the Federal Government to protect the rights and well-being of individual citizens, thus rhetorically linking the welfare of the people to the Federal Government. Oppression could and did occur at local and state levels, therefore, a higher power was needed to redress individual grievances. But that was a rationale without end; oppression can and does occur at the federal level. Is a higher level representing a community of nations therefore needed to protect individual citizens? Contemporary Progressives would argue that it is, and other nations or international organizations must step in to protect "human rights" as defined by those same nations or international organizations. Self-determination is eliminated, and although "diversity" seems to be championed by Progressives, by design, the end result of their efforts must be a dreary and stultifying sameness under dictatorial rules making "one size fit all."

As power is concentrated in remote organizations, and the Federal Government is an extremely remote bureaucratic organization; its application becomes increasingly arbitrary. With distance, organizations always become less responsive to the people subject to their authority. Sooner or later those remote organizations become so autocratic that a revolution takes place, breaking out at the lowest levels—rural areas, families, towns, tribes, states, or wherever definitional lines exist in a population. History provides no examples where this cycle has not—or *is* not—taking place. The only question remaining is whether or not the Federal Government has overreached to the point that a revolution might be imminent.

Perhaps the single most disturbing aspect of the Progressive movement that has controlled the Federal Government for the last eighty-six years is the replacement of God in American culture with the Government. Rights that formerly came from God now come from the Federal Government, and one needs only to review Roosevelt's second bill of rights in his State of the Union speech in 1944 to see the outline of what has occurred since then.

In the early 1930s, Protestant Christianity began moving lock, stock, and barrel into Progressivism and humanism, replacing the principle of salvation through God's grace to salvation being obtained by living according to Progressive and liberal principles. Even atheists became able to earn salvation in whatever afterlife one envisioned (if any), and the Christian God as the judge of what was right or wrong was ignored. Christians who insisted that the Bible was the revealed word of God were marginalized, ridiculed, and even oppressed by federal bureaucrats who dispensed favors like petty tyrants, or even more accurately, like petty gods who lived on Mount Olympus (commonly called Washington, D.C.).

Under common law tradition, authority moves upward from the people who are sovereign, whereas under civil law, it descends from the sovereign (king, emperor, or supreme religious authority) downward for the people to obey as subjects. No better example of this difference is that the U.S. Constitution begins, "We the People of the United States..." whereas the Treaty of Lisbon, normally considered as the Constitution of the European Union, begins, "His Majesty the King of the Belgians, The President of the Republic of Bulgaria,..." In literally every country except the United States, the head of state is sovereign. In the U.S., it is the people—or at least, it has been until now.

To Progressives this is anathema; the Constitution, as well as all American documents and laws, are considered time-contextual, and must change with the times in conformance with Progressive interpretations. According to Progressive ideology, the world is currently too complex and dangerous for the people to be sovereign— only the highly educated and trained individuals that would emerge in a meritocracy are qualified to rule, command, and interpret. Common law must be replaced by civil law and the messy trials by jury eliminated. The involvement of the common people should be limited to approving or certifying officials through their vote—and only when absolutely necessary. Progressivism would also move the United States more into line with the rest of the world in order to make a true world government more feasible. The vast majority of the world's nations currently have difficulty understanding the American system and see it as alien to what they know. That must be resolved by changing the United States, not by exporting the American way.

Protestant Christianity dovetails with common law, and may indeed be necessary for common law to be effective. In

17

Protestantism, particularly as it developed in the United States, every believer is in a personal relationship with God, and church hierarchy is more for administration than for developing and controlling dogma. Charity and volunteerism are important concepts, valuable not the least because a democracy only functions well when enough citizens are sufficiently virtuous to provide politicians and bureaucrats that resist becoming destroyed through corruption. Virtue is tied to morality as defined by a religion, and without religion, self-absorption and greed become the primary motivation for human activity. By the twenty-first century, universities were teaching morality in their colleges of education, to be taught to the children in public schools without reference to God or a higher authority than government.[11] The church had been replaced by secular schools for teaching morality.

While many other countries have developed free-market economies to some degree, none have fostered entrepreneurism as extensively as the United States. In the U.S. until recently, the primary determinants for a person to become successful were his own energy and expertise. European concepts of a "free market" have been and are dramatically different, involving heavy regulation, socialized labor unions, and daunting interference from government. In the European Union, the operative business environment more closely resembles the crony capitalism practiced in China, a model that some American companies have been moving toward in the last two decades. Progressives see free-market capitalism as inimical to a well-run authoritarian meritocracy or dictatorship, and promote private-public partnerships such as Herbert Hoover recommended during the 1920s, to give Government more power to control business cycles, produce higher employment, and redistribute the wealth on some basis defined by Progressives.

And lastly, American property rights, as noted in the Land Ordinance of 1785 and Northwest Ordinance, established individual land ownership as not only an economic goal for all citizens, but also a social goal to be advanced by Government. The idea that anyone can own property and receive a legal title or deed immediately after tendering payment is unknown throughout the vast majority of the world, and once again, Progressives wish to bring America into line with the rest of the world.

Today the concept of American Exceptionalism is utterly and uncompromisingly rejected by Progressives seeking to remake America. After the opening of Ellis Island in 1892 to handle the enormous influx of immigrants from Southern and Eastern Europe, the Federal Government took on new dimensions and began to copy European institutions. The Progressive Period, generally identified as beginning in 1898, has lasted to the present day, and it is Progressive initiatives that have brought the nation to the brink of extinction. Accordingly, it is these failed and harmful Progressive programs that need to be adjusted, re-directed, reversed, or eliminated.

In the Middle Ages, the estates of the realm that defined citizen functions were the clergy, nobility, and commoners. Today, the clergy has all but disappeared in the West, although in some Muslim nations the three estates are still present as originally conceived. In the West, a more appropriate current definition of the estates would be the lawyers, government bureaucracy, and people. The lawyers make up the three lesser estates of government, the executive (including the time-serving bureaucracy's leadership), legislature, and judiciary, and anyone interested in obtaining a part of the government pie generally must pay his entry fee by becoming a lawyer. In addition to the formal government estates, three more must be included: the press or media, the education establishment, and the non-government organizations (NGOs). These organizations include foundations, associations, and corporations that exist to champion some cause or political movement and influence not only Government, but also the citizenry. Normally NGOs are run and controlled by lawyers, so this sixth lesser estate could be considered a subset of the first primary estate, since they are effectively, but not officially, part of government. Reorganizing for discussion and discarding "the people," the estates become: (1) Lawyers; the Presidency, Congress, and the Judiciary; (2) the Government Bureaucracy; (3) Non-Government Organizations; (4) the Media; and (5) the Education Establishment. All are tightly controlled in the United States by East Coast Progressive elites and cannot be influenced or countered by the people. Supporting this monstrosity of fat cats who recognize no authority but their own are the Dependents, the people beholden to the Government for their well-being.

## Lawyers: The Imperial Presidency

The imperial presidency can be dated from the inauguration of President Theodore Roosevelt in 1901, but he actually represented the Progressive movement from the time he was governor of New York. It is important to note that the general political strategy of Progressives concerning any issue always involves controlling the debate over the issue and its solution. He who controls the debate controls the political process, as opponents are forced into responding to the formulations of the controller. No better example exists than using the word "Progressive" for a political movement, because the word's root is "progress," and who can be against that? Actually, the word should carry the meaning it has as an adjective for describing a disease: when a disease is progressive, it is getting worse and will ultimately kill the patient.

The standard definition of Progressivism used by Progressives is, "a general political philosophy advocating gradual social, political, and economic reform through government action." Note the use of the word "reform"—again, who can be against that? Supposedly Progressivism is a broadly based reform movement, based in the middle class. As taught in school to American children, it embraces concepts such as environmentalism, social justice, and a flexible constitution that ought to be changed as society evolves. Actually, it is something much different and more sinister. The word "reform" is nothing more than a disguise for "change," under the assumption that change is always good since the status quo is never perfect. The directionality of that change ending in a dictatorship of the elites is Progressivism's hidden agenda.

Progressivism calls for government action in all things and at all times—following a top-down model of decision-making, mirroring the European structure of civil law. In short, all problems are to be solved by government, and none fall into the realm of religion. That translates into full government control: elites adhering to Progressivism are to dominate the Government, society is to be changed by social engineering, social justice, and redistribution of wealth, and economics are to be controlled by state planning. At the very least, economic control is to be accomplished through state capitalism, though communism or socialism are generally preferred.

Only three presidents since Teddy Roosevelt have defined

themselves as something other than "Progressives." Warren G. Harding, Calvin Coolidge, and Ronald Reagan. With those three exceptions, all presidents in the twentieth and twenty-first centuries have automatically sought to increase the size, scope, and power of the Federal Government.

At the same time, the term "liberal" underwent a change, and now no longer stands for the Jeffersonian definition meaning, "to provide a maximum of individual liberty with a minimum of government interference." The modern term is synonymous with Progressive, though some Republicans would say they are Progressive but not liberal. Beginning with the presidency of Woodrow Wilson, all Democrat presidents have said they were not only Progressives, but also liberals, although Bill Clinton liked to say he was a "moderate" liberal. This non-historical use of terms has led to substantial confusion, as Alan Colmes demonstrated in his book, " *Thank the Liberals* *For Saving America (And Why You Should),*" by conflating Jeffersonian liberalism with modern statism and Progressivism, even though he must have known the difference.[12]

The key aspect of modern liberalism or Progressivism as understood by the vast majority of Americans is that serious problems are facing society in the status quo and the only possible solution involves government action. In actuality, Progressives always say the status quo is inadequate, and "reform" is required. Conservatives attempting to defend the status quo against Progressive initiatives are at a substantial disadvantage. They must defend an actual program (or non-program) against a utopian proposal that is always purported to solve the alleged problems and usually decrease costs. After the new Progressive program is implemented, it is usually found to be counter-productive, have unintended consequences, and cost far more than anticipated. Progressives then "double-down," and starting from the new status quo, initiate a new and improved Progressive program designed to correct and expand the previous one.

Facing the second program, the conservatives are unable to even offer the previous status quo for consideration, as such an idea would be reactionary or "turning the clock back." In the modern age, one can only "go forward," which is, of course, the dictionary definition for "progressive." Once again, Progressives cleverly control the debate through terminology. Hitler, Stalin, Mussolini, and Mao all took their countries "forward," doubling-down when their ideology made life under their regimes worse, and never taking a step "backward." President Barack Obama, following the fascist and communist examples, along with those of Woodrow Wilson and FDR in the United States, has consistently followed the same Progressive methodology. And make no mistake, Hitler, Stalin, Mussolini, and Mao were all Progressives in their ideologies and political strategies.

Progressives see only two major obstacles to implementing their program: the Constitution and religion, especially Protestant Christianity. They don't dare to draw attention to the Preamble of the Declaration of Independence, as they do not believe its words. Woodrow Wilson publically rejected the Preamble and recommended it be ignored. The offending words were, "We hold these truths to be self-evident, that all men are created equal, that they are endowed by their Creator with certain unalienable Rights, that among these are Life, Liberty and the pursuit of Happiness. That to secure these rights, Governments are instituted among Men, deriving their just powers from the consent of the governed."

Progressives, like Woodrow Wilson, do not believe in God-given rights, but instead, believe that all individual rights are bestowed by Government as temporary social expediencies that may be withdrawn at any time by Government. Progressive theorist, Frank Goodnow, even wrote that the theory of natural God-given rights had no historical justification.[13] Faith, based in religion, does not enter into his, or any other Progressive's, equation.

To Progressives like Wilson, FDR, and Barack Obama, the Constitution was strictly time-contextual and is no longer relevant to the present day. It should be considered a living document, not an absolute blueprint for Government and the authority and responsibilities of governmental bodies. At this point, they believe the Constitution should be replaced with a document like that proposed by Rexford Tugwell in his Ford Foundation funded book, *The Emerging Constitution*.[14] In the Progressive view, the common citizenry is incapable of dealing with the fast pace of modern life and modern government, and an oligarchy is needed so elites can rule benevolently on behalf of the people. Today, this oligarchy is nearly in place, and firmly backed by Progressive theorists in academia to provide it with morality, ideas, and legitimacy. This academic and intellectual involvement has been present from the early days of

Progressivism in the late nineteenth century. Frank Goodnow, the founder of the American Political Science Association and a president of Johns Hopkins University, unabashedly said that the duty of the university was to place greater emphasis on social duties than individual rights, thus promoting the supremacy of the collective over the individual. The student's duty was to bring this "truth" home to his fellows.[15] Goodnow said this in a speech in 1916, and, since that time, Progressives have been beating the drum relentlessly in American schools.

American Progressivism was imported from Germany from 1885 to the 1930s, and almost all early Progressive leaders and theorists were either German or students of Germans (Wilson, Goodnow, and John Dewey, for example). They followed the lead of German scholars who had little understanding of American democracy, having never lived under anything but an autocracy. For whatever reason (perhaps because they believed everything in Europe was superior to its American version), American Progressives sought to copy the European lead. This still goes on today, and as President Obama said in Strasbourg, France, on April 3, 2009, "In America, there's a failure to appreciate Europe's leading role in the world."[16]

In Germany, an aristocratic political elite was formed after Prussia swallowed the other German states from 1864 to 1871. It was supported by an enormous and ever-growing governing bureaucracy ( *Beamtertum*), and became a model of efficiency. But that was not the end, nor was World War I. Hitler rose to power, in part by utilizing the propaganda techniques developed by Wilson's wartime propaganda machine, the Committee on Public Information, and Edward Bernays, a committee member. Bernays produced a book in 1923, *Crystallizing Public Opinion*, where he explained how political ideas of parties could become public opinion through propaganda. Not only were the people to be controlled, they were to *like* being controlled.

Hitler co-opted the bureaucracy, put Bernays's theories to good use, and unleashed fascism on the people. Ordinary Germans lost the right to vote and retained only the right to obey. The culmination of Progressivism was experienced in Nazi Germany, Soviet Russia, Communist China, and other totalitarian states, but by 1970 ,Progressivism had taken over the United States as the primary political theory, held in check only by the Constitution and Christianity.

Using the tactic of misdirection in public, Progressives suppressed the fact that Hitler, Stalin, and Mao were all Progressives, having simply modified Progressivism to fit their nations. The differences between fascism and communism were only in state control versus state ownership of the means of production, and the only difference between fascism and Progressivism today is a strong nationalist element in fascism versus a strong globalist element in Progressivism.

Conservatives have attempted to fight Progressivism by citing history. In nearly every case except for prosecuting wars on a national basis, private enterprise has been able to accomplish every mission cheaper, faster, and better than a government program. During World War I, President Wilson attempted to manage the war production effort from the White House, and the result was gross inefficiency, sky-rocketing costs, and the non-delivery of essential weapons and supplies. Having learned from Wilson's mistakes, FDR created a War Production Board, staffed it with industrialists, and sat back and let private industry run the show. The Government supplied money and placed orders; the rest was up to the "arsenal of democracy." His decision was correct, and the result was the greatest wartime productivity ever seen in the history of mankind.

Even national, state, and local infrastructure is best left up to private enterprise. James J. Hill's Great Northern Railway, built without a dime of government money, became the most successful trans-continental railroad in the U.S. Cornelius Vanderbilt proved time and again that private enterprise could provide faster, better, and cheaper steamship and packet service than Government. But historical arguments became losing arguments by the twenty-first century because Progressives had been propagandizing American children in school since the New Deal to ignore history. Historical facts (if known or understood at all) are deemed irrelevant for modern American politics because "times have changed" or "the world is different now." But human nature and the faith of Christianity haven't, so under Progressivism, the former must be modified and the latter eradicated.

The term "statism" has made no impact at all on the American public because its use in American schools is anathema. It is identical with Progressivism in practice, but since it implies a static condition rather than promoting "progress," Progressives shun it like the plague. To put all this into an historical term that everyone would understand (and which would be devastating to the Progressive movement) is

24

simply to call Progressivism a variation of fascism. It is closer than most people realize, in that fascism, as defined by Benito Mussolini in Italy, simply combined nanny state or democratic socialism with nationalism. The state controlled the means of production through central planning and regulations, precisely as done today in the European Union. We call this system crony capitalism or state capitalism, where the means of production are owned by the private sector, but control and regulation rests with the government. To a large degree, this is the economic system functioning today in China, and certainly the one the U.S. is moving toward.

The only apparent difference between twentieth century fascism and twenty-first century democratic socialism or Progressivism, is the lack of a nationalistic component. Yet appearances are deceiving. The new nationalism in Progressivism is globalism, or in a simpler term, supra-nationalism. Elites, both in the U.S. and Europe, now consider themselves citizens of the world, not merely citizens of their respective homelands. Environmentalism is their religion, the globe is their country, and socialism their economic system. That adds up to Supra-National Socialism, or SNAZI for short. It only remains for conservatives and American Patriots to "out" their opponents with this new, but very correct term. SNAZI makes a great term for controlling the debate and strips Progressives of all their rhetorical camouflage.

From Wilson to FDR to Johnson to Carter to Clinton to Obama, there is a straight line in which each president becomes more Progressive, more powerful, and more imperial (meaning emperor-like). The "establishment" Republicans have not been far behind, and the Department of Health, Education, and Welfare was created by Eisenhower, the Environmental Protection Agency by Nixon, Veteran Affairs by George H. W. Bush, and Homeland Security by George W. Bush. The White House staff has grown to unimaginable proportions, and the use of executive orders to implement laws that Congress never passed, as well as foreign treaties the Senate never ratified (as required by the Constitution), has become commonplace.

In addition, presidents since World War II have increasingly resorted to appointing individuals with near-cabinet rank to oversee various initiatives. Such appointees are normally called "czars" due to their nearly unlimited power and being answerable only to the president. FDR was the first president to appoint such individuals, and over his long presidency, created eleven such positions. Truman had six, Eisenhower one, Kennedy zero, Johnson three, Nixon three, Ford two, Carter two, Reagan one, and George H.W. Bush two.

Then the technique of governing through czars took off: Clinton had eight, George W. Bush thirty-three, and Obama thirty-eight and counting. The presidency itself has become insulated from the actions of the president's administration, his power has become nearly unlimited, and, with so many departments and decision-making executives having over-lapping areas of responsibility, the U.S. executive branch has taken on the appearance of an organization in which no one takes responsibility for anything. Indeed, it has become almost impossible to find out who is doing what. Re-elections have become exploits in obfuscation and the dissemination of propaganda, rather than holding the sitting president responsible for policies and actions in his first administration.

America now has an unaccountable president, whoever he is, and an imperial one at that. He has hundreds of people at his elbow willing to do anything he asks. The citizens are increasingly remote—just faces and bodies to be brought out for speeches and political events; window dressing and impersonal objects to help display the greatness of the president himself. At one "spontaneous meeting" with "ordinary citizens," presidential candidate Hillary Clinton met a number of folks in a popular fast-food restaurant and chatted about their issues. It was grand theater, except that everyone she met were hand-picked Democrat Party members with phony questions and orders to swoon over the candidate.

When have Americans had a president who ever mowed a lawn, worked flipping burgers, did manual labor, had a newspaper route, changed a tire or replaced his car's brakes, shopped at Walmart, watched Judge Judy, or cut his own hair? Reagan did some of that, but he was the exception that proved the rule. Somehow, one of us—Americans from middle class culture—can no longer become president. The president must be a product of elite Ivy League schools, live in a superzip enclave surrounded by elites such as himself, and never have worked at a job where he could be fired without "due process."[17] We've created this monster ourselves, and he's not one of us, he's one of them.

And he's not on our side.

But is the descent into a dictatorship or an oligarchy inevitable? Not necessarily, but it depends on the morality of the society as determined by the dominant religion in that society. Since the 1920s, Progressivism and liberal teaching from the pulpit have steadily marginalized Christianity as the source of morality. Moral equivalence became the buzzword for proper thinking; one religion was as good as another, as were all cultures and ideas. Not surprisingly, Harry Emerson Fosdick, America's most famous liberal minister in the thirties, preached that Hitler and Fascism came into being because of the faults of America and its policies.[18] At this point, morality appears to be a thing of the past, and there is nothing standing in the way of the U.S. falling into an oligarchy—nothing that is, except the Constitution and the remnants of Protestant Christianity.

Progressivism, with its quasi-theological component, humanism, has long been identified as representing the anti-Christ. As early as 1928, Dietrich Bonhoeffer taught that humanism was Christianity's most dangerous enemy. Under humanism, God orients himself to human wishes rather than humanity being oriented to God's, thereby enshrining self-absorption and the authority of secular bodies as absolute.[19] With God subordinated to serving the people, Christianity becomes a belief that can be adapted to the political posture of the state. Germany's Evangelical Church, went along to get along with Hitler's Nazi regime, attempting to survive on the fringes. The Vatican was no help; Pope Pius XII praised Nazism.[20]

By 1937 Christian activities were severely curtailed in Germany and Nazi ideology had become the new state religion. In the U.S., Progressivism has continued to grow until it defines curricula and substance in every public school, and nearly every college and university. Education promotes social justice, environmentalism as the religion of the elite, and that the Earth is god. Humanism, with a slightly Christian adaptation, had been embraced by the vast majority of pastors preaching in the U.S. by 2012. With the subordination of religion to the power of the state, the Progressive Federal Government has become no less powerful than the Nazi Government in 1933, and the president supposedly leads the people instead of the state—words identical to those spread by Nazi propaganda. Truly, the United States has moved close to despotism.

27

## Lawyers: The Congress of Interests

The framers provided for a popularly elected House of Representative every two years to provide the nation with a constantly churning chamber of individuals representing the popular will of the people. At the time, there was no thought to representatives becoming career politicians; instead, the task of representing the people of one's district was thought to be a duty to which a person might be called. Most states had provisions in their constitutions for "rotation" in government; that is, an individual would be required to rotate in and out of public office versus private employment, and political parties were loose alliances of people with various political beliefs. There were no party organizations, and little party-oriented campaigning. The Senate positions were filled every six years by individuals elected by their respective state legislatures, hopefully older and wiser than congressmen, and representative of their states as a whole. Several events later overtook these fine and noble sentiments and reversed the idea that government served the people to what is seen today: that people serve the government.

In the early republic the designations of Federalist and Democrat-Republican were labels instead of political parties, and represented whether a person believed in a strong federal government or a weak one. Adams and Hamilton favored a strong federal government, hence "Federalist," while Jefferson and Madison, who wanted the primary power to be held by individual states and the national government to be as small as possible with very limited powers, were Democrat-Republicans. In the first election, the electors each had two votes, and whoever received the most would be president, the second most, vice president. It was possible for them to be from different parties. Washington's first cabinet featured Jefferson as Secretary of State, though Jefferson was a Republican and Washington a Federalist.

True political parties as we know them today made their appearance due to the efforts of Martin van Buren, later the eighth president of the United States. In 1819, then New York State Senator van Buren created a new political machine called the "Bucktails," more or less in agreement with Hamilton's or Madison's James Madison Federalist Number 51 that parties were probably necessary,

28

and as promoted by the Bucktails, parties existed to check "the passions, the ambitions, and the usurpation of individuals."[21]

Van Buren built a party organization starting at the state level in New York, then drilled down to districts, wards, and election precincts. The state organization coordinated and funded candidates and directed the districts or counties. Lower down, the district and county organizations made sure that every ward and precinct was staffed with "captains" who walked the streets and got out the vote.[22] Later, van Buren added partisan newspapers that rallied the faithful.

Van Buren became a U.S. senator in 1821, and immediately set about building a national party along the lines of his organization in New York. His avowed purpose was to create a party across sectional interests that would control the question of slavery and prevent it from becoming the divisive issue on which the U.S. would flounder. To tie individuals to his new organization, he needed patronage positions at all levels, and, therefore, set Government on the road to becoming continually larger as the population grew.

In 1820, the Federal budget was less than twenty-two million dollars, one-half to defense, one-fourth to debt service, and one-fourth to the states and various federal agencies. There was exactly *zero* spent on welfare or education. Nonetheless, big government's camel had poked its nose into the tent; the institutions were present, and with time, America would arrive at where we are today.

Another earth-shattering event was the passage of the 17th Amendment, which was ratified immediately after the 16th (income tax) in the spring of 1913 under Woodrow Wilson. The election of senators was changed from being conducted by state legislatures to a popular vote by the people. This put a new dimension on the Senate—the senators were no longer representatives of their state legislatures and forced to remain in close contact with those bodies. Their election became a matter of money and popularity with the people in general. Senators could now be elected on the coattails of presidential candidates, and the unintended consequence was that senators became even *more* dependent on special interests and their party due to the costs of running state-wide races than members of the House of Representatives.

Without term limits or rotation requirements, senators and representatives could—and did—remain in office for very long periods, effectively becoming career politicians with little or no attachment to the private sector or even their home state. In addition, representatives were kept in office by their party's gerrymandering of districts, so much so, that by 2008, many districts had become "safe" for one party or the other, at least during presidential years. One analyst determined that in 2008, only fifty-five out of the four hundred and thirty-five seats in the House were competitive—that is, a candidate from either party might win on his own merits.[23] Only fifty-eight other seats were considered as leaning one way or the other and subject to an upset. The remaining three hundred and twelve seats would more or less automatically re-elect their incumbents, or the candidate from the party controlling the district. Clearly, there was no longer a mechanism for voters to keep their representatives accountable for their actions.

As Congress became increasingly partisan and irresponsible, staying in office became a matter of being in the right party, satisfying the demands or dictates of special interests that contributed heavily to election campaigns, providing constituent service to the home folks, and bringing pork home to one's district. National politics faded from consideration, as did any thought about what current actions might have on the future. Representatives rocketed along from one election to the next, and, becoming pure politicians, simply did whatever was necessary to win the next election. Incumbents became nearly unbeatable under ordinary circumstances, and, as they gained seniority, they gained power and could obtain greater amounts of pork for their state or district. Under these conditions, spending was bound to increase beyond all reason.

But none of this fully explains why a conservative candidate who is successful in his home district with his message of reducing the size of Government and restoring fiscal sanity very often becomes a Progressive after arriving in Washington. Unknown to voters in mid-America—or wherever the congressman or senator comes from—the city and environs of Washington, DC, are overwhelmingly Progressive, and the new arrivals face daunting challenges.

Politicians must be at least somewhat narcissist to run for political office, and as such, inevitably desire to be liked and appreciated. At home in their districts or states, they are big fish, and for representatives, the pond is always rather small. Upon arrival in

Washington, however, the representative finds that he is one of many, all of whom are members of a privileged, governing elite, fêted and pampered, and hobnobbing with moneyed interests willing to go to great lengths to help a congressman, so long as the congressman supports their agendas. The differences between Washington and their districts are stunning: in Washington everyone they meet is intelligent, well-informed on issues, attractive, often powerful, and certainly have money or access to money that they are willing to make available to the politician. At home are ordinary folks, mostly with little money to support candidates, and while it is not unusual for a freshman congressman to raise a million dollars from his district through a lot of hard work, in Washington, five, ten, fifteen million dollars and more are readily available to a congressman seeking re-election.

But there is a catch: the newbie must help grow the Government so the special interests can continue to feed at the trough. Literally *everyone* in Washington is dependent on the Federal Government, and cutting expenditures is seen by everyone—from taxi drivers to university presidents—as negatively affecting them personally. Simply put, if the candidate who campaigned on reducing the size of government is elected, he is thrown into an environment where every single person is his friend if he signs on to Progressivism, or his dedicated enemy if he stands by his principles and campaign promises. And make no mistake; this extends to every aspect of his life and that of his family. Few, if any, individuals can withstand this pressure.

At best, it can be expected that the conservative will posture on issues by "fighting for" fiscal sanity or whatever, but without ever actually achieving his goals or even doing much about them. He'll buy off his folks at home by obtaining a few government grants, and quietly go along to spend more money and grow Government. He quickly acquires a wonderful pension, and, if accepted by the elites, can look forward to a very remunerative life brokering deals and influence after his political career is over. If a politician becomes a lobbyist when out of office, the voter can assume he was corrupted.

A perfect example was Blanche Lincoln, a former senator from Arkansas. A very attractive lady with marked social skills, she attended a finishing school in Virginia, then worked on the staff of her home district's congressman, became a lobbyist in Washington for various clients, and built her Progressive credentials. After her

31

former congressional boss was implicated in a House banking scandal, she returned to Arkansas for a short time, ran for Congress, and won his seat. She married a medical doctor with a practice in Virginia, and, after taking a year off to give birth to twin boys, returned to Arkansas and ran for the Senate. Winning again, although now only nominally an Arkansan, Ms. Lincoln returned to Washington, completed two terms as a senator, then was defeated for a third term.

Naturally, she returned to being a lobbyist—where what she actually has to do is not something the people at home would care to know. In Arkansas, Ms. Lincoln sounded conservative and appeared to represent her constituents by continually pumping money back into the state, particularly for the rice farmers in her home area, but she voted Progressive on all important issues. What finally defeated her was that she had spent very little time in Arkansas after reaching the age of twenty-one—estimated to be less than three years over the following thirty (i.e. ten percent of her time as an adult.) Her life was in Washington among the Progressive elites, not in Arkansas, a conservative, Christian state. The different allegiances finally showed through.

So, it clearly is possible to elect individuals to Congress who seem to be representing conservative principles and values, but more often than not, conservatives are disappointed in the results. The representative goes his own way once in office, becoming a team player on a team the voters aren't on and don't even know exists. To gain social acceptance, contacts for future (and present) earnings, political power, and funding for future elections, the newly-elected conservative goes along with—or even promotes—Progressivism. Whatever conservative principles he had are left by the wayside, only to be taken up during elections or when back in his home district.

In Washington, good intentions and morality are in short supply, while corruption and self-gratification are endemic. The majority of senators and congressmen spend their time gaining SMP (sex, money, and power) by becoming a player in the Washington establishment, which liberally spends the money it receives from the Federal Government on its friends. Progressive Washington society virtually guarantees lifetime employment dealing with Government, and wealth beyond all expectations. For males there is the added bonus of nearly unlimited numbers of beautiful girls at their beck and call, sometimes expensive and sometimes not, and away from home and the prying eyes of constituents, politicians often find these temptations irresistible.

In short, there is little hope for Congress, regardless of who is elected. As religion and morality recede, they no longer determine Congressional behavior. Today, elected officials are no longer bothered with principles—they have been replaced with constituents to be purchased and transported to the polls as needed. Once elected, a congressman is free to ignore the wishes of the people in his district. Part of the problem is the culture and temptations of Washington, which would ruin Mother Teresa. The remainder is all about money—Washington is awash with it, all of it coming from Government, and it votes much more effectively than human beings.

## Lawyers: The Court Goes Ideological

To many people, the Supreme Court is the court of last resort, the people's last hope to restore one's sanity in an increasingly alien and pathological world. Such faith is misplaced for many reasons, but not the least because the Court has long been a leader in the Progressive movement and likely to remain so for the foreseeable future. Since the New Deal and FDR's abortive court-packing scheme, justices have been appointed for ideological reasons, not for their expertise in jurisprudence.

The first of nine justices FDR appointed was the Progressive Hugo Black. Formerly a senator from Alabama who had supported FDR unconditionally, Black was a rabid New-Dealer, staunchly anti-Catholic, and a member of the Ku Klux Klan. He is revered, along with his associate William O. Douglas, by Progressives for always ruling in accordance with his Progressive ideology even if he had to invent historical facts to support his case. Not since Chief Justice Taney, who ruled in the Dred Scott decision that helped catalyze the Civil War, had a justice been so partisan and deaf to argument. Black was responsible for two vitally important decisions that significantly altered the U.S. Constitution, both coming in a single ruling: *Everson v. Board of Education* in 1947. This ruling effectively reversed the meaning of the 1st Amendment to the Constitution from protecting religion from government to protecting government from religion. To accomplish this feat, Black relied on a single letter Thomas Jefferson wrote to the Danbury Baptists in 1802 while he was president,:

"...I contemplate with sovereign reverence that act of the whole American people which declared that their legislature should 'make no law respecting an establishment of religion, or prohibiting the free exercise thereof,' thus building a wall of separation between Church & State. Adhering to this expression of the supreme will of the nation in behalf of the rights of conscience, I shall see with sincere satisfaction the progress of those sentiments which tend to restore to man all his natural rights, convinced he has no natural right in opposition to his social duties. I reciprocate your kind prayers for the protection & blessing of the common father and creator of man, and tender you for yourselves & your religious association, assurances of my high respect & esteem."

Seizing on the phrase, "wall of separation between Church and State," and claiming that Jefferson was representative of the majority opinion and intent of the writers of the 1st Amendment, Black wrote in the majority opinion that there must be this strict wall of separation between all government in the U.S. and all religion, in particular, that religion had no place in government and government was not to be influenced by religion or take the least notice of it. Black apparently was ignorant of the fact that both Jefferson and Madison, while serving their respective terms as president, regularly attended Sunday church services in the chambers of the House of Representatives. Jefferson was also not present in the Constitutional Convention that produced the original Constitution, nor involved in writing the Bill of Rights. Both times he was in Europe and was hardly influential with regards to the 1st Amendment.

Second, Justice Black invoked the 14th Amendment to make his interpretation of the 1st Amendment applicable to state law, thus opening the door for federal law to trump state law in all situations. The 14th Amendment contained the clauses, "...nor shall any State deprive any person of life, liberty, or property, without due process of law; nor deny to any person within its jurisdiction the equal protection of the laws." The intent of the Congress in 1866 was to secure civil rights for negroes, not to enable the Federal Bill of Rights to overturn state law. Nonetheless, Everson was henceforth used to invalidate state and local laws with respect to religion, and even to support suits against government bodies allowing any representation of religion on public property—such as displaying a nativity scene in front of a county court house at Christmas or a monument to the Ten Commandments. Not only did Black make law, he made law contrary to the wishes of the vast majority of American citizens.

The Supreme Court involved itself and the lesser federal courts in administering law—supposedly the province of the executive branch. This first developed in the aftermath of the 1953 decision in *Brown v. Board of Education of Topeka, Kansas*, dealing with school segregation. The Court held that "separate but equal" was "inherently unequal," and school systems were ordered to desegregate. This was easier said than done, especially since racial self-segregation was present in city neighborhoods, and school assignments were made according to location of residence. Many schools in white areas were overwhelmingly composed of white students while schools in Negro neighborhoods were correspondingly black. The Court held that neighborhood schools did not achieve the desired result, which according to the Court, was that all schools in a school district should have the same proportion of Negroes to whites. Schools could no longer represent the neighborhood in which they were located—each had to represent the whole district proportionally.[24]

Using the interpretation of the 14th Amendment in Everson, the Supreme Court went far beyond its constitution powers by usurping the power of enforcement of its decision which was previously held by the Executive Branch (the President). Most Federal judges, particularly in the Courts of Appeals, interpreted Brown not as a prohibition of segregating students by race, but as an order to integrate the races in all schools. In 1963, the Court ruled in *McNeese v. Board of Education* and *Goss v. Board of Education* that positive plans for integration were required to end segregation. Federal district courts began requiring desegregation plans to be submitted to them for approval before implementation.

In *United States v. Montgomery County Board of Education* (1969), Judge Frank Johnson's desegregation order that a ratio of the races was to be established by a district judge was upheld, effectively making a judge the administrator and enforcer of the law. Ideas were few, and District Courts ordered busing of children to and from schools, sometimes for long distances each day. Transportation costs skyrocketed, but that was not the Court's concern—social engineering was.

Times had changed from 1832 when President Andrew Jackson refused to enforce the Supreme Court's ruling in Worchester v. Georgia, and began the forcible removal of Indians from the South to Indian Territory in the current state of Oklahoma. Jackson maintained that since the Court had no enforcement power, the mode and amount of enforcement was solely at his discretion. That modus operandi continued until the Civil Rights Act of 1964 and the Voting Act of 1965 were passed.

Although proponents of those bills stated repeatedly that the bills did not authorize busing and quota systems, in 1966 the Department of Health, Education, and Welfare put racial quotas and busing requirements into effect. Federal courts attempted to impose metropolitan plans, encompassing cities and their suburbs into a single plan, but the Supreme Court finally put a limitation on such overreach in *Milliken v. Bradley* in 1974. The result was white flight into the suburbs, and in spite of busing, school districts in the North sometimes became even more segregated than prior to 1964. Progressive elites, both white and black, sent their children to private schools, and the vastly expensive debacle only affected the middle and lower classes stuck in multi-racial cities and counties. The road to serfdom had made its appearance and would be traveled by all those unable to become Progressive elites.

Following the de facto move by the Court into the legislative and executive realms in the 1960s and 70s, the power of the Court became greatly magnified. Federal bureaucracies found that allying themselves with the Court and interested NGOs in what has become called "friendly lawsuits" could give them extra-constitutional authority. Court decrees sometimes required vastly increased powers, funding, and personnel in a bureaucracy, all of which a bureaucracy could blame on some judge's ruling. Congress, the people, and even the President had become irrelevant.

The political affiliations of the justices became as important to both sides of the political spectrum as winning the presidency. Congressional and presidential initiatives have to pass the scrutiny of the Court, and after Franklin Roosevelt's National Industrial

Recovery Act was declared unconstitutional in 1935, no president has neglected an opportunity to put friendly justices on the bench. Surprisingly, however, Republicans have been much less successful in selecting conservatives for the Court than Democrats, and whereas no Democratic appointee since Eisenhower's presidency has been conservative, many Republican justices have turned Progressive after being appointed. The record is so astounding that one wonders what mechanism has been at work in the selection of justices by Republican presidents.

Perhaps the most far-reaching impact of the Supreme Court's increased Progressivism has been the replacement of Christianity with humanism as the determinant of what was right and good in the country. Charity, formerly the province of the churches, has been increasingly handled by secular charitable foundations, and federal tax laws and their adjudication have promoted those foundations and institutions without restraint. In order to remain relevant—or so America's pastors thought—churches had to acquire corporate tax-exempt status (501c3) to function, but when they did, they became subject to a host of federal regulations. Separation of church and state became a one-way street; churches could not engage in political activity, but the Federal Government could and did regulate church activities, while promoting atheism and humanism, and working to marginalize the role of religion in American life. Since 1947, every Supreme Court decision in which the 1st Amendment's freedom of religion clause has been involved has gone against America's Christian churches.

With respect to preserving and protecting the Constitution, five of the current justices on the Supreme Court take the view that it is a living document, meant to be interpreted as time-contextual, and subject to re-interpretation. Two have stated that the opinions of foreign jurists should be considered in the Constitution's interpretation, and three believe it must come more in line with international law. The United States is perilously close to having its Constitution being considered inferior to international law, and if Progressivism becomes more virulent, that outcome is inevitable. At that point, individual freedom, as it is understood in the United States, will have been abolished, and it will have disappeared one little freedom at a time.

Three rulings in 2012 and 2015 have firmly positioned the Court as ideologically Progressive. The first ruling on Obamacare on June 28, 2012, *National Federation of Independent Business v. Sebelius,* was concerned with the individual mandate that required an individual to pay a penalty to the IRS for not purchasing health insurance. Since the Constitution has no provision for Congress to assess penalties on citizens for not buying something, this feature of the law was unconstitutional. The court decided for the Government: first ruling that the mandate was not a tax so it could rule on the mandate's constitutionality, and then determining the mandate was indeed a tax, and so fell under the enumerated powers of Congress—therefore, the act was not unconstitutional.

The second ruling came on June 25, 2015, when the Court held in *King v. Burwell* that the Patient Protection and Affordable Care Act authorized federal tax credits for eligible Americans living not only in states with their own exchanges, but also in the thirty-four states with federal marketplaces. The language of the act clearly required such credits to apply only to citizens of states which had set up insurance exchanges (as an incentive for states to participate with such exchanges), but the Court, recognizing that the Congress had written a law that wouldn't work unless the incentive proved effective, elected to re-write the law itself rather than sending it back to Congress for modification. As a result, subsidies and credits could be paid through federal exchanges as well as state exchanges.

The third ruling, in *Obergefell v. Hodges* and three related cases, dealt with homosexual or "same-sex" marriage on June 26, 2015. The court held that homosexual couples, stalwart supporters of Progressivism, had a "fundamental right to marry inherent in the liberty of the person, and under the Due Process and Equal Protection clauses of the 14th Amendment, couples of the same sex could not be deprived of that right and that liberty."[25] That this was at odds with the Constitution, America's Judeo-Christian tradition, and religions that defined marriage as solely between a man and a woman, was of no consequence. The five justices—three Jews and two Catholics—were ruling as they did because they believed it was the right thing to do, regardless of the law, the Constitution, or any precedence. Therefore, the Court ordered all states to issue marriage licenses to any same-sex couple that wished to marry.

Justice Thomas, in his stinging dissent, argued that the petitioners in this case were not deprived of their liberty, as they have been allowed to travel and settle freely without government intervention. The Progressive majority worked around this problem by substituting the petitioners' "dignity" for "liberty." But as Thomas said, there is no "dignity" clause in the U.S. Constitution—and that, even if there were, Government could not bestow it upon a person or take it away. One's liberty and dignity should be shielded from Government — not provided by it. Thomas wrote, "Today's decision casts that truth aside. In its haste to reach a desired result, the majority misapplies a clause focused on 'due process' to afford substantive rights, disregards the most plausible understanding of the 'liberty' protected by that clause, and distorts the principles on which this Nation was founded. Its decision will have inestimable consequences for our Constitution and our society."[26]

## Bureaucratic Governance

The growth of the Federal Government is perhaps best illustrated by the growth of executive departments, the number of cabinet level executives, and the number of people dependent on government pay, contracts, pensions, and welfare for their economic viability.

| Department | Formed | Employees | History |
|---|---|---|---|
| State | 1789 | 19,000 | Formerly Foreign Affairs |
| Treasury | 1789 | 116,000 | |
| Defense (War) | 1789 | 3,000,000 | Formerly War & Navy |
| Justice | 1789 | 113,000 | Formerly Attorney General |
| Post Office | 1792 | 546,000 | Now US Postal Service |
| Interior | 1849 | 72,000 | |
| Agriculture | 1862 | 110,000 | |
| Commerce | 1903 | 44,000 | Formerly Commerce & Labor |
| Labor | 1913 | 18,000 | |
| Health & Human Services | 1953 | 67,000 | |
| Housing & Urban Dev. | 1965 | 11,000 | |
| Transportation | 1966 | 59,000 | |
| Energy | 1977 | 109,000 | |
| Education | 1980 | 5,000 | |
| Veterans Affairs | 1989 | 235,000 | |
| Homeland Security | 2002 | 208,000 | |

Other Employees and Employment:

| | |
|---|---|
| Defense Contractors | 7,800,000 |
| US Postal Service Contractors | 350,000 |
| Homeland Security Contractors | 600,000 |
| Obamacare Expansion | 700,000 |
| All Other Department Contractors | 2,500,000 |
| Total Federal Employment | 13,382,000 |
| Total State & Local Employment | 5,285,000 |
| Total State & Local Contractors | 2,100,000 |
| Total Federal, State & Local Employment | 20,767,000 |
| Total Work Force | 155,000,000 |
| % of Total in Government | 13.4% (1 in 7.5 Employed) |

Outside of the employment figures, the breadth of the Federal Government has widened considerably over the years, and increased the president's span of control well beyond the maximum an executive is normally expected to manage effectively.[27] Other than his cabinet, the president must supervise numerous other cabinet level executives such as the White House Chief of Staff, Director of the Office of Management & Budget, Administrator of the Environmental Protection Agency (17,000 employees), trade representatives, Ambassador to the United Nations, Chairperson of the Council of Economic Advisors, and Administrator of the Small Business Administration. In addition to this list are sixty-nine independent agencies that report to the president, such as NASA, the Peace Corps, Social Security Administration, General Services Administration, Central Intelligence Agency, etc.

Several of these agencies were formerly represented by cabinet level executives: the Director of the Federal Security Agency (1939-1952), Director of the Federal Emergency Management Agency (1996-2001), Director of the Central Intelligence (1995-2001) (24,000 employees), and Director of the Office of National Drug Control Policy (1993-2009). Four more cabinet executives or departments have already been proposed: Peace (2001), Global Development (2003), Culture (2009), and Business (2010).

With such a cumbersome organization and its vast number of employees, the presidency is simply an impossible task for even a highly intelligent, experienced individual to master. Unfortunately, the egos of presidents prohibit them from delegating power through a collection of vice presidents in some order and hierarchy. For example, there could be a VP for Legal, as well as ones for Finance, Foreign Relations, Defense, Technology, Welfare, Economics, Health, and Communications. All agencies in the executive branch should be made subordinate to those group VPs. Agencies must be streamlined and greatly reduced in size, and most especially, the "turf" for each agency defined explicitly so overlap is reduced as much as humanly possible. If this cannot be accomplished under the current American political system, it is doomed by its own structure that renders it ineffective.

There is a solution to bureaucratic dominance and arrogance, of course, but probably not one possible in a republic. All entitlements from government must be eliminated, and strict term limits put in for all government employment, elected or otherwise. A rotation between the government and private sectors is required, something like limiting government employment to ten years, and then having to be in the private sector for another eight years before becoming eligible again for government employment. This has to encompass all government employees, including teachers and civil servants. In the words of Mercy Otis Warren criticizing the Constitution in 1788, "There is no provision for a rotation, nor anything to prevent the perpetuity of office in the same hands for life... to the exclusion of men of the best abilities from their share in the offices of government. By this neglect we lose the advantages of that check to the overbearing insolence of office, which by rendering him ineligible at certain periods, keeps the mind of man in equilibrium, and teaches him the feelings of the governed, and better qualifies him to govern in his turn."[28] Mrs. Warren might have added "regulate" and "serve" to "govern," thereby including civil service personnel.

Yet there is a feature to bureaucracies that is rarely mentioned and certainly never broadcast to the citizens—the problem of bureaupathic behavior on the part of bureaucrats. Originally a theory developed by William Niskanen in the early 1970s, it has come to define why government bureaucracies grow and why bureaucrats exhibit the behavior that they do.[29] A bureaucrat's primary mission is to grow his organization, a goal not unlike that sought by many managers in private industry. But the environment is totally different, and success does not come through efficiency or effectiveness; indeed, such important concepts to private corporations are counter-productive in government.

The size of a bureaucracy can only be increased by increasing the bureaucracy's budget, either by showing a need for more funding to achieve the stated mission, or by taking on new projects, functions, and missions. Acquiring new programs and responsibilities often leads to destructive turf wars between organizations, adding greatly to the costs borne by taxpayers, and generating hard feelings, efforts that are at cross purposes to others, and sometimes cause massive duplication and inefficiency.

The budget is the sale, with the customer being the Ways and Means Committee in Congress, and, to a lesser extent, the Office of Management and Budget reporting to the president. All the other bureaus and bureaucrats are competitors, though, to be successful, powerful alliances are formed to spend the citizens' money. These alliances are made between the bureaucrats, members of Congress and their staff, private corporations, foundations, and various NGOs for the benefit of those in the alliance at the expense of the taxpayer. Since Congress must allocate the funds for the bureau's activity, it is necessary for bureaucrats to bribe key members by locating facilities in their districts, granting regulatory exemptions to certain constituencies, and, of course, arranging for huge campaign contributions from the NGOs that profit from the bureau's expansion.

Some of this is built in automatically through the process of base-line budgeting. Rather than having to justify a bureau's budget each year from scratch, the previous year's budget is used as a starting point—or base-line—and only increases—and rarely decreases—need to be considered. Often an increase is an across-the-board percentage, keeping up with the rate of inflation, increased cost of living, or originally planned step increases, and once a program is instituted, it is literally home-free for eternity. Planned increases in following years are particularly insidious, as Congress can—and does— then claim it has reduced spending by reducing the amount of the previously planned increase. Often, these planned increases are greatly inflated for just that purpose—to make Congress look good while the bureau maintains its expected rate of growth. If Congress fails to reduce the rate of increase for whatever reason, the bureau experiences a windfall, and not only for one year—all subsequent years are affected as the base-line has advanced beyond expectations. And, of course, the public is none the wiser.

The only opposition to the growth of a bureau or government department comes from other bureaus and their bureaucrats. If one considers that the total budget will be held at a certain level—which it isn't—then *every* bureau wants a larger slice of a fixed pie. This often leads to extraordinary inter-agency turf wars almost unknown to the public except when there are extremely negative consequences. An example was the abortive rescue mission mounted by the Carter Administration to recover the American hostages in Iran. All of the armed services—Army, Navy, Air Force, and Marines—clamored to be included under the assumption the operation would be successful, and their service would receive great publicity and be looked upon with favor during the budget-making process. No single individual was placed in charge—since that would result in one service getting most of the credit—and the operation was a fiasco. In short, inter-agency rivalry doomed the mission and killed American servicemen.

Some bureaucrats have found a new way to avoid competition for funding called "sue and settle" or "friendly lawsuits" as mentioned previously. This works particularly well for agencies like the EPA where bureaucrats encourage an outside NGO to bring a suit against their agency for failing in their mission to protect some feature in the environment, like a snail darter fish. Working hand-in-glove on the lawsuit, the EPA and complainant work out a settlement in which the complainant is paid well for its involvement, while the EPA agrees to enforce stricter regulations and add enforcement personnel. A federal judge signs off on the settlement, and the EPA enters into the appropriate consent decree. Viola! The EPA must spend additional money to satisfy the decree—now having the force of federal law (and one not passed by Congress), and the funds are automatically approved by Congress in perpetuity. The entire deal is worked out behind closed doors, the machinery of the republic is circumvented, the complainant and involved bureaucracy both benefit, and the taxpayer picks up the tab.

The power of a bureaucracy often does not relate to its size. The three most powerful bureaucracies with respect to their impact on the lives of ordinary Americans are: the EPA, the Treasury Department (the IRS), and Homeland Security. To that must be added the Federal Reserve System, the shadowy central bank that is actually an incorporated NGO, which sets monetary policy for the Government.

Homeland Security already has plans and procedures for the internment and resettlement of millions of American citizens (U.S. Army FM 3-39.40 dated February, 2010) in place. The IRS is responsible for enforcing Obamacare and persecuting conservative organizations and individuals, and the EPA is dedicated to implementing Agenda 21 and making private property a thing of the past. The members of these organizations, so much at odds with constitutionally guaranteed liberties, have been given a clear mandate by the Federal Government. That power is now based on elitist, Progressive values, and criminality has become normal. Federal agents are above the law, suffer no moral guilt, and are convinced they are doing the right thing. For their own protection and well-being, they work to always increase the Government's power and reduce that of ordinary citizens. Such agencies can no longer be fixed—they must be abolished.

**NGOs behind the Scenes**

Citizens generally think of non-government organizations as being non-profit corporations, and that assumption is generally correct. However, that does not mean such corporations do not make a lot of money—they just spend it on acquiring assets, paying high salaries, and rewarding their friends. Most NGOs are foundations, associations, and corporations that exist to champion some cause or political movement and influence not only government, but also the citizenry. Others are more or less charities, but often pay their executives on a scale that rivals major public for-profit corporations. For example, a state-wide lottery in a southern state was sold to the voters as a fun way to provide large sums of money to education, in particular grants to students to help pay for college educations. But for every dollar the lottery took in, fifty cents were paid out in winnings, forty-seven were consumed in operations, and only three percent went for education. In the FBI's definition of fund raising schemes that are considered scams due to an extremely low percentage going to the designated charity, this lottery more than qualifies. Not coincidentally, the executive director of the lottery makes nearly a million dollars with bonuses, and the benefits to lottery employees rival that of Washington bureaucrats.

But the NGOs that should concern most citizens are those that influence (some would say "control") Government to spend money for something the NGO deems important, assist in writing bills and regulations, or help get legislation passed. Generally, citizens do not even know NGOs are involved, as all the discussions and agreements are made behind closed doors in the most un-transparent way possible. For example, consider who wrote the American Recovery and Reinvestment Act of 2009, commonly known as the "Stimulus" or "Porkulus." The answer is that it was written, in large part, by the Apollo Alliance, a project of the Tides Foundation, an organization heavily funded by George Soros who also funds Media Matters, a radical, far-left Progressive pressure group.

Among those on the board of the Apollo Alliance have been Leo Gerard, International President of the United Steelworkers; United States Congressman, Jesse Jackson, Jr. (D-IL); Carl Pope, Executive Director of the Sierra Club; Van Jones, a self-proclaimed communist; Gerald Hudson, International Executive Vice President of the Service Employees International Union (SEIU); Joel Rogers, a founder of the Marxist political coalition known as the New Party; John Podesta, President and CEO of the Center for American Progress; and key figures from the Laborers' International Union of North America.

Van Jones described Apollo Alliance's mission as "sort of a grand unified field theory for Progressive left causes." A director of New York state's chapter of the Apollo Alliance is Jeff Jones, one of the four key leaders of the Weather Underground terrorist organization, along with Mark Rudd, Bill Ayers, and Bernardine Dohrn. The Apollo Alliance also has a long list of endorsers, including ACORN, Greenpeace USA, the League of Conservation Voters, the National Wildlife Federation, the Progressive States Network, the Rainforest Action Network, the Sierra Club, the Union of Concerned Scientists, and the Working Families Party. Not to be overlooked are its union endorsers, the AFL-CIO, AFSCME,

Electrical Workers, Food and Commercial Workers, Machinists and Aerospace Workers, Mine Workers, SEIU, Sheet Metal Workers, Steel Workers, Teamsters, Transportation Workers, and the United Auto Workers. Somehow, Environmentalism and big labor unions were tagged to receive a major slice of the stimulus pie. One does not need to wonder why.

How about the Patient Protection and Affordable Care Act, also known as Obamacare? The primary godfather of the bill was Robert Creamer, a convicted felon and husband of Congresswoman Jan Schakowsky from Illinois. Creamer apparently wrote almost a third of the act while in prison, and became an inspiration for many left-wingers. Creamer advocates deception to impose socialism on a recalcitrant nation and wants a "democratization of wealth" and "Progressive control of governments around the world." The object of Obamacare was to turn many more people into wards of the state, much like Indians on their reservations, and create a large new constituency for the Democrat Party. Creamer heads an NGO, the Strategic Consulting Group, a political consultancy whose clients include ACORN, the Service Employees International Union (SEIU), the AFL-CIO, the United Steelworkers Union of America, the Democratic Congressional Campaign Committee, and dozens of other leftist organizations.

There are also the NGOs that work hand-in-glove with the federal bureaucracy on "friendly suits," and agree to consent decrees that award them millions of dollars for their trouble. Others set themselves up to do the work that bureaucracies should do, often by putting elected officials on their boards to ensure non-competitive bidding. In Arkansas, for example, there are regional planning and development districts (RPDDs) that are actually 501(c)3 corporations that write grant requests for cities and counties. The mayors and the chief administrative officers of the counties—the RPDDs' customers—serve on the RPDD boards. There is no competitive bidding, and the RPDD takes a percentage of the grant for its fee. The RPDDs also grant loans with funds from several federal departments such as Agriculture and Interior, acting as agents for the Federal Government, granting loans to Progressives and supporters at their sole option. They operate landfills and waste disposal companies in non-competitive environments, but the worst is that they also function as regional clearing houses for grant applications, and all requests for grants form state and federal agencies must be processed through them. They have a say in recommending or denying every grant—in effect, stopping all those not written by them. This is the very model of corruption.

Another insidious NGO in most states is the [state name] Association of Counties. Supposedly, they represent the county governments in the state legislature instead of the elected state representatives (whose districts are rarely—if ever—drawn on county lines), and their fee for such activity is a percentage of the money collected by the state to be sent to the counties. In order to tamp down citizen complaints about this extralegal NGO, the money it receives is taken off the top. The expense is not included by county officials in their budgets—and, therefore, never seen by the citizens.

Unfortunately, there is practically no limit to the number of NGOs attempting to insert themselves into governmental processes. They take money—usually unbeknownst to the citizenry—in very large amounts, while ensuring their connections through various mechanisms, like hiring a county administrator's daughter, members of a congressman's family, or the best of all, a family member of a president. Snubbing their noses at voters, they fail to comply with the Freedom of Information Act by claiming private corporation status, but, in order to function, promote their quasi-government status. Somehow, they obtain the best of both worlds.

## Watchdog to Lapdog Media

As can be seen from the foregoing discussion on bureaucracies, there is little restraining their continual growth. Bureaucracies sometimes even form alliances to increase their budgets, thus eliminating all competition. At that point, only the media, or "press" as it was formerly called, functions as any sort of brake on the unbridled expansion.

Before World War II, newspapers and magazines were open about their political preferences, newspapers sometimes even putting the word "Republican" or "Democrat" on their masthead. With almost no exceptions today (the Arkansas Democrat-Gazette is one), newspapers attempt to maintain a fig leaf of impartiality, but in reality, large national and city newspapers are nearly all Progressive, with perhaps over eighty-five percent being Democrat. Two of the three major national newspapers, the *New York Times* and *USA Today* are unabashedly Progressive, and the third, the *Wall Street Journal*, primarily features business and economic news. All of the major television networks are Democrat, with the sole exception of Fox and its two cable channels, Fox News and Fox Business News. With respect to political commentators on television, the ratio of Democrats (all Progressives) to Republican is probably ten to one.

This dominance by Progressive Democrats in the media leads to the question of why journalism has taken this cant.

The answer is simple—Progressives are what American journalism schools have produced since World War II.

Two of the largest daily newspapers, the *Los Angeles Times* and the *Chicago Tribune*, both conservative and Republican, were relentlessly castigated in the 1950s as being the two worst newspapers in the country—just because they were Republican. The *Times* went Progressive Democrat after the ascension of Otis Chandler as publisher in 1960, to a large degree to gain acceptance by East Coast elites.[30] The *Tribune* capitulated in 1969 under the leadership of publisher Harold Grumhaus, at first changing the news to politically neutral, but retaining Republican editorials, but soon thereafter, the editorials followed the paper's irreversible drift to the left. To no one's surprise, the two papers became acceptable to the Eastern elites, and the *Tribune* even began to participate in the leftist-oriented and fully Progressive Pulitzer Prize competition.

It was President Franklin D. Roosevelt, however, who first put the media firmly in bed with the Democrat Party and Progressive politicians. Roosevelt became the greatest newsmaker America had ever seen.[31] Stories were released every day from the White House, many of them personally by FDR and individually to selected reporters, all of the stories being favorable to the president. Purposefully, there was no time for fact-checking because the next story was on its way, and if a reporter *did* check and find inconsistencies or inaccuracies, he was risking his career if that information was published. Roosevelt was punitive, and when reporters wrote articles he didn't like, that reporter's career with respect to White House news was over.[32] Reporters and news outlets soon learned to go along to get along.

Under Eisenhower, the press was tolerated rather than

manipulated, and with civil servants in the Federal Government having begun their federal careers under FDR, reporters found that more news could be obtained by taking a Progressive Democrat position than anything else.

Concurrently, the press learned to protect and cover up for Democrat presidents and personnel in their administrations. That FDR was crippled and couldn't walk unaided was covered up, as was Sumner Welles's homosexuality and trysts with black porters on train trips. FDR's numerous affairs with women in the White House were never reported during his presidency, though they became a lively subject after his death.[33] The press invariably took the side of the Communists in FDR's administration, even extending decades-long support to Alger Hiss, and covered up Truman's minimal cognitive abilities and ties to the Pendergast political machine in Kansas City. JFK's suffering from chronic Addison's disease and repeated outbreaks of various venereal diseases were overlooked, as were his extraordinary number of affairs with women, right under the nose of his wife and children. The repeated group sex episodes involving JFK and his brothers were simply winked at and covered up.

Both JFK's and Johnson's election frauds were squelched, along with Johnson's infidelities, MLK, Jr.'s infidelities, and Jimmy Carter's minimal intellectual capacities (they celebrated him as extraordinarily bright when the reverse was true.) Carter's co-dependence on his wife for decision-making was a major unreported problem, but the dam finally broke over Clinton's many infidelities. Even then, the media overlooked Clinton's outright boorishness and defended him by ignoring probes into his involvement in scams and illegalities.

But the capstone proof of the media's total subservience to Progressive administrations is the current near-criminal blindness to President Obama's negatives: his communist upbringing (his father, maternal grandmother, and grandfather, and his primary mentor, Frank Marshall Davis, who may also be his birth father, were all communists, and his mother was a fellow-traveler), his questionable birth, academic record, studious avoidance of decision-making, dependence on Valerie Jarrett (daughter-in-law of Frank Marshall Davis's best friend), etc.

By 2012, the traditional media had extended its activities to include near-universal support for Progressive Democrat candidates, globalism, socialism, Agenda 21, and the movement to a world government. Whether the media sees itself as a king-maker or merely a handmaiden is hardly relevant—it does the bidding of the Progressive Democrat Party. Outlets that are out of step, such as Fox News, talk radio, and various bloggers on the Internet, are routinely denigrated, and, from time to time, efforts are made to eliminate them. Dr. Josef Goebbels could not have been happier with the German state-controlled press than Obama is with the American media. All opposition to Obama and his actions will be automatically vilified in the media.

## Education as Conditioning

The history of education in the United States is one of home-grown schools administered by local communities, and inculcating the community's values in its children. In addition, such schools provided their students with a liberal education. Although the definition of "liberal education" has morphed considerably over the years for political reasons, it was formerly an education that gave individuals broad knowledge and transferable skills; it trained them to think for themselves rather than simply submit to a higher authority.

Then came John Dewey and Progressive education at the end of the nineteenth century. Dewey, an atheist who hated Christianity with a passion that was pathological, said the purpose of education was to develop the child to take his place in society. Knowledge was not absolute, but rather, a social condition, and students needed to be in command of their own learning. He said it was impossible to prepare a student for any precise set of conditions, and it was, therefore, important to prepare him for life and to deal with the problems life would throw his way.

Dewey's take on education became firmly implanted in the U.S. by World War II, and liberal and Progressive education became, for all practical purposes, synonymous. Children were not to be taught facts, but rather, how to think. Engineering was felt by many educators to be vocational training and not worthy to be taught at universities. On the other hand, universities wanted federal grants for research, so science and engineering were grudgingly accommodated for the dollars they generated.

Progressive President Woodrow Wilson gave the store away when he further clarified how education was to be organized. In 1909, he said, "We want one class of persons to have a liberal education, and we want another class of persons, a very much larger class... in every society, to forego the privileges of a liberal education and fit themselves to perform... manual tasks.[34] This set the stage for truly educating only the ruling elites and condemning the serfs to receiving only indoctrination and training for manual labor. Wilson's division is more in evidence today than at any time in the past.

Since Dewey's education theory stressed present society as the milieu to which the student should adapt, it was a very small step from Progressive education to outright psychological conditioning and propagandizing. With federal funds flowing to "improve" education, schooling was detached from local control and given to federal bureaucrats. In 2013, thefederally developed "Common Core" was pushed onto the states. It effectively dumbed-down a high school education from twelve grades to ten and a half, but it fostered an appreciation for "diversity," tolerance of non-Christian religions and immigrants from all parts of the world, and an acceptance of non-American ideas. Mathematics was made relative, and if a child could give a good defense of why four times five equaled twenty-five, his answer was accepted as correct. History before 1898 became irrelevant because the U.S. had supported slavery, murdered Native Americans by the millions, and the Framers of the Constitution (if mentioned at all) were slave holders and land developers raping nature. In effect, American history began with the Progressive Era.

Key takeaways from Common Core instructions to teachers included that there are no absolutes, inflation was caused by greedy capitalists, the United States should pay reparations to third world countries for using their raw material resources, and that "social justice" and "environmental justice" were the most important concepts a child should learn. That this curriculum was a prescription for brainwashing children into accepting and believing in humanism, socialism, and Marxism, was underscored by the insistence that morality had to be taught in the schools, not in the churches. Christianity—the thing Dewey most hated—was superstition and myth, something to be discarded in the twenty-first century.

All this begs the question: what is to replace the American

believing in American exceptionalism? In 1980, the answer would have been "the new Soviet Man." But in 2012, the answer was "the global citizen," working for the good of mankind as a whole, protecting the Earth and its resources, implementing Agenda 21, and establishing peace forever throughout the world. The global citizen would believe in socialism and social justice for all mankind, excepting only the elite who, by virtue of their education, intelligence, and adherence to Progressive principles, would necessarily rule the world for all the people, supposedly at all times keeping the people's welfare in mind.

This is so idealistic and so potentially powerful that it has greatly appealed to the immature mind. Any problems that might arise are written off as due to older generations that are not as enlightened as younger ones, and they must be made to see the error of their ways. It is the same approach as was used in Nazi Germany, Soviet Russia, Communist China, and Kampuchea, and there is no reason to expect a different outcome from these historical examples. The only solution is home schooling one's children. However, universities also preach all this to great effect, and future American leaders will come from those completing sixteen or more years of such indoctrination. Obviously, the Federal Department of Education should be abolished, and control of schools returned to local jurisdictions and the children's parents. The subjects of morality, environmentalism, global social responsibility, and social justice must be moved out of K-12 curricula.

Unfortunately, opponents of these programs have been marginalized through the use of professional "facilitators" (trained to maneuver groups to a desired "consensus" which is the pre-determined desired outcome) hired by school boards and school districts to handle undesirable opinions and individuals at relevant meetings. These same facilitators instruct teachers how to further their agenda in the face of parental objections. Teachers are taught to build a teacher-determined "consensus" in the classroom through controlling discussions and marginalizing alternative viewpoints. Students taught differently by their parents become isolated, and give in to fit back into the group. Ones who don't are sent for sensitivity training or anger management classes to make them better parts of the collective.

Consensus-building is not a process wherein there is any compromise; it projects the collective opinion and then builds solidarity in the class or group for that opinion. Few children can withstand the psychological intimation, and they readily conform with little administrative difficulty. In actuality, this is mind control based on techniques developed by philosopher George Friedrich Hegel. In his technique, opposition is marginalized after the consensus is announced as being counter-productive and retarding "progress." Other teachers use Karl Marx's Theory of Alienation, which states that human beings will do almost anything to avoid isolation and ridicule and gain acceptance by the group. The thinking environment is controlled, and facts and truth are made interchangeable and unassailable. Television commentator Bill O'Reilly uses this technique frequently on his program, creating consensus on facts by saying, "Everyone knows that." The interviewee doesn't object because he doesn't want to appear contrary, and O'Reilly's unchallenged statement becomes fact for the discussion. In the classroom, most facts are presented to children as inviolate and not up for discussion—most certainly not if the child wants to stay in the group and get a good grade.

Climate change and environmentalism are being sold today in our public schools, packaged in slick textbooks and teaching materials, without parental knowledge or approval. Even worse, parents are often demonized. For example, a parent might work in a coal mine, but his child is taught that coal mining is a rape of nature, an unsustainable activity causing the world great harm, and people associated with the coal industry are criminals escaping proper justice. Children are made to see and relate to their parents as being ill-informed, behind the times, obstructionist, and often racist. Under Progressivism, non-Progressive parents are the enemy to be overcome; their sole reason for existence being to give birth to children on behalf of the state, and then giving their children to the state to educate and condition for the state's purposes.

The result of this indoctrination in school is a population that denigrates the nuclear family and their fathers and mothers, and values expediency and group approval over independent thought. It is one that eliminates judgments, concepts of right and wrong, morals, and faith in God. People hide in their local groups and submit to the will of authorities who make all the decisions. Serfdom and the nanny state become realities.

Ask your child what is wrong when a TV news anchor says; "Scientists are now wondering just how much global warming is responsible for these monster storms we've been having." The statement is pure mind control on three counts: (1) the anchor has established that global warming is a fact, (2) that monster storms are only a recent phenomenon, and (3) he never identifies who the "scientists" are. But most Americans are taken in by this technique, and start believing that global warming and the monster storms are linked. All because of Progressive Education—thank you, John Dewey.

## The Dependents

Not the least of the problems facing reformers of the Progressive Federal Government is the sheer number of people currently receiving money from the government:

| | |
|---|---|
| Total Federal, State & Local Employment | 20,767,000 |
| Social Security Recipients | 67,600,000 |
| Welfare Recipients | 108,592,000 |
| Federal Pensioners | 1,900,000 |
| Military Pensioners | 2,300,000 |
| Federal Subsidiary Recipients | 2,000,000 |
| State & Local Pensioners (incl. Teachers) | 7,000,000 |
| Dependents of Government Employees | 35,000,000 |
| Total Dependent on Government | 245,159,000[36] |

With a total population of three hundred and seventeen million people at the beginning of 2014, over seventy-seven percent of all Americans receive money from the Government, and are wholly or partially dependent on that stream of income for their well-being. This number is only an estimate, as there are no statistics on dependents in households receiving money from the government other than those of direct government employees. On the other hand, some people are counted more than once. In the case of some politicians for example, they receive social security for their years in private legal practice, then a pension from their time as a prosecutor, another as a county judge, another as state attorney general, another as a congressman, another as a senator, and maybe a few more. It is not unusual for a lifetime politician to enjoy as many as four or five pensions, adding up to much more than he ever earned while employed. Sometimes elective offices carry accelerated accrual of taxpayer-paid pensions, such as receiving two years credit for a pension for each year in office to some number of years.[37]

The point of the above analysis is that there is an overwhelming number of citizens who will do anything to retain their stream of income from government. Beginning in 1862, the federal departments began providing services to citizens (only the post office dates from before that time), and the provision of benefits and services went into high gear when the Department of Health, Education, & Welfare was created in 1953. By 2015, there were only one hundred and fifty-five million Americans in the work force out of a population of three hundred and seventeen million. Of those employed, only one hundred and twenty-seven million were employed full-time in a job or profession reflecting their skills, training, and education—meaning that the number of Americans fully employed was about half the number of those receiving funds from the government and declining.

Clearly, most voters have a vested interest in keeping the government money spigots wide open. Elections under any circumstances other than total economic collapse are futile for changing the course of government spending and its ever-increasing growth. Progressive politicians have carefully crafted a near-total dependency on government for the citizenry's well-being and the continued profitability and viability of private enterprise. This has ensured a docile and pliable citizenry in both the public and private sectors.

Progressives certainly know they are driving the United States into a catastrophic economic collapse and are counting on the citizenry approving the most drastic measures to maintain the flow of their government benefits. Those attempting to reduce the size of government and substitute honest work for a government check will certainly be vilified as the enemy, just as Stalin blamed mythical "wreckers" for all his economic failures. Progressives, controlling all of the estates except, possibly, the people, will blame honest Americans who are attempting to feed their families for their own failures.

Yet the answer to the U.S.'s problems is practically self-evident: Progressivism must be defeated, and government by, for, and of the people restored. The way to combat Progressivism and save America is, of course, the subject of this work.

# Chapter 2

## How America's First Congress Resisted Tyranny

In 1774, agitation throughout the thirteen American colonies had reached the point where many colonists were openly defying the British government. Their grievances were many, but primarily the colonists felt they had built their towns, cities, and colonies by their own hard work, sweat, money, and, in many cases, blood. More than a few grievances had originated in the British Isles. Tyranny by the crown, rent racking, religious persecution, and various other restrictions and practices, had driven many poor souls to America. Braving all the New World's risks, trials, and dangers, they had built a new life for themselves and their families in liberty and under self-government. The colonists had tamed the wilderness, fought off Indians, cleared the land, built their homes, built their churches, raised their children—all with little or no help from the royal government. And they were moving west, in spite of the royal proclamation of 1763 that reserved all the land west of the Alleghenies to the Indians and the Catholic colony of Quebec.

That was, of course, the colonial viewpoint. Parliament and the royal governors saw the situation quite differently. Great Britain had financed the war against the French and Indians at great expense, with little recovery from the colonies. They now wanted the colonies to not only pay for the troops quartered in America for frontier defense, but make good on England's war with the French.

Until 1773, a variety of acts to produce revenue from the colonies had been enacted, all with less than satisfactory results. Then the fat was thrown into the fire with the Tea Act of 1773, triggering the Boston Tea Party and other acts of defiance of British authority.

Angered beyond endurance, Parliament passed the Coercive Acts, a series of punitive laws designed to punish Boston after the tea party outrage in December of 1773. The port of Boston was closed, Massachusetts was stripped of its historic rights of self-government, assemblies were limited, and the governor could move trials to Great Britain for offenses in Massachusetts, thereby denying Americans an historic right—specifically, to a jury trial by their peers.

To a very large degree, the American colonists viewed the mother country and its government as providing little or no services of value to the American citizenry. Defense against the Indians and their depredations was almost exclusively home-grown, and representatives of the crown were more interested in enriching themselves than aiding the colonist. Parliament and the king were seen as remote and as taking actions against the colonists, rather than on their behalf. There was a strong belief that if a government could not or would not defend its citizenry and promote the general welfare, then the citizens had a right—even a duty—to render that government a nullity. Citizens had and still have a natural, God-given right to protect themselves, not only from armed attacks, but also from threats to their culture, language, traditions, religion, and well-being. If the king could not fulfill his obligation to protect his subjects in all those particulars, the bonds of allegiance to the king were void. This principle applies today, especially now that the Federal Government has evolved into a remote, elite dictatorship much like the government of George III, and does not protect American citizens from assaults in these six areas. In fact, the Federal Government is enabling those attacks, all in the name of Progressivism. Clearly, Americans are facing the same situation today that caused American Patriots to rise up against George III. There is much to learn from what transpired in the early days of the formation of the American republic.

## Generating the Articles of Association

The first Continental Congress was called in September of 1774 at the instigation of Virginia to coordinate a protest throughout the colonies, because what was done to Massachusetts could happen to any colony. Twelve of the thirteen colonies sent delegates—Georgia was the only one missing—and the Congress that met in Philadelphia was a meeting of eagles. The attendees included George Washington, Samuel and John Adams, Patrick Henry, John and Edward Rutledge, Silas Deane, John Jay, and many other notables.

Peyton Randolph from Virginia presided over the group, and, by October 20, the Articles of Association (generally called the Association) had been produced. Significantly, Congress possessed no authority from the mother country to make laws or function as a government, so everything about it was pushing colonial administration into uncharted territory. Nonetheless, the Association put the American Revolution down the path of no return, and, eventually, all the colonies except New York and Georgia formally approved the proceedings.

The Association was truly a revolutionary document, actually, one that would have surely put all members of Congress on the scaffold in the Tower of London if apprehended by British authorities. The Declaration of Independence almost two years later was hardly more treasonous, yet the Association has been overlooked almost without exception by writers of history texts.[38]

The Association said in part:

"We... affected with the deepest anxiety, and most alarming apprehensions, at those grievances and distresses, with which his Majesty's American subjects are oppressed; and having taken under our most serious deliberation, find that the present unhappy situation of our affairs is occasioned by a ruinous system of colony administration, adopted by the British ministry about the year 1763, evidently calculated for enslaving these colonies... Various acts of Parliament have been passed, for raising... revenue in America, for depriving the American subjects,... of the constitutional trial by jury... for crimes alleged to have been committed in America: And in prosecution of the same system, several late, cruel, and oppressive acts have been passed..., also an act for extending the province of Quebec, so as to border on the western frontiers of these colonies... discouraging the settlement of British subjects in that wide extended country; ...to dispose the inhabitants to act with hostility against the free Protestant colonies...

To obtain redress of these grievances, which threaten destruction to the lives, liberty, and property of his majesty's subjects,... we are of opinion, that a non-importation, non-consumption, and nonexportation agreement, faithfully adhered to, will prove the most speedy, effectual, and peaceable measure: And, therefore, we do, for ourselves, and the inhabitants of the several colonies, whom we represent, firmly agree and associate, under the sacred ties of virtue, honor and love of our country, as follows:

1. That from and after the first day of December next, we will not import, into British America, from Great-Britain or Ireland, any goods, wares, or merchandise…, as shall have been exported from Great-Britain or Ireland; nor… import any East-India tea from any part of the world; nor any (there follows a list of items)… from… British plantations…

2. We will neither import nor purchase, any slave imported after the first day of December next; after which time, we will wholly discontinue the slave trade, and will neither be concerned in it… nor sell our commodities or manufactures to those who are concerned in it.

3. As a non-consumption agreement… will be an effectual security for the observation of the non-importation, we… solemnly agree and associate… we will not purchase or use any tea, imported on account of the East-India company, or any on which a duty hath been or shall be paid… or use any of those goods, wares, or merchandise, we have agreed not to import…

4. (After) the tenth day of September, 1775… if the said acts and parts of acts of the British parliament herein after mentioned, are not repealed, we will not directly or indirectly, export any merchandise or commodity whatsoever to Great-Britain, Ireland, or the West-Indies."[39]

More details on the no-exportation and non-importation of goods to and from England and British possessions followed. The Articles also emphasized the raising of sheep in America to provide wool for clothing that had previously been imported, stressed frugality and economy on the inhabitants of North America, and outlawed extravagance, entertainments, andprice-gouging.

Then came Article 11, the one that created the mechanism by which all this could be implemented and controlled:

"11. That a committee be chosen in every county, city, and town, by those who are qualified to vote for representatives in the legislature, whose business it shall be attentively to observe the conduct of all persons touching this association; and when… any person… has violated this association, that such majority do forthwith cause the truth of the case to be published in the gazette; to the end, that all such foes to the rights of British-America may be publicly known, and universally condemned as the enemies of American liberty; and thenceforth we respectively will break off all dealings with him or her."[40]

In accordance with the Association, local committees were set up throughout the colonies that enforced the "no trade with England" policy. Signing the Association agreement as thousands did was an act that put the committee members' names on record as supporting treason—certainly earning them a traitor's death at the end of a British rope. With everything to lose, the committee members worked constantly and vigorously to keep the revolutionary spirit alive, and gave it the necessary permanence to see the country through eight long years of ruinous war. The colonists themselves suffered greatly from this policy, but English imports went from a value of three million pounds in 1774 to two hundred and twenty thousand in 1775, a decline of ninety-three percent, while exports from the American colonies declined by ninety-five percent. In a single year, the Patriots established themselves as economically independent from Great Britain.

The committees were patently illegal, as neither the Continental Congress nor the Articles of Association had been authorized by royal governors, Parliament, or the Crown. Although colonial governments had previously attained a measure of self-government, such powers had been specifically granted by Parliament and the Crown under the proviso that all acts by colonial assemblies were subject to approval or rejection in England. No authority had been given to the colonists to form a continental congress, and decrees from such a congress had no legal status. In no respect could the colonies be called sovereign—sovereignty rested definitively with the king of England, George III.

Nonetheless, the local committees authorized by the Articles worked wonders, and, as a result of often high-handed actions, trade with Great Britain essentially disappeared for the entire time of the Revolutionary War. The Articles forced the common people in every locality to take a stand: Patriots for an independent nation; Loyalists for the Crown; and neutrals who supposedly took neither side, but whose neutrality greatly benefitted the British. There was no turning back: it was victory or death.

## How and Why

Self-government already had a long history in America. It appeared during the earliest days in Plymouth with the Mayflower Compact, and in 1619 when the House of Burgesses convened for the first time at Jamestown, Virginia. Colonists had seized the reins of government from royal governors a number of times, sheltered supporters of Cromwell following the restoration of the monarchy under Charles II, and even resisted giving up those identified as regicides.

The first attempt at forming a multi-colony American government took place in 1643 and produced the United Colonies of New England, or, as it is more widely known, the New England Confederation. This confederation was an alliance of the Puritan colonies of Massachusetts, Connecticut, Plymouth, and New Haven for mutual defense against the Indians and the Dutch colony of New York. When the Catholic King James II revoked the colonial charters in 1686 and established the Dominion of New England under Royal authority, the confederation dissolved.

Following the Glorious Revolution of 1688, the citizens in Massachusetts overthrew James's governor, Sir Edmund Andros, and restored self-government in New England until royal authority was re-established by William and Mary. At the same time, Leisler's Rebellion established an independent government in lower New York, while another faction in upper New York, the Albany Convention, declared for William and Mary. Jacob Leisler, formerly a captain in the New York militia, called an inter-colonial convention in New York to organize coordinated action against the Indians and French in 1690, but it dissolved almost immediately. William III's new governor arrived in New York in 1691, and, after a short confrontation, Leisler surrendered to British troops. Leisler was later executed for treason, but his rebellion demonstrated the capriciousness of British rule in the colonies and reinforced the idea that a remote power could not legitimately govern a people who, by their own industry, developed and defended their land.

Into this long-simmering situation came five great waves of Scotch-Irish immigration from 1710 to 1775. Over a quarter-million Presbyterians from Ulster and other regions in Ireland came to escape political, religious, and economic persecution by their British overlords in Ireland, and they found the wilds of America much to their liking. They recognized children as having great asset value in their agrarian culture, and large families became normal. Not surprisingly, the Scotch-Irish were the primary reason the population exploded in the colonies during the pre-Revolutionary period. They were also anti-British to the core, and not only did they agitate for rebellion, they later formed the backbone of the Continental Army, at times comprising up to sixty percent of the army. The importance of this entire group of colonists would later be minimized by Progressive historians and sometimes labeled simply as "Irish" by Catholic historians to infer they were Catholic instead of Protestant. One historian even tagged them as "the people with no name."[41]

Egged on by the newly arrived Scotch-Irish, local leaders began turning more and more to home rule. Various conventions were held, of which the Albany Congress in 1754 was the most important. Representatives from seven of the thirteen colonies, New Hampshire, Massachusetts, Rhode Island, Connecticut, New York, Pennsylvania, and Maryland, met for almost a month, discussing mostly Benjamin Franklin's "Albany Plan." This was a proposal to create an association of eleven colonies to deal with the problems of the Indians and the French, with a president appointed by the Crown. It provided for a colonial assembly with legislative powers, and was, therefore, rejected by the individual colony legislatures as well as the Colonial Office. The Albany Plan was not intended to forge a new nation, but certainly would have been a step in that direction.

The first Continental Congress was not a union of the colonies either, but in October, 1774, it sent a Declaration and Resolves enumerating the rights of Americans and asking for the repeal of the Coercive Acts to King George. In part, the Declaration said:

"That the inhabitants of the English colonies in North-America, by the immutable laws of nature, the principles of the English constitution, and the several charters or compacts, have the following RIGHTS:

Resolved, 1. That they are entitled to life, liberty and property: and they have never ceded to any foreign power whatever, a right to dispose of either without their consent.

Resolved, 2. That our ancestors, who first settled these colonies, were at the time of their emigration from the mother country, entitled to all the rights, liberties, and immunities of free and natural-born subjects within the realm of England.

Resolved, 3. That by such emigration they by no means forfeited, surrendered, or lost any of those rights, but that they were, and their descendants now are, entitled to the exercise and enjoyment of all such of them, as their local and other circumstances enable them to exercise and enjoy.

Resolved, 4. That the foundation of English liberty, and of all free government, is a right in the people to participate in their legislative council: and as the English colonists are not represented, and from their local and other circumstances, cannot properly be represented in the British parliament, they are entitled to a free and exclusive power of legislation in their several provincial legislatures, where their right of representation can alone be preserved, in all cases of taxation and internal polity, subject only to the negative of their sovereign, in such manner as has been heretofore used and accustomed: But, from the necessity of the case, and a regard to the mutual interest of both countries, we cheerfully consent to the operation of such acts of the British parliament, as are bonafide, restrained to the regulation of our external commerce, for the purpose of securing the commercial advantages of the whole empire to the mother country, and the commercial benefits of its respective members, excluding every idea of taxation internal or external, for raising a revenue on the subjects in America without their consent.

Resolved, 5. That the respective colonies are entitled to the common law of England, and more especially to the great and inestimable privilege of being tried by their peers of the vicinage, according to the course of that law.

Resolved, 6. That they are entitled to the benefit of such of the English statutes, as existed at the time of their colonization; and which they have, by experience, respectively found to be applicable to their several local and other circumstances.

Resolved, 7. That these, his Majesty's colonies, are likewise entitled to all the immunities and privileges granted and confirmed to them by royal charters, or secured by their several codes of provincial laws.

Resolved, 8. That they have a right peaceably to assemble,

consider their grievances, and petition the king; and that all prosecutions, prohibitory proclamations, and commitments for the same, are illegal.

Resolved, 9. That the keeping a standing army in these colonies, in times of peace, without the consent of the legislature of that colony, in which such army is kept, is against law...

All and each of which the aforesaid deputies, on behalf of themselves, and their constituents, do claim, demand, and insist on, as their indubitable rights and liberties, which cannot be legally taken from them, altered or abridged by any power whatever, without their own consent, by their representatives in their several provincial legislature."[42]

This petition was a bombshell in London, and the king responded by sending additional troops to the colonies. Up to this point, Parliament had reacted indulgently to American complaints, especially when they were backed up by boycotts of British goods after lobbying and petitions proved ineffective. There had been two earlier boycotts that had proven at least partially successful in reducing British trade; the first in 1765 following the Sugar and Stamp Acts which Parliament then repealed, and the second in 1768 which caused Parliament to repeal all of the Townshend duties except the one on Tea.[43]

The Tea Act, designed by Parliament primarily to enable the British East India Company to sell tea cheaper in the colonies by removing transshipment taxes on tea in Great Britain, was passed in May of 1773. However, it also contained a not-so-hidden political motive. If the tea tax still in effect from the Townshend Acts was paid on the cheaper tea in Boston and elsewhere, the colonies would have implicitly agreed to paying taxes "without representation."

Economically, the Tea Act created price competition to tea smuggled into the colonies on American ships since the East India Company was allowed to ship tea directly from India, and any tea shipped through Great Britain would not be subject to a British export tax. Opposition to importing the tea immediately developed in the four major colonial ports. In New York and Philadelphia, the tea was shipped back to Britain, and in Charleston, it was left to rot on the docks. In Boston, Patriots refused to allow the tea to be unloaded, while the governor refused to allow the tea ships to leave port. The

Americans responded with the Boston Tea Party in December of 1773. Led by the members of the Sons of Liberty, a revolutionary group consisting primarily of freemasons in Boston, a party of men dressed as Indians boarded three East Indian ships and proceeded to throw all three hundred and forty-two chests of tea into the harbor. This time, British reaction was more severe, and after Parliament's passage of the Coercive or Intolerable Acts, the first Continental Congress was called.

One cannot underestimate the importance of tea and its distribution in the American colonies at the time. There was literally no surface water on the eastern seaboard that was fit to drink, and customarily all water was boiled before drinking. Tea made the boiled water palatable, and was the primary non-alcoholic beverage. Coffee replaced tea as the drink of choice by the 1850s, but in 1773, tea kept the colonists in good health. If the Royal Navy tightened down on the endemic smuggling of Dutch tea into the colonies, the result could be a disaster. Nor was tea the only issue. It might have been the flashpoint, but the British Navigation Acts also prohibited the colonies from trading with any country other than Great Britain or its possessions. The colonies were hardly self-sufficient on more than a subsistence level, and to defy Great Britain meant that economic catastrophe was likely to be the result. Yet the cause of liberty was so important, Patriots were willing to risk everything in its defense, including economic collapse.

**Controlling the Debate**

As English authority was simply not recognized by many towns and localities where Association committees were established, the committees' decrees and actions became the de facto law of the land. Although actual sentiment to establish a new nation free from British control was distinctly in the minority, Patriots used the Association to seize control of county and town councils, often by intimidation and the threat of force, and create committees composed solely of Patriots. Kangaroo courts were set up to try people for trading with the British, and offenders who staunchly defended the king or showed Tory (Loyalist) tendencies were often run out of town or the county. This was not a pretty period in American history, as the liberties the

Patriots said they were fighting for were exactly those they denied to Tories. The best that can be said is that women and children were rarely harmed, but males were tarred and feathered, businesses destroyed, contraband confiscated, and heavy fines imposed. As Tories were run out of towns and rural areas, they fled to cities on the coasts or sought safe haven with relatives in quieter areas. In many cases something approximating mob rule took over, and America endured its version (much milder, of course) of the French Terror.

As the population divided itself into three distinct groups, Patriots, Tories, and neutrals, towns, and areas took on political orientations; some became hotbeds for patriotism, some Tory, and some unable to be roused by either side. Country of origin and religion played major roles, as the towns and areas had often been settled by relatively homogenous groups, and there were Quaker towns, Puritan towns, Scotch-Irish areas, etc. This was seen in the militia formations, and often full companies were Scotch-Irish, Congregational, Anglican, and the like.

In short, there was "ethnic cleansing" to use the modern term, but rarely by assassination. As an individual's business was shunned or no one would help bring in the harvest or plow in the spring, families would pack up and move to a friendlier area, or endure in isolation and silence. Before long, everyone in an area knew the feelings of everyone else, and they acted accordingly. The scene in the movie "The Patriot" accurately depicted a Scotch-Irish town and its Presbyterian church. Soldiers were recruited in the church and it appeared that the whole town supported the rebellion. If anyone didn't, they held their tongue.

In modern terms, the committees "controlled the debate," generally with the assistance of the county sheriff and militia. In particular, the committees made sure the elected sheriff and volunteer militia were firmly under their control before rousting individual citizens for trading with the British. That was all a committee needed to have power—the colonial (later state) militia was made up of county militias, and there was no other body of police. At the national level, only the British occupying forces were available to suppress the committees, but to use British troops was a governor's last resort.

During all this, the Patriots controlled the information the citizenry received, although much of it was wrong, exaggerated, or simply anti-British propaganda. There were only two means of communication: word of mouth and printed material in the form of newspapers and pamphlets. Word of mouth from official or trusted sources, such as spreading the warning that the British were marching toward Lexington, was readily believed and acted upon without hesitation. Rumors were usually dealt with more tentatively, such as by sending a rider to a neighboring town to check out a rumor before calling out the militia. Pamphlets were considered as truth in most cases simply because the news or opinion was written—anything written was first thought to be true. In all of this, it was difficult for Tories to know what was happening if for no other reason than no one would tell them.

Controlling the information flow was probably the primary reason the Patriots were able to shut down all commerce with England. As the war progressed, which side (or neutral) a person was on became a defining characteristic, and outsiders to a community were looked upon with suspicion until their true sentiments could be determined.

The Continental Army may have been a relatively weak force, always poorly supplied and inconsistently led, but nonetheless, it outlasted the British. In the end it won because the home front was secure. Wives and families supported their menfolk away in the war, and Patriot communities remained dedicated to seeing the rebellion through to victory. In modern eyes there might have been no alternative but victory or death, but at the time, there was always the West into which an individual could disappear. Later, for example, the leaders of the Whiskey Rebellion and Shay's Rebellion simply vanished into the West when the Federal Government regained control. On the other hand, such flight on a large scale was probably not feasible, and British retribution would have been severe had the Patriots lost.

In the first Continental Congress, a rumor initially ignited the delegates' passions to make their petition to the king and produce the Association. Immediately after the Congress convened, a report was heard that Boston had come under British cannon fire. It was a false report, but readily accepted as something that could happen.[44] Emotions did not recede rapidly, and the idea of a total boycott gained ground steadily until the Association was passed.

The existing militia officers frequently were not enthusiastic about signing the Association, in many cases because they held royal commissions that would definitively brand them as traitors. Often, local militias had to be reformed from those who would sign the Association, and if local government officials refused to sign, they were by-passed—por worse. These new militias were no longer focused on Indian problems and local emergencies, but on aligning the population with the Continental Congress and taking action against British tyranny. Although they professed loyalty to the Crown, their actions were rebellious, and they forced citizens to declare themselves and make choices. In some areas, notably the Hudson Valley and New York City, the Association committees initially were dominated by Tories. Connecticut militia units took swift action and marched into New York and other Tory areas to set up Patriot committees and militia units, and western Pennsylvania units did the same in eastern Pennsylvania counties.

Although the founding fathers often get the credit from modern historians for successfully catalyzing public opinion and pursuing the war for independence, the committees were made up of the citizenry, who took risks absolutely on a par with the signers of the Declaration of Independence. This might have been a minority revolutionary movement, but large numbers of ordinary citizens were willing to stand up and risk their lives, property, and their family's survival to win their liberty. The Association of Tyron County in North Carolina was a typical example. On August 14, 1775, nearly a year before the Declaration, the Association declared:

"The unprecedented, barbarous, and bloody actions committed by the *British* Troops on our *American* brethren, near *Boston*, on the 19th of *April* and 20th of *May* last, together with the hostile operations and treacherous designs now carrying on by the tools of Ministerial vengeance and despotism, for the subjugating all *British America*, suggest to us the painful necessity of having recourse to arms, for the preservation of those rights and liberties which the principles of our Constitution and the laws of God, nature, and Nations, have made it our duty to defend. We, therefore, the subscribers, freeholders and inhabitants of *Tyron* County, do hereby faithfully unite ourselves under the most sacred ties of religion, honour, and love to our Country, firmly to resist force by force, in defence of our natural freedom and constitutional rights, against all invasions; and at the same time do solemnly engage to take up arms, and risk our lives and fortunes, in maintaining the freedom of our Country, whenever the wisdom and counsel of the Continental Congress, or our Provincial Convention, shall declare it necessary; and this engagement we will continue in and hold sacred, till a reconciliation shall take place between *Great Britain* and *America* on constitutional principles, which we most ardently desire; and we do firmly agree to hold all such persons inimical to the liberties of *America* who shall refuse to subscribe to this Association." (emphasis in the original)[45]

This declaration was signed by forty-eight individuals, mostly of Scotch-Irish origin, and is representative of the declarations produced by a large number of counties throughout the colonies. Notably, there was no constitution at the time in North Carolina, nor had the first Continental Congress produced one the preceding year. North Carolina, however, had called a provincial congress together in August, 1774 in New Bern, and become the first of the thirteen colonies to form a revolutionary legislature in defiance of British authority. This congress approved a boycott of British goods and trade and the formation of a continental congress, electing three delegates from North Carolina to serve when one was formed. A second provincial congress met in April of 1775, and, after the British actions at Lexington and Concord, a third met in August to provide the state with self-government.

In the August meeting in 1775, North Carolina set up a Provincial Council (Committee of Safety) to administer the colony when the provincial congress was not in session. The Provincial Council took action to form town and district Committees of Association and organized North Carolina militias. A Constitution came later after the Declaration of Independence was signed. The "constitution" referred to by the various Association committee writers was not a written document, but the existing arrangements of government, the laws, charters, customs, and institutions together with the principles they incorporated.[46] All this became the basis for the "common law" of the emerging states and nation.

Far less numerous were towns like Ridgefield, Connecticut that voted down the Articles of Association, and declared their firm allegiance to King George and the British government. A meeting was held in Ridgefield on January 30, 1775, and adopted a series of resolutions:

"That we do acknowledge his most sacred Majesty, King George the Third, to be our rightful Sovereign; and do hereby publickly avow our allegiance to him and his legal successors; and that we will, to the utmost of our power, support his throne and dignity against every combination in the universe.

That we acknowledge that the three branches of Legislation, to wit; the King, the House of Lords, and the House of Commons, concurring and acting together, have a constitutional right of government over the whole and every part of the British Empire.

That the Governour, Council, and representatives of this colony... having an established right of legislation... in and over this Colony, and do hereby acknowledge and avow their right of Government and legislation in and over this Colony...

That it would be dangerous and hurtful to the inhabitants of this Town to adopt said Congress's measures; and we hereby publickly disapprove of, and protest against said Congress, and the measures by them directed, as unconstitutional, as subversive of our real liberties, and as countenancing licentiousness."[47]

Three days later, a dissenting group of citizens from Ridgefield met and produced the following:

"Whereas, in a Meeting of the Town of Ridgefield, held on the 30th of January last, the question was put, whether the town would adopt and conform to the Resolves contained in the Association of the Continental Congress, or not; which Question was resolved in the negative. We, subscribers, inhabitants of the society of Ridgebury [an area in Ridgefield], within the said town, do hereby declare, that we were not on the negative side of the above question, and are very sorry that the Town did not adopt the above said Association, as we think it of importance to the cause of American freedom that it should be faithfully observed, and do accordingly purpose to observe it ourselves, as far as we can, under our present circumstances, and stand ready to concur with the Town, if a majority could be obtained for that purpose in appointing a Committee of Observation."[48]

This document was signed by twenty-nine individuals. Help came from the county which called a county-wide congress for

Fairfield County at the town of Fairfield on the 14th of February. All of the towns sent delegates except two, Ridgefield and Newtown. This congress catalyzed action on the part of a number of Ridgefield citizens, and lines were drawn in the sand. A group calling themselves the Ridgebury Liberty-Men produced another document on March 20th:

"Whereas the Delegates from all the Towns in this County (except two) met in Congress, at Fairfield, on the 14th day of February last, being deeply affected to hear of the defection of the Towns of Ridgefield and Newtown from the Association of the Continental Congress, yet finding some who heartily adopt the peaceable measures recommended by Congress, did strongly recommend it to the inhabitants of each of the aforesaid Towns who are warmly attached to the rights of their country, to notify a meeting of said inhabitants, and proceed to choose a Chairman and a Clerk, and fully adopt the doings of the Continental Congress, and publish and transmit the same, with their names thereunto affixed, to the several Towns in this County."[49]

The remainder of the document approved the Association of the Continental Congress, and bound Ridgefield and the signers to supporting it. The Liberty-Men stressed that they [wholly disapproved] "and protest against everything contained in the Resolves passed by this town on the 30th day of January last which is contrary, or in anywise repugnant to the rights of the American Colonies, as states by the late Continental Congress."[50] This declaration was signed by fifty-four citizens, and Ridgefield was in for a difficult war. Newtown, the other holdout in Fairfield County, passed a resolution signed by seventy citizens supporting the Resolves of the Continental Congress on April 13, 1775.

A holdout in New York, the town of Newburgh on the Hudson River, finally subscribed on July 14, 1775:

"Whereas we, the subscribers, have refused to sign the Association within the time limit by the Provincial Congress, and whereas our troubles with the Mother Country continue to increase, and we are now convinced that we have no other alternative left but to repel force by force, or submit to be slaves; Sensible that this is our deplorable situation, and in order to link our chain of friendship still more firm, and to convince our friends and the friends of American

71

liberty in general, we do hereby solemnly and sincerely swear on the holy evangelists, that we will, from henceforth, heartily agree and consent to whatsoever our Continental and Provincial Congresses have, or may do, direct, ordain, and appoint, for the preservation of our constitutional liberties, and that we will, as much as in us lies, discourage the spirit of opposition that has too unhappily prevailed in some parts of this County."[51]

Some committees were set up as essentially trade associations, such as the butchers of Philadelphia who agreed to not butcher lambs at certain times during the year to help improve the breeding of sheep: "We whose names are underwritten, Butchers in the City and Suburbs of Philadelphia, being fully convinced that every thing we hold dear depends on the faithful execution of the Resolves of Congress..., and being glad of having an opportunity to show our zeal and attachment to the liberties of our country..."[52] Their declaration was signed by sixty-six individuals.

Another committee's resolution was representative of many with a heavy religious content. In December, 1774, the Bute County Association of North Carolina formed a militia company and wrote:

"We...do most seriously, Religiously, Join our hearts and hands in embodying ourselves in to an Independent Company of free Men to be in readiness to defend ourselves against any violence that may be exerted against our persons and properties to stand by and Support to the utmost of our Power the Salvation of America. And do most humbly beseech our Lord Jesus Christ of his great Goodness that he will be pleased to govern and guide us to his glory...do engage to stand by Each other with life and fortune, and through whatever fate should befall either, to cherish each other in sickness and in Health. And do furthermore ...promise to each other...that should either of us survive the dreadful Calamities of War, that we will Religiously Cherish and support to the utmost of our power each other's desolate and loving wife, and tender affectionate Children, being poor orphans, from poverty and want, and for the faithful proformence, of this our Brotherly and friendly Covenant, which we mean to proforme So help us God."[53]

These committees and militia units essentially provided the Patriot cause and its armies with the manpower and support to carry the country through the war. Generally, however, the leaders themselves did not serve except for short periods, but they saw to it that their county quotas were filled with volunteers, conscripts, or substitutes, who were generally from the less prosperous members of their community. In many areas, this manpower was culled from the Scotch-Irish inhabitants—men who possessed an abiding hatred of Redcoats for the institutional persecutions the British regularly had carried out earlier in Ireland and the lowlands of Scotland against non-Anglicans.

Typical was a volunteer named James Dougherty in Lancaster County, Pennsylvania. He arrived in America during the winter of 1774-1775 with his wife and infant son, and had been sent to Sunbury with a letter of introduction from his pastor back in Antrim, Ireland. He enlisted in June of 1775, and served to the end of the war in 1783 as a rifleman, artillerist, and in the Commander-in-Chief's Guard, during which time he spent less than a month at home, once on parole after his capture in the Battle of Quebec, and another short leave during which he fought Indians in the Susquehanna Valley. Like most of the long-serving men lacking property and social status, he never rose higher than the rank of private.

## The Association in Action

The committees suppressed Loyalist activities in their towns and counties and were the recognized revolutionary leaders, contending for the hearts and souls of the population. It was hardly a contest, as the British were not present in most cases, and although the British government possessed overwhelming force, it was concentrated in those towns it occupied, as well as on the high seas. In the countryside, the militia and committee leaders could always be where the British weren't. Even in the South, where there was a substantial Tory population, pacified territories rapidly reverted to Patriot control after the British moved out.

The boycotts of 1774 were extremely successful, in part because wealthy planters in the middle and southern colonies supported them. For openers, the Association rendered their debts to British merchants uncollectable, or at least deferred payments until much later. The Navigation Acts restricted them to trading only with the mother country and its dominions, but if independence was won, they could trade anywhere in the world. And there was the West to be won. The Proclamation of 1763 prohibited settlements west of the Appalachians, and after independence, it would be null and void. Indian lands would be available for speculation and development by Americans, not British and Canadians, and in particular, the French Catholics. Even the boycott on the importation of slaves was seen in a positive light. The big landowners already were maintaining or increasing their slave holdings through domestic reproduction, and a moratorium on slave importation would make their slaves more valuable.

On the other hand, small farmers in the middle and southern states were devastated by the lack of trade, and in December of 1775, a series of salt riots broke out in Virginia. Salt had become unavailable, and the small farmers were faced with either re-opening trade for salt by returning to Britain's good graces, or winning complete independence so trade could be established world-wide. It was a dilemma that was only resolved eight years later after incredible hardships.

The British position was perhaps best summed up by Samuel Johnson in his pamphlet, *Taxation no Tyranny, An Answer to the Resolution and Address of the American Congress*. He decreed that since Great Britain had always protected the Americans, obedience was stipulated, and that England, therefore, enjoyed the right to govern. "British dominions were governed by English laws, entitles to English dignities, regulated by English counsels, and protected by English arms," and therefore, the English Parliament had a perfect right to impose taxes on the American colonies.[54]

In April of 1775, Lord Dunmore, the royal governor of Virginia, seized the Virginia gunpowder supply in Williamsburg, threatening to emancipate the slaves and burn Williamsburg. Reports of Dunmore's actions and threats raced through Virginia and the South, enraging whites of all social classes. Dunmore offered freedom to any slave who signed up with the British army in November 1775, and this act, seen by most colonists as directly endangering their lives and property, turned many ambivalent whites against the British. Johnson's pamphlet also received wide distribution, particularly his statement, "[L]et us give the Indians arms, and teach them discipline, and encourage them now and again to plunder a plantation..." Other British leaders recommended arming slaves and inciting them to revolt against their masters.[55]

During the war, the British pursued a series of strategies to win back the colonies that are worthy of study for their application to modern revolutionary conflicts.

From the beginning, British commanders tried to win over the people by maintaining a certain benevolent posture that would enable the colonies to take their rightful place as British dominions after the war was successfully concluded. The Howe brothers, one commanding the British Fleet and the other the British Army, were also peace commissioners and charged with trying to bring the rebels to submission by whatever means possible. That influenced General Howe to attempt to crush the rebellion through a demonstration of raw British power by an overwhelming assault at Bunker Hill. Rather than flanking and capturing the American army by cutting it off at the Charleston neck, Howe opted for a frontal assault to show the colonists that the British Army was unstoppable. His gambit failed, and the Americans took heart at the sight of heavy British casualties. After severely defeating General George Washington at New York the following year, he became dovish, and exhibited a curious reluctance to finish Washington once and for all through ruthless pursuit.

Although many British officers in the colonies considered the revolution to be primarily a religious uprising by Scotch-Irish Presbyterians, others understood that New England Congregationalists and tidewater low-church (vestry control) Anglicans were in the fight as well.[56] John Adams split the Americans into three equal parts, one-third Patriot, one-third Tory, and one-third neutral.[57] A better approximation from the almost 2.78 million American population in 1780 as estimated by the Census Bureau would be five hundred and seventy-five thousand slaves, seven hundred thousand Patriots, five hundred thousand Tories, and a little more than a million who were neutral or ambivalent.

The Patriots turned out in large numbers to fight the British, and about a hundred and twenty thousand served in Continental Army formations. Another eighty thousand joined militia units that actually saw action for short periods of time. Approximately seven thousand were killed or mortally wounded in battle, eleven thousand died of disease or wounds in camp, and eighteen thousand succumbed as prisoners of war. To this toll must be added another ten-to-fifteen thousand that were so enfeebled from wounds or captivity, they expired within a year of leaving the army or being released from captivity. Patriot military deaths therefore totaled forty-six-to-fifty-one thousand men, or about one-fourth of all Patriots who took up arms. This number still understates the total American losses, as it doesn't include civilians killed by Indians, Tories, or British as they burned and pillaged, nor does it count civilian deaths caused by privation and sickness brought on by wartime conditions. Another ten-to-twenty thousand deaths would seem to be probable and possibly low, especially considering that about fifty thousand Tories took up arms for the British.[58]

Tory deaths are estimated at eighty-nine hundred, bringing the total carnage to most likely about seventy-five souls. Moreover, since only a fourth of the population would have been of military age and male, the numbers indicate that a very high percentage of eligible Patriots served during the war, even accounting for multiple enlistments and that many neutral individuals probably served as well. All this suggests that about three and a half percent of the free American population died during the war from its effects, higher than any war in American history. Another hundred-to-a hundred and fifty thousand Tories and fifteen thousand slaves left with the British before, during, or after the war, so the human toll was enormous.

Adding to the people's sufferings, the economy of the colonies declined dramatically, both from the effects of the Association and the war itself. The colonies' real per capita income may have declined by as much as twenty-two percent from 1774 to 1800, but that includes seventeen years of high growth rates following the war's conclusion in 1783.[59]

During the period of the war itself, the decline may have reached over fifty percent, the greatest slump in America's history. Contributing to this slump were the boycotts, the destruction of the war, a dysfunctional financial system, the loss of overseas trade, British occupation of major cities, and the loss of Tory productivity through emigration. British armies occupied New York, Boston, Penobscot, Charleston, Savannah, Augusta, Philadelphia, and many other cities at some point during the war, and severely restricted trade and business activity among the colonies. In real per-capita terms, New England's commodity exports rose by slightle over one percent from 1768/72 to 1791/92, and the Middle Atlantic's by almost ten percent, indicating the extent of the war's economic devastation in the North. Offsetting even those modest gains was the disappearance of overseas trade below Delaware: exports fell by thirty-nine percent in the Upper South, and almost fifty percent in the Lower South.[60] Economically, the war had been a catastrophe.

Urban areas were devastated, with Boston, New York City, Philadelphia, and Charleston being hit particularly hard. Their share of total white-collar employment fell by a third from 1774 to 1800, and the percentage of earnings that could be considered white collar fell from five percent to below two percent The formerly prosperous middle-class nearly disappeared, and clearly, the United States had not recovered from the economic disaster brought about by the Revolutionary War even by 1800.

There were serious shortages in certain staples that Americans were forced to do without or scramble to provide for themselves. Tea, of course, disappeared as the Royal Navy regularly patrolled to stop smuggling, and people began to use almost any plant that could serve as a substitute. Salt was an especially vital commodity, particularly because it was used to preserve foods. Before 1775, it had been imported from Great Britain or Turks Island in the Bahamas, under the control of Bermuda.[61] Turks Island was officially closed by the British to American shipping early in the war, and salt supplies rapidly began to disappear. A very real fear of a salt shortage arose, and various states took measures to spur salt production. North Carolina rationed existing quantities in the state and offered bonuses to encourage the construction of salt works. All along the seacoast, salt works sprang up, boiling seawater in large iron pans—a primitive method perhaps, but the Patriots were desperate to alleviate the salt shortage.

The Bermudians, dependent on the American mainland for grain and flour, petitioned the Continental Congress for an exemption to the American embargo, and, in the fall of 1775, Congress allowed trade with Bermuda and the Bahamas.[62] That action hardly solved the problem, however. The Royal Navy understood the importance of salt and effectively interdicted much of the merchant traffic. In 1778, for example, the Commissary Department of the Continental Army contracted with Miller and Tracy of Boston to sail to Turks Island and obtain salt. Of the thirteen vessels sent, seven were captured on their outward voyage by British vessels. Nor was the domestic production of salt able to meet American needs. The Royal Naval units closed down many of the coastal salt works in New Jersey and Virginia through constant patrolling, and, throughout the duration of the war, salt remained in critically short supply.

All this had taken place following a period of extraordinary economic growth that Parliament might have thought would make the colonists extremely happy to be a British dominion. After all, the gross national product (GNP) of the thirteen colonies had increased by a factor of twenty-five between 1650 and 1770, allowing American colonists to enjoy the highest standard of living in the world.[63] Exports to overseas markets and imports of finished goods had made the colonies increasingly prosperous, and Britain's restrictions under the Navigation Acts were having minimal economic impact, although the lack of freedom to trade with non-British dominions was a festering political issue. Domestically, inter-colony trade had also burgeoned. Unforeseen by Parliament, however, was that such trade between colonies fostered both economic interactions and increased intercommunication, and tended to push them into closer association with each other—the prerequisite for becoming a nation.[64]

So great was American prosperity before 1775 that arriving Hessian soldiers considered America a paradise. One German wrote in his diary, "...we could perceive the radiance of freedom which the inhabitants of this new world had previously enjoyed...Every plantation, every farm, seemed a shelter in a fool's paradise; the good harmony between neighbors, where a beggar was never seen on the street and certainly never encountered. All this made us think it to be a blessed land when compared to Germany." Dazzled by the wondrous bounty, the diarist exhibited great sympathy for the Patriots, "...among those inhabitants, love, faith, and freedom of speech were to be found, and now, through war, to have their customs and well-being completely destroyed."[65]

Such extraordinary prosperity was hardly a cause for revolution, but, of course, the economy wasn't the issue. The colonists felt threatened by Parliament and the king ideologically and religiously. They were willing to risk their economic well-being for the sake of ensuring their liberty to a degree higher than that enjoyed by citizens in Great Britain itself. Obviously, America was inferior to the mother country in almost every way except the degree of individual liberty, but the upstart Americans thought they were superior. They were ready to confront the world's greatest military power with nary a qualm. American exceptionalism can do that to a people.

In addition, there was the thundering effect of religion—specifically the sermonizing by American pastors from their pulpits. Although these were generally confined to Presbyterian, Congregational, low-church Anglican and, to a much lesser extent, Lutheran, Baptist, and Dutch Reformed ministers, their effect went far beyond that normally reported by Progressive historians.[66] As one Hessian diarist noted upon entering Philadelphia in 1777, "I have seen few churches and those few are mostly in ruins, because their preachers have joined the rebels and led their parishioners into their evil beliefs."[67] Congregational minister William Starnes told his church attendees that "...these lands by them first settled they purchased by fair bargain of the natives. The rest was obtained by conquest, in a war entered into them for their own defence, and they defended their acquisitions by themselves alone for a long time with inconceivable expence of blood and treasure...these lands are clearly ours... What any man acquires by his own labour and toil, he has an exclusive right to." (Spelling as original.)[68]

English colonial policies were repeatedly depicted with words meant to enflame the population: "oppression," "despotism," and "tyranny." The Congregational minister, Oliver Noble, railed at "the oppressive hand of despotic power." the President of Harvard stated, "America...[was]...threatened with cruel oppression." The Presbyterian president of Princeton, John Witherspoon, spoke of, "The ambition of mistaken princes, the cunning and cruelty of oppressive and corrupt ministers." And the Reverend Samuel West said that the people of Massachusetts, "find themselves cruelly oppressed by the parent state."[69]

God was clearly on the side of the Patriots. Reverend Noble thundered, "commit our cause to God and stand fast... The cause of America is the cause of God, never did Man struggle in a greater, or more righteous cause." The Presbyterian minister, John Carmichael, told a company of Pennsylvania militia on June 4, 1775, "[I] congratulate you...on this day, on the certainty we have, for the justice and goodness of our cause...he [God] is on our side..., and if God is on our side, we need not fear what man can do unto us." Ministers often remarked on the future greatness of America, a land that would replace the tired lands of Europe suffering under their tyrannical institutions.

For some, America was the new Israel; America was to be "a holy people unto the Lord our God" and an example to the world of the righteousness of liberty. Virtue and patriotism became inseparable; virtue on the part of the citizenry made a democratic republic work, and patriotism was the obligation the citizen had towards defending the republic and its institutions in accordance with God's wishes. Secular happiness depended on a vision of a Christian future. As John Adams wrote to one minister about preaching against the tyranny of Great Britain, "It is Religion and Morality alone, which can establish the Principles upon which Freedom can securely stand...You cannot therefore be more pleasantly, or usefully employed than in the Way of your profession, pulling down the Strong Hands of Satan."[70] The modern reader should consider if America has changed from the vision spoken of by these early voices.

After all these words, the American people would have to fight to obtain (or *re*tain, in their minds) their liberties. Perhaps foremost among their cherished liberties were those so definitively and eloquently stated by James Otis in 1761 and expanded in 1764: that no King or Parliament has the right to deprive a man of his life, liberty, or property.[71] Otis also made no mistake as to the origin of his rights: "All power is of God."[72]

To ensure their liberties and God-given rights, Patriots were willing to suffer massive economic hardships, risk life and limb and everything they owned. Even if they prevailed, the resulting regime would be untried and uncertain at best, and could be much worse than the situation in 1774. They might be exchanging one despot thousands of miles away for many despots around the corner. But it was truly a religious war, a war over ideas generally only partly formed.

Thomas Jefferson, James Otis, Samuel Adams, John Adams, and Benjamin Franklin might articulate with great erudition the principles of liberty and democratic self-government that were so noble they were able to convince some men to lay down their lives for such ideas, but, for most revolutionaries in the local committees that signed their names to the Association, the issue was much simpler: either a man could determine his own destiny between himself and his elected representatives, or he wasn't free. All else was slavery, in some form or another, and such a life was readily visible in the poor Negro wretches who toiled without pride, honor, stature, and hope. Even the Indian was better off. He could die free, and was worthy of respect as a man, as someone who would stand up for himself. This was a fight to the bitter end, and the men like James Dougherty would have to be killed before the colonies could revert to British rule.

We are left with only one question: "Is modern America made up of lesser citizens?"

# Chapter 3

## Correctable Defects

A number of problems may be correctable even with the present Progressive control of Congress, the executive branch, Supreme Court, federal bureaucracies, education, NGOs, and even state and local government. These corrections may or may not require drastic citizen action, but, at the very least, citizens must besiege their representatives and the president with calls for action to reform government.

The operative theory behind all these actions is the assumption that American politicians still retain a vestige of morality from the times their parents dragged them to church. Perhaps Progressives don't realize where they are taking America, or perhaps they do, and still have nagging doubts. Gnostics believe the earth is the realm of the demiurge—Satan—and perhaps they are right. If so—and the decline of Christianity and the rise of atheism seem to indicate they are—then Progressives are Satan in the flesh, and there is nothing to be done. But for the moment, let us believe rehabilitation is possible.

It is all about framing the debate. Republicans often say the situation outlined in Chapter 1 came about strictly through the Democrat Party. But that is not true. It has become increasingly obvious that the Republican Party is tightly controlled at the national and even some state levels by what is often termed "the Republican Establishment." This is a group of moderate Progressives whose political position is only slightly less stridently Progressive than that of the Democrat Party. Senator John McCain, Speaker of the House John Boehner, Senate Majority Leader Mitch McConnell, and presidential candidate Jeb Bush represent the Republican establishment as moderate Progressives and differ with far-left Progressives like presidential candidate Hillary Clinton, Senate Minority Leader Harry Reid, House Minority Leader Nancy Pelosi, and Chair of the Democratic National Committee Debbie Wasserman Schultz only in the speed in which they would take the United States into a Progressive dictatorship of the elite. The term, "Democrat-lite" definitely seems to be applicable for them.

## Survival Issues

The national Republican party seems unwilling or unable to confront any of the seven most important issues since Obama took office: (1) the survival of the four great features of American exceptionalism; (2) Agenda 21 as promoted by Progressives; (3) Government growth and its intrusion into the lives of Americans at all levels; (4) the education of America's children; (5) economic stability providing opportunity for all citizens; (6) security of the citizenry from lawlessness, demographic changes through immigration, and foreign aggression; and (7) the survival of the United States as a political entity, true to its principles as laid down by its Founding Fathers. None of these issues have been addressed by the Republican Party in the last twenty-six years with definitive statements of policy, much less any coherent action.

The Democrat Party, however, has taken a position on these issues, framed the debate, and forced the Republican Party to play catch-up on the Democrats' home field. For anyone who doubts that the debate on all issues is controlled by Progressives/Democrats, one only needs to consider how "political correctness" dominates one's choice of words and approach to problems. Political correctness always reflects Progressive ideology, and is so pervasive in the U.S. today that no one remembers that it originated to describe slavish adherence to the Stalinist line in the Soviet Union. Today, political correctness describes slavish adherence to Progressive ideology, and doing and saying everything accordingly. These seven primary issues must be addressed with politically incorrect approaches by the Republican Party and all citizens who desire the survival of the United States. These people will henceforth be identified by the term "patriots" in this work. Let us address the primary issues one at a time.

(1) **American exceptionalism**. Progressive/Democrats have rejected American exceptionalism, a concept they don't understand and don't like. Accepting no standard definition of the concept, they belittle it and frame the debate on details rather than the underlying pillars that make America exceptional. They have rejected morality based on Protestant Christianity in favor of humanism, moral equivalence, and the denial of any standard, and right to be judgmental. Morality is no more than whatever fits current circumstances to promote the Progressive agenda. Democrats favor instituting civil law, and see private property as no longer sustainable under Agenda 21. They have moved the U.S. economy into a system of crony capitalism, and are tempering it with European-style state socialism. President Obama has actually likened the American feeling of being exceptional to the Greeks or the French likewise feeling exceptional. In so doing, Obama has shown himself as not being culturally an American, and his treatment of the armed forces, historical memorials, American historical figures, common law, and America's Christian heritage, has certainly fallen woefully short of representing and furthering American ideals and culture.

First and foremost, the concept of American exceptionalism must be recognized and acknowledged by everyone in government, but with a new definition used throughout by all citizens. The four features defined in Chapter 1 are what make the United States exceptional, and the debate must be limited to these elements. Any expansion or deviation from stressing these four elements misdirects the debate into areas in which Progressives can effectively marginalize the entire concept.

The British author, Godfrey Hodgson, openly attacked American exceptionalism in his *The Myth Of American Exceptionalism*, but like other authors who have mocked American exceptionalism, offered no definition. Some Progressives have attacked what they have thought was the basis for exceptionalism: the myth of rugged individualism, the "can-do" spirit of a youthful culture (now long gone), and the unique natural resources available in the lands conquered and settled by the Anglo-Celts in the New World. Others dismiss the concept and point to Europe as having created the political system the Founding Fathers adopted, making America little more than a democracy of amateurs following in Europe's footsteps. Not surprisingly, this position is one assumed by many historians and political scientists in Britain and France, even though both featured monarchial governments at the time of the American Revolution.[73]

Patriots must change the debate, and demand American exceptionalism be defined and discussed in terms of the four great underlying pillars. Anything else is to let Progressives frame the debate and allow the United States to devolve into a European-style, failed socialist state.

(2) **Agenda 21** is being pushed by Progressive Democrats at all levels, from ICLEI (International Council on Local Environmental Initiatives) in county and city government, to the Department of Interior, the EPA, and all other bureaucracies in the Federal Government. Since two of the major goals of Agenda 21, are the abolition of private property and total control of the citizenry, Progressive Democrats supporting Agenda 21 seek to destroy traditional American concepts of individual liberty and citizen rights, regardless of all rhetoric to the contrary. To realize the goals of Agenda 21, a depopulation of the world to only one billion persons is required, of course tightly controlled and monitored by Progressives. Unable or unwilling to stand up against Agenda 21, Republicans are silent. They apparently fear the Progressive juggernaut cannot be stopped, and want their families to be among those selected to survive. It is a fool's hope; Americans are being blamed for all mankind's problems, and the survival of any American other than a certified Progressive is doubtful.

Congressmen, senators, presidents, and all state offices must be filled with individuals pledged to opposing Agenda 21 with every fiber in their beings. ICLEI must be labeled and taxed as a subversive organization responsible to a foreign power (the United Nations). The Federal Government must remove all Agenda 21 initiatives from its executive departments (put there by Bill Clinton), and the United Nations expelled from its New York offices along with all attendant organizations and personnel. The United States must lower its contributions to the United Nations to a level less than fifty percent higher than the average of major nations representing all parts of the globe. Agenda 21 means the destruction of the United States, and any person supporting it should be considered subversive, and working for a foreign government. All NGOs advocating Agenda 21 must lose their tax exempt status and be required to denote their status as a subversive organization in all literature and public disclosures.

(3) **Government Growth**. Progressive Democrats always push the growth of government—the Government is the putative solution, not the problem. Today, an extremely strong case can be made for the abolition of the EPA, the Federal Reserve, and the departments of Agriculture, Energy, Education, and Homeland Security, plus many agencies within other departments. Base-line budgeting should be replaced by zero-based budgeting as a bare minimum, yet no Republican has yet espoused this step. Progressive leadership fears tha,t in the cataclysm of universal shortages of food, water, and energy in the next decade, believed by them to result from uncontrolled American liberty, only a strong federal government will be able to save the select. Draconian measures will be necessary, and government functionaries will have to sacrifice the citizenry in order for the elite to survive. That's also why gun control is so important to Progressives; it must become a reality for them to be able to suppress the citizenry and construct the new Progressive oligarchy. Progressive dogma assumes that taxes on wealth and property must become confiscatory as, eventually, all property is to be owned by the state. Government growth is always good, regardless of the nation's economy. If the economy is good, government grows; if is it bad, government grows faster.

Progressive John Kenneth Galbraith led the way in promoting the approved Progressive solution to all societal ills—have the government spend money. Involved in price controls during World War II, he found the U.S.'s war economy thrilling and highly successful. A government-controlled economy did not adhere to useless economic principles of the past, and the future of state capitalism was golden. He forgot what Utopian Socialist Charles Fournier had pronounced a hundred and fifty years earlier: "What the State promotes, withers; what the State protects, dies." The modern corollary was simply: "What the State promises, never happens."

The people must begin to elect legislators, governors, and presidents who are committed to reducing the size and extent of government. Constitutional amendments such as those contained in the Appendix must be proposed and approved. Government bureaucracies should be moved out of Washington, DC and environs as soon as possible, and relocated around the nation in areas experiencing slow economic growth. The government must be moved into closer contact with the citizenry, not become increasingly remote. Washington may continue as the legislative capital of the United States, but all other aspects of government should be at least a teleconference away.

(4) **Education.** Progressive Democrats have pushed Common Core into most states and school districts, and, using the leverage of federal funding, have been able to effectively dictate curricula, school textbooks, and what should be taught through the Department of Education. Common Core sets standards that are unreasonably low, and makes all teaching follow Progressive political correctness. Worse than that, it dumbs-down American high school graduates by a year and a half, and replaces competence and accuracy with "free-thinking" compatible with Progressive ideology. There is little difference between what is happening today in American classrooms and what occurred in the Soviet Union under Stalin.

Already a vast amount of Progressive propaganda has been accepted by school-trained young people as fact: that man is responsible for global warming, twenty percent of all female college students are subjected to a sexual assault on campus, raising the minimum wage raises employment, illegal immigrants in the U.S. deserve a job and government assistance, Christianity is myth for the uneducated, homosexuality is an approved lifestyle, abortion rights empower women, and gender differences should be ignored. All of this is simply Progressive propaganda, expertly promulgated and disseminated, and supported by Progressive educators in line with their personal agendas. Americans wonder how the Germans under Hitler were able to swallow his rantings as fact, but they only have to look at Americans accepting what Progressives are teaching to see Hitler's techniques in action.

Ninety-five percent of university professors are Progressives, and daily, the trained elite becomes more misanthropic, more convinced that they should rule in place of God, and more sure that personal liberty is a luxury that can no longer be allowed for the common people. All is to be allowed for the elite, however, as they are the ruling class, the nomenklatura. The rest of Americans are to submit in order to survive as subjects rather than as citizens.

The people must take back control of education, first by abolishing President Carter's misguided idea, the Department of Education. Second, Common Core must be eliminated for being substandard and an insult to all Americans. Politicians in favor of Common Core must be removed from office when they come up for re-election. All initiatives by the Federal Government in education that have attempted to promote social justice must be terminated. These initiatives, however flawed, belong to the states and their local governments. Tenure in educational organizations must be abolished and simple procedures installed to terminate bad or even poor teachers in all public schools, universities, and colleges that take public funds. That means essentially all universities, colleges, and public schools.

If citizens are paying for their children's education, they must have a voice in who teaches the students, what they teach, and even how the teaching is accomplished. To require the citizenry to finance schools and then have no say in the educational process (another practice imported from Imperial Germany and currently being defended to the death by Progressives), is a gross violation of democratic principles.

The lack of rigorous and high standards in the teaching of teachers is a national scandal, and allowing teachers' unions to dictate how, what, and when teachers will teach is unconscionable. Students are not wards of the state to be propagandized at will, they are members of families, with mothers and fathers, and the state only educates them as a service to a student's parents, and on the parents' behalf. Somehow, all this has been forgotten and replaced with subservience to receive government grants. As Americans, we must do better.

(5) **Economic stability**. Progressive Democrats have lost all credibility as to their ability to steer the economic ship of state. One Progressive idea after another has been floated and foisted on the American public with inevitably disastrous results. The New Dealer Franklin Roosevelt, a man who was never able to support himself in private industry and throughout his life lived off his mother's money, first decided to introduce capital controls on American citizens and confiscate all holdings of bullion gold. He followed that act by massive public works programs, hiring unemployed individuals in

great numbers in the several months prior to elections and laying them off a few months later. He introduced wage and price controls, setting the wages a worker could earn in private industry as well as the prices for which a company could sell its products. This unconstitutional act (the NIRA) was abolished, but the damage had been done. From that point onward, a significant number of American citizens looked to the Federal Government for support. Social Security was introduced, with FDR's solemn pledge that it would never cost a citizen more than one percent of their earnings. By 2000, it cost a self-employed person 15.3% of his earnings, and it was called self-employment tax.

The Keynesian theory of economics was heralded as the key to solving all economic problems. Supposedly, it enabled governments to control business and economics so that prosperity could be shared across the income scale, wealth could be redistributed, and recessions and depressions banished forever. It's never happened. The Austrian School of Ludwig von Mises offers a much better chance at dampening business cycles and should be given a try.

England dove into socialism following World War II with disastrous results. By 1978, the pound sterling had been devalued and was no longer the world's reserve currency. Once ruling the world's greatest empire, Britain was in a depression and nearing full economic collapse. Fortunately for Great Britain, Margaret Thatcher became Prime Minister. She broke the power of the unions, privatized most of the government's enterprise assets, and restored prosperity.

The Soviet Union finally woke up to the fact that communism didn't work, moved to capitalism and a market economy, and gave up its dream of world domination. Now, it's the U.S.'s turn. The Progressives are taking the American economy down the well-trodden road to collapse, and not making a single move to head off the inevitable. The only question is whether this is folly or by design. Cries for a balanced budget and spending cutbacks go unheeded, and the end of the dollar as the world's reserve currency is in sight.

The correction of this course is austerity in government spending and rebuilding the industrial giant that was once America. Yet, this is hardly possible without a sea change in the political atmosphere from Progressivism to classical Jeffersonian liberalism. The product liability problem alone practically eliminates all American manufacturing and dictates that goods be manufactured in China or some other overseas location where the liability for faulty product design or manufacturing enters a black hole. The most important position in a U.S. corporation is no longer found in engineering, but in the legal department. Tort reform is an absolute necessity.

Although Progressives continue to say that U.S. is the world's second largest manufacturer, that statement, like all Progressive propaganda, is highly misleading. The largest industries in the United States included as "manufacturing" are petroleum, steel, automobiles, aerospace, telecommunications, chemicals, electronics, food processing, consumer goods, lumber, and mining. But petroleum, chemicals, lumber, and mining are not "manufacturing," and telecommunications equipment, electronics, and consumer goods are universally outsourced to third-world countries but included in the gross revenues for American companies. America's true manufacturing sector had fallen to twelve million jobs in 2014, down from over seventeen million in 2000.[74] Major incentives are clearly needed to revitalize the American economy, and elected representatives must be in favor of such incentives.

(6) **Security.** Progressive Democrats have sought security for American citizens through international agreements and reliance on international bodies of politicians and bureaucrats beholden to no one but themselves. International agreements are what brought about World War I and World War II, and the United Nations is arguably the most corrupt organization in the world, although the European Union and the Obama Administration might mount challenges.

Progressive administrations have subordinated the American justice system to the International Criminal Court and the World Court, both part of the United Nations. While other nations close their borders to illegal aliens, the U.S. Federal Government refuses to protect Americans, even suing a state (Arizona) for attempting to enforce immigration law when the Obama Administration would not meet its constitutional obligations.

On the other hand, the Federal Government refuses to prosecute "sanctuary cities" such as San Francisco that refuse to cooperate with federal authorities to deport illegal aliens. Between the Federal Government's policies and sanctuary cities, drug cartels, enemy agents, terrorists, smugglers of all types, and simple illegal aliens flood into the United States. The Federal Government looks on with apathy… or is it by design?

The U.S. is still active in NATO, with over sixty-five thousand troops stationed in Europe. Against whom are these troops deployed? For whose security are they on station? Altogether in 2013, the U.S. had almost two hundred and eighty thousand troops either stationed in foreign countries, or abroad in "contingency" operations.[75] The American military is making all this effort in foreign lands while illegal immigrants flood into the U.S. and receive benefits not easily available to the average working American or veteran of the armed forces.

The Department of Homeland Security was established in 2002, and, by 2014, had two hundred and forty thousand employees, plus many more private contractors. Yet, the armed forces were established to provide the nation's security. If they are not to be used in this capacity, what are they for? Apparently, Progressives did not trust the military—much like Hitler did not trust his—so they have set up a civilian agency, like Hitler's RHSA and SS, to handle the nation's internal security.[76] First, came the Department of Homeland Security under George W. Bush, and then Obama called for a Civilian National Security Force to be created by greatly expanding Bill Clinton's AmeriCorps, "to be as well funded and trained as the military."[77] Once again, the Federal Government had set up competing bureaucracies, muddied the waters, and promoted turf wars. Even worse, on July 7, 2015, President Obama announced a reduction in the armed forces of forty thousand soldiers over the following two years, while at the same time, he was increasing employment in the Department of Homeland Security.[78]

Military personnel were restricted from carrying weapons on government property or in recruitment offices and the like beginning in 1991; Islamic terrorists have seized on this creation of soft targets and have slaughtered American military service personnel seemingly at will. The Department of Defense's answer in 2015 after the attack in Chattanooga was to have military personnel wear civilian clothes so they wouldn't be a provocation.

This seems to be in line with Lenin's strategy in 1918: "As Marx and Engels have frequently insisted, the first commandment for those who would carry out a successful revolution is to bring about the destruction and disintegration of the old army and its replacement by a new one."[79] As the American armed forces have become smaller, a civilian bureaucracy fully controlled by Progressives has grown accordingly. Why?

For true believers in Christ, security is not a physical concept. Radical Protestantism says that absolute security cannot be found on earth in any form, not in a church, the Bible, a dogma, confession, metaphysics, absolute norms, truth or values, or any such things. Absolute security is only to be found in God, and Christians should abandon the search for absolute physical security because it is only found through salvation by virtue of God's grace.[80] That will bring comfort to some, but not to all. And in the demise of the U.S., Christianity is also likely to disappear. Is that God's plan? Patriots will find that difficult to believe, but they will have to fight to keep the military around to act as a counter-weight to Progressive ambitions.

(7) **Survival of the U.S.** Progressive Democrats have been attacking and destroying every structural aspect of the United States including its society, religion, legal foundations, economy, morals, and political institutions. The nation is now reliving 1933, and the United States is Nazi Germany. The Progressive Federal Government has become all-powerful, and Americans are ruled by sycophants of a pathological narcissist, who is interested in only one thing—his own august being. And Republicans cannot figure out what to do, if anything

Immigration changes the demographic nature of the country, for better or worse, unless it is restricted to the ethnic, religious, and racial composition of the current U.S. But no Republican promotes restrictions, afraid of alienating minorities in his district or state and being voted out of office. He will do anything to stay in office, and is even willing to see the nation become a third-world country, so long as it does not happen too quickly and affect his life style. After him comes the deluge.

Becoming sheep and accepting the demise of the United States due to citizen apathy is unacceptable to a patriot. Immigration must be suspended until the country gets a grip on its problems. Changing America's demographics is not a solution to its current problems, it exacerbates them in every instance. The proposed amendments to the Constitution in the Appendix further address this problem.

## Combatting The Sins of Progressivism—Ideas and Initiatives

Christianity is under siege, while accommodations are illegally being made for other religions such as Islam. The courts are in disarray, with Progressive judges sentencing child rapists to thirty days, a fine, and other light sentences. Illegal aliens convicted of violent felonies are let loose in the U.S. due to prison and jail overcrowding, and aren't even deported. Others who are deported return and hang out in sanctuary cities to continue a life of crime, including murder.

Progressivism stresses rehabilitation rather than punishment in accordance with its atheistic denial of sin. In prisons, Progressive administrators literally have put the prisoners in charge of the prisons, coddling them excessively, and facilitating their criminal careers. Progressive politicians and the Federal Reserve have destroyed any semblance of fiscal responsibility in government, and the inevitable result will be financial and economic collapse.

In 1913, when the Federal Reserve was created, the dollar stood at ninety-five cents compared to the Continental dollar when first issued in 1774, a drop of only four cents in value. In 2009, the dollar was only worth four cents. Progressive bankers and economists had destroyed the dollar, causing it to lose over ninety-six percent of its value, and causing prices to rise by nearly twenty-three hundred percent—or, in other terms, what cost ten dollars in 1913, cost two hundred and forty dollars in 2009. All this is not a picture of progress.

There is the decline in American morality that is closely linked to the Progressive war on Christianity. Moral relativism rules, and the American treatment of blacks since 1865 is considered the same as Stalin's murdering sixty-one million people in the Soviet Union.

Reinforcing their denial of American Exceptionalism, Progressives claim that the United States is no longer a force for good—it is arrogant, condescending, and must look to Europe for world leadership. This lack of moral values plays out in the political arena, where politicians routinely lie, fabricate, and issue highly misleading statements. Bills are introduced in Congress under titles stating nearly the exact opposite from their true purposes. The "Fairness Doctrine" was the bill to gut conservative talk radio since Progressives found it too revealing.[81] Obamacare was titled the "Patient

Protection and Affordable Care Act," but actually provided neither. Patients lost their doctors, and health care costs increased.[82] Unconstitutional measures are routinely ruled constitutional—and vice-versa—by a Supreme Court pursuing ideological agendas.[83] The president takes action unilaterally and without authority, simply assuming it when Congress fails to do what he wants.[84] In any other society, President Obama's actions would be termed dictatorial, but to Progressives, they are necessary and beneficial (to Progressives).

The Democrats/Progressives have a clear overall goal: the creation of a world government in which the U.S. will be a charter member with a socialist autocracy and new Constitution.

Under the United Nations Agenda 21 Program, there will be no such thing as private property or individual liberties as Americans have known them.[85] Instead, there will be "human rights" following the UN declaration, determined and administered by government. Against that agenda, the Republican Party has put up nothing, as it has no guiding mission or goal beyond winning the next election.

At this point, there is little reason to support a party that is unable to recognize any of the diseases that ail the United States, much less do anything about them. In every case, the Republican Party allows Democrats to frame the debate, entering into it at a decided disadvantage, and losing in discord and confusion. That's why deals are made: to win at least *some*thing, if only just a sterile bone. A sorrier state of affairs cannot be imagined.

The Republican Party must either be jettisoned or taught to frame all issues as part of the seven given above, and insist on debate according to these issues. This will not stop the march toward an autocracy, but it can win adherents to the patriot cause when the country dissolves into factions fighting for resources. As pointed out in Chapter 1, at the current time patriots are in a decided minority. People must be detached from their dependence on federal and state money, or they will fight on the side of serfdom as the only way to survive. They must be taught that surrendering to totalitarianism is not in their children's best interests, and that a successful fight against the elite can only be accomplished by patriots rising up and framing the debate so the "low information voter" can understand the true issues in play. The issues must be clearly delineated so that the actions taken in Chapter 5 can be undertaken as fully justified, and that every such action will have a legitimate philosophical and democratic basis.

Patriots must promote a renaissance of the four great pillars of American exceptionalism, not only to make the United States great again, but also to make it reflect true American values.

Common Law is no longer a given, as a majority of justices on the Supreme Court as well as a majority of lawyers throughout the land already favor making American common law subservient to international law, which is civil law. Attempts to introduce civil law (except in Louisiana where it is already the basis for state law) or non-Christian religious law (such as Sharia Law), must be treated as unconstitutional. This will take a new amendment as listed in the Appendix. The common law process of making law must always be followed—the law originates with God, is put into practice by the traditions and actions of the people, and only then encoded into legal statutes by representatives of the people. All orders emanating from the executive branch such as presidential orders, secretarial orders, and agency regulations that do not have a clear origin and mandate from the people and their legislative bodies must be null and void. International law must become unenforceable in the United States unless codified in domestic law, making the laws of other nations and the opinions of foreign jurists meaningless. The issue must be the re-establishment of common law as the basis for all American law, framed in a way the people can understand, and in accordance with our heritage.

A law that cannot be understood by those it affects is patently invalid, yet most federal laws are incomprehensible to the average American. Only the most wealthy Americans can afford to hire the legions of lawyers necessary to be compliant or avoid such laws. Most likely, an amendment to the Constitution should be promoted to clarify the principle of common law, thereby prohibiting law-making by the executive branch, its departments and agencies, and the judiciary branch. Such an amendment would suddenly frame the issue of the separation of powers correctly from the people's viewpoint, putting Progressives on the defensive.

The Constitutional separation of powers requires voluntary compliance by government officials to work, and, under Progressive administrations, that is no longer a given. Progressives currently recognize no meaningful separation of powers as intended in the Constitution, and this point is expanded more fully in Chapter 6. But without an enforcement and penalty structure that is not unduly messy and impractical for violations by individuals and agencies, the principle of separation of powers will become increasingly meaningless.

Virtue and morality were originally defined by Protestant Christianity, and still, today, Protestants make up half of the American citizenry. The Roman Catholic Church claims sixty-five million members in the U.S., the largest single denomination in the country, and its growth has significantly altered the demographics from the first forty years of America's existence. The difference between Catholicism and Protestantism may seem minor, but Catholicism features a strict hierarchy of authority and there is a much reduced emphasis on an individual's personal relationship with God. Catholics, therefore, more readily accept hierarchical political systems since they mirror those in the Church, and authoritarianism more easily emerges in Catholic states than Protestant. There is always the danger that papal dictates can interfere with domestic secular government, and Pope Francis has indicated his willingness to do just that. Until becoming Pope, Francis had lived his entire life in Argentina, and, as a result, believes socialism should be the political system for all countries. He abhors capitalism, and has little or no understanding of American exceptionalism, a situation that bodes ill for the survival of the United States.[86]

Protestantism, in comparison, features a history of latitudinarianism, which Catholicism only did in the United States from 1750 to 1800. Both, however, are vastly preferable to humanism, as humanism subordinates God to humans, and the highest level of government takes on the role of God. There is no penalty for wrong-doing to be paid after death, so if a person can get away with a crime on earth, he is home free. Such a system destroys virtue, and, more importantly, all basis for a moral code for people to live by.

Ultimately, Progressivism as a secular faith is plainly and inherently doomed, but it can destroy the United States on its way out. Social development can and does take place under Progressivism, but its achievements are always insecure and subject to being reversed as situations change. Like the communist party line in the Soviet Union, Progressive dogma is only valid until changed—often without notice beforehand. It is always possible to misunderstand what America has achieved—and forfeit what previous generations gave us after so much sacrifice.

Political systems based on citizen participation require that the citizenry be informed and have a common religious and social base (maybe even ethnic) in order to be successful. Nations with diverse populations will always be rent asunder along the fault lines of diversity, be it religion, language, ethnicity, race, or culture. Nations with heterogeneous populations are inherently empires rather than nation-states, and holding a diverse people together in an empire requires a strong authoritarian rule to keep competing factions under control.

Truly successful empires always concentrate on focusing the citizenry on great challenges such as a competing empire or over-riding issue such as environmentalism or Agenda 21. In so doing, emperors introduce simple cultural patterns through conditioning the citizenry to make sacrifices in the name of defeating the competitor or resolving the great issues. "Everyone knows that..." becomes the mantra of supranational government's propaganda as it remakes the people's belief systems and reduces them to subjects. Individual liberty, the hallmark of the United States and its exceptionalism, then disappears and becomes a thing of the past.[87]

Common to the totalitarian communist and the parliamentary state-socialism systems in the West is the conviction held by every country's elites: that the welfare of the masses can only be achieved by an enormous concentration of power—political, economic, and cultural—in the hands of the state, or to be more exact, the hands of the small elite that controls the machinery of the state. Inherent in this conviction is that religious beliefs must be subsumed into believing in the state, which should be worshiped for its power and venerated and loved for the bounty distributed to the citizenry.[88] With over forty percent of American citizens already dependent on subsidiaries from the Federal Government, the full conversion of the American republic to a totalitarian state cannot be long delayed after Christianity is fully marginalized.

A modern dictatorship initially gains control over a population by promoting differences in the population, effectively Balkanizing the citizenry based on various factors such as race, ethnicity, politics, religion, region, etc. People are set against each other, then power is concentrated at the national level to ensure order and security. In Nazi Germany, street warfare between the Nazis and communists disappeared when the Nazis gained power. Political strife was eliminated as political parties were banned, and the public's attention was focused on over-riding issues to solidify Hitler's support. In all realms of social interaction, however, the government, corporations, universities, and others there were subgroups that differentiated themselves from the rest, and were only subsumed into the great mass of the Volk (the people) under the external pressure of World War II.

In Nazi Germany, diversity provided the foundation of the aggregate. Focusing on a very few issues, the Jewish question, the Versailles Treaty, and the economic failure of the Weimar Republic, the regime reformatted moral standards, bringing about national solidarity while changing what people considered normal and deviant, good and bad, appropriate and outrageous. Conflict with the Jews replaced class warfare, allowing all of the Volk to be included, thus reducing social anxiety. Hitler promised to eliminate all social barriers, and indeed, much progress was made in accomplishing just that. The German people collectively, via each citizen in his own individual way, produced a common social reality that permitted the horrors of the Nazi regime to take place.[89] Clearly, the Progressives in the United States learned much from the Nazis as they are pursuing the identical strategy with different over-arching issues.

The side effects from the Progressive/SNAZI (Supra-Nationalist Socialist) strategy are already making their presence known, but, for the moment, in a milder form than in Nazi Germany. As the Holocaust and the Nazi war of annihilation showed, the vast majority of civilians, as well as soldiers, behaved in discriminatory, violent, and inhumane fashion if the situation at hand seemed to encourage and promote such behavior. Sane people who saw themselves as good were capable of deviant and brutal behavior if they considered such behavior to be the norm, appropriate, sensible, or correct. Yet the proportion of Germans who were psychologically inclined to such behavior was not greater than average, but actually *normal* for people regardless of their society and times.[90]

Progressives have unleased the same demon of institutionalized violence in the United States, but are still to acquire a monopoly on the control of that violence in the U.S. due to the 2nd Amendment. Notably, the Federal Government condones—even encourages—violence by blacks, liberals, and Hispanics, but cracks down hard on white perpetrators of unrest. This is the same policy pursued by the Nazis, as Nazi violence was encouraged and condoned, whereas communist and what was called "reactionary" was not.

With a new paradigm of political correctness having been instituted by Progressives and far-left individuals in the United States during the twentieth century, the ideas of individual responsibility and self-government have nearly disappeared. This has also substantially lowered the role of Christianity in the lives of many Americans. Believers can only become true Christians by traveling the difficult road of personal experience, decision, and awareness, a road that currently has the effect of isolating Christians from the common man espoused by the government.

Today, the Christian is a kind of social outlaw, someone who does not accept the latest government line of political correctness. Indeed, even the language has been changed to reflect the new American man (think new Soviet man) promoted by Progressives, and the use of many terms such as "handicapped" and "homosexual" have been effectively outlawed. Christians are now seen to be bigoted and even radical, no longer mainstream in a country founded as a Protestant Christian nation. Being a practicing Christian has become very difficult outside of rural communities where evangelical churches are still going strong.

In their assault on Christianity, Progressives use every possible resource at their command, but primarily rely on American education institutions and the media. Many of the attacks feature conditioning through propaganda, and here diversity is promoted to degrade Christianity as an opponent. What is new under Obama is the promotion of other religions to the exclusion of Christianity—for example, Islam is being accommodated while Christianity is not. Non-Christian religions such as Islam, confront Americans with a novelty and freshness Christianity no longer seems to possess. Progressives are solidifying their efforts through citizen-conditioning by calling the twenty-first century the "post-Christian" era. They have already moved on beyond Christianity, supposedly to a more enlightened age, and all those left behind are no longer worthy of life or consideration.

This Progressive campaign is having surprising success. To Americans seeking a relatively undogmatic, ethical faith which concentrates on the importance of our social duties, Confucianism and some Eastern religions offer an alternative to Christianity. If spiritualism is foremost in the mind of the seeker, Buddhism and Lamaism offer attractive alternatives since they are not bound up in Western political history and their own historical impacts are unknown. Yet, the features of Christianity to which many academics and Progressive/atheist thinkers object come from Christianity's refusal to isolate itself from secularism and the spiritual from the material. Christianity is fully involved in the human experience, in the trenches fighting over issues of morality and ethics, faith and works, good and bad, right and wrong. These are issues for Progressives, just like they were for Nazis, and Christianity is viewed as imposing on Progressive prerogatives.

On the other hand, religious cults and religions based in science, modern rationalism, and charismatic leaders are also on the rise. Some are centered on secular objectives or organized around certain semi-political/theocratic and self-righteous leaders who concentrate on only a few gut issues, but, by their sanctioning of hatred and cruelty, they represent a real challenge to Christianity. They offer Americans a religious experience without requiring theological study or understanding a broad breath of concepts and issues. For Progressives, they can be tolerated during the war on Christianity and used against Christians until they, too, will fall to the needle after Christianity is neutralized.

Part and parcel of Progressivism is yet another religion cloaked in a Progressive cape—totalitarianism. It is founded not only on the will to power by elites who expect to reap all its benefits, but also on the will to be secure and the impulse to please and adore leaders on the part of the general citizenry. A slave, if he is well-behaved, can expect to have all his security needs met by the benevolent master, rather than having to worry about the safety of his family himself. So it is with totalitarianism—the leader provides safety in return for the population's obedience and adoration—and this was exactly the same position taken by George III that the Founding Fathers rejected. Totalitarianism, actually the end point of Progressivism, leaves the common man stripped and helpless in the presence of unlimited power wielded by the elite. Progressives are the new George III, but instead of a monarchy, they are pushing a dictatorship of the elite.

As De Tocqueville noted, political excitement can extinguish religious excitement if religions are allowed to decline.[91] His comments have never been truer than they are today. In the 1770s, religious fervor was at a high pitch; today it is at a low ebb. Progressives have substituted political excitement for religious excitement as they fundamentally change America, and, indeed, this excitement is making the destruction of the United States probable. Hitler showed how it was done in Germany, and the Progressives are doing it in America with only slight variations in messaging and techniques.

Many modernists and Progressives refuse to acknowledge the concept of sin as defined in Christianity and replace it with the twin categories of evil and guilt. The elite impute guilt to the citizenry for failures in socialism, Progressivism, communism, Hegelism, and the like. According to Progressive ideology, it must be the fault of human nature that these ideologies had problems. The inevitable solution is to double-down on the ideology, and increase the conditioning of the citizenry to accept what didn't work in the past and won't work in the future. To Progressives, evil only applies to people who oppose Progressivism.

Progressives normally cite the cumulative nature of technical development as proof that Progressivism is on the right track. Yet until recently, philosophers have displayed a pessimistic outlook on the impact of technical progress on society. There is no consensus as to the proper form of progress, nor its control (if at all desirable). Social change has become quite rapid, but physical evolution is still quite glacial. The savage is still present in every human, and the technified savage with scientific training has made the last century the bloodiest and cruelest in human history.[92]

For all of the above reasons, Progressivism is the mortal foe of Christianity. One cannot be a Christian and a Progressive. Of all our modern illusions, the most damaging is the idea that we can compensate for our helplessness, spiritual deficiencies, and frustration with our secular insignificance by adopting a godless and anti-individualistic collectivism. The true meaning in life comes from being someone, not merely a unit in a social collective, but a leading character in a breathlessly exciting metaphysical and religious drama of salvation and eternal life, played out on the beautiful and inspiring—but exacting—stage of physical and temporal existence. This is true humanism, and, as analyzed and understood by philosopher Soren Kierkegaard in his greatest moments, is seen to demand—and even necessitate—Christian theism as its indispensable foundation.[93] Progressive humanism that rejects Christianity as its foundation is an illegitimate remnant, but ,unfortunately, that is precisely what is promoted by Progressives.

Progressive psychologists and sociologists often add their weight to the attack on Christianity, claiming it is bad for individuals' psychological balance and bad for the stability and orderly development of a social system. Following this line, anti-Christian propaganda usually stresses various problem-riddled episodes in the long history of the Catholic Church. Those periods have existed, and, at times, corruption seemed the primary feature of the Church organization, but the worldliness of the Church was not, and *is* not, greater than the worldliness of the world. Its record is not worse than that of other human regimes and associations, and, indeed, very much better than most of them.[94] Nor does the Catholic Church figure prominently in history as causing or condoning democide in spite of the often mentioned Crusades. The Crusades hardly rate a mention in comparison to the Progressive regimes in the twentieth century that have murdered over a hundred and fifty million people on government orders, not counting war losses.[95] As always, Progressives misdirect the debate by accusing their opponents precisely of what they themselves are doing—this time murdering human beings.

Progressives usually assail Christianity as being responsible for more deaths, mostly through wars, than any other religion, political entity, country, or force in history. They cite no statistics unless they make some up. But the casualties in religious wars have been vastly overstated. Only one-to-three million people died in the crusades, while the Soviet Union murdered sixty-two million, abortion (so loved by Progressives) has killed forty-five million and its number is increasing every day, Communist China exterminated thirty-five million, the Manchu Empire probably thirty million, Nazi Germany twenty million, and the Mongols empires all together about ten million. The United States is at the bottom of the list for democide, regardless of the Progressive claim that the U.S. is a "violent nation," as it incurred only six thousand deaths from intergroup or collective violence from 1900 to 1987.[96] Communism and dictatorships have caused the vast majority of violent deaths in history, not Christianity, and not even religion per se. When there is no authority higher than government, government kills.

As a bare minimum, patriots must continually hammer Progressives by asserting that the United States is a Christian nation, and what made America great was its moral structure based on Christianity. In every confrontation with a Progressive, it should be stated that Progressivism and humanism are inherently evil because there is no recognition of a power superior to government.

The people must continually support free-market capitalism, and fight government interference wherever it rears its ugly head. There is no personal accountability in government, and when regulations are issued by governmental bureaucracies that harm people in the private sector, no one pays any price except those victimized by the regulations. The people must clamor for the elimination of personal immunity for government employees as well as introduce the regular sun-setting of all government regulations issued by bureaucratic departments. Programs that directly compete with private industry must be eliminated, as they pay no taxes, and the government agency delivering those services does so less efficiently and effectively than private industry.

Patriots also must become the champions of private property ownership and the general elimination of government restrictions emanating from the Department of the Interior, Department of Agriculture, the Department of Homeland Security, and the EPA. Zoning laws everywhere should require a super-majority of two-thirds of the citizens owning property in the affected zone in order to restrict what a person can do with their property. Building codes should be reduced to guides, rather than immutable laws. Where building codes are desirable, a two-thirds majority should be present. The principle at work here is that government is not to protect people from themselves and their failure to use common sense. In addition, patriots should champion the reduction of property taxes for the poor and middle class by increasing homestead exemptions on non-income producing property.

The Democrat/Progressive positions currently causing so much distress should be met head-on with new legal initiatives. Agenda 21, for example, presumes that a coterie of internationally recognized elites, such as the Bilderbergs, will firmly control every nation and the world governing body yet to be created. All governments are to become benevolent dictatorships of elites, and some form of socialism shall be the governing philosophy in every nation. Private property will not exist, and all private enterprise will be licensed by the government. Homo sapiens will be made to fit into a contrived schema of nature, and no activities will be allowed to use resources that cannot be regenerated by the earth within some specified period of time. To achieve this state, a mass extinction of humans must take place, and the world's population reduced to not more than one-seventh of the current number. Deciding who will select the humans for sacrifice and on what basis, are things no one wants to talk about (except in Obamacare where age seventy is a brick wall after which health services are focused on "end-of-life.")

All this is to come about under the guise of environmentalism, global warming, and saving the earth. But citizens are already pushing back. Laws have already been passed in some states (such as Missouri) that prohibit any state official from enforcing a law that had its origin in or is compatible with Agenda 21. A federal law is needed to that effect, and all states should pass similar statutes. All citizens should learn about Agenda 21, as many still believe it is some sort of "conspiracy theory." In June of 2014, a web search on "Agenda 21" returned a hundred and forty-eight million hits. Such high numbers suggest Agenda 21 is hardly a conspiracy theory, and as early as 2008, over four hundred and fifty U.S. cities and counties in forty-six states had signed up to be members of ICLEI USA, Local Governments for Sustainability. By 2012, the number had reached nearly seven hundred and was growing rapidly while the citizens of the U.S. continued to know little about the initiative.

Government employees must also rejoin the general citizenry with respect to obligations, legal status, pay, and benefits. Civilian government employees and elected officials should be required to fund their retirement and pension plans entirely from their own wages or resources. In the current situation, many citizens are forced to pay for the pensions of government employees, even though those same citizens are unable to put any money of their own toward their own retirement. This situation is the very essence of a two class system: the elite and the serfs.

With regard to the Federal Government's role in managing the economy, one of two things must happen: (1) the Federal Reserve becomes a national central bank, responsible and answerable to the executive branch under full oversight in Congress and transparent to the people through regular reports; or (2) the Federal Reserve is abolished. That the primary institution managing monetary policy in the United States is a private and highly secretive corporation with no requirement to report to the citizens or their government cannot be tolerated. During the twenty-first century, Americans have seen how a small cabal of Wall Street bankers and elites subverted the entire political and economic system to their own benefit and escaped all penalties. Bailing out "banks too big to fail" did little for the U.S. economy, but it made certain politically-connected individuals fabulously wealthy. This was corruption, pure and simple, and cannot be allowed to continue. The "Occupy Wall Street" activists actually had a point, but individuals openly doing drugs and students who were still living on Daddy's nickel were the wrong ones to make it.

With respect to the security of the United States, Americans must fall back on themselves and their own resources. Sad to say, the U.S. simply cannot continue honoring Emma Lazarus's poem on the Statue of Liberty:

"Give me your tired, your poor,
Your huddled masses, yearning to breathe free,
The wretched refuse of your teeming shore,
Send these, the homeless, tempest-tost to me,
I lift my lamp beside the golden door."

This sentiment was sustainable only while the vast majority of Americans put more into the American system of government than they asked from it. Since the advent of Progressivism, the United States has been marching inexorably toward becoming a nanny state, in which most people assume they are entitled to money and benefits from the Government—money and benefits they did not earn by the sweat of their brow.

Since the 1960s and the "War of Poverty," entitlements have been the driving force in American politics. As the American economy stagnated under feckless politicians believing in the false promises of Keynesian economics, the United States could not take care of its own, much less a vast wave of immigrants seeking a part of the riches freely passed out to them by government. Those immigrants have changed the demographics of the nation to where descendants of the original patriot base of Scotch-Irish that signed the Articles of Association constituted less than eight percentof Americans in 2010.

The nation had already lost its affiliated Protestant Christian majority by 1900, and by 2000, the number of affiliated Protestants had shrunk to only twenty-three percent and the number of independent Christians, many nominally Protestant, were twenty-eight percent resulting in a bare majority of fifty-one percent of the U.S. population.[97] By 2025, affiliated Protestants are forecast to decline further to twenty-one percent.[98] The fastest growing segment of the population by religion is Muslim, with the U.S. following a trend that is already a serious problem in the formerly Christian nations in Europe. The second fastest growing segment is atheist, truly a frightening statistic for a republic.

Given the demographic changes in the citizenry, security within the borders of the nation has become a contentious issue. Most immigrants who are Muslim, Hispanic, and Asian are more loyal to their home countries than the United States, regardless of their citizenship status.

In effect, America has allowed the country to be overrun by people inimical to the health of the country, in spite of the Progressive line that these immigrants are valuable new citizens. No doubt some are, but most are not. When a plebiscite is held in the American Southwest, as it surely will after the American economy collapses, many Americans will be shocked to discover that most Latinos will vote for forming a new nation called Aztlan comprised of California, Nevada, Arizona, New Mexico, Utah, Colorado, and the greater part of Texas, along with several northern states of Mexico.

The current Obama administration refuses to close the southern border, and seeks to give foreigners illegally in the United States a path to citizenship (amnesty). That most do not wish to become

American citizens seems to be a fact the Administration has not yet processed. What they want are government benefits. The Government has acknowledged that a substantial number of people already in the United States pose a large risk to the nation's security, but Progressives believe the U.S. will be combined in a few years anyway with Canada and Mexico in a North American Union (following the example of the European Union). Open borders are just a matter of time.

Surely, the greatest issue for patriots today must be the survival of the United States as a political entity, defeating all enemies, foreign and domestic. At the present time, little can be done without first Starving the Beast, but is it instructional to enumerate a few necessary initiatives in which citizens can get involved. For example, the illegal immigrants must be encouraged to go home, and the quickest way is to sunset the federal programs that are enticing them to come to the U.S.

The military must remain populated with conservative Christians—a task becoming more difficult by the day—and young patriots must enlist or enter officer programs in greater numbers than today. Morale in the military has sunk to an all-time low in 2015, mostly due to the Obama Administration's misuse of the military and constant denigration of its members. There is also a segment of the military that can be impacted readily by patriots, and that is the National Guard. Young men and women from patriot families must be encouraged to join their state's National Guard, so that when the collapse comes and Progressives organize their dictatorship, the National Guard will be the nucleus of an army of resistance.

Many patriots treat the Constitution as a seminal document and the guiding light for the American republic, and so it is. But it has defects that have allowed American exceptionalism to wane, particularly in the last hundred and twenty years, and efforts should be mounted to make necessary changes.

One defect came from the fact the country was in formation at the time the Constitution was written: the lack of a definition for a citizen and citizenship. The Founders were striving for inclusivity, and instead of assigning citizenship based on an individual's parents and the country and culture they adhered to, an individual's place of birth was used. In order to give American citizenship to the population in 1789, all free residents of the new United States at the time were grandfathered in as citizens regardless of birthplace.

In all but a very few countries, President Obama is considered a citizen of Kenya according to the nationality of his father under the legal principle of *jus sanguinis* (law of blood) instead of the U.S.'s *jus soli* (law of soil.) Determining citizenship is one of the very few cases where the U.S. should come more in line with the majority of nations: *jus soli* should be replaced by *jus sanguinis*. Overnight, the anchor-baby problem would disappear, and the amendment should strip citizenship from people who became citizens by birth in the U.S. when both parents were citizens of other countries. Abolishing *jus soli* would also eliminate the problem of dual citizenship.

Perhaps the most significant defect in the Constitution is the lack of term limits for elected and appointed officials. At the time the Constitution was written, the principle of "rotation" was well-established in states, where—usually—certain officials could not succeed themselves in office, and elections occurred frequently. There was no concept of civil service, and officials such as judges tended to have short times in office, in part to lessen corruption. Starting with President Martin van Buren, however, political parties became much stronger and the spoils system went into effect, the abuses of which were addressed by the introduction of civil service in 1883 under President Chester A. Arthur.

As long as the Federal Government was not busy writing intrusive rules and regulations to govern the activities of private American citizens, the civil service system functioned rather well. With the advent of President Franklin D. Roosevelt, the Government hardened into fiefdoms ruled by civil servants, which, over time, became almost exclusively Progressive.

By the mid-1970s, it had become practically impossible to fire a federal employee for lack of job performance, as the procedure took a minimum of several years of documented failures and reasons for termination. At the same time, many bureaus acquired nearly unlimited power that elected officials could not or would not rein in.

One of the major problems inadequately treated by the Constitution is the removal of elected officials at the federal level. The Senate functions as the judiciary in an impeachment trial of the president, but since the 17th Amendment changed the election of senators from state legislatures to a popular vote, it is most likely that the Senate majority will be of the same party as the president. Accordingly, a special body should be constituted for impeachment trials, one individual from each state, elected by state legislatures. Members of Congress should be subject to recall by state legislative action or by a referendum of the people, and all federal judges, including the Supreme Court, should be similarly subject to removal through a vote of "no confidence" by state legislatures or popular vote.

Other amendments are needed and they are listed in the Appendix. The "welfare clause" should be redefined as only applying to the overall benefit of the citizenry rather than any individual. The president should not have the power to implement initiatives without Congress's authorization and funding of those initiatives. The burden of family and individual welfare must be put where it belongs following a hierarchy of responsibility: individual, family, church, locality, state, and, finally, the Federal Government in that order. In literally every research inquiry into the efficiency and effectiveness of government, it has been found that the closer a government agency is to the people, the more effective that agency is in providing services.

The 1st Amendment's clause on religion should be changed to unmistakably protect religion from government rather than government from religion. This amendment would strip Progressives of the cover courts have provided for their jihad against Christianity and help promote morality and virtue in the nation. Voluntary religious observations without cost to the government should be allowed on government property and by government bodies as both Jefferson and Madison opined.

The 2nd Amendment should be clarified to eliminate the American Civil Liberties Union's (ACLU's) argument that the right to keep arms is limited to those in the National Guard (a well-organized militia). The ACLU, a pressure group originally formed to advocate for the Soviet Union and defend communism and communists in the U.S., blindly overlooks the definition of the militia as "the body of the people" by several states at the time the 2nd Amendment was written.

The 14th Amendment needs clarification to avoid double jeopardy and restore state prerogatives instead of requiring all state laws to conform to federal acts. The modification must restore the powers granted and reserved by the 10th Amendment by eliminating the conflict the 14th Amendment currently poses through judicial activism, and reduce the Federal Government to its proper place in the hierarchy of law-making while providing a better balance between state and federal power. Since the Supreme Court redefined the concept of liberty to what any individual or group believes it should mean in *Obergefell v. Hodges* in 2015, an adequate definition must be spelled out to prevent the Court from ruling according to ideology rather than common law.

An amendment is needed to clearly state that treaties and international agreements are, and always will be, subordinate to the Constitution and must be ratified by two-thirds of the Senate in order to take effect. Treaties and international agreements must not be allowed to become law through executive orders, secretarial orders, administrative rulings, or court judgments as is currently the case. The judiciary and executive branches should not be allowed to make law under any circumstances, and the judiciary should be restricted from assuming oversight power on the compliance of its rulings instead of passing that function to the executive branch.

Americans have learned that the president and his attorney general selectively enforce Supreme Court decisions, and there must be a penalty applied severally and individually through the Constitution for such action. Only by making bureaucrats and elected officials personally responsible for their failures—and with penalties involving incarceration, fines, and restrictions on future governmental employment—can malfeasance in government be reduced.

The civil service retirement system should be rolled into Social Security and all separate retirement plans for civilian employment by the Federal Government abolished. Government employees must not be a privileged class of people who are allowed to avoid paying into Social Security. Since the employer of government civilian employees is actually the taxpayer, such employees must be responsible for both the employee's and employer's contributions to Social Security in the same fashion as self-employed individuals. Service in government should be a privilege, and, as such, there should be no union or bargaining unit allowed for government employees.

There are many other amendments that might be considered to make government more efficient and accountable to the citizenry, most notably the off-proposed "balanced budget amendment." Proposals for this amendment usually state that the Federal Government cannot borrow money except during wartime to meet its obligations, and income must always be greater than expenses. As the Federal Government has not had a balanced budget since the Eisenhower Administration, the problem is what services or payments must be eliminated in order to avoid incurring debt.[99] Most likely, a balanced budget amendment is infeasible given the complexity of the Federal Government's operations, but the single most important objection is that it would give lawmakers a mandate to raise taxes to fulfill their constitutional obligations when operating in the red. They would simply pass a budget, and, when revenues failed to match expenses, invoke the amendment as requiring a tax increase.

Obviously, few of these ideas will come to fruition under the current Progressive majority in the United States and the overwhelming percentage of Americans dependent on government checks. But the problem is that no one is even talking about these solutions. No Republican has brought them up in Congress, nor are they on any talk show, and the citizenry cannot be expected to support something no one is championing. The above has to come from the ordinary people, the people seeing their America destroyed before their very eyes, with nobody in government even lifting a voice in protest.

Declaring the current Constitution as sacrosanct means than none of the above can be implemented, yet that is precisely what many conservatives are doing. Even worse, many are retrenching on Biblical concepts, reacting to Progressive attacks on Christianity. Involving oneself in arguments over evolution versus a strict interpretation of Genesis and saying the earth is only six thousand years old is counter-productive in secular politics. Abortion may well be murdering a human being, but there is little common ground to construct a bridge between pro-lifers and those pro-choice. The issue is a religious and moral one, best solved at the very local level where communities can set rules in line with the religious beliefs of the local majority. The Supreme Court should overturn its ruling in *Roe v. Wade*, and remand the issue back to the states. Unfortunately,

111

Progressives force a "one size fits all" mentality at the national level, and local democracy—so long the hallmark of the United States—is nearly deceased.

The situation is much worse than in 1774, because, at that time, Patriots possessed leaders, some even inspired, whereas today, both sides are enfeebled and just drifting like the Weimar Republic into totalitarianism. Obama, our worst nightmare, will not be done in 2017, and he will be either moving to a higher level where he can do even more damage, or possibly staying on as president after evoking emergency powers.

The possibility of Obama continuing as president and delaying the 2016 elections follows a scenario he put into place in 2012. On June 25, 2012, Obama declared a National Emergency that gave him the authority to wield extraordinary powers.[100] The stated reason was because Russia had accumulated a large stockpile of fissionable material. That was clearly bogus since the stockpile had existed for a long time. However, at that time, Obama believed he would lose the election in the fall. Under his powers in a national emergency, he could forestall the Republicans from coming into office by suspending the electoral college, declaring martial law, and ruling as a dictator. It would all be completely legal, just like the steps Hitler took to seize control of Germany in 1933. Instead, Obama won the election, and the National Emergency was allowed to expire on December 25th. No action was ever taken to meet the "emergency" during the six months the declaration was in effect.

On July 1, 2014, the Foreign Assets Tax Compliance Act (FATCA) was due to go into effect, a move believed by many economists to be the trigger for an economic collapse. It was concealed as part of President Obama's stimulus act, the $17.5 billion Hiring Incentives to Restore Employment Act (H.R. 2487), brilliantly abbreviated by the administration's propaganda experts as HIRE. It was passed in March of 2010, as merely one of an endless stream of initiatives designed to expand government. Had anyone read it, the act would have been known as the Capital Control Act, because it included a section entitled "Foreign Account Tax Compliance," that instituted capital controls on American citizens. Foreign banks and financial institutions were required to withhold thirty percent of all outgoing capital flows and disclose full details on accounts owned by American citizens and corporations to the IRS. A threshold of $50,000 was established for an individual to come under the new law, but it included all depository and custodial accounts, such as currency, gold, stocks, bonds, and all other investments maintained by the financial institution. If this provision was illegal according to a foreign nation's domestic laws, the account was required to be closed.

There were some exceptions to this law: money flowing to foreign governments and their agencies, international organizations, foreign central banks, and accounts owned by "any other class of persons identified by the [Treasury] Secretary...as posing a low risk for tax evasion." Presumably Secretary Geithner, already discovered to have evaded paying taxes, would be exempt, as would Congress, federal officials, unions, and all the usual suspects normally favored by the Progressive Obama Administration.

Costs incurred by foreign financial institutions would go up sharply for handling accounts owned by Americans, and benefits would probably be illusory. Some six million Americans resided abroad, and understandably, were greatly concerned. Two outcomes were probable: foreign institutions would stop handling accounts owned by American citizens; and they would reduce their dollar accounts overall. Use of the dollar as the world's reserve currency would come under great pressure, thus forcing the government and American corporations to buy foreign currencies to trade in international markets. The result could very well be a substantial devaluation of the dollar.

FATCA was akin to Roosevelt's executive order banning the private ownership of bullion gold in 1933, and was the first institution of capital controls since FDR died in 1945. In effect, government put in controls to stop Americans from moving their assets overseas to protect themselves in an expected economic collapse due to government policies and feckless spending. As a harbinger of things to come, it could hardly have been worse.

But on May 2, 2014, the IRS announced the FATCA implementation would be delayed until January 1, 2016, for foreign banks making "good faith" efforts at complying with the new law. In effect, the impact of the law was moved back eighteen months, and put whatever effects the law would have squarely into an election year. During the tax season of 2015, it is expected that many foreign banks will cease handling dollar accounts for American citizens, causing major disruptions, and possibly necessitating another declaration of a National Emergency by President Obama late in the spring of 2016. As in 2012, Obama could delay the fall elections, this time to handle the economic collapse. If all this happens—as it certainly could—it might mean the end of the United States as a republic.

# Chapter 4

## The Awakening Need

Since the beginning of the Progressive period in 1898, Protestant Christianity, the most powerful force in the United States in maintaining the tenets of American democracy and American exceptionalism, has been steadily marginalized by Progressives.[101] In particular, Progressivism and liberal teaching from the pulpit has steadily marginalized evangelical doctrine—that an individual is saved by God's grace. Inherent in the idea of salvation is that one is to do his best to live by God's law, honor God, and do God's will. The Bible is the revealed word of God, although normally room is left for the canon and its precise words to be somewhat time-contextual in order to be understood by contemporary believers. Such was the religion of the majority of Americans in 1900, but no longer.

Liberal (Progressive) Protestantism has adopted a form of Progressive humanism that subordinates God to serving the people, not the other way around, and makes Christianity a belief to be adapted to the political posture of the state. History teaches us that subordinating religion to the state causes the emasculation of religion. Germany's Evangelical Church went along to get along with Hitler's Nazi regime in the 1930s, and today Protestant ministers in the U.S. are teaching humanism. On the Catholic side, Pope Pius XII praised Nazism, and today Pope Francis openly promotes socialism. The situation in Germany under Hitler and America under the progressives are precisely parallel. Change "Nazism" to "Progressivism" and "Germany" to "the United States" and we have the current situation in America.

Today, Americans are re-living 1933, and the United States is

Nazi Germany. Americans have elected a president who is uncritically supported by his party and promotes a Progressivism far more intrusive than ever before. Progressivism has continued to grow until it impacts many of the sermons in Protestant churches. The next step is to require the submission of sermons to political authorities before they can be delivered. The city of Houston has already come close to this by issuing subpoenas to various Protestant pastors to turn over "all speeches, presentations, or sermons related to [the] Houston Equal Rights Ordinance, the Petition [for repeal], [Lesbian] Mayor Annise Parker, homosexuality, or gender identity prepared by, delivered by, revised by, or approved by you [the pastor] or in your possession." Clearly, churches were seen as opposing individuals in power and needed to be brought to heel.

Humanism, with a slightly Christian adaptation, has been embraced by the vast majority of pastors preaching in the U.S. today. Christianity today is no more than an inconvenient relic for the Democrat Party of Obama, Pelosi, and Reid, and evangelical Christians are dismissed as a minor constituency, the religious right. Germany paid an enormous price for their folly, and so will America.

Modern sociologists who have fallen under the sway of Progressivism generally relate the contemporary success of religion and pseudo-religions—where they occur—to anxiety and fear in the search for meaning in life or to one's existence. Hence the rise of gangs, cults, jihadism, and religions stressing the "leader principle" whereby the ordinary people simply obey sacred writings, leaders, and commands. The exception that proves the rule is American evangelism which is gathering adherents in opposition to Progressivism and cultish movements that are undemocratic and seek to enslave their followers.

In reality, Progressivism itself is essentially a religion; certainly it abates existential anxiety in its believers and followers. Theologian J. V. Langmead Casserley explained the rise of Progressivism in 1952, "Totalitarianism [the terminal political system of Progressivism] is founded not only on the will to power of autocratic statesmen, but also on the will to security, and the impulse to adore and propitiate, on the mass of citizens...The pseudo-divinity of the modern state is perhaps not so much a divinity which it has arrogantly usurped, as a divinity thrust upon it by masses of insecure and frustrated people, insistently demanding some powerful and venerable object of faith and trust."[102]

One has only to note the pseudo-divine status accorded Barack Obama and Progressivism in the United States by legions of people to see that Casserley was thoroughly correct in his analysis. Citizens by the millions are voluntarily subjecting themselves to a "nanny-state" political system in return for federal handouts and an imagined security.

The dilemma for Christianity is perhaps best understood by comparing the contemporary campaign of Christianity's destruction with other historical examples. When a totalitarian secular government becomes established, whether it be Progressive, fascist, communist, or socialist, (all minor variations of the same totalitarian ideology), organized Christian churches are eventually eradicated—or at least, effectively marginalized. The reason is simple: Christianity empowers the individual and fosters democracy. It is a de facto threat to the existence of an elitist government because it stands as an outside organization meeting not only the spiritual needs of its adherents, but also, in part, their economic needs through Christian charity. Protestant Christianity is the greatest threat of all due to its inherent democratic structure running not only through its dogma, but also in its organizations.

**The War on Christianity**

To meet the Christian threat, all powerful elitist governments stress that citizen security can only come through an efficient government, able to meet the challenges of fast-changing times (whereas Christianity does not change with the times). Progressives rant that, in an increasingly complex world, protecting the citizenry from itself, as well as various external and internal dangers, is the job of government. Providing health care, education, retirement, housing, food subsidies, and even entertainment, become enabling strategies to tie the citizenry ever tighter to government in "moving forward" rather than backward to individual liberty and Christianity.

The first state to obliterate Christianity was the USSR, beginning immediately after the Bolsheviks felt relatively secure following the defeat of the White armies. The second was an attempt to marginalize

117

Roman Catholicism in Italy under Mussolini which was largely unsuccessful. Mexico took a very Jacobin stance in the 1920s, followed by Nazi Germany under Hitler, Spain under the anti-clerical socialists that spawned the Nationalist/Catholic revolt in 1936, Red China, and the Eastern European communist states under Soviet control, with the exception of Poland. Other examples abound where religions other than Christianity were extirpated, such as in Cambodia under Pol Pot. Genocide involving non-Christian religions became common in the twentieth and twenty-first centuries such as that against the Armenians in Turkey in 1917, in various actions by tribes and dictators in Africa, and the jihadists in Islamic states during the last twenty years,

Soviet Russia's de-Christianization proceeded under a new god—communism—and its prophet, Vladimir Lenin. Whereas the Eastern Orthodox Church had supported Russia's involvement in World War I, Lenin brought the war to an end. Much of the 1917 revolution's impact on the Russian people was negative, but with unrelenting propaganda, promises, and a vast amount of smoke and mirrors, hope and change were in the air. The Orthodox Church was robbed of its relics and valuables which were sold in international markets to provide food for the peasants. In actuality, the amount of funds obtained was small, and, in any case, all monies gained went to support the communist nomenklatura (the ruling/elite class).

There were two primary strategies used by Soviet communists to eradicate the Russian Orthodox Church: attacking the Church's structure and dogma through repression and ridicule, and discrediting its personnel by mocking their beliefs through scientific materialism.[103] Both were used with great success in turning the country to atheism, beginning with the widespread shooting of Orthodox priests and ten Orthodox hierarchs, all occurring while the Orthodox patriarch of Moscow, Tikhon (born Vasily Ivanovich Bellavin), sought an accommodation with the Bolsheviks.

Tikhon failed to understand the immensity and horrific nature of the threat to his Church, and became the first of many Christian leaders to insist on fighting by the rules and credit his adversaries with Christian humanity when, in fact, there was none. Using similar tactics in the Russian and Spanish civil wars, the communists in Russia and the communists and Republicans in Spain waged wars of extermination against Christianity. Churches were blown up, priests and nuns horribly tortured and executed, and bodies of dead clergy were disinterred and displayed to show their decomposition before subjecting them to gruesome indignities. Icons and sacred objects were smashed to show the impotence of the Christian God. Stalin formed the League of the Militant Godless (LMG) in 1925, and the League became his primary instrument of persecution so the Soviet government could present itself to Christians in western nations as not being the genocidal beast it actually was.[104] This tactic was a great success, and, even today, Progressives deny that such atrocities ever happened. For Progressives, whatever they say is truth—denial is a river in Egypt.

In Spain, firing squads of Republicans and communists were organized to "execute" statues of Christ and various Catholic saints, but with Britain and France supporting the Republicans, photographs of such events were suppressed. Even in the United States, where the government under FDR tacitly supported the Republicans/communists and allowed American volunteers to fight for the Spanish Republic in the Abraham Lincoln Brigade and George Washington Battalion, criticism of the Republican anti-Christian campaign was muted. The U.S. literary and movie-making worlds turned out propaganda to support the Republicans, and Ernest Hemingway's works dealing with the Spanish Civil War became best-sellers. Although the American government later identified the Abraham Lincoln Brigade as a communist front organization, Progressives in the U.S. lionized its members and still consider them heroes to the present day.

The anti-Christian campaign from the communists, socialists, leftists, and Progressives had an unintended side effect for one group of people on the left side of the political spectrum. Secular Jews (atheists of Jewish heritage) were extremely prominent in the Soviet Communist Party, and they supported the persecution of Christianity and Christians in Russia, Italy, Spain, Mexico, and even Germany until Hitler came to power.[105] When Germany turned to eradicating Jews from Germany, humanist support for minority groups had reached a low ebb, and, in the case of the Jews, what they had sent around in Soviet Russia, Mexico, and Spain came back at them with a vengeance under Hitler. France volunteered to deport Jews to the gas chambers during the Vichy regime, and even Pope Pius XII was less than sympathetic to their plight.[106] For secular Jews in the U.S. promoting Progressivism, there is an historical lesson here to be learned.

The Soviets replaced the Orthodox Church in 1922 with the Renovationist, or Living Church, under conditions that made it little more than a communist party sub-. This "church" lauded the communist revolution as "a Christian creation," its leader as the "tribune of social truth," and said that Stalin had been put in power by God and was, therefore, fully legitimate.

But even this fig leaf of a church suffered extreme persecution in the late 1930s, leaving an embarrassingly tiny remnant to show the world the Soviet regime's "tolerance" for Christianity. Following World War II, the fully communist-controlled Renovationist church was used as the model for setting up churches in Warsaw Pact nations that became little more than Potemkin villages of religion.

In stark contrast to Soviet propaganda abroad, individual priests and lay believers at home were constantly subjected to harassment from LMG flying squads that roamed the countryside and rooted out remnants of believers and their Christian symbols. Christian holidays were abolished to give the people more time to be productive, and the League celebrated an anti-Christmas, mocking Christ and God, finally burning images of religious figures in a bacchanalian festival. People were urged to change their Christian names to ideological meaningful ones, and pseudo-christenings were instituted to give newborns proper communist names.

The Progressive war against Christianity in the U.S. adopted the same marginalization strategies used by Stalin but on a more benign scale. Blacks, such as Cassius Clay, rid themselves of their "slave" names, in Clay's case for "Mohammed Ali." "Christmas Trees" became "Holiday Trees" and greetings were changed from "Merry Christmas" to "Happy Holidays."

Perhaps the best indicator of this Progressive campaign occurred in 2014. In the Presidential Museum and Library of George W. Bush in Dallas, a special Christmas exhibit was put on display in three rooms. It featured a Christmas tree topped with an eagle and with decorations of birds and colored balls, but also three exhibits of Jewish menorahs, two of the recently-invented celebration of Kwanza, and two of the last day of Ramadan, which, according to the displays, was the Islamic equivalent of Christmas. Other than the highly secularized tree, Christmas was not included in the exhibit at all; there was no nativity scene, no Christian cross, no angels, no mention of the birth of Christ or even Christ himself, and no mention of why Christmas was celebrated in the United States. As an indication of the public's acceptance of Progressivism, the exhibit was up for nearly two weeks before a visitor noted the omissions and complained. Nothing changed, and the exhibit remained as it was until taken down in January of 2015.

In addition to the communist extirpation of Christianity in the Soviet Union and other communist nations, fascism showed in the 1920s how the Progressive movement could evolve into an atheist religion. According to Progressive dogma, modern governments needed to be comprised of highly educated elites to eliminate the spiritual, social, and economic ills that had brought about World War I. As no such elite existed under a unified banner, least of all in Soviet Russia, it fell to Benito Mussolini to show the world how such an elite could be created.

The result was fascism, and as defined by Mussolini, it was less of a party than a religion. Fascism, similar to Soviet communism, called for an anthropological revolution, sometimes referred to as a "palingenesis" (the Stoic word for the re-creation of the universe) by leftists, creating a new fascist man and a government-controlled economy, utilizing very large corporations. Democracy was considered obsolete and no longer appropriate to the modern age, government would be conducted through hierarchical organizations (much like the Catholic Church), and private property was to be eventually abolished through systems of taxation of wealth and governmental eminent domain. In short, there was little in Mussolini's agenda other than his nationalistic component that differs from modern American Progressivism.

Mussolini's social policies generated many tensions with the Catholic Church, but he lacked sufficient power to bring it to heel. With the ascension of Pope Pius XI in 1922, the papacy became a formidable opponent. Pope Benedict XV had spent lavishly during World War I and left the papacy in dire financial condition, but support from American Catholics for Pius XI re-invigorated the Vatican and put it beyond Mussolini's reach. Mussolini reached an accommodation with the Vatican and left the confrontation with the Church that his development of a new atheistic man and the deity of his state would make inevitable to a later, unspecified, time.

Adolf Hitler was more fortunate in his position vis-à-vis the two denominations he faced, Lutheranism and Catholicism. Both could (and were) won over to his support to face communist Russia, held to be more dangerous to Christianity that Nazism by both denominations. Both denominations had become enfeebled in Germany by World War I and the following period of unrest and hyperinflation, and Hitler was able to neutralize both. The Catholic Centre Party actually voted for the Enabling Act in 1933 that allowed Hitler to become the dictator of Germany, and both denominations sought accommodations with Hitler rather than to oppose him. In the event, both were oppressed and marginalized, having contributed to their own demise through a lack of backbone and clear thinking.

Perhaps the most relevant example of a Christian country in which Christianity was nearly eradicated is the German Democratic Republic (communist East Germany.) During the 1950s, Protestant church leaders in the GDR sought a *modus vivendi* with the communist regime, believing such a strategy would allow the churches to survive. By the 1970s, church leaders spoke about the church and Christianity "in socialism" rather than against, alongside, or superior to the secular regime.[107]

This effort at accommodation, actually a variant of appeasement, failed disastrously, and by 1989, only ten percent of the East German population acknowledged any religious affiliation at all.[108] The key to the successful effort was educating the young. All schoolteachers were required to be Marxists, and the remorseless and relentless atheist propaganda by the state against all forms of Christianity was extremely effective. Christian holidays were eliminated (Christmas became "winter vacation"), Sunday became a work day, and the state determined when, where, and what religious instruction could take place. The GDR provided the *Jugendweihe* (youth consecration) to replace baptism and confirmation rites in Lutheran and Catholic churches, and as promoted by the Humanist Association of Germany, it became the standard initiation marking the transition from youth to adulthood. Christians were subjected to systemic discrimination in education, isolated and ridiculed as "superstitious." The Progressive campaign in the United States to replace Christmas with a non-specific "holiday" time had its origin in the GDR, and Progressives in the U.S. are simply following in the GDR's footsteps.

What Christian opposition to totalitarianism can achieve is demonstrated by the history of Poland from 1980 to 1991. Communist Poland had been unable to marginalize Roman Catholicism after its leaders assumed power in 1945, and leftists in Great Britain and the U.S. were deeply embarrassed over the strong religious sentiments of ordinary Poles fighting at great risk to themselves to establish a democratic government. The Polish trade union, Solidarity, received a great deal of support from two Western titans of conservatism, Margaret Thatcher and Ronald Reagan, but none from Progressives. The ultimate success of the anti-communist and pro-Catholic Poles in Poland helped bring down the Soviet Union in its entirety. That ended the Cold War, and put egg on the faces of most American Progressives who had assumed all along that the Soviets would prevail.

In an unmitigated rage following the demise of the Soviet Union, American Progressives turned on Christianity, redoubling their efforts to remove Christianity from American politics and even as a domestic moral force. They quickly replaced the Christian God with the earth, Agenda 21, and environmentalism. The war against Christianity went from the back to the front burner.

From 1990 to the present, Progressives have seen the war on Christianity succeed beyond their wildest expectations. By 2010, Protestant Christianity no longer underpinned the morality of the courts. With Elena Kagan joining the Court in 2010, there were no longer any Protestants at all on the Supreme Court bench; the Court became composed of six Catholics representing slightly less than twenty-two percent of Americans, and three Jews representing less than two percent. Majority rule had been abolished, as least as far as religion is concerned. That few, if any, Protestants noted the religious composition of the court and reflected on what it meant for religious and cultural interpretations, demonstrated to Progressives how well their efforts were succeeding.

But even worse was the growing power of government. Nazi Germany clearly demonstrated what people can do when given a clear mandate by the state. When state power is based on the wrong values, criminality becomes normal. Most agents of government are above the law regardless of what various politicians say, suffer no moral guilt, and are convinced they are doing the right thing.

Consider the actions by the EPA, Homeland Security, NSA, and Lois Lerner; that is what happens when Christian morality no longer matters. When the Department of Justice settled with Bank of America over possible wrongdoing in mortgage lending, it received sixteen billion dollars. The main recipients turned out to be President Obama's special interests: the ACORN network of agencies, National Council of La Raza ("The Race" in Spanish), Operation Hope, National Community Reinvestment Coalition, and the Neighborhood Assistance Corporation of America. These were the very organizations that had created the mortgage crisis in the first place.[109]

Only the bell tower of the church in Berlin where German Evangelical pastor Dietrich Bonhoeffer preached survives as a monument to man's folly under Nazism. What will be America's monument to its folly under Progressivism, or does it even deserve one after failing to heed the lessons of history?

Americans are copying Europe today, walking the same plank to oblivion. Pastors are silent or preach Progressivism and humanism, they support the half-baked ideas that enslave citizens to federal handouts, agree that rights come from the state instead of God, and that salvation comes through supporting the government, charitable works, tithing, or sitting in a pew—actions of man rather than of God. Obama may think he is God, the Fuehrer of the "free world," but, according to Christian teaching, without God's grace. the United States is doomed. The survival of Christians in America has become political, as in Germany in 1933. Germany succumbed to totalitarianism, a political order was established in which social justice supposedly prevailed, and devout Christians died along with Jews.

It is instructive to review the decline of Protestantism in the United States. As Progressivism grew during the first half of the twentieth century, American Protestants were enfeebled by its spiritual leadership that moved the churches away from what they derisively called "fundamentalism" to concentrate on social and economic justice.

This started under the Social Gospel movement that sought to politically implement the Lord's Prayer, "Thy kingdom come, Thy will be done on earth as it is in heaven." That neither the Bible nor any other source could enlighten anyone on what exactly the "The Lord's will in heaven" was producing with respect to the issues on earth was considered irrelevant. The principle was put into effect to fight all sorts of social problems (assumed not to be present in heaven), such as income inequality, crime, racial persecution, inadequate pensions, poor working conditions, poor public facilities, hunger, and the like. The agency to eliminate all these social evils was government, and its size and scope needed to be increased accordingly. Christianity would set the example from the pulpit, and parishioners were expected to support the activist government programs.

This intellectualizing of Christian theology for secular action made for strange bedfellows as noted atheists such as John Dewey and church pastors began singing the same songs. Harry Emerson Fosdick, preaching at Rockefeller's Riverside Church in New York City, almost literally declared war on fundamentalists in the Presbyterian church, the largest Protestant denomination. He was supported by such stalwarts as Henry Sloane Coffin, the president of Union Theological Seminary in New York, and Reinhold Niebuhr, and everyone in New York societal circles took notice.

By 1970, the five doctrines that had been considered necessary and essential to Christianity as defined in the 1910 Doctrinal Deliverance had been sidelined as irrelevant and unnecessary by the governing bodies of all major Protestant denominations except Southern Baptists. Heretofore, these principles of faith had been at the heart of Christianity: (1) the Bible being inspired by the Holy Spirit; (2) the virgin birth; (3) that Christ's death was an atonement for the sins of mankind; (4) the resurrection of Christ; and (5) the historical reality of Christ's miracles. These principles were discarded, leaving the major Protestant denominations nude before the state. The result, of course, was a mass exodus of Christians from mainstream Protestant denominations. Modernity may have been a fine intellectual exercise for unworldly dreamers on 5th Avenue, but it was heresy for the laity.

Harry Fosdick was one of the first to espouse "moral equivalency" between ideas and ideology. He was an early apologist and appeaser of Hitler and Nazism, saying that the phenomenon of Hitler and fascism came into being because of the faults of America and her policies. Rockefeller admired Mussolini, and the Rockefeller Center has artwork memorializing and praising the Italian dictator. Fosdick was also an anti-Zionist, a friend of the Islamic Middle East, and apparently an anti-Semite. His sermons did not always come from the Bible; sometimes they came from secular and philosophical works such as those by William James.[110] Christianity simply got lost somewhere along the way for the intellectual elites of New York City. Visiting German cleric, Dietrich Bonhoeffer, described one such sermon in 1939 as, "Quite unbearable. The whole thing was a respectable self-indulgent, self-satisfied, religious celebration…Such sermons make for libertinism, egotism, indifference…Perhaps the [Americans] are really more religious than we [Germans] are, but they are certainly not more Christian."[111]

Reinhold Niebuhr was often held out as American's foremost theologian, and President Barack Obama referred to him in an interview in 2007 as "one of my favorite philosophers."[112] Like Obama, Niebuhr was not culturally an American. Although born in the United States shortly after his family immigrated in 1892, he grew up in a German household, speaking German, and his father was a pastor in the Prussian Church Union. Niebuhr never worked a day in private employment—following his seminary work, he became a pastor in a German church in Detroit, skipped World War I, , by 1928, was a teacher in New York City at the Union Theological Seminary. In Detroit, he became a socialist, preached Social Gospel, and took up the cause of the workers at Ford's new plant without ever having met a single Ford worker.

At heart a pacifist, Niebuhr supported intervention in World War II only after tortuous logic identifying Christ's position as against resistance in both deeds and words, but allowing that resistance could be justified by weighing its harmful effects versus its favorable outcome. As such, one could have a "just" war, and World War II was one such example. Later, Niebuhr decided the Vietnam War was not. Somehow, with Niebuhr's superior Prussian intellect, he could tell the difference even before realizing any outcome. Niebuhr stayed on the far left of politics and avoided all moral absolutes—a very safe position—and his sermons greatly disappointed his friend Dietrich Bonhoeffer.

The upshot of the foregoing discussion is that no help should be expected from the leaders of any Christian church to restore American exceptionalism and secure American democracy. Protestant as well as Catholic leaders seek only order, and are willing to sacrifice their parishioners as necessary to maintain an orderly society and government favor. Almost all Christian denominations are wedded to secularism and are willing to render unto Caesar literally everything just to exist. Many Protestant churches have been convinced by lawyers to become 501c3 non-profit corporations, and believe that, if a pastor makes political statements from the pulpit, his church will lose its non-profit status. That is untrue in the vast majority of cases, as churches are specially exempted. However, churches were certainly ill-advised to form non-profit corporations and subject themselves voluntarily to the IRS's corporate taxation rules, and should now dissolve their corporate bodies.

Meanwhile, non-Christian religious groups grew without restrictions. One would think that Jews would have allied themselves with evangelical Christians who have been unwavering in their support of Israel, but, almost without exception, Jewish groups have routinely denigrated evangelicals.

Over the last three decades, Jewish citizens have voted solidly for Democrat/Progressives; all ten Jews in the Senate are Democrats, and all twenty-two Jews in the House are Democrats. Apparently, Jews are highly suspicious of Christians, and therefore, support the party that is the least Christian.

Another reason often advanced is that Jews see themselves as a minority and simply vote for the party that seems to care most about minority rights, regardless of what that minority is. Amazingly, they apparently do not see the threat of their sworn enemies—Muslims—overtaking them in population in the United States, as current populations of Jews and Muslims are nearly equal, though Muslins may already be more numerous. That Progressivism means the establishment of dictatorial power at the federal level, just like in Nazi Germany and the Soviet Union (where communism was nearly universally supported by Jews) does not yet seem to be on their radar. The extermination of Jews in America is nearly inevitable due to the rise in Muslim influence in the U.S. and Progressive power, yet most Jews continue to side with their eventual executioners.

It is important to understand why Christian leadership has failed

127

and the great bulk of people in the West have turned away from Christianity. For without Christianity, there can be no American-style democracy.[113] Parliamentary democracy as designed in the West, including the American variant, was constructed to function only within a dominant Christian structure. Democracy was not made for the strictly secular state, as it cannot survive the ensuing corruption of pure secularism, and, sooner or later, democracies or republics must fail and slide into totalitarianism if Christian morals and virtue are not the foundation of the state.

Unfortunately, American Protestant churches have positioned themselves to be ready targets for Progressivism. Mainstream Protestant denominations have attempted to promote "Social Gospel," stressing good works to the exclusion of salvation through God's grace, thereby negating a large portion of Christian teaching. This renders their congregations unable to withstand Progressive dogma, and they are easily seduced into the collective. On the other hand, Evangelical pastors have attempted to promote literal scripture, and by doing so, alienated teachers and academics who have then attacked them with science as unlettered and backward. Social Gospel promotes Progressivism, and literal scripture provokes Progressives into a fury of opposition. By the twenty-first century, Christianity, in the United States and throughout Europe, had become isolated from the state and politically impotent.

The error in evangelical preaching of interpreting Scripture literally misses that New Testament writings are essentially testimony on what the early followers of Christ had seen and heard. As such, the Scriptures are contextual, at least in part, and it is the essential substance of the testimony that is important. The Bible is a guidepost and intimate ally to man in his life, providing values and standards on which man is to conduct his life. It contains truth, but to argue that truth is also fact is to automatically invite criticism. Literal application of Bible texts causes isolation as atheists can ridicule believers by applying pseudo-scientific humanist standards to confrontations with Christians. Humanism should only come through God's will, according to Christianity, and all things in the natural and human realms are what they are because of God.

It must be remembered that all men objectify their values within some sort of religious or David Hume-oriented framework of a priori knowledge to give life purpose and direction.[114] If Christianity does not provide this framework and value system, an individual will obtain it somewhere else. Individuals have a very human need to love and devote themselves to something or someone that transcends themselves in value, position, or spirituality, and that need must be fulfilled to avoid descending into nihilism. If Christianity makes the mistake of ignoring this need to concentrate on form rather than substance and meaning, something other than Christianity will take its place.

The subject matter of Christian theology must be life— encompassing both mankind and the universe in relation to the will and purpose of God. Instead, Christians argue over whether the Holy Spirit enters the human body at birth, at conception, at confirmation, baptism or some other time. Some Evangelicals argue over the age of the earth and promote creationism over evolution in passionate discussions. None of these positions are relevant to the truth in Christianity. God as He is known to Himself is a mystery to man, and transcends man in every particular. Not everything is made clear or scientifically provable in the Bible, and a position can be found where the Bible is compatible with evolution.

The Bible sees the world inhabited by man as a part of God's world and work, and man is called to love life as a chapter in the human drama in accordance with God's will. The stage is temporal, but the theater is the eternal universe. Man is a being made and loved by God, possessing an eternal purpose and a nature oriented toward the fulfillment of that purpose. This concept is not difficult to understand, but is obviously nearly impossible to fulfill in all particulars. But that is as intended; it is the striving that is important, not the attainment.

As Christianity has receded, rationalism and humanism of a modern type have emerged to provide alternatives to religion in dealing with life's purpose. Prior to the eighteenth century, rationalism (such as that by Thomas Aquinas) saw God as the ultimate rational being rather than man himself. But modern rationalism has defined itself as the antithesis of faith, and fostered agnosticism and atheism. God is not promoted as the ultimate creator of reason (and physical structure), but rather, that all things can ultimately be known to man through science and investigation.

Unfortunately for atheists, science does not contain reality, but is itself contained by reality. Science cannot interpret life and its meaning, but Christian faith can allocate to science its place in the realm of all things, including faith and reason. Science seeks to discover the nature and composition of all things and what can be done by man. There is no way of determining what must be or what things and physical properties ought to be like, for only God possesses the fundaments and reasons for all things in nature. The limitations are clear when one understands that science only attempts to understand nature and experience then applies generalization and rules. In no case can science attribute values to nature or its principles.

Today, science is often thought to be the universal panacea—the solution to all problems—and mankind's salvation and provider of the good life. This belief is literally a kind of superstition, and is all the more irrational without acknowledging the presence of the hand of God.

Attacks on Christianity by Progressives have been noted in American literature for some time; in the modern age beginning with Dr. Hugh Schonfield who published his landmark attack, *The Passover Plot,* in England in 1965. Schonfield called himself a liberal Hebrew Christian, immersed himself in Messianic Judaism, then became a pacifist and founded the Commonwealth of World Citizens. Although he claimed *The Passover Plot* was not an attack on Christ and Christianity, that's exactly what it was.[115]

In Schonfield's theory, Christ's crucifixion and resurrection was planned by Christ, and Christ was given a potion that put him into a coma on the cross. Then he was entombed so that he could be revived. Either he was revived successfully, or he died in spite of the precautions, and his body stolen. In either case, he had fulfilled all messianic predictions, and could be celebrated as the messiah. Whether he died in the tomb or months or years later was inconsequential; the story was complete, and Christianity arose. Essentially, Christians have all been duped. Christ did not die in atonement for mankind's sins, he died because he miscalculated or led a subsequent life in obscurity, possibly with Mary Magdala and a daughter.

This screed was outdone by a Progressive writer named Eric Zuesse in his work, *Christ's Ventriloquists,* in 2012. Admitting that he was a Progressive and calling himself an investigative historian, Zuesse supposedly invented a new technique to study the New Testament and separate truth from fiction. He called his great advance, "scientific legal/forensic methodology." By not assuming writers of the New Testament books were honest in their intent to write truth, he claimed it was now possible to discuss the honesty and deceptiveness of Biblical statements.[116] A key to Zuesse's purpose was that he sought funding help through exchristian.net, a website and organization for de-converting Christians and helping former Christians. Its express purpose as stated on its website was to "encourage those who have decided to leave Christianity behind."[117] Obviously, they were to move forward into Progressivism. The purveyors of the site claim that, "It [the site] is not an open challenge to Christians to avenge what they perceive as an offense against their religious belief." The purveyors of this anti-Christian material need not have worried; anti-Christian rants are normal for Progressives, and are protected speech.

Zuesse concluded in his book that Paul had hijacked Christianity from Jesus and his disciples, and he and his followers produced a New Testament that bore little resemblance to what Jesus might have said and taught. In short, Christianity was all a hoax, one perpetrated by Paul.[118] Paul, therefore, created Christianity, and Zuesse assumes his motivation was to become the most powerful man in history. This "insightful" work was given a heartfelt endorsement by noted atheist Richard Dawkins. Such attacks and ridicule are what Christians can expect to see increasing exponentially in the near future.

Progressives in American education maintain that religion, per se, is only for the uneducated and unintelligent. Karl Marx said that religion is the opium of the people, and if so, then Christianity is certainly the most powerful drug and to be avoided at all costs.

Progressive Politicians attempt to dilute Christianity's poison by welcoming other religions into the U.S., and even giving them special privileges over Christianity. Examples include Islam, for which President Obama declared the month of November as "National Muslim Appreciation Month" to celebrate the Muslim community and the Quran. Obama has gone out of his way to glorify Islam, even to the point of telling National Aeronautics and Space Administration (NASA) Administrator, Charles Bolden, that the foremost mission of NASA was "to find a way to reach out to the Muslim world and engage much more with dominantly Muslim nations to help them feel good about their historic contribution to science... and math and engineering."[119]

On July 14, 2014, Obama put out a statement honoring the Muslim holiday of Eid-al-Fitr at the end of Ramadan that said "[Eid] reminds us of the many achievements and contributions of Muslim Americans to building the very fabric of our nation and strengthening the core of our democracy."[120] That, of course, is a gross distortion of American history. Muslims formed an insignificant percent of the population until the end of the twentieth century, with the first mosque being built in 1915, and few (maybe twenty) followed before 1960. The vast majority of mosques were built since 1990, when the Muslim population in the U.S. began to burgeon due to immigration. Muslims are overwhelmingly supporters of Democrat candidates, although their numbers are controversial. In 2001 the American Jewish Committee estimated the Muslim population in the U.S. had reached less than two million, and in 2011, the Council of American Islamic Relations (CAIR) stated there were seven million.[121] In comparison, the Jewish population was less than seven million in 2013.

President Obama has moved heaven and earth to marginalize Christianity, forcing Catholic colleges to fund activities considered crimes by the Catholic Church and working to eliminate parochial schools. His prepared speech on June 28, 2006 at the Call for Renewal Conference in Washington said, "Given the increasing diversity of America's population, the dangers of sectarianism have never been greater. Whatever we once were, we are no longer just a Christian nation; we are also a Jewish nation, a Muslim nation, a Buddhist nation, a Hindu nation, and a nation of nonbelievers."[122] Obama has steadfastly opposed Christian influence in education and government. On June 17, 2013, Obama told a town meeting in Belfast, Northern Ireland, "If Catholics have their schools and buildings, and Protestants have theirs… that encourages division. It discourages cooperation."[123]

## The Awakenings

What is apparently needed is another Great Awakening, but one that fits the times. Historians differ on the number and dates of "Great Awakenings" in American history, but there have been essentially six periods of substantial Protestant revivals, starting with the Puritan immigrations in the seventeenth century.[124] Generally speaking, the

First Great Awakening began around 1730 and lasted until 1770, and was driven by Scotch-Irish Presbyterians who would later become the backbone of Revolutionary fervor. Preachers promoted an Age of Faith in opposition to Europe's Age of Enlightenment, stressing salvation through faith and biblical teaching rather than human reasoning. In the 1770s, those same preachers delivered rousing sermons against the tyranny of king and Parliament, and stayed on message throughout the Revolutionary War.

The Second Great Awakening is normally considered to be the period from 1815 to 1850. This was an evangelical movement primarily among Baptists and Methodists which formed interdenominational missionary societies to carry religion into the West. Christian education was promoted, and abolition groups appeared along with temperance and women's rights movements.

From this point onward, further awakenings are controversial. A Third Great Awakening is often defined as occurring in the late nineteenth century, promoting the Doctrine of Social Gospel, and spawning a number of new religious denominations such as the Christian Scientists, Seventh-Day Adventists, and Jehovah's Witnesses.

The Fourth Great Awakening in the 1960s and 1970s is generally not considered to be of the magnitude of the earlier three, but it does denote a period of great change in Protestantism. The mainline denominations lost membership in great numbers, while conservative evangelical churches grew rapidly. Churches and ministers promoting Social Gospel teachings failed to oppose atheistic Progressivism, and their members either flocked to evangelical churches or looked to secular Progressivism for guidance and salvation.

Yet, all is not well among evangelical denominations, as often their actions play into Progressive agendas of ridicule and marginalization. Fundamentalist Christians who fight the teaching of evolution in schools do themselves irreparable harm, and they would be much better advised to fight for the establishment of charter schools where subject matter can be more closely monitored and controlled by parents. Day after day, television networks run programs discussing how the Bible is at odds with archeology, and movies show corrupt or philandering Christian ministers versus devout rabbis. Bar Mitzvahs are regular fare, but a confirmation hasn't been shown since movies began. In spite of thousands upon thousands of sermons being delivered every week, the image of Christianity on TV and in social media remains negative and confining. Christianity has the most uplifting message of any religion and any group that meets on Sunday, but is there no positive message affecting the American political conscience. Why?

The answer is because most college students lose their Christian faith while in college and don't regain it for many years, if ever. And if and when they do, their pastor preaches a message of Social Gospel. A perfect example is Hillary Clinton, a conservative, attractive, God-fearing girl when she went to Wellesley, a radical humanist Progressive fully steeped in far-left and communist ideology when she came out. If people need an example of what universities can do to impressionable students when ninety-five percent of their professors are Progressive, they have to look no farther than Mrs. Clinton.

Hillary Clinton allegedly wrote her senior thesis on radical community organizer Saul Alinsky, then, while at Yale Law School, she interned at a communist law office and worked on behalf of the Black Panthers—so closely that wags would later say Bill Clinton was the first black president. With long brown hair, granny glasses, and oversized sweaters in the standard hippie style, the dumpy Hillary invaded Arkansas where she savaged the conservative rural culture as being beneath her. Especially galling was that it abounded with cheap-looking, big-chested blondes who her husband seemed to prefer. Fortunately for Hillary, Vincent Foster and Webb Hubbell were by her side while honing her style to play up to those above her and tyrannize those below. By the time she became Secretary of State in 2009, she had lost all remnants of the moral compass she had acquired from her parents and was the poster child for atheistic Progressivism.

In order to re-establish Christianity as the fundament for the nation's morality and return God to the position of respect he enjoyed before Progressives became dominant, no less than another Great Awakening is needed. But, this time, the Progressive opposition is well-organized and funded. Even worse, at every step in the educational process, from kindergarten to post-graduate degrees, Progressive teachers and faculty hammer home the message that

Progressive humanism is the proper religion for intelligent people, and Progressivism the only correct political stance.

The Bible spoke of camels, sheep, kingdoms, lifestyles, and political structures present from 800 B.C. to 150 A.D., and Progressives dismiss the Bible as hopelessly outdated. Biblical situations may be archaic, but the Bible merely needs to be taught so its truths and lessons are related to modern situations. Progressives contend that the Bible is not factual history, especially the Old Testament, and, therefore, must be rejected.

Not so, as the answer is simple—the Bible contains many stories demonstrating the love of God and His teachings that should be more properly considered metaphors, parables, or simply truth, as distinguished from fact. Not everything can be proven in black and white; Christianity requires its believers to have faith—as do all religions—while the defining trait among Progressives is an absence of faith, love, and morality that can only be acquired by the grace of God.

For example, Genesis states that the universe was created by God. Today, we need only to consider the "Big Bang" was a work of God. After all, proponents of the Big Bang contend that the universe began nearly fourteen billion years ago from an infinitesimal volume with extremely high density and temperature to a universe that is still expanding over enormous distances. But was that the first time? Where did that original mass come from, and will the universe someday begin to contract? And what is fourteen billion years to God? Why not a trillion years?

Light came from the release of energy from elements as they were transformed, the sun was formed, and the earth captured to go around the sun. The elements to make water were in the atmosphere as the earth cooled, perpetual rains came to create oceans, and the cycle of evaporation and rain established, which also allowed the continents to form, and even move over the earth's surface. With the earth wobbling on its axis, seasons came into being. Why could all that not be created by God? More to the point, doesn't that extraordinary process and its natural laws reveal the hand of God in creating the universe, its elements, and properties?

God next created life, first in simple plants and animals, which, with time, grew into mighty forests and highly evolved creatures. Finally, God created man, the most advanced and complex living thing on the earth, supposedly in God's image. But man is only a small part of God's creation, and so it is right that man is only a small part of God's image. Actually, God's image is everywhere, everything is a part of God, or better put as Quakers do, God is in all living things. Genesis is, therefore, truth, though not necessarily historical fact as thought by the Hebrews three thousand and more years ago. God did create the universe, the sun, earth, and moon, and all living things, of which man was his most advanced creation. And that is the truth written in the Bible.

There is no need to depart from the tradition that the Bible is the word of God, but, more properly put, it was written by man divinely inspired by God, or, as some define him, the Holy Spirit. With time and translations, minor errors may have crept in, but God would not have allowed major errors—those affecting His truths—to mar His work. We must remember, the Old Testament used by all Christians was and is a translation from ancient Hebrew into Greek, a work commissioned by Ptolemy II, King of Egypt in the third century before Christ.

Ptolemy assembled some seventy Hebrew scholars (hence the name, the Septuagint) at Alexandria, and, over ten years, they produced a Greek translation of the Old Testament. One can only imagine the infighting between those scholars while attempting to produce a book of the most sacred Hebrew writings for Gentile use, and since the earliest texts used in the Jewish Masoretic Bible date from two centuries later, controversy will always rage over the purest form of the Old Testament. But that controversy does not alter the substantive truth in the Old Testament if one does not take the stories as historical fact.

With respect to the New Testament, general agreement can be reached on principles of faith that define Christianity: the writing of the Bible was inspired and overseen by the Holy Spirit and contains Christian truth, Christ's earthly death was in atonement for the sins of mankind, Christ was resurrected and lives today with or within God. That should be enough to define a Christian, and the remaining tenets are more properly the realm of denominational doctrine.

## Social Gospel, Social Justice, & Christianity

The concept of Social Gospel must be firmly rejected even though Jesus stressed the performance of many acts (but never "redistributed wealth") that fit into that category. At the heart of the matter is a simple truth: no human being is God, and we must act as humans, not as God. No group of humans should coerce others to provide charity or in any fashion fulfill some task of Social Gospel at the others' cost. By definition, that reduces those others to serfs or slaves, as all action fulfilling ideas of Christian charity must be accomplished voluntarily. In effect, Obamacare is against God's law in that individuals must pay for others against their will. It is exactly the same as if the Federal Government would levy a tax on every American of a thousand dollars per year to be used to feed the needy in Africa. Such action might be very laudable under Social Gospel, but it cannot be compulsory. Even more telling is that Obamacare contains exemptions for favored groups such as Congress—the very body that passed the law—unions, and other friends of the government. If it is such a wonderful program, why isn't everyone subject to its provisions?

God put man on the earth to function in a social setting run by man, and the New Testament teaches God's way with respect to social ills and problems. However, man is to solve those societal ills as man, not as God. The Christian is to do the best he can, for God, his family, himself, and his larger group—his country—following Biblical teaching, but always dealing with worldly problems as a citizen living in the world, not a God living in heaven. Therefore, a war may be a just war, and service rewarded. Individuals who commit evil acts can be executed, to be forgiven by God if He so desires.

Man's law is based on God's law, and God and Christ do not require suicidal non-action instead of defending oneself with all necessary force. All life is not precious—some lives are so evil that they should be removed from society as expeditiously as possible to reduce their negative impact. Man is to judge in all things, for that he has been given free will by God to use as appropriate. Christians must stand for these principles, because as a committed Christian, an individual is God's agent on earth, and he must live up to that responsibility. An atheist or humanist fears death as the end to everything, and, therefore, opposes capital punishment; the Christian does not fear death, and capital punishment simply moves the wrong-doer or person wrongly convicted to God's level for disposition. That is why today theocracies readily embrace the death penalty and

Progressive governments do not.

In the New Testament, John 8:7, Christ says in the matter of the adulterous woman, "He that is without sin among you, let him first cast a stone at her."[125] Christ could not judge the woman based on Hebrew (man's) law because he was the son of God, as he says later in John 8:15. Focusing solely on what Jesus said instead of looking at the Christological aspects of the story misses the point; Jesus challenged Hebrew law and the authorities who claimed power from the law, and gave the woman grace, thus establishing his position as being a superior authority, bringing freedom and enlightenment to all who would follow him. The phrase in Matthew 7:1, "Judge not, that ye be not judged," is quoted often, but the qualifiers that follow clearly indicate that Christ does not expect judgments to be omitted in secular affairs. Men are to be judges and judge, but care should be taken in making those judgments by collecting evidence and taking testimony rather than being arbitrary. Progressives do not get support from Christian theology in their refusal to judge, or by putting criminals back on the street to commit more crimes. Even the concept of forgiveness implies judging before forgiving what has been judged.

The Democrat/Progressive/atheistic world is simply unworkable, and if it does succeed in destroying Christianity in the United States, power in the world will soon pass to two competing entities: a very nationalist China, seeing its opportunity to seize world hegemony with its huge population, industrial base, and technological expertise; and Islam, still somewhat medieval, but commanding much of the world's energy resources. Europe and the United States will become totally absorbed in a struggle to recover some level of prosperity, but Europe, beset with an increasing Muslim population, will be little more than the northwestern part of Islam. With little democratic tradition and lacking systems respecting private property, Africa and Latin America will continue to be mired in genocide, coups, and totalitarian governments.

What makes the United States increasingly unmanageable is the declining virtue and morality in its citizenry —think Hillary Clinton. Eighty years of teaching Progressivism in American public schools has taken its toll, and God and Christianity have been relegated to the past. The destruction Progressivism has wrought cannot be overestimated—America is now filled with pathological narcissists, headed by President Obama, celebrities, and many politicians. Historically, Christians could be called upon to sacrifice, even give their lives, for their Christian country. Death was simultaneously an ending and a beginning, and certainly not the termination of one's existence. So death was not to be feared, and many Christians have been seen to die peacefully, even happily, apparently already seeing where they were going and liking what they saw.

But for atheists and secular Jews, death is the termination of all life, the end of experiencing, something to be feared and delayed to the last possible moment. For the Progressive, life is a one-shot thing, and it is dog-eat-dog, with victory to the cleverest, the most ruthless, and the greatest narcissist. Sacrificing is for chumps, for the ignorant, and not for intellectuals. Every life is held to be priceless, survival worth any amount of money. Not that the Progressives care about any of the lives they crow about, but if some amount can be spent for someone else, it can be spent for them.

Nor can an atheist be content with his life—after all, it is soon to end, and there is much left to be experienced. Life is a rat race: win the most beautiful woman or most handsome man, make the most money, attain and exercise the most power. Failure and self-criticism is not an option—all failures are due to others: their failures, their incompetence, and their mistakes. The Christian doesn't blame others, he blames himself for sinning. In fact, that's how to tell a Progressive from a Christian—a Progressive always blames someone else for his own failures.

One of the greatest contemporary Progressive heroes is Robert Creamer, who wrote *Listen to Your Mother, Stand Up Straight! How Progressives Can Win*. Like Adolf Hitler, Creamer wrote this Progressive bible while in prison. Convicted of two felony counts for fraud, Creamer could have been given four years in prison, but being married to the furthest left Progressive (some say Marxist) in the U.S. House of Representatives, Creamer got off lightly. The indictment alleged that Creamer swindled nine financial institutions out of at least $2.3 million by writing rubber checks and wire transfers on accounts he controlled as executive director of the Illinois Public Action Fund, and used the money to pay his own salary and expenses. Creamer pleaded guilty to one count each of bank fraud and failure to collect withholding tax, and, as part of the plea bargain, prosecutors dropped several other counts. As reported at the time of sentencing, the judge allegedly had a personal and political relationship with Creamer's wife, and he received an unusually light sentence.

The relevance of Creamer's work, outside of page after page of outright lies and miss-characterizations of conservatives (usually referred to as "radical conservatives"), is that he re-formulated Christianity into two wings, one good and one bad. The Social Gospel mainline Protestants and Modernist Catholics were good, and fundamentalist Evangelicals were bad. He maintained that "ultra-fundamentalists represent a distinct minority among American Christians, but they have come to have a disproportionate voice."[126] Creamer himself was raised as a Social Gospel Presbyterian, but married a secular Jew.

He does not see the Jews, with less than two percent of the adult American population but being over seven percent of Congress, as having a disproportionate voice, nor the Catholics with less than twenty-two percent of the adult population, and twenty-nine percent of Congress. Baptists and Pentecostals, however, with almost twenty-two percent of the adult population, but less than thirteen percent of Congress have a disproportionate voice?[127] Math is simply not a Progressive strength.

Creamer, representing the Progressive view of Christianity, wrote, "[American fundamentalists] conceive of God as a 'strict father' who demands disciplined adherence to his commandments and punishes those who disobey. Humans are viewed as innately sinful and in need of redemption that only a commitment to God, as manifested in Jesus and their view of Christian faith, can provide. Fundamentalist faith calls for the execution of the 'strict father' family model at home as well as in the broader society...[There is a] fundamentalist unwillingness to separate church and state..."[128] In Creamer's view, there is little if any difference between fundamentalist Christianity and fundamentalist Islam. The "strict father" becomes the "leader," the tyrant, and the autocrat. Clearly, Progressives see fundamentalist Christianity as fostering a dictatorship, again imputing their own designs on others. (Transference is the psychological term for this disorder.)

On the other hand, Creamer wrote, "Progressive Christianity sees God as a nurturant (sic) parent, offering unconditional love and grace. Jesus, in the Progressive tradition, is a model for living. His life was the embodiment of Progressive values, of empathy and responsibility…Ethically Progressive Christians seek to live life in Christ's footsteps—to live a Christian life not founded on rules and commandments, but on one's responsibility to help lift all of humankind to flourish and succeed."[129]

This view is fascinating, as Bible teachings are carefully cherry-picked to support Progressivism, and dogma is framed in such a way to make Progressivism extremely popular. Rules and commandments are eliminated and replaced with the totally impractical altruism that it is the Progressive Christian's ethical charge to help lift all of humankind, without reservation, to flourish and succeed in all their endeavors. Salvation comes exclusively through good works in the secular realm, faith is held to be of no consequence, and, in this brave new world, there are to be no rules coming from God. God is completely replaced by the largest government body affecting a citizen's life—in America's case, the Federal Government.

Creamer believes this is totally benign as bureaucrats are drawn from the people and will have been educated in Progressive schools with Progressive values and morality. In his democratic society, individuals should never fear government or its actions. The government, in looking out for the collective, automatically will be looking out for its individual members. This same philosophy was used as a basis for Stalin's, Mao's, and Pol Pot's communism, and for Hitler's fascism, yet Creamer sees no parallel he wishes to mention.

Under the Progressive agenda, the public sector must be expanded to provide goods and services that are not provided efficiently in the private market. This can mean almost everything under a Progressive definition of "efficient," from food production to insurance, with the rump private sector heavily regulated and controlled by government. In Creamer's major battles for the near term, he includes "universal higher education and preschool," and most tellingly, "the battle to expand public revenues to fully fund key government functions—especially critical social priorities and public infrastructure." In his view, "Over the last twenty years, key government services have been starved for resources—both at the federal and state levels."[130] The Federal Government is to become much, much bigger, and increasingly remote and unaccountable to the citizens.

141

For Progressives it is imperative that revenues for the Federal Government be greatly increased. They say they are going to tax the rich. But the majority of the richest one percent of people in the U.S. are Progressives, feeding off the government as crony capitalists. Progressives want that system to continue because it ensures that the Progressive Federal Government holds the reins of power while being able to blame the semi-private, but government-controlled, industry for all societal problems. So who pays the bill?

Middle-class America, of course, is to foot the bill for the rich and the poor, but most especially for Progressives who will be the government functionaries living without rules or accountability. There is essentially no difference between the Creamer's Progressive vision for America and Mussolini's fascist vision for Italy or Stalin's communist vision for the USSR.

Meanwhile, Americans will not even have their faith to sustain them. Progressive Christianity of the type devoted to moving power to unions (Creamer's primary strategy to move the putative political power of corporations to the people) will be tolerated, but fundamentalist Christianity is to be marginalized and suppressed just like the Tea Party, whose representatives were famously shrieked at by Creamer's wife at a town hall meeting. If one believes in the Lord and salvation through the grace of God, he is to be re-educated or liquidated—but it won't be the individual's choice; it will be up to Progressives with the same mindset as those who decide under Obamacare if one's life is worth the cost of a certain operation or the supply of some particular medication.

Underpinning all of this is the Progressive belief that the average American is not capable of running his own life, and it must be managed for him by government. As early as 1909, Progressive philosopher, Herbert Croly, stated in his Progressive bible, *The Promise of American Life,* that the average American was simply not bright enough and not well-educated enough to manage his own affairs.[131] Croly's work was the first of many espousing Progressivism, and he also believed, as literally all Progressives do, that the Constitution is a "living" document, to be altered by government as necessary to meet changing conditions. A monarchy is no more paternalistic than Progressivism, and citizens are to be treated as children and reduced in status to helots.

Later Progressive writers have taken issue with the inevitability of the emergence of totalitarianism in Croly's thesis, but *none* bemoan the loss of individual liberty necessarily fostered by an all-powerful Federal Government managing a "nanny state." No one steeped in Progressive dogma was surprised by Jonathan Gruber's elitist stance that the American people were too stupid to understand Obamacare as presented to them, and their stupidity was critical for the law to be passed. Nonetheless, it was rare to hear so directly what the eastern Progressive elites think about the American citizen and how they can be controlled against their best interests.

Although President Obama has said he is a Christian, he has been remarkably antagonistic toward Christianity and sympathetic to Islam. With respect to Christianity, for example, he has stated, "We do not consider ourselves a Christian nation... If all it took was someone proclaiming 'I believe in Jesus Christ and that he died for my sins,' people wouldn't have to keep coming to church, would they?... Those opposed to abortion cannot simply invoke God's will; they have to explain why abortion violates some principle that is accessible to people of all faiths....We have Jews, Muslims, Hindus, atheists, agnostics, Buddhists, and their own path to grace is one that we have to revere and respect as much as our own."[132]

With respect to Islam, President Obama said, "The future must not belong to those who slander the prophet of Islam...The sweetest sound I know is the Muslim call to prayer... Islam has always been part of America... America and Islam...share common principles of justice and progress, tolerance, and the dignity of all human beings.... Islam is not part of the problem in combating violent extremism; it is an important part of promoting peace... In ancient times and in our times, Muslim communities have been at the forefront of innovation and education... Ramadan is a celebration of a faith known for great diversity and racial equality... I consider it part of my responsibility as president of the United States to fight against negative stereotypes of Islam wherever they appear."[133] In addition, the president has been repeatedly noted for observing the Ramadan prohibition for wearing jewelry, including his wedding ring.

Given a president who promotes Islam so openly, even speaking favorably of Sharia law, it is not surprising to see public accommodations, such as making a provision for Muslims to wash their feet in American airports, introduced specifically for Muslims. Yet, at the same time, the Supreme Court's faulty interpretation of the 1ˢᵗ Amendment is used like a club against Christianity and its observances. The ACLU rarely misses an opportunity to clamp down on Christian nativity scenes on public property, and the Federal Government has even allowed atheistic signs lampooning and ridiculing Christianity as myth to be erected while taking down crosses.

With Christianity fast becoming marginalized and American exceptionalism ridiculed from the White House, one historian said in 2013, "The battle for the soul of the United States is over; the battle for the spoils of victory now begins."[134] The great American tradition of individual liberty embodied in American exceptionalism has received the final nail in its coffin from Barack Obama, and an unsustainable system of universal welfare for various citizens who vote in easily controlled blocs, has become actuality.

So who is battling for the spoils from the dead soul of America? There are several groups, but Progressives in the Democrat Party have the inside track. Christians are nowhere in the running, and Christian beliefs and morality have been pushed aside. But who exactly is doing the pushing? Who are the enemies of Christianity?

At the top of the list are the Progressives, but there are others that either wish to see the U.S. collapse economically and spiritually into an atheistic Progressive state, or don't care.

Control of the Democrat Party was fully attained by its Progressive wing by 2010, and the principles enumerated and set out by Saul Alinsky in his *Rules for Radicals* in 1971, along with the Cloward and Piven Strategy (C&P) to remake the United States into a welfare state, had become the methodology and means to destroy Christianity and exceptional America.[135] Alinsky, early on in life an orthodox Jew but later an agnostic, was a community organizer who developed his rules to empower the poor, who, in his view, were a vast untapped resource in the United States. His goals were not important and could be modified from campaign to campaign, and his organizations lacked any basis in morality or religion. He advocated direct action through mobs and supposedly non-violent force in demonstrations targeted at the enemy—anyone or anything opposing Alinsky's initiatives. Such opponents were to be demonized without mercy, and truthfulness was discarded whenever a gain could be made through falsehood. Perhaps more than any American, Alinsky promoted the saying, "the end justifies the means."

Richard Cloward has often been described as a Marxist, and, after a short time in the American armed forces, spent the rest of his life in academia, specifically Columbia University, living in a far-left cocoon with guaranteed employment. His wife, Frances Fox Piven, was born in Canada to Russian Jewish immigrants like Saul Alinsky, and became a naturalized U.S. citizen in 1953. A member of the Democratic Socialists of America like Cloward, Pivin joined communists Howard Zinn and Murray Levin at Boston University in refusing to cross a picket line to teach, and also signed the "Writers and Editors War Tax Protest" pledge, protesting the Vietnam War by refusing to make her income tax payments. No doubt she would approve of the tactics in *Starve The Beast*, but not if they were used against a communist, socialist, or Progressive government.

The C&P Strategy called for the overloading of the American welfare system by recruiting all possible claimants to register for benefits, thus causing government to collapse. For some reason, they believed the U.S. welfare system would then be revamped into a system guaranteeing every citizen with a minimum yearly income that would eliminate poverty. They belittled the idea of social mobility that had been one of the hallmarks of American exceptionalism, opting instead for European and communist class warfare. The result has been to make the U.S. financially insolvent while creating vast numbers of people dependent on government for their livelihood. The entitlement state C&P so earnestly desired has come into being, and the productive segment of the economy cannot and will not produce the funds to keep it going for much longer. It would not have gotten this far, except for the dollar being the world's reserve currency. The delusions of a couple of very far-left professors, securely protected from the consequences of their beliefs and actions in New York City, have damaged the remainder of the country beyond all belief.

C&P brought into focus the injury being done in America's universities by irresponsible academics. Buttressed by perhaps the best retirement plans of any industry, America's highly-paid professors were and are free to dabble as activists for the poor, unions, unwed mothers, drug users, prison inmates—literally, any group that might be having problems that could be solved by more government programs. The solution is always the same: throw money at the perceived problem (but make sure that a substantial amount ends up with the usual suspects.)

Professors are often arrested adolescents to a great extent; they receive pay and benefits out of proportion to their contributions to society: free athletic facilities, subsidized trips, conferences in exotic places, an academic schedule that only requires six hours of teaching per week for thirty weeks per year, and often only six hours per week of required office hours. That works out to three hundred and sixty hours per year, as opposed to the normal private employee's regimen of working one thousand, nine hundred and twenty hours, or five and a third times as much. It also means that a full professor at Columbia (like Cloward was) who currently averages $264,500 per year in salary (not counting perks), earns $735.00 per hour.[136] An average assistant professor (the lowest rung) at Columbia earns $132,900 per year, still in the top twelve and a half percent of American earners, and if married to another assistant professor, the family is in the top two and a half percent of American households just in salary income alone. Being a university professor has become a very lucrative profession, particularly as most academicians supplement their incomes by writing books, making speaking engagements, etc.

In addition to Progressives, the Democrat Party, the usual anti-Christian fanatics, the educational establishment, and the various voting blocs that traditionally vote for Democrat candidates to receive their share of entitlements, three other groups in the U.S. exacerbate the economic, spiritual, and political situation.

The largest group is made up of the seniors terrified of adverse changes in their Social Security and Medicare entitlements, while believing they have earned them through their own payments while working earlier. Many of these citizens consider themselves good Christians, but they have been deluded by government's senior entitlement system. What a citizen paid in to Social Security is paid back out within six years of retirement on the average. After that time, Social Security checks are welfare, pure and simple, and those seniors are a powerful drain on the nation's resources. Social Security, once intended strictly as a safety net for seniors in their old age, has become a substitute for retirement planning, even though payouts are often insufficient to maintain a senior's lifestyle in retirement.

In effect, the government created a monster, and the citizens fell for the government's propaganda. In so doing, the people trusted the untrustworthy, since Congress spent literally every dime of Social Security contributions as soon as they were received. After Lyndon Johnson's presidency, there was never any retirement nest egg being put aside by the government for people paying in to the program.

But there are two other groups also assisting in bringing about an economic and spiritual collapse in the U.S. The most obvious is made up of welfare cheats and those simply angling for government assistance and benefits instead of contributing to the economy. Welfare payments were intended to be temporary—to help a person or family over a rough spot (replacing the church in this responsibility). Unfortunately, the system has evolved into a giant festering boil, sapping the life blood of the nation while reducing many people to full dependency on government for extended periods of time—in some cases, a permanent dependency. At the current time, little can be done about this group as they produce large voting constituencies for many politicians, and actively trade their votes for continued government payments. As long as the government has money, the people on welfare rolls will receive their dole.

The second group is made up of the business owners and large corporation executives against which most leftists rail because of their high salaries and benefits. To be sure, executive compensation has gone off the charts in the last two decades, and the key driver of income inequality is the growth of chief executive officer earnings and compensation and high compensation in the financial sector. Much of this is outside of the productive sector because it is dependent on government contracts, although the financial Ponzi-like world of derivatives has made billionaires out of many Wall Street traders in recent years. The average compensation for a chief executive officer in the United States was a high $739,500 per year in 2013, including stock options and other elements in the total compensation package.[137]

The growth of high incomes for executives while middle-class income declines means that American society is separating into two classes, the wealthy elite and a dependent worker class. In the short range, middle class America can expect further erosions of its earnings, especially relative to the top one percent of earners, and increased calls

147

for class warfare from the left. With this increasing gap will come increased pressure for a redistribution of wealth from the rich to the poor. Sooner or later, all extremely wealthy people who are not aligned with the leftist elite and crony capitalists will be sacrificed and their wealth confiscated to be used to placate the poor and maintain the elite in power. Unfortunately, many of these elites are Progressives and will be protected (for example George Soros), and even confiscating the wealth of the others would only cause a momentary blip of income to a government that spends eight billion dollars a day.

Many wealthy individuals already see—and fully understand—the recent phenomenon whereby a chief executive officer (CEO) such as Obama confidant, Jeffery Immelt at General Electric, received $25.8 million in pay and benefits, four hundred and ninety-one times the average compensation for an employee of General Electric.[138] Such pay ratios became required reporting under the Dodd—Frank Wall Street Reform and Consumer Protection Act of July 21, 2010, and eight corporations reported ratios greater than one thousand for 2012, fueling outrage across the political spectrum. Even worse, a study of fifteen hundred corporations which compared CEO compensation against company performance from 1994 to 2013 concluded that those corporations with the highest-paid CEOs performed the worst. This negative relationship held true across the entire spectrum of CEO compensation and industries, but was the most pronounced in the top one hundred and fifty companies in executive compensation.[139] The study, conducted at the David Eccles School of Business at the University of Utah by finance professor Michael J. Cooper, with co-authors Huseyin Gulen of Purdue and P. Ragha Venda Rau of Cambridge, found that corporations with CEOs averaging more than $20 million per year in compensation also averaged yearly losses of $1.4 billion.[140]

The situation is akin to other historical periods when aristocracies or elites became so excessively greedy that revolutions took place which not only caused regime changes, but an entire restructuring of the government in the countries affected. And lest the reader believe the problem is confined to the corporate world or private enterprise and crony capitalism, government functionaries also earn astounding sums of money and enjoy perks hardly dreamed of by the middle class. Hillary Clinton stated in 2014 that she and President Clinton were "flat broke" and couldn't even meet the mortgages on their "houses" when they moved from the White House in 2000, were heavily in debt, and forced to "struggle." Although *technically* true, the statement was highly misleading. The Clintons were only in debt for deferrable campaign expenditures and the like, to the tune of $13 million that would be paid by donors—and Mrs. Clinton had already signed a book contract with an $8 million advance.

In addition, within a year, President Bill Clinton garnered $20 million in speaking fees and other income, and the Clinton Foundation practically printed money to be put at the disposal of the Clintons. By 2013, the Clinton fortune was estimated to be somewhere between $100 and $200 million, with minimums of $15 million for their young daughter Chelsea, $22 million for Hillary, and over $80 million for Bill.[141] Hillary's net worth is all the more amazing when one considers she was a U.S. Senator from 2000 to 2009 and Secretary of State until 2013, supposedly working for her constituents and earning her government salary. Yet at the same time, she increased her net worth by over $20 million.

Board directorships have rained on the Clintons like manna from heaven, most of which pay extremely well for the time involved; essentially paying for the Clinton name. No one makes the slightest pretense that young Chelsea, born in 1980, possesses any business acumen, yet she earned an estimated $40 million in five years, three as a "consultant" with McKinsey & Company from 2003 to 2006, and two years with the Wall Street hedge fund, Avenue Capital Group. Since 2000, she also attended graduate school at Stanford, Columbia, and Oxford, and took a year out to campaign for her mother's presidential bid in 2007-8.[142]

Such earnings for politicians and their family members are common. For example, Senator Dianne Feinstein's entire working career has been in public service, yet she has a net worth somewhere between $70 and $200 million. Congresswoman Nancy Pelosi is another politician who has spent her entire life in the political arena, and is worth from $100 to $300 million ollars. How these two women amassed such fortunes while supposedly working for their constituents in elected positions boggles the imagination. In Pelosi's case, it should be noted that she is the daughter of Thomas D'Alesandro Jr., a Congressman from Maryland, Mayor of

Baltimore, and former godfather of the Baltimore Democrat Party machine, one that rivaled Chicago's machine run by Mayor Daley. Machine politics and corruption were what she learned at home, and apparently she paid close attention. By no stretch of the imagination are these people representatives of middle-class America, and, indeed, only pretend to be when campaigning.

What is occurring today in the United States is a fascinating display of two groups of fabulously wealthy people accelerating their wealth and influence in order to comfortably survive what they know is coming but are unwilling to admit publically—the collapse of the United States. Crony capitalists such as George Soros, Jeffery Immelt, Bill Gates, and others such as the deceased Peter Lewis (Progressive Insurance) have been driving the Progressive agenda forward using their wealth as an entrée to the Progressive ruling elite and as a club against the middle-class that might rain on their parade.

Politicians are bought and sold, and sometimes, such as in the case of Barack Obama, the powers behind the throne are hidden from the public eye. Progressive politicians assume they will be in the surviving ruling elite, and continually jockey for position among true believers to ensure that they will be major players after the collapse. They may even take the most extreme positions on issues that push the country faster toward collapse, but always couch their positions as being on the high moral ground and certainly not ones that will endanger traditional Americanism.

On the other side are the self-made men and money manipulators, who are amassing as much money as possible before the collapse, trusting in their ability to flee to a safe haven or use their money to buy their way out. When in politics, often these individuals seem only slightly less Progressive than the "fundamental transformation" Progressives, as they put up only a nominal fight as loyal opposition to avoid becoming targets of the Progressives in power. In the Republican Party, they are called "RINOS" for "Republicans In Name Only." They sometimes stun their constituents by making deals to put themselves in a favorable light with Progressive power blocs, and leave their own followers stranded. After all, there is nowhere else for conservatives to go, so RINOS attempt to ensure their own survival at the expense of their supporters.

In addition to middle-class people simply attempting to protect their assets, it is the self-made men and money manipulators that FATCA (Foreign Account Tax Compliant Act) is aimed at. Their days are clearly numbered. To a very large degree, they are becoming ever more desperate and frenetic, constantly accelerating their acquisition of money. They will probably continue to do so until the collapse, then run and hide like members of the Nazi SS did in 1945. The actions by the SS contributed to the collapse of Nazi Germany, and the money men of Wall Street will do the same to the U.S. Many are Progressives and expect to be in the ruling class that will emerge, but many will have no place to go. In either case, they are committing mass suicide, as the socialist governmental model that will emerge will have few positions for them.

The need for these individuals to self-regulate and forego their astronomical salaries and stupendous perks is beyond calculation. They must do the Christian thing and share their wealth one way or another for the very survival of the nation. Unfortunately, that seems to be a forlorn hope as only the Koch brothers and a few others seem to realize that taking huge salaries make them part of the problem rather than part of the solution.[143] As long as extremely high-earning individuals exist, Progressives have an issue against capitalism and a call for redistribution of wealth. Yes, many of these individuals are Democrats and Progressives, but as long as any Republican or conservative earns over 20 times the average earning in his company, Progressives win their point. Perhaps Christianity can cause them to forego their riches, perhaps they are already too far gone. At any rate, Christianity is the only force that has any chance at all to convince rich and powerful individuals to change their destructive ways and work to save the United States from destruction. This issue must be pounded from the pulpit and included as critical to the Great Awakening that is so desperately needed.

Many entrepreneurs and great capitalists attempt to atone for their greed in part by funding enormous charitable foundations, spreading the wealth to the people in poverty or throwing their money away at Third-World countries. Some of this philanthropy results from a feeling of guilt, not for having made so much money, but for having made it with unfair competition or using underhanded methods.

IBM, for example, was generally a follower company that

maneuvered competitors into sharing their technology (or in the case of Eckert and Mauchly, simply beat their opponent's excellent case with the highest priced lawyers in the legal arena), and then out-marketed their opponents using their political clout to keep better ideas from coming into the market.

Microsoft was able to catapult itself into a major player by purchasing a reverse-engineered copy of another inventor's operating system, and then craftily writing a contract that gave the company rights to market the system under special circumstances. In neither case did the best technology win out in fair competition, and the information technology world, particularly in database management, still suffers today with inferior products. Rather than pricing its operating system products to produce the best technology for consumer and industrial use, Microsoft reputedly skimmed the cream, making as much money as the market would bear, costing everyone more than a truly competitive marketplace would have allowed. That those reaping the benefits of such practices now assuage their consciences by funding foundations is simply too little, too late.

In addition, these "greed-guilt foundations" almost invariably exacerbate the nation's problems. The propensity to help only non-Americans has further penalized Americans, both employees and customers, who created the excess wealth in the first place by being paid too little or paying too much. The Christian approach would be to first take care of one's family, then one's church, employees, customers, neighbors, and people in one's community. Nearly always missing are donations to one's church, particularly in the amounts wealthy people can easily afford. In addition, the charity provided through a foundation in a rich person's name does not dispense charity—it is purchasing promotional exposure. Christian donations should always be anonymous, otherwise they are self-aggrandizement.

The responsibility of successful industrialists and entrepreneurs to treat their customers, users, and employees fairly is present throughout their careers, not just after they have become fabulously rich. Unfortunately, they almost never do it even then. What is the answer to the age-old question of "how much is too much?" or when does responsible success morph into unbridled greed? Clearly there is a point, but only for individuals in the private sector since no government or public servant can ever be paid too much according to current Progressive wisdom. Of course, corruption is bad, but rarely are federal employees or national figures prosecuted, as long as they stay active as Progressives.

The idea behind the Sherman Anti-Trust Act was probably valid, but its implementation was only against individuals who had offended Progressives. Perhaps an updated version might be appropriate, and ceilings placed on earnings that do not require some certain level of effort and responsibility. That is the key—the individual responsibility of the earner to the republic at large, both while he is earning and after he has made his pile. Starve The Beast must starve wealth manipulators as well as government, but, in all cases, innovation and risk-taking must be rewarded with the opportunity to gain wealth. In a capitalist society, wealth must be a proper and attainable goal, but not at the cost of swindling people or retarding the growth and prosperity of the nation in general. Once again, Christianity must provide the moral basis for making proper decisions, rewarding contributions, and punishing wrong-doing.

Modern man, whether in a capitalistic, communist, or socialized welfare state is, above all, a regimented man. His working life is superintended by an elite corps of managers, his leisure life planned and provided to him by professional makers of movies, television shows, entertainment events, sports, and whatever the political elite feels is socially expedient. The tragedy is that what makes man human is incompatible with the regimented existence. The most successful planned societies are to be found among insects. Modern man of all classes is thus a cheated and fragmented man. Through no fault of his own, he exists in an incipiently neurotic and hysterical condition. As we have seen in the Soviet Union, communism could only continue to exist throughout its reign in an atmosphere of wild hysteria, pathological suspicion, and sadistic persecutions.

To remedy the modern inhuman condition, however, mere "social justice" is not enough. The welfare state is crudely materialistic, essentially bourgeois, and based on the idea that providing creature comforts satisfies all human needs and make citizens happy and content. One is reminded of the Roman imperial policy of "bread and circuses" when looking at the U.S. policy of "welfare and sports."

It is clear that the U.S. needs much more than "social justice" to escape collapse and the slide into a totalitarian government. It needs a plan to end all planning, the restoration of individual liberty, responsibility, and initiative to the individual. Most of all, the nation needs its citizens to love one another again, a Christian love, born in Christ, and emulating Christ as well as humans can. A revitalized society is needed in which individual consciousness expands, and where one can realize what it means to be a human being in all his glory. Genuine social freedom means that each personal life is a little oasis of responsibility and self-government, and social, non-political groupings of individuals—the most important being the churches— are free from political control. What the U.S. needs is simply more religion—most particularly, Christianity. The nation is where it is because it has lost its Christian morality, one person at a time.

As political theorist Sebastian De Grazia said, "Unless a human being is welcomed into the world with love, he might as well have been still-born; unless his widening horizon continues to assure him of that love, he will not grow; and unless the religious and political beliefs which secure this love are left unfouled, he will wander through life as in a maze."[144]

Modern man under Progressivism experiences and interprets existence as an impersonal process rather than a highly personal drama. The Gospels do not seem to him to be about anything of which he is conscious. Christianity must, therefore, combat Progressivism with all its forces, and help the modern American to realize the meaning and depth of his own humanity. This is not emotional evangelism, but rather a quiet philosophy of Christianity that helps modern man become human again—a necessary first step to hear God speak. A psychological transformation is required, one also necessitating a social change focusing on the individual as a sovereign entity rather than as a cog in the great wheel of Progressive "progress."

The best way to transform the lives of the great majority of citizens is to create and support wholesome social traditions and culture patterns through which they can be led to Christianity early in life, becoming sheltered by Christianity from the cradle to the grave. That means the family is all-important, and religious instruction is the duty of every father and mother. Unfortunately, in Western society, the family, Christianity, and tradition have become enfeebled and are declining forces. The mobility and power enjoyed by individuals have declined as government has increasingly exhibited a "plantation philosophy" in which citizens are seen as slaves, serfs, or supplicants dependent on government subsidies for their livelihood.

The tradition of being highly mobile, able to move anywhere to work and support their families, has generally disappeared for most middle- and lower-class individuals in American society. According to Mobility Theory as developed by this author, lack of physical and geographical mobility causes great dissatisfaction in personal lives if Christianity is not present to support people in maintaining their essential humanity. During the growth of the United States, the frontier automatically provided that mobility as men and families were always free to head West and start new lives, to a large degree free from government interference and control. Today, there is no place to go, and support systems—most importantly, the Christian congregation of a local church—must provide that comfort and renewal without travel.

The need for another Great Awakening of American Christianity cannot be overstated. Progressives frequently stress their support of the common man in their rhetoric, but, deep down, they simply don't like people, much less love them. Not only do they favor abortion, but a hallmark of the Progressive program and Obamacare in particular, is euthanasia. Old people who have lost their usefulness to society are not to receive the medical care given to more productive elements since the return on investment is lower. In Progressive dogma, people are commodities, to be manipulated and controlled at will. There is no honesty or caring for people, and under Agenda 21, it will be interesting to see which six billion people are eradicated to bring the world's population under control.

Recently, a Progressive lawyer stated that the loss of a single species on the earth was a tragedy, yet the earth has lost more species in the past than are present today. The earth's climate is forever changing, and species must adapt or go extinct. Somehow, Progressives are willing to spend more effort to rescue an obscure and minor mussel on the endangered species list than to fight for individual liberties for the citizenry. The focus must swing back to people and their freedoms and away from considering people as interchangeable parts that exist only to do the Progressives' bidding. Slavery or serfdom should not be the lot of the common citizen, and the two-class society—the Progressive ruling elites and the serfs—must be fought against as un-Christian, with the teachings of Christ held foremost.

As historian Norman Stone stated in regard to the Communist revolution in Russia, it was accomplished by "Latvian rifles, Jewish brains, and Russian fools."[145] Today, the Progressive takeover of western governments is being accomplished by Muslim money, Jewish brains, and Western fools. The Federal Government increasingly resorts to outright lies to control the American citizenry, some, such as the excuse that Lois Lerner's emails were irretrievably lost due to a problem on her computer and the seven other personnel who received those emails, not only strains credulity, but is soundly refuted by legions of computer experts.

History has taught us that man needs religion as surely as he does food and water, and C. G. Jung even wrote that all of his patients over thirty-five years old had problems that could only be solved by finding a religious outlook in life.[146] Clearly, religion is a human necessity, without which man is capable of the most inhuman acts.

On the other side, the Progressives believe they have progressed beyond Christianity morally, intellectually, and socially. Maybe, but there is no empirical evidence supporting such a claim. Dreams like world socialism, world peace, and democracy for all are supposedly wonderful concepts, but are actually more socially expedient slogans than concepts. For socialism requires a heavy dose of government centralization and totalitarian structures, which are completely incompatible with democracy. World peace requires the absence of competition for resources and the homogenization of mankind.

In comparison, Christianity eschews slogans and enriches itself and its believers through a dialectical process involving fruitful friction with all kinds of thought and research. The essence of Christian development is the confrontation of Christian thought with truth and knowledge derived from all sources, and any disharmony is ironed out into a new truth that is built into an expanding and encompassing Christian synthesis. These actions reflect the Christian understanding that truth can come from many sources, and that all truth belongs in principle to God.

In the modern era, Christian growth has been stunted. Modern Christians have lacked the intellectual and spiritual robustness and moral courage to recognize the fact of their failures and sin. American Christians prefer to fall back on the words of Aesop's frustrated fox, "The grapes I cannot reach are sour." This is terribly craven and corrupt. Today it is, "The United States cannot be saved, but is corrupt and not worth saving." What sophistry! The almost certain fall of the United States into totalitarianism is our fault, and we cannot assuage ourselves with self-righteousness and complacency. Christ's prayer, "Father, forgive them, for they know not what they do," hardly applies to modern Christians and not at all to Progressives. Progressives are truly evil, and the American citizenry knows what to do, but we're simply too lazy or craven to do it.

When President Obama said on September 25, 2012 in an address to the United Nations, "The future must not belong to those who slander the prophet of Islam," he apparently had nothing against having it belong to those who slander Jesus Christ and Christianity.[147] And Christians, must make no mistake; Obama's viewpoint reflects the Progressive mainstream.

The Beast must be Starved, and Christian morality must be revived through another Great Awakening.

# Chapter 5

## The Winning Strategy

What motivates and keeps the Federal Government growing is money—funds taken from citizens to be used by government officials at their discretion. One way or another, all money raised by government for its use or misuse comes from the people. The United States is the most heavily taxed nation in the world, although most people only think about income tax as being their portion. What people forget is state and local taxes, the tax component in everything they buy, all the government-mandated expenditures that should be considered as taxes. Adding all that together, taxes account for fifty to seventy percent of an average citizen's income. The only strategy available to private citizens who are not in organized lobbying or pressure groups is to deny government a significant portion of the revenue it needs to fund its programs, much as Patriots in 1774 and 1775 eliminated the vast majority of funds going from the colonies to support the British crown.

The situations in 1774 and 2015 are remarkably similar in some respects. In 1774, American citizens demanded more self-government because they had built America with their own hands, often in spite of British rule. Conversely, King George and Parliament felt the colonists had prospered only because of England's actions, and demanded the colonists pay their due. Today, the Federal Government is King George the Third, and President Obama rejects American exceptionalism and the primacy of the private sector in economic life. As he said on August 13, 2012, "If you've got a business—you didn't build that. Somebody else made that happen."[148] In his mind, that "somebody else" was government. King George could have spoken those same words in 1774.

Under Obamacare, a citizen is required to pay a tax if he doesn't purchase a product the government requires him to have. If the tax is not paid, the citizen's property is seized. In 1774, American citizens were faced with British monopolies on critical goods, and were required to pay taxes on those goods. Americans were not allowed to provide those goods (tax free) for themselves, and attempts to do so were stamped out by British troops and the Royal Navy. As in 1774, at issue is nothing less than who is sovereign, the people or government? Or in other terms, does government serve the people, or do the people serve the government? Progressives clearly say the most important thing is the collective, and individual rights exist at the whim of government and the collective. Nothing is absolute, all things are relative, including liberty, and judgments should be made only against recalcitrant individuals who believe in immutable individual rights from God. By 2014, this political philosophy was in the ascendency, and the people clearly served the government, or more properly stated, the people could do certain things at the pleasure of government, and pay government for the privilege.

All this was made even more poignant by President Obama's attitude toward the people of America. When he inferred at Roanoke in 2012 that no one could accomplish anything without government having provided training, finance, or made available infrastructure so the accomplishment could happen, he was stating one of his deepest convictions. Obama obviously thought the "self-made man" was a myth, and betrayed his total lack of comprehension concerning the private sector. Government was the foundation on which America became great, not its people, their religion, morality, or industry. Somehow, everyone was dependent on government and the collective, and not on their own talent and efforts. If those statements are a correct rendering of his beliefs—and they are—Obama is obviously unfit to be President of the United States, and is guilty of malfeasance in office. Opposition to such incompetence, malfeasance, and misguided thinking is not a choice—it is the duty of every American.

The strategy of living one's life to minimize the amount of a citizen's financial assets going to government to fund its unconstitutional, incompetent, and treasonable activities is certainly not seditious by any stretch of one's imagination, although

Progressives would say it is "un-American" not to keep them in power with inexhaustible funding. It is not un-American to provide for one's family instead of the government, and to live honestly and righteously instead of lying, cheating, and stealing one's way "forward" to success. Only a Progressive could call the small, grass roots Tea Party groups un-American for believing the Constitution should be upheld and that people should live godly and honest lives. Such groups were even called "Astro-turf," implying they were phony, and this came from Nancy Pelosi, a person raised in the Baltimore Democrat machine that routinely stole elections and lived on corruption.

No doubt the following tactics for living will be assailed by Progressive politicians and government employees, but precisely those individuals seek to dominate and enslave the common citizen. Who is more righteous: the person who seeks to enslave another, or the person who seeks to live his life in liberty and self-determination? The Progressive would say that liberty is no longer viable in this modern age—when left to their own devices, the common people would destroy themselves and planet earth. The patriot would answer, if you can't live in liberty, why live at all? A serf or slave would exist only to feed a Progressive's lifestyle in far greater luxury than anything available to the common man. Charity is the most Christian of virtues, but it must be voluntary or it is not charity. What government does is extortion, and, as such, must be condemned by every Christian. Yes, Christ said Christians were to help the less fortunate, but he never said to set up a government that would extort and seize one citizen's assets against his will to give to someone favored by government or its policies. Social justice is and will always be a Christian tenet, but it is not to be achieved by government re-distributing the wealth.

The Progressive Achilles' heel is that all government funding is ultimately taken from the people—the end consumers—one way or another. If government taxes the corporations, their prices are raised to cover the cost of the tax. The matching tax paid by an employer, along with an employee's Social Security and Medicare payments (FICA and MED tax), represents money that could otherwise go to the employee in pay. For self-employed individuals, the sham is dropped completely, as he must pay 15.3% of what he earns in "self-employment tax." Ultimately, every tax on anything is ultimately paid by the people, either directly or as a consumer paying for an item with all the taxes hidden in the price of the item.

The idea of starving government of funds to bring it under control has been endorsed by Senator Harry Reid of Nevada, Senate Majority Leader during the Obama Administration. On February 7, 2009, he attempted to dampen criticism of the many Obama appointees who had purposely evaded paying their income taxes. He said, "Look, the country was ground under the heel of George Bush's despotism for eight long years. Who can blame these patriotic Americans from seeking to fight this tyranny by starving it of funds?"

Who indeed? Since the Obama Administration has been much more tyrannical and acted illegally in many more instances than the Bush Administration, no doubt he would see the situation even clearer today.[149]

There are six primary ways to shut off the flow of money to government: (1) minimize all unnecessary spending, particularly those items bearing high tax components, (2) reduce income tax obligations, (3) downsize lifestyles to lower taxes and insurance on wealth, (4) eliminate wealth in instruments subject to government control, (5) form associations wherein citizens help each other through providing non-remunerated services, and (6) go off the grid and become completely self-sufficient. All of these strategies impact the inflow of funds to the Progressive Federal Government and are worthy of consideration, and only strategy 5 requires planning to be on firm legal ground. However, it can be anticipated that Progressive elites will attempt to pass laws making all of them illegal at some point rather than cease their program to enslave the American citizenry. These strategies to rein in government are extensive, and an individual's implementation of the ideas contained therein is only constrained by his imagination.

## Minimize Spending

Rural residents have an advantage in reorganizing their lives to reduce the amount of money going to the government, but city dwellers can still significantly lower their contributions. For example, an employee could agree to a lower salary or wages in return for the employer providing free or subsidized lunches, transportation, work clothes, uniforms, tools, cell phones, computers, eyeglasses, company recreational and athletic facilities, employee discounts, complementary tickets and coupons, various memberships, periodicals, newspapers, training sessions at vacation sites, office supplies (for working at home), and many other items the employee would normally have to provide himself. Vacations can be timed with business trips, effectively eliminating the transportation and some of the housing costs. Some of the above benefits may be taxable under certain conditions, and the advice of a tax specialist is recommended.

City dwellers can also buy into suburban truck farms and receive part of the produce for their cooperative efforts, rent suburban agriculture land for "victory garden" farming like that done during World War II, or use the science of aquaponics to grow food at home and even in apartments. Ownership in other cooperatives can also provide various valuable services for which the citizen would otherwise pay money (and taxes). Married people filing jointly should always have one spouse heading a limited liability company, partnership or proprietorship, and incur significant tax benefits to lower the couple's income tax. Buying items on the Internet is a way of avoiding sales taxes, and that can be significant. The list of ideas is essentially endless, and most, if not all, of these ideas can be found in various survivalist or preparedness websites, books, periodicals, and even IRS publications. Note that some of these techniques to avoid paying taxes might be illegal in the U.S. or in your specific state, and this work is not recommending you break the law. It is, however, saying that every citizen and every family can take steps to reduce retail purchases for whatever they are accustomed to purchasing. For example, a single person may be a member of a fitness center, at a high monthly cost which carries a substantial tax component. Community colleges often offer the same service to their communities for free, but even if that is not available in your area, you could take a class at low cost (possibly one you really need) at some educational institution, and, for very little money, gain access to its athletic facilities.

A citizen may own several dogs or cats, and be paying retail prices for pet foods at a retail grocery store. Yet feed stores servicing rural farmers carry those items in bulk and at a much lower cost. Bird seed prices are high in pet stores, but corn and seed can also be found much cheaper and in bulk in feed stores. Even if your vehicle gets good gasoline mileage, gas has an enormous tax component, so plan your trips to minimize gas consumption. Cars and trucks themselves are huge tax liabilities and expense generators, including insurance, repairs, personal property taxes, gasoline, and licensing. Cut down on the number of cars in your household—not every non-working child of driving age needs a vehicle. Insurance companies currently offer huge discounts to bundle homeowner's insurance with vehicle coverage, sometimes nearly saving the cost of insuring one vehicle altogether.

Government employees are probably the most effective group in avoiding income taxes because they are provided substantial perks by their government agency for which they pay no tax. For example, in Arkansas, county employees are traditionally sent to Little Rock for "training sessions" conducted by the Arkansas Association of Counties in December. These are little more than paid holidays with reimbursed travel to allow employees to do their Christmas shopping in the capital. Not surprisingly, attendees refuse to carpool in order to maximize their reimbursable travel expenses which more than cover the actual costs incurred. Elected officials are also reimbursed by the state for travel expenses, but rather than submitting detailed expense vouchers, they create a company to handle such expenses and bill the state on undetailed invoices. If their dummy companies are ever audited—doubtful for Democrats—they'll dummy up cash expenditures for backup.

There is also a reason why Denver has the second highest number of federal employees in the U.S. It allows Washington bureaucrats to visit Colorado in the summer on taxpayer money and enjoy a piggy-backed vacation, as well as ski on vacation in the winter, once again with the travel being on the taxpayer tab. The IRS conducted a truly egregious training session in Las Vegas in 2013 that cost millions of dollars, and it was little more than an outstanding paid vacation for the attendees. IRS employees know how to play the game, although $400 and $500 hotel rooms drew unwanted attention to the opulent lifestyle enjoyed by the supposed servants of the people.

Michelle Obama and her two kids have jetted all over the world in the president's first six years in office, so much so that they have outspent any other three presidential families put together in history. Progressive bureaucrats and lawmakers are over the top in spending; they attend seminars and conferences at the Aspen Institute of Humanistic Studies in Aspen, Colorado (a ski resort), or at one of its campuses at vacation spots like Berlin, Paris, Rome, Madrid, or Tokyo. Aspen promotes Agenda 21, and, although it advertises itself as "centrist," it is absolutely Progressive, throwing in a few conservatives as tokens. It partners with Columbia University and the Council of International Human Rights Policy in the Ethical Globalization Initiative whose aim is to put human rights values and principles at the heart of global governance and policy, to ensure that the needs of the poorest and most vulnerable are addressed. If that sounds like a Progressive program, it's because it is.

There are several categories of expenses that every person and family has, but, even there, expenses can be reduced along with the money sent to government coffers. In order of importance they are: food, shelter, energy, clothing, health, and all other expenses. When food comes to mind, most preppers think of survival food, and that is certainly possible, but President Obama has issued an executive order that the Federal Government can seize private food supplies in an emergency and distribute them to whomever they wish.[150] Nonetheless, an excellent assortment of dried foods with up to a twenty-five year shelf life, providing five thousand calories per day (two adults) for one year is available commercially for $4,900, or about $6.71 per day per person.[151]

A more long range food-producing system for less than $200 called aquaponics can be constructed, producing vegetables in high quantity and seven hundred pounds of fish per year from one fish-vegetable system.[152] Of course, one is not limited by the number of systems, and there are ones small enough to be in an apartment, and larger ones for a backyard. This system can then be supplemented by dried foods, wheat, and corn in bulk for bread-making, and rice for filler. With that, two people can have a ten-year's supply of good, nutritious food at a cost of about eighty-two cents per day per person. The tax money going to the government on food drops by about ninety-three percent.

Not surprisingly, the Federal Government has stepped in to regulate aquaponics systems, limiting the type of fish to tilapia, and seeking to regulate and license such systems. Bureaucrats claim to be protecting consumers from various health hazards by clamping down on producers of milk and restricting farmers' markets and the roadside sale of garden vegetables. Sooner or later, the sale of any food will take a license and be closely regulated by the Federal Government, regardless of whether any putative health hazard is even remotely involved. It is all about money, including the revenue from licenses and taxes. Even the traditional sidewalk stand where a child sells lemonade is endangered. The government may not be able to keep Iran from acquiring nuclear weapons (to keep Americans safe), but it can surely put little kids and their lemonade stands out of business.

In many jurisdictions, it has become illegal to sell raw cow's milk and goat's milk, and, again, the authorities claim this is due to health concerns. There are various issues here, but when milk is homogenized mechanically, the process can cause arteriosclerosis because it frees the enzyme xanthine oxidase. Raw milk has its supporters, and raw goat's milk is definitely a winner as it can help prevent diseases such as anemia and bone demineralization, and assist in the digestive and metabolic utilization of minerals such as iron, calcium, phosphorus and magnesium.[153]

It is illegal to sell meat that has not gone through the FDA-approved processing in sterile facilities, but it is absolutely legal to purchase a live calf or goat and then have it slaughtered for one's own use. Sometimes, rural residents continue to raise the animal for a while, but that is not necessary. Even more important is that several individuals or families can go together to buy an animal, each owning some part, and then have the animal slaughtered to their specifications. With the cost of a calf currently two dollars per pound, and hamburger slated to go to seven or ten dollars per pound shortly, everyone with a freezer should be considering this strategy. The same can be done with a hog, goat, or other animal slaughtered for the dinner table.

Another tactic is to make use of the various farms that allow people to come in and pick their own strawberries, blueberries, raspberries, watermelons, squash, etc. Doing the picking oneself saves a lot of money as the labor component in harvesting is precisely the element that produces extensive federal tax receipts. If the citizen is adept at gardening, a victory garden of sorts is recommended, but heirloom and GMO (genetically-modified organisms) hybrid seeds should be used in separate patches. The heirloom seeds will give the grower less yield, but the resulting seeds can be used in following years (the hybrid seeds produce plants with good yields, but unusable seeds), freeing the gardener from the tyranny of Monsanto and the producers of GMO seeds. Besides, doing one's own gardening can also keep a person more fit and be very rewarding.

Canning, dehydrating, and other home-processing can be used to good effect to lower retail food costs. Some bread-makers are excellent, and with the homemaker purchasing flour, yeast, and a few other ingredients, the home-made bread can be a real winner at the dinner table. There are skills to be learned here, but the more mouths a cook is preparing for, the cheaper the preparation becomes on a per-person basis. Some preparedness stores and websites also sell foods in large cans and even fifty-pound sacks (such as wheat, rice, beans, and corn), and preparing food from bulk can seriously lower a family's food bill.

Shelter is somewhat more difficult to lower, but there are two elements one can attack to lower costs. Traditionally, American families of four live in the amount of space two European families would require, and three or four families in third world countries. Consider adopting the rule that husband and wife share a bedroom, male children share one, and female children one. One and a half bathrooms should be adequate, so based on the size of your family, consider moving to a smaller house following the foregoing rule. Remember, we're not talking about impressing someone, we're discussing the survival of the United States. Secondly, consider relocating to a cheaper area, either in property taxes or transportation costs to work, or both. Remember that transportation energy costs are likely to skyrocket under subsequent Progressive administrations (the only ones Americans can expect), so the use of public transportation should be considered. In any case, one should not locate more than thirty minutes from work, if at all possible.

Retired couples should seriously look at moving to a rural environment, not only to lower their taxes, but also for health reasons. The differences in taxes can be enormous: a fourteen hundred square foot house on an eighth of an acre in Carol Stream, Illinois incurs a property tax of \$6,000; a forty-five hundred square foot house on four hundred acres in Sharp County, Arkansas is only \$830.[154] The only caveat to consider in moving to a rural location is that retirees might need to be close to a hospital or medical provider to ensure the availability of prompt and effective medical care. In all cases, retirees should look to living with, or in close proximity to, their families, relocating if necessary. Many services can be provided to family members within the family, and when the United States collapses, being close to family members may mean the difference between life and death.

Schools are rapidly becoming a non-issue in choosing a location as almost all of America's K-12 schools have adopted Common Core. In the Progressive scheme of things, one size fits all, and local control of schools is fast becoming a thing of the past. In particular, all of the highly taxed northern cities will be like peas in a pod, all teaching Progressivism, morality, and "finding oneself" rather than the three "Rs."

In relocating, housing costs should be considered together with energy costs for heating and air conditioning (if necessary). The best a retired person can do at the present time is relocate to an low-housing cost area in which solar or wind power is sufficiently feasible to greatly lower the electric bill. In other locations, a geothermal system could possibly be used to advantage, and the best areas feature mild winters, not excessively hot summers, and low humidity. Such climate considerations limits one's choices to Hawaii, some areas of California, Oregon, Utah, northern Arizona, northern New Mexico, southern Colorado, West Texas, Arkansas, southern Missouri, and Tennessee. The West Coast and Hawaii are extremely expensive in housing costs and have far-left Progressive governments in place that will not be going away in the near future. But the rest include several where housing costs are low along with living costs, property, state income, and sales taxes. For example, Tennessee and Texas have no state income taxes, and the high sales taxes can be avoided in other ways such as purchasing on the Internet.

Obviously, another available option is relocation to a foreign country, but this is not recommended unless it fits your situation. Foreign countries, notably Poland, English-speaking Belize, Costa Rica, and a few others are more than happy to accept retired or

167

wealthy Americans as the pensions, social security, and capital provides a boost to their economies. Over six million Americans now live in foreign countries, and this is a financial drain no Progressive wants to mention.

A very large number of immigrants from Latin America who were legal and who built up substantial Social Security benefits have returned to their home countries and live high on the hog on the funds contributed every year to Social Security by current American workers and their employers. Repatriated Hispanics often drop their American citizenship to avoid American taxes, while continuing to receive American benefits.

As America becomes progressively less free, other countries look better every day, particularly since the retiree's funds will go much farther. The only reason this option is not recommended is that, when the United States collapses economically, the devaluation of the dollar will probably make paupers out of many Americans living on fixed incomes from the United States, and who wants to be a poor person in Costa Rica?

Nonetheless, every year a number of retired couples consider moving to a foreign country where the costs of living are substantially lower than in the United States. However, American citizens living in foreign countries are required to pay American income taxes, and the IRS tends to look at retired people living abroad as tax-evaders. This was part of the reasoning behind FATCA. As mentioned previously, this act requires all foreign banks to file a large amount of forms and documents with the U.S government if they accept U.S. citizens as clients. U.S. citizens who don't provide full documentation as required by FATCA will be subject to a thirty percent withholding tax on any payment credited to their accounts that could possibly be considered income by the IRS. Many foreign financial institutions have already opted to deny services to U.S. citizens, and it remains to be seen just what effect these unprecedented capital controls on U.S. citizens living abroad will have. Needless to say, FATCA has put a major damper on moving abroad unless one also renounces American citizenship.

Corporate executives and financial personnel still well below retirement age appear to have little fear of FATCA since their employers will be handling all their financial transactions for them and will be able to avoid the more onerous aspects of the law. No doubt George Soros and other major players will be able to bet against the dollar unencumbered by FATCA, but middle-class Americans attempting to protect themselves against Obama's tyranny will be firmly caught in a mesh of laws and regulations they can't understand or escape. Once again, the man in the middle is firmly in the cross-hairs of government with no place to go.

At the same time, one of the consequences of Progressive action to allow illegal Hispanic aliens to remain in the U.S. and receive benefits is that a new time bomb has been created in Social Security. Many, if not most, Mexicans and Central Americans in the U.S. legally (and soon illegally) are building up Social Security credits and planning to move back to their homelands for retirement. The Social Security payments will be going out of the country, further exacerbating the U.S.'s balance of payments, and losing the tax revenue on that money as it is spent. Green card holders only have to build up forty quarters of credits to be eligible for payments, and this is a drain that has not yet been analyzed for its effect on the unfunded debt.

Another option is for the retiree to rent his house in the United States and buy a second home in the foreign land, then, when the crash occurs, rent the foreign property and return to live in the U.S. As was learned during the German collapse in the 1920s, the availability of foreign exchange made some Germans wealthy since the mark declined drastically against the currency they held. The dollar is likely to be devalued multiple times against other currencies, and having rental income from foreign properties may be the best hedge available. The operative rule is to live where the money is worthless, and receive income from where the money is valuable.

To make this option work best, the retiree might well be advised to form a corporation in another country that provides substantial security to owners of corporations, regardless of citizenship. For certain immigrant groups that still speak their home country's language, this option is especially attractive, particularly if they have the means and contacts to get around FATCA. Asians such as Japanese, Filipinos, Indonesians, Indians, Koreans, and Chinese can do very well under this scenario. Blacks could move to Liberia or South Africa to live in relatively well-to-do circumstances at the current time, then return to buy properties cheaply in the United States after the

169

crash. For all of these options, the British Commonwealth islands in the Caribbean are highly attractive to everyone.

Another possibility is for the retirees to go in with a group of like-minded individuals and build multiple houses in a foreign country, and hire a local manager to watch over the investment. That reduces the risk and amount of work for each family, and there is safety in numbers. Even before retirement, such a facility can make a good vacation location, One should also look to Canada as a possibility, and having sources of income in two countries usually provides good opportunities for tax savings.

The only problem for expatriates deals with continuing their American citizenship. Obviously, many Americans have never thought of moving out of the country to reduce costs of living, but the Federal Government has, and in the future may well crack down on people seeking to emigrate from the U.S. Already a bill has been introduced in Congress that, once a citizen leaves the U.S. and takes up permanent residency in a foreign country, he can never return. How's that for freedom, Mr. Progressive? If a person decides to expatriate, the move must be planned appropriately, as the tax laws applying to Americans renouncing their citizenship after June 16, 2008 are relatively punitive, and legal help on this issue is highly advised. Contrary to the policies of most nations, U.S. citizens, regardless of where they live, are required to file tax returns and pay the appropriate tax. The beast is fighting for its food.

Forming a foreign corporation might be well advised, but it should be noted that this work is not recommending any person break any laws, nor is it dispensing financial or legal advice. But perhaps an example can be illustrative. A corporation can be created in the principality of Lichtenstein that might make foreign asset operations simpler. One must first open a numbered account in a Swiss bank, and that can be accomplished by mail with the proper introduction, or in person. Often, the naturalized U.S. citizen has a relative in Europe that provides an address other than in the U.S., to which the signature cards and necessary forms are mailed. The account is opened with a draft from the relative who is not a U.S. citizen.

The Swiss banks provide other services, such as assisting an account-holder to form a corporation in Liechtenstein. They will contact the Liechtenstein state agency, and a letter from the

Liechtenstein Praesidial-Anstalt should follow, welcoming the interest in Liechtenstein. It acts as a domiciliary agent for those interested in establishing corporations in Liechtenstein, and it will furnish the names of lawyers for the potential corporation owners to contact who can handle the incorporation. The two Liechtenstein lawyers act as local corporation directors, and other than the Praesidial-Anstalt, are the only people aware of the true owners. The same rule of secrecy is maintained in Liechtenstein concerning corporate and banking information as with Swiss bank accounts, and any credit check shows only the two lawyers as directors and the corporation's legal liability. As a corporation, this entity and its bank accounts then (apparently) do not become subject to FATCA.

A registration certificate shows the corporation as registered and incorporated, and its holder is the corporation owner. The certificate can be passed to another person, effectively changing ownership without the knowledge of the Liechtenstein lawyers. It is the ultimate cut-out, insuring complete secrecy, and has been widely used by the very rich and intelligence agencies operating clandestinely. There may be some variations on this procedure as the laws change from time to time in the various countries providing such services, and anyone contemplating such arrangements is well advised to check them out thoroughly.

After food and shelter comes energy, and it is normally broken into two components, home heating and air conditioning, and fuel for transportation. With respect to home heating, President Obama has seriously impacted energy costs, and not for the better. Traditionally, the options are oil heat, natural gas, coal, wood, and electricity. But the three fossil fuels also produce electricity, so unless your home is located in a forest, a windy area serviced by wind turbines, or an area where water generates electricity, you will be dependent on fossil fuels. Oil, coal, and wood are under attack by Progressives, and if Obama has his way, in a few years, coal-fired electric power plants will be a thing of the past. Nuclear power plants cannot be built since Progressives do not believe nuclear energy can be made safe, and besides, there is the thorny problem of disposing of nuclear waste To which the Progressives have no solutions.

Wind turbines require an average wind velocity of ten miles per hour all year around to be effective, and solar power is in its infancy.

171

Notably, there are no engineers saying that solar power is feasible on a large scale, and today the cost to provide a home with solar power is out of reach for most homeowners even when taking advantage of federal subsidies. In addition, the bill from the electric company for on-grid systems does not go away, it just gets somewhat smaller. Off-grid systems must have battery banks to provide power when the sun is not shining. Unfortunately, in areas of little sunlight during the winter, solar power is generally not yet, and may never be, a feasible solution.

If solar power is infeasible and geothermal systems impracticable for some reason (usually space), the best bet is natural gas. It and propane are the cleanest environmentally so they draw the least amount of opposition from environmentalists. But natural gas's availability is limited to urban and suburban locations. Heating oil, coal, and wood-burning will be outlawed sooner or later, and costs to replace them are simply unimaginable. In rural areas, wood furnaces and wood-hot water systems are commonly used, and the EPA is attempting to eliminate wood furnaces and stoves as of the date of this work. Although the energy source is renewable, the culprit is particulate matter and $CO_2$ in the smoke, considered by the EPA to be a pollutant. That trees depend on $CO_2$ to grow and use in the process of photosynthesis is apparently irrelevant. Propane is available for rural applications, however, its cost has gone up two hundred percent in the last ten years, and, with its production ties to the refining of gasoline, can be expected to rise enormously in the future.

President Obama, in his jihad against the American middle class, has also signed on to reducing American energy consumption and limit fossil fuel emissions. The Paris accord of December, 2015, enshrined the European plan of reducing emissions by 60% from the 2010 levels prior to 2050, and for the United States, that would most likely mean the end of burning coal or wood. Obviously there will be an increased dependence on wind power generation, but otherwise there will have to be radical breakthroughs in energy technology. What this will mean is for the moment unforecastable.

For most people, potential actions to reduce home heating costs are limited to adding insulation, installing weather-stripping, replacing windows with non-metallic frames and double- and triple-pane glass, adding storm doors, sealing light fixtures and cracks, and finishing the basement walls and floor. Unused rooms should be sealed and left unheated. Actually, all this just makes good sense, whether you're trying to Starve The Beast or not. But after the one-time tax bonanza (to the government) from the government's approved home modifications, heating costs, with their high tax component, will be significantly reduced.

Since the cost of electricity is slated to skyrocket, it is incumbent upon everyone to reduce their use of electricity to the greatest possible degree. All light bulbs in a home should be replaced by LED bulbs that produce no heat and use a fraction of the kilowatts of normal tungsten filament bulbs. They are expensive at the current time—$5.00 to $10.00 per bulb—but energy use is cut by about eighty percent. Electronic equipment and appliances that use energy constantly should be minimized, and turned off rather than allowed to enter "energy-saving" mode. Dry clothes on a clothesline rather than in a dryer, and stop blow-drying hair. Use wind-up clocks rather than clock-radios, unplug the dishwasher, and clear the hot water heater's elements once each year. In short, there are many, many ways to cut electricity use, and now is the time to put them into practice. After the collapse, power will probably be available only at specific times in an area, assuming it is available at all. A homemaker could do worse than to purchase a tub and washboard for the times when no electricity is available.

Reducing the cost of gasoline can only be accomplished by reducing the need for gasoline. Using a vehicle that gets high mileage is preferable, but a change in lifestyle is far more important. If you have children, cut down on their activities in organized sports—although exercise is good for them, sports activities are generally a waste of time. Only an infinitesimal number of children will be able to later make a living in sports, and there is little to be learned in sports that will be beneficial in life. It is simply entertainment, for the kids and their parents, and following the Progressive dictum that everyone is a winner every time, the participants learn a false set of values. Children need to learn about failure, and how to deal with it.

Sports are no substitute for academics in school, but if parents simply cannot stand up to societal pressure, a child should be allowed to participate in only one sport per year, preferably a cheap one like hunting, camping, soccer or softball. Skiing, football, snowmobiling, scuba-diving, sky-diving, ballet, martial arts, beauty contests, and anything that comes with pricey weekly lessons should be avoided. Far less than one percent of all girls who take ballet continue dancing after age sixteen, and the number of individuals that make any money at all through sports is a tiny fraction of those whose parents have shelled out big money for them as children. The only exception to an activity with weekly lessons that might be considered is music, but, here again, the child must show some talent for it to have any effect on his life. To save gasoline, parents should not transport their kids everywhere (think soccer mom) and definitely not go out of town or any great distance to see their children play. Instead, parents should work with their children on their homework or schooling rather than lionize sports. Remember, Progressives want Americans to focus on sports so they can be more easily converted into serfs.

Activities and shopping should be organized so the family car is not used more than once a week unless it serves as transportation to work. Join carpools, even if only of two people—anything to cut down automobile use. For a couple without dependents, only a single vehicle is needed, and it should be chosen to fulfill all the roles necessary. If the family has children, a second automobile might be indicated, but of the smallest size possible. If the family lives in a temperate climate, consider a motorcycle for the second vehicle. The purchase of gasoline should be as limited as possible: possibly to once every ten days if used every day for transport to and from work, and maybe as seldom as once a month or longer if not.

Always buy the cheapest possible gas, as there is little or no difference between the gasoline marketed by the various oil companies. You should not own a vehicle that requires premium gas or diesel. Nor should there be a reason to own gasoline driven power units unless you own a farm. If you have a large lawn, and zoning regulations require that you keep it cut regularly, consider planting a garden, covering the lawn with mulch, or plant pine trees so you no longer have a lawn, or it is small enough to be mowed by a push mower. Be creative, but work to eliminate costs in the maintenance of your property. At the very least, stop watering your lawn—all that does is spend money and use up a precious resource.

Clothing should be a mix of thrift and second-hand stores and new items. Women's clothes are particularly expensive, but the art of dressmaking still exists among many women who make their own clothes. Hire a dressmaker, and pay in cash to reduce costs for such clothes, or learn how to make your own clothes. Preparedness stores and groups often put on classes to teach such skills. Eliminate clothes that require dry cleaning, and learn to make your own soap to reduce costs. Shoes are another expensive item and should only be purchased when others wear out. Buy the cheapest possible shoes for children so that they wear out before the children outgrow them. If children outgrow their shoes or clothes before they wear out, trade them to someone else for something you need.

Health care costs are a sticky problem, but people may be surprised at the flexibility by some doctors who are generally conservative. Obamacare has destroyed the best option, carrying insurance only for catastrophic illness or accident and paying cash for everything else. But even now with high co-pays, it often pays to bargain with the doctor for a lower charge based on paying in cash. Generally, charges are reduced by twenty-five to fifty percent, indicating just how much cost is added by third-party payment processing, and in particular, by Medicare. Doctors who will negotiate their fee if you pay cash are often the best doctors. Sign an agreement that the doctor and his clinic or hospital are not responsible for mistakes or malpractice of any kind, and watch the costs decline.

Perhaps the best advice is to do your homework before going to a doctor, or, at the very least, before the bills start to mount. The drug companies are in the business of selling medicines and drugs, doctors and nurses are in the business of providing corrective medicine, hospitals are in the business of providing beds and medical facilities to doctors and patients. Only you, the individual, have the maintenance of your health as your primary concern. If your doctor recommends a test, find out how much it will cost, and what he can determine from the test. Doctors are people, and when they understand you have a limited amount of money, they will often attempt to provide effective medical services within your means.

The best health regimen is to eat properly, get lots of physical exercise—through work, chores, or, if need be, by sports—team or individual—don't drink to excess, don't smoke at all, don't do any recreational or addicting drugs, and don't spread or pick up germs through carelessness. Fight obesity with a passion—an obese person is an unhealthy person. Childhood obesity results in nearly a fifty percent increase in health costs during a person's lifetime.[155] Keep everything working, get plenty of sex, go to church often, have fun and do things with others.

In short, live life.

To lower costs, one can refuse all rides in ambulances unless the injured or sick person's condition is critical—and have an agreement with several friends to take each other to the emergency room or hospital as necessary. Calling 911 for a medical emergency incurs a great deal of expense, and it is much cheaper to drive to the emergency room instead. Ambulances are very expensive, and expect a bill of $800 to $2,000 if you use one, and many individuals are released the same day from a hospital or emergence room after being brought there by an ambulance. In rural settings, consider purchasing air ambulance insurance.

America is over-medicated to an extreme, and even over-doctored. Many medicines that are prescription in the U.S. are over-the-counter and much cheaper in Mexico and Canada. Make arrangements with people on the two borders to obtain your medicines. Other medicines are available for animal use at minimum cost, but are exactly the same as for humans. Most doctors no longer practice prophylactic medicine; that is, provide medicine for a situation before it occurs, such as providing a pain-killer or antibiotic for cuts and injuries frequently suffered in the normal course of work, like farm or field work. Such doctors require a patient first to suffer the cut, then come in to the doctor (for a $75-$100 office visit), then write a prescription for an antibiotic only sufficient for that cut (thank you for protecting me, FDA administrators). Self-treating with antibiotics known to be safe for an individual who is not allergic to the medicine reduces costs to a very small amount. It is only since the advent of health insurance that practices have been instituted to everyone's substantial increase in cost.

Health care costs can be substantially lowered by everyone, but require attention to detail by the patient and his family. For example, a sixty-eight-year-old man was suddenly stricken early in the morning by a sharp pain in the left side of his lower abdomen, and although he had never had kidney problems before, it seemed like that was the trouble. After enduring severe pain for several hours, he called 911 (he lived alone), and was taken by an ambulance to an emergency room. He was not given anything for the pain on the half-hour ride to the emergency room, nor did he receive any in the ER for the first hour, even though an IV tube had been attached in the ambulance. X-rays were taken, and about forty-five minutes later, the doctor announced the man had a kidney stone in the tract leading down from his left kidney (no surprise, that was what everyone in the ambulance and emergency room said the problem probably was), and showed the man the x-ray where the stone was clearly visible. The man was given a shot for pain, given a prescription for a painkiller, and told the stone should probably pass in a few hours. He called a friend, who came and drove him home.

In the afternoon, the stone passed and the ordeal was over—except for the cost. The ambulance was almost $900.00, and the total of the doctors and emergency room came to over $5,000. A "walletectomy" had been performed. The bill showed two MRI x-rays, although the man had never been placed in an MRI unit, a urine analysis, even though no sample had been given or taken, $450.00 for a radiologist to interpret the x-rays (apparently the normal doctor was incompetent to spot the stone), and miscellaneous charges. The two MRIs cost $1,600 each, one for the lower abdomen and one for the upper chest. The former patient contested the charges, and was turned in for collection within three days by the radiologists. In confronting the director of the emergency room as to why an MRI was taken (if it was) of the upper chest when there was no indication of any problem there, the doctor replied, "Because of your age—it would have been malpractice if we had not looked for other problems."

Apparently, by the same logic, if the man had come in with a broken ankle, he would be subjected to a heart evaluation. In fact, this occurred three years later when the individual stopped in at a clinic with a sore throat that had lingered for two weeks. The doctor confirmed the sore throat, but refused to prescribe antibiotics as she thought the throat would clear up by itself in another ten days or so. But then, she went exploring, listening to the man's heart and checking his lungs. She discovered a very minor heart murmur the man had had for at least twenty-five years, and suggested she take steps to eliminate it. Her effort at salesmanship failed, and the man went home, having wasted $60 that he paid in cash after bargaining down the office visit from the $115.00 charge for insurance patients.

In the end, the man paid the bill, but learned a valuable lesson:

never allow oneself to be taken to an emergency room by an ambulance, and take a pad and paper to record every service, test, or procedure performed. Some ten years earlier, this man had undergone surgery on his neck, and when the preliminary MRI was done, the technician immediately handed the patient the x-rays to take across the street to his surgeon. A month later, a bill came from a radiologist for having interpreted the MRI. After contacting the surgeon and confirming the x-rays had never been out of his office, the patient refused to pay. The account went into collection, and the radiologist maintained the billing was valid because it was the hospital's *policy* to have all MRIs interpreted by a radiologist. That he hadn't seen the x-rays made no difference.

There was also double billing for another service from the hospital, and, after being turned in for collection on both invoices, the man paid for the single service provided. He found, to his amazement, that the collection company took his first check, and computer-generated another one for the bogus billing, and ran it through the bank a month later. The patient's bank initially honored the check, because computer-generated checks are normal (as in the case where a person purchases something by merely giving the seller his bank account information). Actually, the collection company had engaged in a criminal act—theft by taking—and the man reported the company to the district attorney for prosecution. Amazingly, the district attorney was unaware of this type of crime, and the case became his first one for prosecution. Apparently the collection agency routinely fabricated checks, and waited a month or two before submitting them a second time (they used the same check number as the earlier one) so the account holder wouldn't spot the duplicate.

To say that health care is studded with fraud would not be an exaggeration, but, of course, all industries heavily controlled by the government become hotbeds of fraud and corruption. It has been estimated that one-half of all worker's compensation cases are fraudulent, but that number, in spite of being highly disseminated, does not seem to decline. Supposedly, some forty percent of all Medicare payments entail elements of fraud or waste, but, again, that number never gets addressed. And remember, the single most likely place you'll pick up a bug and get sick is at a doctor's office, clinic, or hospital, simply because that's where the sick people are.

The chance that tort reform will ever be introduced to limit awards in malpractice suits is slim to none. The trial lawyers are firmly Progressive and strongly allied with the Democrat Party. The money at stake is simply overwhelming, and some percentage of lawyers will always be unable to resist becoming wealthy on a single case. It is not uncommon for an award to reach into the millions, but then the lawyer for the plaintiff takes his often greatly inflated expenses out of the settlement or award and also a contingency fee of thirty to fifty percent. Sometimes, in smaller awards, the lawyers walk away with the lion's share. In some states, the loser must pay the winner's lawyer fees, so even if the award is tiny, such as $5,000, the lawyer might take thirty-five percent of that, plus $100,000 in attorney's fees from the loser. That's why settlements are so common.

The tobacco master settlement agreement in 1998 created a number of billionaires from the plaintiffs' attorneys and several friends of Congress who brokered influence. Even worse was the precedent: smoking is addictive, but it is also voluntary, therefore, smokers are taking no responsibility for their own bad choices. In court, only the "hired gun" lawyers win—then they shake hands, and go out arm-in-arm with the opposition's lawyers to have a drink, leaving the loser bankrupt, all witnesses feeling like they need to take a shower, and the winner counting pennies.

Literally, the last classification of expenses, "all other expenses" are optional. Yet, this is where most people waste their money. Why does one need a new car, much less two? If you have car payments for more than three years out of ten, you're wasting your money. A new vehicle loses twenty percent of its value when it is driven away from the dealership. All vehicles are engineered for two- to three hundred thousand miles before a major overhaul, and if the vehicle doesn't dissolve in the salt used by northern states, it should be kept that long. Anything else is spending for vanity.

Auto repairs are sometimes another major item, and the operative rule is to avoid going to dealerships if at all possible. Following the Obama elimination of Republican-owned dealerships for GM and Chrysler, excellent mechanics were dispersed into independent auto repair shops. Spend some time and find the little guy who doesn't charge $75.00 per hour for mechanic work according to a number of standard hours for that job rather than the hours actually worked. The mechanic should also either order the after-market parts himself at one-fifth the price or give you the information to purchase the parts on the Internet. And under no condition should you purchase extended warranties—this is just another way to sell insurance. The seller is betting on the work under the extended warranty being much less than the cost of the warranty, and he is almost always correct, even when the dealer is doing the work at top dollar.

Dealing with a small business or individual opens up another opportunity—that of trading or reciprocal gifting of services. Property owners often provide space or a garage at no charge to an individual or small business in return for free services or products. Cable TV even once featured a show where people traded up on goods until they were able to trade for the item they wanted. It was a game, where the winner was the one who had traded up to the most expensive item.

It has been estimated that one-third to one-half of all items purchased (other than clothes and consumables) are no longer used after the first year. They are purchased for a specific purpose or to meet a temporary need, and are rarely or never used again after that initial need is met. In effect, there is a huge second-hand market present if people would take stock of the items they are storing because they "might need them someday." But instead of selling those items, trade them for what is needed, and then trade those items away for the next necessity when they are no longer needed. Swap meets, garage sales, flea markets, lawn sales, Craig's List, on-line yard sales, etc., all can dramatically reduce the costs of living by making prices more reasonable and reducing wasteful expenditures. The fair market values are much lower than for new items, and income is reduced accordingly.

Even more importantly, in a financial crisis when cash is tight or inflation rising rapidly, trading and swapping may become the only ways to obtain necessities. An urban resident might be able to trade an extra automobile for a plot of rural land for gardening or a partial ownership in such a parcel and receive some of the proceeds of the lot for a designated period of time. Obviously, one is only constrained by one's imagination, but the object is to obtain everything needed while spending the absolute minimum amount of money. It goes without saying that the only use of a credit card should be to purchase items on the Internet that are cheaper than the locally available items and carry no sales tax, and using a debit card is a bad idea at all times. Since credit cards routinely cost the merchant three percent of the purchase amount, an individual buying from a small business should ask for a two percent discount when paying with cash (not a check) on large ticket items.

Obviously, it is desirable to limit credit card use as soon as possible to establish a history of low usage to avoid being targeted when Progressives come after people Starving The Beast. The number of cards a person maintains should be limited to a maximum of two; one for local use, and one for Internet purchases where the card number will probably become compromised over time. As the Progressive government begins to feel the effects of lower revenues, credit cards should be consolidated into one per family or even one per group of families where cooperatives have been formed. These cards can maintain normal use, and pass Progressive transaction count tests to avoid suspicion.

The same strategy can be used for bank accounts. They should be consolidated into as few as possible, and, of course, debit cards should never be used. The best method of converting depositing checks is to cash incoming checks at your local bank or receive a substantial amount of cash at the time of making each deposit. The deposit slips are maintained as images, but are usually not maintained in a media the Federal Government can readily access to analyze accounts. Minimize the number of checks you write.

In addition, people should learn to re-use items, perhaps not for what they were originally purchased, but in lieu of purchasing another item. For example, wash aluminum foil for a second time of use, use a wash cloth to wipe up a spill instead of using a paper towel, use jelly jars for glasses, butter containers for food storage, and milk jugs for the storage of water and other fluids.

Purchasing anything advertised on national television is costly. Such companies count on dealing with unsophisticated buyers, and shipping and handling charges can become extreme. A test was made of nationally advertised gold and silver suppliers, and the prices varied from very good to totally unreasonable. One company advertised prices at one percent over dealer cost—a meaningless statement as dealer cost could mean replacement cost today, or what the dealer paid three months ago for the specific gold or silver. In the test, the spot silver price was $29.78 per ounce, and the quote for a bag ($1,000.000 face) of pre-1965 American silver coins was $37,000.00. Since the uncirculated coins by weight were only 723.4 ounces, worth at spot $21,543, a quote of not over $26,000 was expected (if circulated, they would have contained 715 ounces.) It was definitely up to the buyer to do his homework first to avoid paying such a huge and unconscionable premium. But the advertisement might have been accurate—the silver price had fallen greatly during the previous weeks, and the dealer might have paid $36,600 for the silver.

Another area is insurance where a veritable army of salesmen descend on the citizen, selling all types of policies. Other than federally required medical coverage and automobile liability mandated by almost every state, there are few others to legitimately consider. If the individual is a homeowner, there is homeowner's insurance that will be mandated by the mortgage holder, but it should have a high deductible, in no case less than three or four thousand dollars. The protection should only be for a catastrophe, not for minor damages. Automotive insurance can often be purchased from the same carrier at a substantial savings, since car insurance is extremely lucrative for those companies (i.e. overpriced.) There should be an umbrella rider or policy with the homeowners insurance for liability, such as for when the neighbor's kid sneaks into your swimming pool and drowns.

If you are relatively young with many mouths to feed, you might consider a term life policy (only pays on the death of the insured) to give your family a running start if you die unexpectedly. But in no case should a person be worth more dead than alive. Universal insurance, whole life, or any plan with a "cash value" that can be borrowed against or builds equity, should never be purchased as they are extremely bad investments. The one thing the agent is trained to do is never tell you the actual interest rate you are getting by putting money into such a policy. Nor should you purchase "mortgage payout insurance" or any insurance on paying for anything you buy over time. These are all just schemes to sell policies, using one hook after another, and if such a policy is required by a lender or seller, go somewhere else. You are paying to provide the lender or lien holder the assurance he will get his money, and if he wants more protection, he should pay for it, not you. Generally speaking, America is grossly over-insured, and that has produced many astronomically wealthy insurance companies.

One company stands out due to its ownership. Progressive Insurance was owned by Peter B. Lewis until his death in November, 2013, and he ranked with George Soros as the biggest financier of Progressive politicians and causes in the United States. He was a very substantial donor to America Coming Together, Moveon.org (matching George Soros's contributions), the ACLU and the Democrat Party. A dedicated and leading Progressive, Lewis referred to himself as a secular Jew. At his death, Lewis was worth over $1.25 billion. As Progressive Insurance continues to be one of the two primary cash cows of Progressivism, it is recommended that no one purchase policies of any type from Progressive Insurance. The name of the company is no accident, and reflects the Lewis family's commitment to Progressivism.

Vacations are another area where a significant impact can be made. The state and city taxes on the travel and hospitality industries are enormous under the theory that the taxes are falling on people who do not vote in the locality or state levying the taxes. Surprisingly, this is an area where costs can be avoided or lowered by bargaining. Obviously, all air travel should be avoided if at all possible, especially if more than one person is traveling. Motels, particularly locally-owned and managed motels, both franchised and not, will often bargain late in the evening when they have vacant rooms, sometimes to as low as half price. One can also develop a relationship with a local motel operator, and obtain lodging for a trip through his connections. Motel operators sometimes even trade rooms with each other, and the traveler might be able to arrange lodging through his local connection. Forego high-priced national chain motels, and particularly those owned by foreign corporations such as Holiday Inn (Great Britain). Rent an RV, camp out, and tell your children this is your way of getting closer to nature.

There is actually very little a person cannot obtain through trading or bargaining, but it requires a change in one's lifestyle. One must eschew the idea of always possessing the "latest and the greatest," and learn to live with fully functional, but not necessarily the newest or most modern items. The test should be, "does it do the job," not how fast or how elegantly. If an item is used regularly, it should be used until it wears out, and, even then, it is possible that it can be sold to someone else, and some value recovered. America has adopted a "throw-away" culture in response to incessant advertising, and all that is needed to save enormous amounts of money is to ignore the siren songs to spend.

Pets are another huge cost in the average household. As noted earlier, feed stores are the proper places to purchase pet foods, not your neighborhood grocery store. Diatomaceous Earth (DE) should be purchased in bulk, either large cans or fifty-pound sacks, particularly if one is also doing gardening. DE dusted on pets and plants kills ticks, fleas, and other undesirable insects, and mixing it in pet food will control worms and other parasites. People can also eat DE (food grade only) without ill effects (any effects will be good), and it is often referred to as "nature's magic bullet." It contains no harmful chemicals and works strictly mechanically.[156] Nonetheless, the quickest way to reduce costs is to reduce the number of pets in the household.

In 2011, there were at least two hundred and eighteen million pets in the United States, and the cost of maintaining them was over sixty-one billion dollars.[157] Most households with at least one pet actually had two or three as an average, and cutting down to a single pet per household could save more than thirty billion dollars annually. Pets may be very good medicine for their owners, but they do not need expensive toys or clothes to make them look like little humans.

Two items of expense should be categorically eliminated: donations to higher education institutions and charities other than church or faith-based charities. Progressive academicians have seized control of our schools and universities through two aspects of their employment: tenure and academic freedom.

Tenure essentially guarantees teachers and university professors lifetime employment—peven if they are incompetent or bad teachers. Many professors burn out in the process of producing a PhD dissertation, and never again perform research or add to mankind's knowledge. Unfortunately, it is impossible to terminate bad or incompetent professors except for moral turpitude or conviction for criminal activities in a court of law, and often not even then. Nor are teachers and university professors underpaid: even in Arkansas, forty-fifth in student achievement, the average starting salary for K-12 teachers is over $35,000 for less than a hundred and eighty days of teaching, and the average assistant professor at the University of Arkansas earns $75,000 for nine months.

Academic freedom is a concept that was transplanted from German universities to America in 1892, first arriving at the University of Chicago. At the time, German universities were felt to be the best in the world, and German principles of tenure and academic freedom had been developed to minimize interference from princes and nobles who were supporting the schools. The evolution of faculty responsibilities and privileges proceeded from that point, and, in 1915, the American Association of University Professors was formed.

Edwin R. A. Seligman, a Progressive political economist championing the income tax, headed a committee to draw up the principles of academic freedom. Seligman believed in Marxist economic theory and wished to limit administrative interference with faculty research, teaching, and other activities. He also pushed for the concept of tenure, wherein a faculty member was granted lifetime employment. This principle became formalized in 1940.

All this raises serious questions. Should anyone in a government bureaucracy be granted a sinecure for life and be secure from economic factors when these benefits are paid by the taxes of citizens who do not enjoy the same benefits? The idea that a faculty member is free to inquire into any line of study is at the heart of academic freedom, but is he then allowed to say and teach anything he wants? Is he to be unconstrained by facts and allowed to distribute propaganda for his own agenda to young minds? Should those paying his salary have absolutely no say in his conduct and use of their facilities? Are universities to be havens for those who can't contribute to society? For Progressives, the answer to all these questions is, "yes."

The American Association of University Professors (AAUP), a very Progressive body, produced the following principles: "Neither an individual, nor a state, nor the church has the right to interfere with the search for truth or with its promulgation when found… A donor has the privilege of ceasing to make his gifts to an institution if, in his opinion, the work of the institution is not satisfactory; but, as donor, he has no right to interfere with the administration or the instruction of the university."

There is a significant problem here; the primary donor to educational institutions is government, followed by the individual states, and none of them penalize education institutions for malfeasance, corruption, and outright propagandizing of our children. Even worse, the primary way citizens contribute to colleges and universities is through support of their athletic programs, when they are little more than semi-professional teams. And that is in higher education. High school athletics are essentially entertainment media, misdirecting parental attention onto sports to avoid calling attention to a school's deficiencies in academics. It is not unusual for a high school to have six football coaches and only a single science teacher.

On the other hand, the AAUP appears to approve of Starving the Beast. Donors (American citizens) have the right to cease making contributions if "the work of the institution is not satisfactory." Well, it isn't, and patriots must not only cease making personal contributions, but also funding government so long as it makes contributions!

The AAUP continued, "The greatest single element necessary for the cultivation of the academic spirit is the feeling of security from interference. It is only those who have this feeling that are able to do work which in the highest sense will be beneficial to humanity. Freedom of expression must be given the members of a university faculty, even though it may be abused, for the abuse of it is not so great an evil as the restriction of such liberty."

According to the AAUP, the citizenry must pay teachers' and professors' salaries, and for the schools, universities, libraries, and all expenses for the conduct of scholarship, but citizens have absolutely no right to say what they should teach or how they should teach it. This is taxation without representation. Citizens have to pay for the educational monster, but have no say in the use of taxpayer funds. Of all the systems in the United States, this one is the most undemocratic. The education of American children is in the hands of people who work for government, not for the people. They are not elected, and there is no way to affect what they teach, how they teach, or if they teach at all. Support for education is the biggest component of your property tax, whether or not you have children. And you have exactly zero influence on what America's children are taught.

All support of high school and college athletics, and all contributions of any type to schools, colleges, and universities must cease. They are a critical part of the Beast, and reducing those expenditures not only starves the educational establishment part of the Beast, but allows parents to unequivocally send a signal to the educational establishment that parents are dissatisfied with teacher and administrative performance. Parents will not be bought off through entertainment by high school and college athletics, and no money will be forthcoming until schools concentrate on their primary mission which is to educate. And that does not mean Progressive education, but education in the basic skills needed by all productive members of society.

There is only one expense that should be increased—that of donations to one's church. But there must be a test made to determine whether one's church is on the Progressive side or not. If a minister or priest speaks of "social gospel" or shows any empathy at all with Obama and his Progressive Democrats, refuse all donations and seek another church. Already Progressivism has all but destroyed most Protestant denominations, as members flee churches teaching social gospel for evangelical churches preaching salvation through Christ and God's grace.

If a pastor refuses to take a political stance and condemn Progressivism, he should be fired by the church. Establishing a dictatorship of the elite is not part of Protestant Christianity, and anyone supporting such an abomination should not receive church funds. Nor is moral relativism, another concept taught by Progressive ministers. One aspect of Progressive ideology says that the teachings of the Koran that specify death to non-believers are the moral equivalent of Christ's teachings and should be given the same weight in all determinations of morality.

With respect to human behavior, Christianity teaches moral absolutes, and many behaviors are simply wrong and sinful in the sight of God. It is the role of the church to bring sinners to God and help them seek redemption, but the church must not excuse immoral and unethical behavior in order to curry favor from Progressives in power. If necessary, donations to a church should be earmarked for specific purposes, and supporting a pastor who counsels understanding and acceptance of actions by Progressives should not be among them.

Christians should look at the sad case of the Lutheran Church in Germany during the Third Reich. It split in two, with the Confessing Church becoming the sanctuary for anti-Nazi Christians, while the traditional church adapted to Nazi ideology and went along with Hitler in the hopes of surviving. It survived, but had compromised itself so greatly that it was never again a moral force in Germany. Today, it is a shadow of its former self, and its impotence is speeding the drift to atheism in Germany. The exact same phenomenon is occurring today in the United States, as Progressive ministers seem to have learned nothing from history.

## Reduce Income Tax Obligations

Income taxes are usually the first thing citizens think about in reducing payments to government, but it probably should be viewed more as a by-product of changing one's lifestyle. Nonetheless, there are many perfectly legal ways to reduce one's income tax, particularly if one pays more than $25,000 in income taxes. Remember, it is important to live well, not to maximize one's income. Maximizing income maximizes income taxes, federal, state, and, possibly, local. Of course, there are many dubious measures that can be taken to lower income tax obligations with little risk, but these are not discussed in this book other than to mention that they are not recommended.

One needs only to look at government employees, who already earn substantially more than their privately employed counterparts, to see how lifestyles can be improved without increasing income. Government provides its employees with free day care, libraries, gym and fitness facilities, subsidized cafeterias, uniform allowances, free parking, car-pooling connection services, free counseling, free vacation opportunities while attending schools, skill-enhancement training sessions, free schooling, free newspapers, free magazines, conferences at exotic locations, subsidized retail stores, free or partially paid investment plans and pensions, free health care or health insurance, including dental, free life insurance, free or subsidized higher education, extensive personal leave, sick leave, long vacation time, subsidized vacation facilities, subsidized or free vacation travel, many holidays, free student loan forgiveness, free computers, free cell phones, and, the best perk of all, receiving all this for working anywhere from two to seven hours per day, four and a half days per week.

The military is on duty for much longer hours, but professors in taxpayer-funded universities often are on campus only two or three days a week, and teach a total of only six hours per week with homework and test grading accomplished by assistants. To say that colleges and universities provide secure sinecures to age seventy for faculty and to age sixty-five or higher for staff would not be an understatement, but so does government civil service employment. Government also provides for early retirement, and it is not unusual to meet couples who were both employed by government with combined pensions of $150,000 to $200,000 per year, and who retired at age fifty-five. Everybody should be so lucky.

So how can an individual serf obtain such a "life of Reilly" in private employment? Serfs have to band together, trade with each other to the benefit of each other to begin to enjoy the benefits the ruling class enjoys at the serfs' cost. Make no mistake; serfs currently send the majority of their earnings to government to enhance the lifestyle of the ruling elite class. Serfs need to keep and use the majority of their earnings, even the vast majority, for their own benefit and that of their families.

This is indeed class warfare at its finest. It is not class warfare as envisioned by Karl Marx—the proletariat versus the bourgeoisie—but serfs against their masters. Communism in the Soviet Union eventually produced the same class war; the common people versus communist party members, specifically the nomenklatura. And this is the same situation we have seen arise in the United States—just replace the word "communist" with "Progressive."

At all times, the serfs must remember that government creates no wealth.Iit derives its revenue solely from the people, and returns only a portion—sometimes a very small portion—to the people under the false rubric of a "benefit." But such benefits have already been earned by the people. Everyone pays in, willingly, unwillingly, and often unknowingly, and only a small portion comes back in services, roads, infrastructure, and the like. A huge portion goes directly to the ruling elite or is wasted to no good purpose. Through the payment of taxes and having to do the Progressive elites' bidding through regulations and laws, serfs are increasingly unable to rise above a struggling subsistence level.

The benefits described above must be delivered to the people by the people, working together to retain their wealth and way of life at the most local level, and living as if the Progressive Federal Government does not exist. Community garden areas need to be established, parking meters abolished, and home-schooling promoted, with retirees lecturing on various subjects. Local government buildings and properties should be made available free of charge to community organizations, and libraries opened for extended hours. Schools should become community centers anyone can use, and staffed by volunteers. Property taxes should be minimized, even for businesses of all types, and those businesses should sponsor various community activities. Schools must be uncoupled from government through the establishment of charter schools, and teachers' unions should be abolished. Teacher pay must be awarded for performance, and tenure stricken as a feature of employment. Local zoning laws and building codes should be eliminated, and local ordinances passed to nullify federal laws and provide a legal basis for resisting federal interference by executive branch agencies. In particular, the office of sheriff is critical, and a devout Christian and strict constitutionalist must be elected as sheriff to provide a bulwark against Progressive dominated federal and NGO encroachment.

The serf class will never be able to enjoy the perquisites of the ruling class under Progressivism with any amount of income. The system is set up to force people to maximize their earnings, followed by maximizing their expenditures so that property taxes, wealth taxes, sales taxes, income taxes, and all hidden taxes are maximized. In the end analysis, all members of the ruling class live well and enjoy terrific benefits and pensions, while the serfs struggle to exist under their crushing tax burden. The serfs must live so they pay little in taxes by reducing expenditures as discussed. But while the people are Starving The Beast, local cooperation can go a long way toward alleviating hardships and ensuring everyone survives hard times in reasonably good shape. When the national economy collapses, hardships will arise as the ruling class seeks to perpetuate its standard of living at the expense of the serfs, and the class rupture described above will come into sharp focus.

It is also important to understand that all bartering or trading for goods and services comes with one enormous caveat: IRS rules say that the value of any item acquired by trade or barter is taxable as income determined by the fair market value of the item. Barter income is taxable. Barter income is also a huge red flag to IRS, greatly increasing the possibility of an audit, even more than having a conservative non-profit corporation. In addition, the IRS has won several cases where barter income was considered net of costs—that is, barter income is a "commission" and not subject to deductions such as the cost of the item traded away.

In fact, according to the IRS, the fair market value of the goods and services exchanged must be reported as income by both parties. If a barter exchange service is used, something that is absolutely *not* recommended, the exchange is required to issue a *Form 1099-B, Proceeds from Brokerage and Barter Transactions* annually to all clients or members as well as the IRS.

Bartering may also result in liabilities for self-employment tax, employment taxes, and excise taxes. The risk of bartering with unknown individuals is tantamount to walking into a minefield so long as the IRS's activities and competence are high. There is really no way of safeguarding oneself in direct barter transactions, and Starve the Beast does not recommend bartering except in desperate and extreme circumstances. Bartering brings all sorts of legal problems, and, once again, the reader should consult with a tax specialist, as this information is not intended to aid anyone in circumventing the law.

There is, however, another way to trade items and services: a person simply gives them away. An individual can give up to $14,000.00 in gifts to another individual in a single year without having to report those gifts or pay any gift tax.[158] Generally, a person receiving a gift will not have to pay any federal gift tax or income tax on the value of the gift received. This regulation opens up new options, particularly in light of the stance by IRS and the Federal Government on donations made to the Clinton Foundation that were apparently directly linked to quid pro quo services provided by Hillary Clinton as Secretary of State. If a person gifts items or services worth less than $14,000 per year and receives items or services valued less than $14,000 in that same year, the gifts are allowed to go unreported and are not subject to gift or income tax.

The key is not to make any barter or trade transactions. They are all taxable whereas gifts below the taxable exclusion are not. Follow the example of the Clintons and do not break any laws. Do not link gifts received with any quid pro quo services or goods provided. Most important is to avoid even the appearance of wrong-doing by trading gifts at the same time, thus linking them and appearing to barter. Remember, you do not possess Mrs. Clinton's connections to escape accountability.

These regulations are subject to change at any time, but they indicate the overall attitude of government to gifts. For many people, the best method for reducing one's tax burden and denying the out-of-control Progressive government any substantial amount of revenue is to donate to one's church as heavily as possible. With donations, the church can increase its services to its congregation using unpaid volunteers, such as sponsoring sports, trips and outings to parks, providing a fitness center free to all members, day care services, game nights, senior meals, parties, etc. All of these services are things that would otherwise cost money and provide tax dollars to the government, but, instead, they come to the individual as a result of a deductible donation, reducing taxes twice--once as a deduction, and the second time by not sending any hidden taxes or even sales taxes to the government. The citizen can gift his services by volunteering with his church to do certain things for charity, and then receive other things from others who are also providing charity. At the moment, the IRS does not tax services as income that are provided to someone by a charity. For example, the repair squad from your church could put a new roof on someone's house with your help, then also repair storm damage that you suffered. In essence, repairs or improvements are made to property at minimum cost, with no one incurring income. The church may own boats, campers, bus, trailers, canoes, paintball guns, sports equipment, a retreat, or other items than can be used by members of the congregation on a rotating basis. One is just limited by one's imagination.

If a citizen is unfortunate enough to be affiliated with a church that promotes Progressivism and social justice, then the answer is to form a

"Survival Circle" with like-minded people to form cooperatives, or simply gift goods and services to each other so that all benefit. One family has chickens and gives their eggs to others in the circle, another has a large garden, still another has pigs or cattle or buys a calf from a farmer and has it butchered. Someone else raises fish with aquaponics, one has a solar power system that keeps freezers going, and another has a pond that provides water. Some wives make clothes, others dehydrate food or perform canning—the potential is limitless. A few vehicles can suffice for a large number of people if they are willing to cooperate for the benefit of everyone in the circle. One family (hopefully with one or two good mechanics among its children) owns all the vehicles, pays low insurance for the fleet, and maintains and keeps the vehicles in good repair. Another pays for the gas and oil. Just make sure than no individual's gifts to another exceed $14,000 in value in a single year. All are gifts, everyone benefits, money going to the government is minimized, and the Beast is Starved!

## Downsize lifestyles

Although reducing one's lifestyle can save an enormous amount of money in expenditures, it also serves to reduce taxes and insurance on wealth. The two primary taxes on wealth are property taxes and personal property taxes, which often include securities, vehicles, and other items depending on individual state laws. In Illinois, for example, the expenditures in municipalities and counties include large pension components for government employees which determine the tax rates rather than the revenue determining the political unit's budget. The only way a homeowner can reduce his property tax is by moving to a cheaper home. During the decline in housing values from 2008 to 2012, property values declined but the requirements for revenue increased, so tax rates were adjusted upward across the board to make up the difference.

Having a nice home is a recipe for high taxes, and, in effect, a person just leases his home from the government, with the property tax being the lease payment. Required homeowner's insurance should also be considered as part of the lease since mortgage holders require it, and the litigious legal environment in the United States makes umbrella liability insurance essentially mandatory.

One of the cash flow solutions offered today is the "reverse mortgage," but this option could cost many homeowners their homes. As taxes skyrocket to meet existing obligations by state and local agencies, a homeowner can easily find himself unable to pay his property taxes under any but the most draconian measures. As a reverse mortgage obligates the homeowner to maintain a current status on taxes as well as insurance, failure to make tax payments on time may trigger the calling of the reverse mortgage. At that point, the reverse mortgage holder would pay the taxes, and take possession of the property. For this reason and many others, a reverse mortgage is a stunningly bad idea.

The best solution is to downsize immediately, staying well clear of gated communities with highly restrictive covenants that force homeowners to spend money, and purchase or build the smallest possible home in the cheapest fashion. But there is an additional reason to downsize one's home that is probably more important than all others: your home must provide you with the means of surviving the collapse. You should plan to reside in this dwelling at least two and possibly as long as five to seven years, the time assumed necessary to span the horrendous dislocations and violence expected in a general collapse.

The home should be in an area or compound sharing space with individuals dedicated to surviving the disorders and home invasions by people who have believed Progressive propaganda, and ultimately find themselves without funds, food, or the means to weather the collapse. Remember, many forecasters of a collapse believe that after merely a single year of disorder and the disappearance of the current logistics system distributing food, gas, electricity, and other necessary items to support modern life, over ninety percent of the American population will have perished. Locating or building a new and appropriate home allows the family to shelter in place during the collapse in addition to Starving the Beast. The home should also be a defensible habitat, built with an eye to home defense. Hopefully, a defense will not be needed, but why take the chance? In warfare, planning and preparation have won a lot of battles.

Since World War II, citizen spending has become increasingly lavish in a race to maintain social position and appearances. "Keeping up with the Joneses" has become a lifestyle for many, thus giving rise to outlandish expenditures, especially for children. Three hundred dollar tennis shoes, fancy cars at age sixteen, vacations to far-away places, and designer jeans are now considered essential to a child's esteem, self-image, and self-respect.

Today, a child without an expensive smartphone or other device to email, handle voice communication, and social media is a rarity. Yet, these devices do nothing to improve a child's life, and certainly are dangerous to his health by taking him away from healthy physical activities and direct interpersonal relations to build social skills. Chores for children are now considered a thing of the past, along with the concept that a mother's job is to prepare her children to leave home. Every other mammal mother in God's Kingdom accepts this as her life's purpose, but Progressives have re-written the cycle of life along with the purposes of mankind and the meaning of marriage.

Patriots living in certain areas of the United States are advised to immediately relocate to those areas that tend to reflect their political and living philosophies when the nation breaks up. One very possible outcome of the current Progressive follies is that the U.S. will Balkanize into at least six states or countries. Although forecasts vary, in general, they assume countries will coalesce around centers of similar race, ethnicity, language, and political outlook.

For example: Aztlan most likely will arise as a new Hispanic nation, encompassing California, Nevada, Arizona, New Mexico, the western and southern portions of Texas, along with probably six northern Mexican states; West Canada could be made up of Washington, Oregon, Alaska, and the Canadian Provinces west of Ontario; Hawaii might become a part of Japan (following its primary ethnic group); South Florida might join a Caribbean Confederation with its capital in Havana or Miami; African America could form from the old South states from Virginia to Louisiana, with Atlanta as its capital; New England might be comprised of the states north of Virginia and east of the Alleghenies, and might join the European Union; and the remainder might become the American Republic, theoretically the most closely aligned politically to the traditional United States before its demise. One should look closely at these future states and decide now where one desires to live and raise a family.

For the current time, the reader should shun California (The People's Republic of California), purchasing nothing being exported from that state, and promote the idea that California should be sold to China in settlement of the U.S.'s outstanding debts. Of course, a major caveat might have to be present in the deal: China will have to take all the current residents.. California currently interprets any company or partnership that advertises in California, sells anything to anyone in California, purchases anything from California, or even invests in a company with any sort of presence in California, as doing business in California and subject to an outrageously expensive California franchise tax, and possibly to California state income tax. Unless the reader is an outright Progressive who loves Chinese food, California is not recommended as a place to live.

## Eliminate Wealth Controlled by Government

Few American citizens know that the Federal Government is already considering converting all outstanding 401K plans and IRAs to a single federally run and guaranteed saving plan where the security will be U.S. government bonds, payable in dollars. That such a scheme would be absolutely terrifying to citizens owning IRAs and 401K investments hardly needs to be mentioned. The impetus for such a move is that the conversion would make nearly 10 trillion dollars available immediately to retire debt, nearly four trillion from 401K accounts and almost six trillion from IRAs.

The major problem of this asset grab is that only about three and a half trillion of the twenty trillion currently in retirement accounts (counting government retirement accounts in addition to the IRA and 401K accounts) would be outside government control and are not already dependent on government policies and its financial health.[159] The remainder is all in government bonds or government backed bonds and securities (the bogus Social Security "trust fund" is recorded as being invested in special non-transferable bonds), none of which represent any marketable asset. Therefore, the government would realize only three point five trillion to be put against the debt, and the entire house of cards might come crashing down.

Obviously, the best plan for investors desiring to remain in control of their own financial destiny would be to cash in all IRA accounts and convert 401K investments into securities off the government's books. Yes, in some cases severe penalties must be paid, but they would be small compared to losing everything. In fact, any investment regulated by government as to its legal yields and when it can be sold is always subject to being manipulated by Progressive financial interests for their benefit rather than that of the citizens'. Government bonds should be avoided at all costs, as they are the lifeblood of the elite lifestyle. Today, the Federal Government has been forced to sell its bonds overseas to foreign countries and investors, and become more beholden to foreign politicians than American citizens. Ultimately, the sham of American politicians representing U.S. citizens will be fully exposed when countries like China flex their economic and military muscles. China enjoys a surplus of three hundred million more males than females (that could potentially all go into an army), and only then will some Americans awaken to the perils of irresponsible Progressivism.

Perhaps the most frightening development in the U.S. banking system during the last three years is the "bail-in" for banks. This first raised its ugly head in Cyprus, where in order to keep Cypriot banks solvent, deposits were converted to non-voting bank equity overnight, leaving only a tiny fraction available to use by account holders. The theory behind a "bail-in" is that all deposits made into bank accounts do not belong to the depositor but to the bank. Legally, they are now considered as unsecured loans to the bank, and in order to keep a bank from failing, they may be converted to ownership shares such as preferred stock (non-voting stock) or some non-demand type of note, on a basis favorable to the bank. For example, if you have $100,000 in your bank account, the bank could declare that only $10,000 is in your account and available for withdrawal or to meet the your financial obligations, and the rest is in a long-term, non-interest bearing note, payable only under conditions set by the bank. In effect, the banks simply confiscate your money, and are free to use it any way they wish.

Can't happen in the U.S, you say? Well, be advised that various banks, including three of the largest banks in the U.S., have already generated plans to provide themselves a "bail-in" the next time their bank is threatened with insolvency. And this is not an "if", it is a "when." A very good case can be made for every U.S. citizen to begin immediately to protect himself by minimizing bank account balances.

For the majority of Americans, savings and investments are miniscule or non-existent, primarily because all family earnings are spent in the course of daily life, and a majority of what is spent ends up going to the government in taxes sooner or later. But as Americans follow the advice in these pages, money will become available to protect one's family, and it will become important to keep those hard-won funds out of the hands of the government.

Gold and silver are touted as historical hedges against governmental theft and rapaciousness, and there is much to be said for their purchase. But there is a daunting precedent for hostile government action toward owners of gold: President Franklin Roosevelt issued Executive Order 6102 in 1933, confiscating all privately-owned bullion gold, and it was illegal for American citizens to own non-numismatic gold until 1974. The order, which was made legal by an act of Congress as an afterthought, forbade the possession of gold coin, gold bullion, and gold certificates within the continental United States and criminalized the possession of monetary gold by any individual, partnership, association or corporation.

FDR, a second- or third-rate intellect, theorized that his action would place a large amount of cash into the economy, thus stimulating business activity and helping raise prices on farm products. Of course, it did no such thing—it only made Americans more wary of government actions and caused wealthy individuals to move their holdings out of the country.

Even though this draconian, anti-populist action was termed an "emergency measure," it remained in effect for forty years, ending on December 31, 1974. As late as 1971, the federal government was still aggressively pursuing the prosecution of people buying or selling gold coins or bars. For example, in the famous case in El Paso, Texas, against coin collectors Paul and Ercell Slone for possessing bullion gold, in Paul's case a quarter of an ounce. Ercell Slone faced twenty-five years in federal prison and a fine of $25,000, and her husband twenty years and a fine of $20,000. In a trial where federal agents attempted to suborn perjury, the Slones were found guilty and the citizens protected from such heinous wrong-doing.[160]

By 2013, the gold depository at Fort Knox had become shrouded in secrecy, and many people, even financial experts, questioned whether any gold actually remained in the depository. When

Germany attempted to repatriate three hundred tons of gold on deposit at the Federal Reserve Bank of New York, the bank refused. After also refusing to allow an audit of Germany's holdings, the Federal Reserve worked out a deal with the German government to return the gold to Germany in increments over seven years.[161] No further information was made available by the U.S. government or the Federal Reserve, and how much gold the U.S. actually possessed was highly speculative. Later, it was found that the required gold shipments for the first two years were made using current gold mine production in the U.S., causing conspiracy theorists to go berserk.

Silver is in high demand for industrial uses, but could also be seized by the government as a punitive measure against its citizens. Like gold, its market price is subject to being set twice each day by international price fixers located in London, and these commodity prices are subject to an extreme amount of control and manipulation by major central banks throughout the world. To a large degree, therefore, individual citizens are at the mercy of government and moneyed interests, but precious metals will probably still be a better hedge against inflation than paper currency. In addition to precious metals, any staple that can be used as a gift, trade or sale item is likewise a hedge against the unsound fiscal policies of government. Food, paper products, ammunition, water, seeds, soap, tooth paste, and the like could all be easily stored as a hedge against hard times.

## Form Cooperatives for Survival

Cooperatives are a sound vehicle for groups that seek to become semi-independent and self-sufficient. Depending on the laws of the state—or states—where the cooperative is operating, various options may be available. There are two major types of legal entities that are available to co-ops, both traditionally having been formed for workers to participate and receive benefits as owners: the Limited Liability Corporation (LLC) and the Worker Cooperative Corporation. Which one is most advantageous to Starve the Beast depends on the state laws applicable for the home locality of the corporation.

State registration and filing requirements for LLCs are usually minimal and can be accomplished without an attorney, and an LLC provides the benefits of limited liability and generally favorable tax treatment. There is usually great flexibility in the structure of an LLC. Individuals forming the co-op sign an "Operating Agreement" which determines the co-op's management and financial arrangements. The agreement is a contract among all members of the co-op, and there are no legal limits on which individuals or types of organizations can be members. There is no requirement that voting power be linked to capital investment or any other particular factor. In some LLC co-ops, worker-owners are paid wages and benefits as employees and receive a share of profits. In others, there are no employees and all workers are also owners. Profits are shared on some contractual basis, and it is important to note that, as owners, the workers are not subject to labor and employment laws such as minimum wage, unemployment insurance, workers compensation, etc. There is no withholding for income tax, Social Security, or Medicare. In the case that the LLC is under Subchapter S, profits go to the owners, whether or not distributed, and each member is responsible for income taxes as appropriate. The beauty of this arrangement is that the LLC can reimburse owners for expenses, operate with very low distributions and prices to members, and, with dedicated effort, legally reduce income taxes to the absolute minimum.

The Worker Cooperative Corporation (WCC) is a form of corporation available in some states that is designed specifically for all owners also being workers in the corporation. The bylaws and shareholder agreements must be carefully crafted, and such co-ops require equal voting rights (a single share) regardless of the amount of invested capital. Distribution of earnings can take place based on hours worked or some other basis, and, once again, expenses paid can be high and wages artificially low. The corporation is required to pay corporate income tax on profits, and workers pay income tax on dividends received, so there is an element of double taxation. The WCC is often held to be the proper model to increase worker job satisfaction, particularly over the long run, but in the scope of this work, the LLC is to be preferred to reduce the amount of tax paid to governments.

In either case, a cooperative corporation, when properly managed for the benefit of its workers and owners, can fairly easily replicate the Federal Government and its treatment of Federal employees, providing many benefits tax free that ordinary citizens would have to purchase with after-tax dollars. Obviously, if the IRS can arrange seminars in Las Vegas on how to line dance and not have to record this as a taxable benefit, the LLC or WCC can do the same thing. It is only necessary to study how the IRS treats its own employees and then follow the same playbook.

The best cooperative, however, is the church-based solution mentioned above in the discussion of reducing expenditures. Co-ops are subject to IRS and state regulations while churches are exempt. Only in the case that a church foolishly incorporates itself as a 501c3 (tax-exempt) corporation does it open itself up to government interference and harassment.

## Go Off the Grid

The "grid" referred to here is the network of power companies and the supply of electric power. Survivalists often have a goal of being able to live without outside-supplied electric power, telephone service, and other services normally expected in an advanced society. Almost invariably, electric power is generated through the use of solar panels and battery storage, with heat being supplied by a wood furnace or wood cooking stove that doubles as a furnace. The dwellings are usually small and often without running water. A certain amount of money must still be obtained, usually through the selling of items made by hand or the providing of casual or regular labor. The necessity for money comes from the obligation to pay taxes on one's property and the few outside services that the survivalists cannot supply to themselves, such as medical care or the purchase of certain materials, clothes, and the like.

A major problem arose in 2014 when the EPA sought to tighten standards on wood-burning stoves and heaters. The goal was to ban all wood-burning stoves and heaters and force Americans to move to other sources of energy.[162] In spite of wood being a renewable resource, burning wood produces carbon dioxide ($CO_2$) and carbon monoxide (CO) gases that are considered by the EPA as pollutants.

Earlier restrictions had banned the sale of wood-burning stoves and some fireplace inserts built after 1988 that didn't limit fine airborne particulate emissions to less than fifteen micrograms per cubic meter of air, but the new proposal lowered the limit to twelve micrograms. By comparison, the secondhand tobacco smoke in a closed car breathed in by a non-smoker can reach three-to-four thousand micrograms. Literally, all stoves being manufactured in 2014 couldn't meet the standard, and the EPA demanded that they be destroyed and recycled as scrap metal. More importantly, earlier stoves and fireplace inserts couldn't meet the standard either, and EPA had all stoves clearly in their cross hairs. The precedent of automobiles that used leaded gas should remind people of what eventually happens.

The EPA dodged Congress and the citizens once again by a friendly lawsuit. Following the issuing of the new rules, seven Progressive state attorney generals and the environmental group, Earth Justice, sued the EPA to regulate outside wood-burning water heaters, and the new standard moved to a judge for adjudication. The U.S. Chamber of Commerce noted that "sue and settle" practices have been responsible for most of the EPA's controversial regulations on power plants, refineries, mining operations, cement plants, and many other industries. The IRS may say "a computer crash eliminated all evidence of wrongdoing, if any", but the EPA says "The court made the rule, not us. We're just enforcing it." And the dog ate my homework.

Although the regulations on wood stoves and furnaces will make it increasingly difficult for families to live off the grid, it may still be possible and worth the effort. Families off the grid usually normally live in remote, rural environments in southern and western states without harsh climates. They can live on less than $4,000 per year, and even if trade items are included in income, would be below the threshold to pay federal income taxes. Such families will still have to pay the Obamacare alternative tax, property taxes, licenses and insurance for vehicles, and all the hidden taxes in everything they purchase, but they will become increasingly important to prove to doubters that living outside government's clutches is worth it.

In addition to the six strategies listed above, every American can hamper the continuous rise of Progressivism in the United States by re-framing the debate from Progressive terminology to more accurate terms and descriptions that will allow apathetic citizens to understand what is going on. For example, the descriptive adjective "good" should always be used as a modifier to the word "Christian," as in, "he's a good Christian" to describe any evangelical Christian. Social justice Christians should always be labeled "secular Christians." Atheists should not be called atheists, but "godless individuals." The term "liberal" should never be used to describe a Democrat—Jefferson was a liberal (and a believer in the smallest possible government). Regardless of individual beliefs, everyone voting for Democrats is supporting Progressivism and must be labeled as Progressive Fellow-Travelers.

Always change the debate and call the people destroying the United States for what they actually are. For example, instead of referring to Bill Clinton as "ex-president Bill Clinton," refer to him as "draft-dodger, sexual predator, Bill Clinton." Organizations should have adjectives that describe their missions or histories. For example, instead of referring to the ACLU as the "American Civil Liberties Union," try "former communist front organization ACLU" or "Atheist, Communist, and Leftist Union." Anyone who attempts to describe himself as a "conservative Democrat" should be called a "delusional Democrat." All government bureaucrats should be called "burcaupaths." Fundamentalist or evangelical Christians should be called "dedicated followers of Christ." When a leftist refers to evangelical Christians as the "religious right," they should be corrected and told that radical Islam is the "religious right," and evangelical Christians simply are on the side of Christ, neither left nor right in the sense of a socialist proletarian dictatorship or a military dictatorship. A table of examples is given in Appendix C.

Perhaps most of all, Progressives should be referred to as SNAZIs, for Supra-Nationalist-Socialists. They are globalist-socialists, and the play is on "supra-nationalist" as replacing "globalist." If that sounds excessively harsh, try "GLZI" for Globalist-Socialist. But as mentioned, except for the racial portion of Hitler's ideology, when one replaces the nationalist component with globalist or supra-nationalist, there is little or no difference between Progressivism and Nazism.

As can be seen, one is only limited by one's imagination. The point is to put every Progressive program and advocate in an unfavorable light, just as the Progressives do when they label Christian organizations as "right-wing" or "radical." This constant drumbeat of pejorative terms used against Christianity, individual liberties, capitalism, and the traditional United States from kindergarten through college has had the terrifying effect of turning America's youth against America. The trend must be reversed to have any chance of saving the United States, and the people need to call a spade a spade. At this point, attempting to be polite is a prescription for extermination, and fire must be fought with fire.

There are other actions that should be taken by every American which are obvious to almost every patriot. Buying foreign-made goods increases our already catastrophic balance of payments, causing China and other countries to repatriate American dollars by purchasing American assets in the United States. Already, most domestic reserves of oil are owned by foreign oil companies such as Shell, BP (British Petroleum), Total (French), and others. The Chinese are rapidly buying up homes through financing reverse mortgages, and Japanese and European companies have developed a stranglehold on what remains of American industrial production. The cry of "Buy American" should be heard every day from every consumer.

The list of the top fifty foreign corporations doing business in the U.S. contains stunning household names, and purchasing products from these corporations should be avoided by patriots. They are: BP (British Petroleum), Shell Oil, Toyota, Honda, Ahold Foods Service, Nissan, ING, Daimler-Benz, Nestle, Siemans, Sony, AEG, HSBC Bank, AXA, GlaxoSmithKline, Volkswagen, Food Lion, T Mobile, Samsung, John Hancock Insurance, Allianz, Novartis, BMW, UBS Financial, BASF, Total Oil, Zurich Financial, Roche Finance, Credit Suisse, Oldcastle, Sanofi-Aventis Pharmaceuticals, EADS, Bridgestone-Firestone, Unilever, Canon, AstraZeneca, ThyssenKrupp, Ito-Yokado, World Net, Panasonic, Bayer, Volvo, Maersk, Philips Electronics, Deutsche Bank, Swiss Re Insurance, Sun Life Financial, BAE Systems, LG Electronics, and Tyco International.

Nor should patriots be investing in foreign companies that compete with American enterprises, and certainly not in foreign currencies. This is "betting against America" like many of the top financiers in New York are currently doing. But even buying American is not enough; citizens need to change their habits. "Brown bag" rather than purchasing lunches, carry coffee from home rather than patronizing Starbucks, and shun high-priced malls like the plague. America can be made great again, but not through citizen spending, especially when the profits from those sales go to foreign entities after government takes its huge cut.

## Summary

Both state and federal governments will rapidly face enormous financial crises due to the lack of revenue if Starve the Beast is successful, but with little money actually changing hands, there will be few records of any type, and nothing to tax. Hiring will have been replaced with volunteerism and donations in kind, so that wages disappear and monetary-purchased consumption is minimized. There are simply not enough IRS agents to stop a person from donating his time and labor to another and tax the benefit or value received. The primary control mechanisms available to the IRS run through the banks. They can monitor all financial transactions, EFT records, checks, debit cards, credit cards, cash withdrawals and deposits, anything and everything. Banks are now extensions of government, subject to their control, and everything they have or do is subject to federal scrutiny.

Financial institution information is supplemented by the federal reporting required of corporations, and investments and such transactions exist in many records and reports made to the government. In short, the Federal Government wants to know everything about you, from your "Real ID" for photo identification at any time, to your complete medical records since birth. For the moment, only higher education transcripts are denied them through the Family Educational Rights and Privacy Act of 1974 (the Buckley Amendment), although that is currently being watered down with respect to state agencies transmitting testing data to federal agencies. The government also wants to know everything you do, from blogging on the Internet to buying a book on Amazon.com. There is currently no realistic limit of government's insatiable appetite for data on its citizens, and that can't be good. The government is only limited by its resources and incompetence, problems that history shows as being solvable under a dictatorship. But the most important of all data concerns money, and when the flows decline or disappear, a brave new world will open up.

# Chapter 6

## Know Your Enemy

The most dangerous enemy the United States has ever faced is not what American politicians tell the citizenry it is. The enemy within has always been more potent than the enemy without, starting with the neutrals and loyalists during the Revolutionary War.

A great deal of animosity was generated during the Revolutionary War against the Quakers who freely traded with the British and declared themselves neutral in the conflict. They didn't adhere to the Articles of Association, claiming they were above politics, and afterward, with the exception of Herbert Hoover, were rarely represented in high office. Richard Nixon's mother was a Quaker, but Nixon himself described himself as a "free Quaker"—a Quaker who does not adhere to pacifism. In any case, he was only nominally a Quaker.

Other than being involved in abolitionism prior to the Civil War, Quakers had little impact on the American political scene, and Philadelphia went from being the most important city in America to one of little importance. Quaker pacifism has come under fire many times, starting with William Penn's secretary, the Scotch-Irish James Logan. When a ship carrying Penn and Logan was chased by pirates, Penn retired to his cabin while Logan armed himself to repel the pirates. After they escaped from the pirates, Penn berated Logan for taking up arms. Logan noted Penn's hypocrisy: Penn was willing to let Logan defend him, but then criticized Logan's resort to arms afterwards.

Two other groups, the Catholic Highlander Scots and Cherokee Indians that fought for the British, were held in contempt in the new nation, in particular the Scots by Thomas Jefferson and John Jay, and the Cherokees by Andrew Jackson.[163] Catholics won a great measure of acceptance under the leadership of John Carroll, elected by American priests as the first Catholic bishop in the United States. He stressed latitudinarianism to an extreme, and even refused to take the Bishop's Oath until the sentence that stated, "I will, to the utmost of my power, seek out and oppose schismatics, heretics, and the enemies of our Sovereign Lord and his successors" was deleted.[164] The Sovereign Lord was the Pope, and Protestant Americans were adamant that no American could recognize an allegiance to anyone other than God and the federal and state governments. John Jay even introduced a bill in the New York State legislature requiring citizens to take an oath repudiating any allegiance to any other power, temporal or ecclesiastical. It did not pass, in part due to Carroll's adherence to latitudinarianism. It was not until the 1830s when Irish Catholics brought in their own priests that anti-Catholic agitation began anew, but this time, against the Irish, not the Scots.

During the Civil War, both sides were greatly hampered by opponents within their borders, in the North by the Copperhead movement, and in the South by Union sympathizers and freed slaves. But the rise of anti-Americanism within the United States in the form of authoritarian manipulation of the political process and actual repression of the citizenry was coincident with the emergence of the Progressivism.[165]

Beginning with Theodore Roosevelt, Progressivism became the political religion of choice among the successful in politics, the arts, press, education, and even business. Only the military and Southern conservatives—by and large the remnants of the truculent Presbyterian Scotch-Irish, now mostly evangelical Christians—resisted the lure of Progressivism. In the military, long the favored career path for Southern heroes, the repudiation of Progressivism was due to three factors among its volunteers: a trust in the Christian God, a strong sense of patriotism and the need for self-sacrifice, and a belief in American exceptionalism.

In spite of Hollywood movies and television shows featuring military conspiracies to take over control of the United States, until the present time, such plot lines have been sheer fantasy. With the sole exception of General James Wilkerson prior to the War of 1812,

207

American military leaders have always recognized and supported civilian control of the military, and there has never been any movement by the military to seize power unconstitutionally for any reason.

That has not been true of American politicians, starting with ex-Vice President Aaron Burr and continuing today with President Obama declaring he was not going to wait for legislation—all he needed to advance his mission was a phone and a pen.[166] In comparison, the military has always represented the best of the nation, and certainly vastly better than the holders of political office in Congress or the presidency. Troop mutinies and refusals to fight have been rare, and the military hasn't been known to surrender readily when the means to resist were still present. Military leadership has often been amateurish and incompetent, yet American troops have fought and died instead of refusing to carry out orders.

Not until after the Second World War was leadership training given priority, and truly effective training for field grade and staff officers introduced.[167] Even then, military personnel have maintained a strong sense of being citizens like everyone else. Service members vote in higher percentages than civilians and are generally known to favor conservative candidates. Not surprisingly, Progressive politicians often attempt to disqualify military votes such as Al Gore did in Florida in 1960.

In 1865, Sergeant William H. Harding of the 5th Ohio Volunteer Cavalry was discharged in North Carolina after almost three years of service, unbroken by a single leave. Sgt Harding, a twenty-one-year-old veteran of over sixty battles and skirmishes and many more scouts and reconnaissance patrols, was left to find his own way home to Ohio. After arriving and eating dinner, he went to work on the family farm as he'd done the day before he enlisted.[168] He was proud to have helped save the Union, but was, once again, a civilian. Almost a century later, four of his great-grandchildren volunteered for the Army in the 1950s and 1960s, one serving in the Infantry in the Korean War, another in the Finance Corps in Korea, a third in the Corps of Engineers, and the fourth in Army Intelligence. They served because it was their duty to serve their country, and when they were discharged, returned to civilian life and became good citizens. The heroes were those who didn't return.

As George Washington recommended, the military was to be comprised of a professional officer corps and cadre of non-commissioned officers, and in times of need, would be fleshed out by the militia.[169] The state and local militias were to be made up of all the male citizenry from ages sixteen to forty-five with no exemptions for education or occupation, and they were to keep and bear arms to maintain their proficiency for military duty as well as restrain tyranny. Several states, such as Virginia, considered the militia to be composed of the "body of the people," e.g. all citizens, and all were to be trained in the use of arms.[170]

After World War II, military duty for the elite (always as an officer) was seen as simply another base to touch in one's career to be eligible for high office, and one's influential family often arranged for such duty to be of maximum benefit to the serving individual. Service had become a necessary stepping stone in a political career, not a duty to be performed without expectation of some gain. The first president to take positive steps to avoid military service was William Jefferson Clinton, but, starting with the Vietnam War, Progressives, with the exception of presidential candidate John Kerry who minimized his service, have avoided military service like the plague. By the time the all-volunteer military was re-instituted on July 1, 1973, military service was no longer seen as beneficial under any circumstances to elite Americans, and, for the next decade, the military was generally considered a highly tarnished shield made up of underclass Americans who couldn't find work elsewhere. President Reagan restored the reputation of the military, but Progressive elites continued to avoid military service.

By 2008, the military had become a professional body of men and women, usable as an effective instrument for political maneuvering on the world stage, and almost like a very large private army for the president/emperor. It had become highly regulated and micro-managed by politicians at the highest level, with operations being run from a "war room" in Washington, complete with simultaneous drone feeds to monitors in the room, allowing staff generals and politicians to see exactly what was happening in real time. "Rules of engagement" determined the actions of troops on the ground, and, even when under fire, troops might not be allowed to shoot back. Initiative had become a thing of the past.

When Americans came under fire in Benghazi in 2012 and called for help, the Chairman of the Joint Chiefs of Staff, 4-star General Martin Dempsey, failed to send either a relief force or order air strikes on the terrorists. Earlier, though apprised of warnings from Ambassador Stevens that the Benghazi facility was in great danger, Dempsey had failed to take any steps to make assistance available if needed. The reason, as he later stated, was "Because we never received a request for support from the State Department."[171] Nor was he ordered to send support by his civilian leaders after the terrorist attack began, in particular the President of the United States (Barack Obama, who was asleep) or the president's representative in the "war room," Valerie Jarrett. The Secretary of Defense was apparently not even a player in the decision-making, and Dempsey was not about to commit troops or aircraft without orders or shared responsibility. The importance of this incident cannot be over-estimated—if a 4-star general can't take initiative, then what should be expected from a captain, lieutenant, or sergeant in the field? Alas, individuals in uniform had become robotic tools to be played with as desired by civilian leaders.

The American military had undergone a radical transformation from the days when generals led from the front. Even in the fluid warfare of World War II, only a single division commander was killed by enemy action, Major-General Maurice Rose, commander of the 3rd Armored Division. Most American generals tended to lead from the rear during World War II, and the effectiveness of American combat units suffered accordingly. An extreme case was General Lloyd Fredendall who was sent home after the disastrous battle of Kasserine Pass when it was discovered he had been far to the rear, building a huge bunker complex for a command post instead of actively commanding his troops. During the First Gulf War in 1991, General Norman Schwarzkopf spent much the campaign in a bunker dealing with the media, yet was welcomed home a national hero. By 2011, control of the military had been transferred back to the White House and Department of Defense, and generals had become corporate managers.[172]

General Stanley McChrystal, probably the Army's foremost expert on counter-insurgency, attempted to reverse the corporate manager trend, but ran afoul of President Obama's sensitivities. After members of his traveling party unwisely made comments critical of the Obama Administration, he was summarily fired and forced into retirement. Such action was extraordinary; since World War II generals had been subjected to ever lessened accountability for their actions and of those around them.[173] In fact, a protection league, even more powerful than the "West Point Protection Association" had come into being, and high-ranking military officers no longer told their civilian leaders the truth, but rather, what they wanted to hear.[174]

President Obama and the ruling Progressives took significant steps to bring the American officer corps to heel, and, as a result, truth did not flow in either direction. Adherence to Progressive ideology is now as important to a field grade officer's career as was the belief in Hitler and the goals of the Nazi Party for a Wehrmacht officer from 1938 to 1945. Serving his Progressive masters slavishly, Army Chief of Staff, General George W. Casey, Jr., issued Field Manual 3-39.40 on February 12, 2010, entitled, "Internment and Resettlement Operations," which specifically dealt with the internment and resettlement of citizens within the borders of the United States and the actions and responsibilities of CONUS (Continental United States Army Command.)[175]

In 2013, it was reported that senior officers in the U.S. military were being given a "litmus test" question to determine who would stay and who had to go as President Obama downsized the armed forces. The key factor in this decision was "whether they will fire on US citizens or not." Those who would not were being removed.[176] This and many other data points indicate that Progressives do not trust the military as presently officered—in spite of Casey's and Dempsey's submissiveness—and are attempting to make it more politically correct (meaning, in line with Progressive ideology) with all deliberate speed.

## Who Is the Enemy?

As can be seen from the foregoing, President Obama is seriously attempting to transform the United States into a nation much more to his liking, but his actions are merely the latest in a long series of anti-American initiatives emanating from the Federal Government and its allies since 1901. Progressives have been attempting (with great success) to transform the United States into a state befitting their supposed genius for meeting the challenges of a modern world. The design of their political system is only nominally a republic and very far from a democracy. It includes an imperial presidency with plenary power, a limited legislature to give the common person a sense of participation, a large professional bureaucracy carrying out all administration functions, an educational establishment to train new generations in Progressive ideology, a media used as a governmental propaganda and manipulation tool, and a controlled judiciary to put a stamp of legitimacy on all government actions. By 2014, all of these institutions were fully present and functioning according to Progressive doctrine and furthering the Progressive agenda.

This development was noticed almost immediately as Progressivism took hold of the political class in America. As Harry F. Atwood so clearly outlined in his 1918 book, *Back to the Republic*, the trend of government has been as follows:

| | |
|---|---|
| From Earliest times to 1788 AD: | Experimental failures |
| From 1788 to 1900 AD: | Progress |
| From 1900 to 1918 AD: | Retrogressive tendencies[177] |

Since 1918, those retrogressive tendencies have intensified.

Atwood promoted the idea of a "Golden Mean" in politics with respect to personal liberty and government power. An autocracy was the extreme form of government for achieving maximum power, democracy the extreme form for power being held by citizens, and the golden mean was a republic.[178] He quite rightly considered the United States as the first true republic, which in his time was clearly the most successful. With Progressivism, moderation and compromise as ideals went out the window, and since 1918, the U.S. has steadily progressed toward an autocracy.

At one time, Progressives were generally confined to the states that remained in the Union during the Civil War, and they represented the elites of industrial, academic, and political America. They looked down on Southerners and people in rural middle America—at best, as objects of pity, products of a limited gene pool, and commoners to be dumbed-down further and emasculated. At worst, those commoners were dangerous malcontents, clinging to their God and guns to maintain their society from being obliterated by outsiders.

Journalist Tony Horwitz epitomized the establishment Progressive when he undertook an extended tour through theO South and produced *Confederates in the Attic* in 1998.[179] He painted the South as only a foreigner could, and failed to understand that the vast majority of Southerners fought in the "War For Southern Independence" for their individual rights and not to be dominated by an outside power.[180] The vast majority of Confederate soldiers owned no slaves, but saw no contradiction in fighting for their liberty while withholding liberty from others. That hypocritical stance prevents most modern Americans, as well as people world-wide, from granting them their deserved respect, even while Progressives, right before their eyes, are destroying humanity in order to save it.

George Will, often considered by Progressives to be "Mr. Conservative," also looked down his nose at Southerners. When northern Virginia began to flourish under Reagan, he crowed, "Where a slavocracy once existed, Northern dynamism now prevails."[181] Evidently, Southerners could not generate their own prosperity, and all credit was due to Northerners. This Progressive attitude actually extends to all the "red" states, as Progressives clearly believe citizens in those states cannot govern themselves. Yet, the truth is exactly the opposite—it is the blue states of New York, California, New Jersey, Michigan, and Illinois, not the red states, that seem perennially to have the worst governments,. It is instructive also to realize that, in military depictions of situations, friendly forces are always shown in blue, the enemy in red—the Progressives have pulled off a major subliminal propaganda coup and control the debate. If anything, the states showing the most communist tendencies—the current blue states—should be called the red states.

Another propaganda coup by Progressives has been to conflate "conservative" with "rightest" and evangelical church members as the "religious right." The terms "right" and "left" are historical and deal with the traditional assaults on government by an atheistic, militant dictatorship of some collective ideology such as socialism or communism on the left, and an autocratic, hierarchical military style junta from the right. Clearly, the first is present today in the U.S., but there is no counter-balancing group on the right.

Generally, when a republic flounders, these two militant and atheistic forces emerge, both bent on the destruction of that republic.

213

From the "left" comes a dictatorship of some sub-group of interests who perceive that they have been victimized by failures in the democratic political structure; and from the "right" emerges a military dictatorship, often aligned initially with some organized religion, but led by individuals interested in their own gain.

Both of these movements espouse dictatorship, develop a cult of adoration for their leaders, and neither are liberal nor conservative. Since the beginning of the twentieth century, for example, Africa has experienced a number of these revolutions, made inevitable by do-gooder westerners attempting to install western-style democracies in societies that possess no concept of democratic political processes.

Remarkably, in the United States, only a leftist movement for the destruction of the American political system has emerged, resorting to violence in varying degrees and espousing socialism, communism or Progressivism. Originally, the "left" was represented by Jefferson and his followers, but they believed in the smallest Federal Government possible and one providing very limited services. Maximum power was to be held at the local level and with the people. There was no "right" except the very mild form represented by some Federalists such as Alexander Hamilton, but the Federalists showed great dedication to democratic processes as time went by, even at their own cost.

Throughout American history, there has never been a "right," or, at least, one espousing a military takeover and the establishment of a militant hierarchy to govern. In Europe, Latin America, the Far East, Africa, and the Middle East, "left" and "right" actually are meaningful labels, as both sides generally take and hold power through mob or military action in which large numbers of people succumb during subsequent disorders.

From its beginnings, the Progressive movement in the United States needed a strawman to oppose and validate its own militancy. As Progressivism was necessarily atheistic, it attacked American churches for any perceived involvement in the political process. But two of their constituencies were religious—Catholics and Jews—and that required making accommodations for their support. Both were lured to the Progressive program with promises of power beyond their minority statuses, and it was not until the recent federal mandates with respect to health insurance covering all types of contraception (some, literally, abortions) that Catholic leadership woke up to the reality that they had been suckered again by a fascist group. Cardinal George of Chicago noted, on September, 2014, that the public creed of the United States was based on the myth of human progress, with little place for dependence on divine providence. "'The ruling class,' those who shape public opinion in politics, in education, in communications, in entertainment, is using the civil law to impose its own form of morality on everyone... those who do not conform to the official religion [Progressivism]... place their citizenship in danger... This is... the self-righteous voice... of the American establishment today who regard themselves as 'progressive'... American civil law has done much to weaken and destroy what is the basic unit of every human society, the family. With the weakening of the internal restraints that healthy family life teaches, the State will need to impose more and more external restraints on everyone's activities."[182]

As stated previously, Progressivism in the United States is little different from fascism in Italy under Mussolini, and Progressives now involve themselves in moral and spiritual issues that the Catholic Church has always claimed for itself—exactly as Mussolini did ninety years ago. But the situation in the U.S. developed differently; here, Protestantism determined morality and produced the primary spiritual positions in politics, and Catholicism was a minority religion allied with the Democrat Party.

Unwilling to attack the Catholic Church except by a stealth campaign, Progressivism took on evangelical Protestant denominations, aided by a Supreme Court that took a huge leap left with the 1947 decision in *Everson*. But even that was not enough, and when the Tea Party movement arose, it was immediately demonized as representing the "radical right." It was a hard sell since Tea Party events produced no casualties or arrests, but the branding stuck. Intellectually, the leap was daunting, as the Tea Party stood for the principles laid down by Jefferson two centuries earlier: small government and limits on government spending. Tea Party rhetoric was hardly "hard right," nor was it leftist. It was classical Jeffersonian liberalism, embodied daily by elderly people demonstrating for fiscal responsibility, less government, and more individual responsibility.

This was a disaster for Progressives, and they had to eradicate the Tea Partiers as soon as possible. The reason was simple:

Progressives had already claimed liberalism as the basis for their own movement. Of course, it wasn't—Progressivism is based on naked authoritarian aggression by elites, in effect, a new nobility, and one firmly set against the common people. It was classical fascism, with the Democrat Party rapidly being the standard bearer for the new authoritarian state.

Progressivism could not be succeeding without the massive support it has enjoyed in the academic world. What citizens forget is that academics are government employees whosee themselves as part of the privileged elite running the country. They dwell on banalities and minutia, and their cloistered existence seems to disable their intellect from maintaining an objective level. In Germany during the 1920s, many academics took the leftist line and compared strong leaders like Frederick the Great and Otto von Bismarck to the puny, squabbling politicians of the Weimar Republic, enshrining "hope" and "change" through their lack of objectivity and any understanding of a proportionally representative democracy.

Throughout France today, universities are arguably the most radicalized segment of French society, harking back to France's woeful history of being unable to govern itself without a dictator, emperor, or extremely strong president. A nation of contradictions, France even has a motto with mutually exclusive elements in their definitions: *Liberté, Égalité, Fraternité*—Freedom, Equality, and Brotherhood. Individual liberties are subjected to government restrictions in an attempt to achieve equality, and "brotherhood" refers to the collective which takes precedence over individual liberties. At one time "equality" meant being treated equally by the law, but after the Paris commune, the word took on meanings of social and income equality as espoused by Karl Marx. This schizophrenia is deeply embedded in the French national character and possibly precludes rational political activity—hardly a reason for Americans to take their political directions from France.

Fortunately for America, Progressives have been usually unable to generate candidates for president who are effective leaders. The best was probably the first, Theodore Roosevelt. He consistently broke new ground, and using his popularity as a rough and tumble leader, was able to create an image that Progressivism was good for the nation and would be the wave of the future. He took action against the Rockefeller Empire (Standard Oil), using the Sherman Anti-trust Act, and, although the people hailed the breakup of the Rockefeller "monopoly" as a great success, Rockefeller actually benefitted, making many more millions as his stock values doubled. Rockefeller was able to set up his family and descendants as leading Progressives and national leaders while he, himself, became a revered philanthropist. If one wonders if it was all smoke and mirrors, yes, it was. But it was great theater.

Teddy Roosevelt was followed by Taft, a Roosevelt-lite president, but even more of a Progressive than Teddy. But then came Woodrow Wilson, arguably the most self-righteous man (other than Jimmy Carter) to ever live in the White House, but with poor administrative skills (again, on a plane with the hapless Carter.) The Progressive program went on steroids, and 1913 was a banner year. First, the Income Tax Amendment was ratified in February, providing the Federal Government with the power to secure whatever funds it needed from the citizenry to implement any program it wanted. Then, in December, the Federal Reserve Act was passed, setting up an American central bank on the European model. The banking system was designed primarily by Paul Warburg, the brother of Max Warburg, head of the Warburg consortium in Europe, to ensure that the banking elites would be able to control monetary policy and economic activity to their own great profit.

The secret meeting at Jekyll Island, Georgia, where the details of the Federal Reserve System—"the Fed"—were hammered out, saw a rapprochement between the European Jewish banking interests of the Rothschilds and Warburgs, and the American J.P. Morgan Bankers Trust, the Rockefellers, and the Jewish firm of Kuhn, Loeb and Company. The six men at the meeting represented one-fourth of the world's wealth, and formed a cartel resting on the backs of the American taxpayers that would ensure awesome profits to their banking consortiums for as long as the U.S. lasted.[183] The Federal Reserve System was not made a part of the Federal Government nor was there to be any congressional oversight. Today, the Fed contains no reserves, and its banks are not banks usable by the public—it is a private cartel of banks for other banks that is protected by federal law, supposedly for the good of all, but, actually, only for the good of the bankers and ruling elites in America.

After a hundred years of operating under the Federal Reserve System, there is no orderly way for the Federal Government to unhinge itself from a banking system that relies on fiat money—the creation of money out of thin air by simply saying that a piece of paper has a certain value—whether created by the Fed (most of it) or the Treasury Department. In 2014, the Fed was creating sixty-five to eighty billion dollars out of nothing every month and inserting it into the U.S. economy to "stimulate" economic activity, and, more importantly, to keep the fiat money house of cards from collapsing. On the other hand, the specter of politicians determining the U.S.'s money supply ought to be enough to deter everyone from the idea of eliminating the Fed and replacing it with the Treasury Department.

Other currently heralded solutions, such as going back on some system of money backed by gold or silver, would require the government to eliminate most of its spending. These solutions would be extremely painful, and probably cannot be considered until the U.S. economy collapses. That day, however, is fast approaching, as the value of the dollar is intrinsically tied to its status as the world's reserve currency. With a number of countries increasingly campaigning to eliminate reliance on the dollar for world trade, economic collapse in the United States, followed by run-away inflation, appears to be a certainty sometime in the next few years.

Following the creation of the Federal Reserve, Progressive President Wilson was faced with World War I and managed to keep the country neutral during his first term. But after America's entry into the war in 1917, Wilson micro-managed the war effort so badly that, to the end of the war, the U.S. was unable to equip its troops with basic necessities. Even more telling was that the U.S., the home of the airplane, never put a single aircraft into service in Europe.

But Wilson did get two unconstitutional acts passed. The Espionage Act in 1917 and its amendments that were generally referred to as the Sedition Act in 1918, and used them to imprison hundreds of thousands of citizens who exercised their right of free speech to criticize the government. Under the Sedition Act amendments, it became a felony to use contemptuous language concerning the United States government, its personnel or its institutions. For example, to ridicule an individual such as IRS employee Lois Lerner for allegedly targeting conservative organizations could earn the critic a sentence of five to twenty years in a federal penitentiary if the Sedition Act's amendments were still fully in force.

The Espionage Act was generally mothballed after World War I, but was unwrapped and used by President Obama in the twenty-first century to stifle criticism of himself and his presidency. Although the Sedition Act amendments were generally repealed in 1921, the Espionage Act is still in force today (and used against whistle-blowers), and freedom of speech as guaranteed by the 1st Amendment is subject to the opinion of a Progressive-dominated Supreme Court. The reader of this work should keep these acts in mind at all times. Nothing in this work should be considered as criticism of the Federal Government except when such criticism could help the government perform its constitutional duties more effectively and efficiently. Criticisms of Progressive individuals should not be construed as extending to the offices they hold.

After the disaster of Wilson came two non-Progressives in the White House, Harding and Coolidge, but, during their administrations, the educational establishment came under the control of Progressives. The Association for the Advancement of Progressive Education (AAPE) had been formed in 1919 to promote the ideas and principles of American atheist philosopher John Dewey. Among other things, it sought to eliminate religion from the educational process, substitute a secular morality and humanistic value system, and promote the education of students about how to live following Progressive ideology. Very rapidly it became necessary for professors to be members in AAPE to advance in their disciplines, and, with the coming of the New Deal, the principles of Progressive Education were nearly universally taught in college education departments throughout the nation. By 1950, religion in schools was on the way out, and Progressivism had become the new state religion in public schools.

Hoover was a Progressive, and although he was a brilliant mining engineer who earned an enviable record in war relief work during World War I, he sought to meld business and government together in what he called "economic modernization," which is known today as crony capitalization. When actions by the Federal Reserve triggered the crash of 1929 and the effects of the Smoot-

Hawley Tariff sealed the economy's doom, Hoover's lack of experience as a politician kept him from making his counter-measures effective.[184] When FDR took over, his actions were generally worse than Hoover's, but he offered a smile and a hope for a better time to come.

Although FDR's programs bumbled along during the Depression with stunning ineffectiveness (the unemployment rate in 1939 was actually worse than in 1933 when he took office,) he very effectively promoted Progressivism and, to a lesser degree, communism. When the Supreme Court refused to do his bidding, he threatened to add six more justices, and it caved in. Never an intellectual or even a notable intellect, Roosevelt believed that a more powerful Federal Government could and would be the answer to every problem. His success in World War II made both FDR and his policies popular, although perhaps his best decision was to off-load managerial control of military research and war production from government to private industry. His War Production Board, which functioned almost without governmental interference, performed magnificently and turned the United States into the "arsenal of democracy."

After the war, neither Truman nor Eisenhower did anything to slow down the spread of Progressivism, and under the philosophical direction of leftist Walter Lippmann and the communist I. F. Stone, the press—soon to be called the media—rapidly adopted Progressivism and became politically correct.

In 1952, the McCarran-Walter Act, written and promoted by Progressive Democrats, combined all previous immigration acts into one, and eliminated the racial restrictions that had existed since 1790 in favor of a quota based on national origin. The Celler-Hart Act of 1965, again promoted by Progressive Democrats, abolished the national origins quota system. The bill's proponents lied repeatedly to get it passed; President Johnson said the bill was relatively unimportant, and Senator Ted Kennedy stated that the demographic mix in the United States would not be affected, and passage would not influence America's culture. It was like saying that had Germany won World War II, Europe would not have been affected.

Although President Kennedy's administration produced few gains for Progressivism, Johnson's produced a tsunami of initiatives. Johnson created only two new cabinet departments, Housing and

Urban Development (HUD) and Transportation, but he passed a host of bills creating a mighty welfare state and declared a "War On Poverty." Like Ronald Reagan said, no sooner had Johnson declared the War On Poverty than it was lost, and, unfortunately, in the long term it was more damaging to America than the Vietnam War. Johnson was a manipulator and a deal-maker rather than an executive, and was probably congenitally unable to be an effective president due to his terminal micro-management, a common Progressive malady.

Johnson's legacy proved enduring as Progressives in both parties were unable to admit his disastrous domestic policies were errors, and refused to repeal or even modify them. Welfare spending went up until Clinton's second term, and poverty increased every year as well. A less effective governmental program could not be imagined. As early as 1965, it was known that the richest inheritance any child could have was a close-knit and loving family, with both a father and mother being present. But the Progressive welfare system had destroyed the family.

According to a report by Progressive Democrat Senator Daniel Moynihan in 1965, the Great Society programs were not helping in reducing poverty, and might be even part of the problem.[185] Welfare de-incentivized marriage, and poverty and crime flourished. HUD was created to introduce sophisticated solutions to the problem of deteriorating cities, and the cities became wastelands. Literally every Progressive program put in under Johnson turned out to be counter-productive, and, as of today, none have been eliminated.[186] They spawned huge and powerful bureaucracies, and no politician has had the courage to demand their elimination.

The failure of Johnson's Progressive Great Society programs was blamed on the Vietnam War by Progressives rather than finding fault with their ideology. Progressive commentator Walter Lippmann simply said that the results showed "how, in the atmosphere of war, it is impossible to pursue the tasks of peace."[187] Richard Nixon strengthened Progressive programs. He created the Environmental Protection Agency in 1970, and took the U.S. off the gold standard in 1971. From that point forward, the U.S. has operated completely on fiat money.

Ford and Carter followed, and where Ford was relatively benign, Carter created the Departments of Energy and Education, both of which have utterly failed to accomplish their missions on any scale and by any analysis. President Reagan set his administration's sights on eliminating the Soviet Union as a threat to the security of the U.S. rather than restoring the economy, which occurred almost as a by-product. Reagan was spectacularly successful in defeating not only the Soviet Union, but also overcoming the fears of war by Progressives and most of the Republicans around him (including the Secretary of State and his wife.) He was unable to stop the Progressive economic juggernaut, however, and even signed an amnesty bill allowing illegal aliens to gain citizenship.

Deterioration of the American economy, its productive capacity, and the people's spirits resumed under Clinton and the two Bushes, but it has been Obama that has driven the country to the edge of total disaster and collapse. Somehow, the American body politic twice elected a truly bizarre individual with no record of achievement or discernible talent other than being able to read smoothly from a teleprompter. Even worse, his administration was fleshed out with ideologues existing somewhere to the left of Lenin, including such notables as Cass Sunstein, Van Jones (an admitted Communist), Elizabeth Warren, John Podesta, and Valerie Jarrett. His Attorney General, Eric Holder, refused to investigate or prosecute anyone even remotely connected with the Obama Administration, and abject lawlessness in the executive branch resulted. Obama's entire cabinet is Progressive to the core, and ideology has clearly won out over ability or competence.

Waiting in the wings is presidential candidate Hillary Clinton, a self-proclaimed "Progressive Democrat," and a substantial majority of the U.S. Senate call themselves either Progressives or "moderate Republicans" (meaning Progressive Republicans.) Among the most committed and virulent Progressives are Harry Reid, Democrat from Nevada, Richard Blumenthal, Democrat from Connecticut, Cory Booker, Democrat from New Jersey, Barbara Boxer, Democrat from California, Dianne Feinstein, Democrat from California, Dick Durbin, Democrat from Illinois, Al Franken, Democrat from Minnesota, Kirsten Gillibrand, Democrat from New York, Pat Leahy, Democrat from Vermont, Claire McCaskill, Democrat from Missouri, Robert Melendez, Democrat from New Jersey, Barbara Mikulski, Democrat from Maryland, John D. Rockefeller, IV, Democrat from West

Virginia, Bernard Sanders, Democrat (actually Socialist) from Vermont, Chuck Schumer, Democrat from New York, and Elizabeth Warren, Democrat from Massachusetts. These sixteen Democrats actively promote the Progressive agenda at all times, regardless of what they tell their constituents. Major Republican fellow-travelers include John McCain (Arizona), Orrin Hatch (Utah), Mitch McConnell (Kentucky), and Lindsey Graham (South Carolina).

Only in the House of Representatives is there any substantial vestige of individuals who recognize any problems with Progressivism or the incomprehensible level of federal spending. Although several Democrats in the House and Senate profess to something other than Progressivism, none have a voting record to back up such a contention. The four most rabid Progressives in the House are all women: Debbie Wasserman Schultz, Democrat from South Florida, Jan Schkowsky, Democrat from the north side of Chicago, Nancy Pelosi, Democrat from San Francisco, and Maxine Waters, Democrat from South Los Angeles. Congresswoman Waters even inadvertently gave everything away when, while questioning the president of Shell Oil, she mentioned, "Guess what this liberal will be all about? This liberal will be all about socializ... uh, uh,... would be about [long pause] basically taking over, and the government running all of your companies."[188]

In American education, the situation is even worse. Besides the vast majority of university and college administrations being Progressives, faculty members are from ninety-three to ninety-seven percent Progressive. Conservatives tend to be clustered in only a few schools, such as Hillsdale College in Michigan. It is not unusual for departments in arts and sciences to contain one or no conservatives, and, if conservatives are present, are often tolerated only if they are prolific publishers. The Progressive percentage is even higher in Ivy League schools, as they are the ones expected to produce future Progressive leaders for the government.

Perhaps the most daunting list of Progressives that affects the daily lives of citizens comes from the media. Of the four major networks, NBC, CBS, and ABC are overwhelmingly Progressive and specialize in commentators clearly identified with the Democrat Party, such as George Stephanopoulos, Cokie Roberts, Keith Olbermann, Dan Rather, Anderson Cooper, Scott Pelley, Charlie

Rose, Morley Safer, Leslie Stahl, Katie Couric, and Bob Schieffer. On cable, networks such as CNN, MSNBC, and others feature Donna Brazile, Julian Bond (to 2015), Jesse Jackson, John Stewart, Sam Graham-Felsen, Fareed Zakaria, Wolf Blitzer, Rachel Maddow, Larry O'Donnell, Chris Matthews, Al Sharpton, Bill Maher, Joy Behar, and Ed Schultz. Only Fox News regularly features conservative commentators, and it is a cable news channel.

Newspapers are even more rabidly Progressive than television networks—if that is humanly possible. Leading the Progressive list is the *New York Times*, followed by the *Houston Chronicle*, *Los Angeles Times*, *Washington Post*, *Chicago Tribune*, *Boston Globe*, *Detroit Free Press*, *Denver Post*, *San Jose Mercury News*, *St. Louis Post-Dispatch*, *Minneapolis Star-Tribune*, *Atlanta Journal-Constitution*, *Philadelphia Inquirer*, *Cleveland Plain Dealer*, *Seattle Times*, and of course, *USA Today*. The *Wall Street Journal* is relatively conservative in its editorials, but its newsroom is decidedly Progressive and selects its news items accordingly. With the lineup overwhelmingly Progressive, it is a wonder that American citizens know the Obama Administration is doing anything wrong at all.

The saving grace appears to be talk radio and the "new media," the web. Yahoo, Google, and the *Huffington Post* are clearly Progressive, but there are many bloggers providing information on the follies of Progressivism, and good stories often go viral. For some reason, the Republican Party is singularly maladroit in using the Internet and social media, and its cyber presence is practically nil. But, on talk radio, conservatives sweep the competition, providing a great amount of information in a short time, and often being among the first to break a story.

Once again, however, the Republican establishment is missing in action, and it disavows talk radio while always seeking to find some mythical middle ground. Rather than attempting to convince the American public of the correctness of traditional Americanism and the extreme danger of Progressivism and its failed ideology, the Republican establishment clings to the idea that one must be moderate to become elected. Unfortunately, "moderate" is akin to "appeaser," as in Neville Chamberlain being moderate in his approach to dealing with Nazi Germany.

Perhaps the American people have been too thoroughly

conditioned by Progressive propaganda to appreciate the existential danger currently facing the nation. Certainly the Republican establishment has. It has ceded the verb "change" to the Progressives through its inaction and lack of backbone, leaving only "hope" to be contested.

## Where They Are Going

What Progressive elites have been taught in school and what they believe is almost a secret because it has not been widely disseminated to the American people. Simply put, Progressive science is based on the assumption that human society can be organized so that all social ills will disappear.[189] This assumption is faulty and belongs to Utopian dreams, as has been proven over and over again since the beginning of time. Progressivism embodies the regimentation of the common man, actually his manipulation or conditioning to give up his God-given rights to the collective, and function as a serf. God has given man free will, at least in Christianity, and free will is anathema to the ideology of Progressivism.

Progressives appear to favor other religions over Christianity. At the moment, that is Islam, Scientology, and Judaism,. But that is merely a ruse to weaken the moral and religious base in the United States. The new global man, like the "New Soviet Man" and the "Nazi SS man" may be a heroic image, but it is actually a non-thinking automaton, doing the bidding of the governing elite without question or humanity. His morality is determined for him by the elites, and anything that furthers their control is automatically good and virtuous.

Even in Christianity, many ministers and leaders have succumbed to Progressivism. A particularly virulent strain of Progressive Protestantism was espoused by Dr. J. Phillip Wogaman, President Bill Clinton's pastor at Foundry United Methodist Church in Washington.

Wogaman was a full-blooded Progressive and a very outspoken advocate of homosexual marriage as well as all the main Progressive issues used in the last forty years to marginalize Protestant Christianity. He was one of the primary supporters of Clinton during the Lewinsky scandal, and refused to believe that Clinton was a sexual predator in spite of the man's long sordid history prior to the scandal. Against all logic, Wogaman counseled the nation to forgive Clinton and ignore the truth of the matter. To a very large degree, Wogaman's views and activities "embodied what has led United Methodism and the mainline denominations astray: denying or minimizing historic Christian doctrines about Christ and the Bible while substituting for them the advocacy of left-wing political causes."[190] Wogaman and many other supposedly Christian leaders have taken the same route to religious oblivion in recent times as some did in the Third Reich. The German Evangelical (Lutheran) Church and the Methodists (under Bishop Friedrich Heinrich Otto Melle), collaborated with the Nazis and accomplished their own destruction. Today, we see the same, only the country is the U.S. and the Nazis are the Progressives.

In addition to Christianity, Progressivism is certain to destroy groups that exist due to rights given by God, enshrined in the Constitution, and strengthened by earlier federal administrations. Since all rights are mere social expediencies under Progressive ideology, to be granted and denied at government's option, such rights will be withdrawn when the elites decide they are no longer needed. Groups such as the Amish probably will be forcibly integrated into Progressive society, and treaties with Indian tribes abrogated. Tribal governments and reservations are sure to be abolished as anachronisms, probably for failing to implement Agenda 21 on their lands. In a nutshell, all groups relying on the American concept of individual liberty and fundamental rights are at risk, and almost none of these groups has yet identified the existential threat contained in the rise of Progressivism.

The focus of the Progressive message is on two crusades: (1) to save the earth, and (2) to eliminate all social problems and unsatisfactory conditions as defined by Progressives. In furtherance of the first crusade, the hoax of man-made global warming was produced. The "hockey-stick" graph was proven fraudulent, and charts in the United States showing the world cooling since the 1930s were arbitrarily changed by the Obama Administration to show exactly the opposite.[191] Swallowing the Progressive hoax, many people still remain true believers in man's culpability.

Animal rights activists, vegetarians, environmentalists, and people seeking meaning in their lives in various "Save the [noun]" causes have been recruited by Progressives to aid in their misdirection. These causes have been ennobled beyond all belief, and serve to elevate Progressives above all criticism. How can anyone be against saving the earth, the lion, the snail darter, etc.? Therefore, the Progressive is working for mankind and all that is of value to humans. The reality is that all this is a sham, being used to maneuver the common people into giving up their God-given rights.

The second crusade, the elimination of all social problems, follows strategies based on a key underlying belief by all Progressives; the nature of man is ever-changing, and that change can be directed by government to create a society in which social problems no longer exist. If this sounds like a foundational belief of communism, socialism, and fascism, that's because it is. One must never forget that fascism in Germany was National Socialism, and all these concepts are based on leftist ideology.

The methodology of these political philosophies is to level the existence of the common man to a point where he cannot provide for himself without the aid of governmental programs, rendering him dependent on the government for his and his family's welfare. Government, at that point, micro-manages people's lives for them (supposedly in their best interests), but in no sense is such a government of, by, and for the people. In order to rule effectively, it must be autocratic—democracy is simply much too messy.

Only where individual liberty reigns can a government be democratic. Progressives know this, and that is also why every communist or authoritarian government labels itself a democracy or republic, usually with the descriptor "people's."[192] It is all misdirection and winning the debate by claiming the high ground when one is really in a swamp.

Following their assumption that the nature of man is changing, Progressives believe the United States must also change and move beyond the principles of its founding. The Constitution, of course, is an outdated and obsolete document. Instead of the Federal Government having limited powers as under the Constitution, they believe government should have all the power without limit. It should be able to tell a citizen whom he may marry… or not; what to eat… or not; what work he may do… or not; what medical procedure he may undergo… or not; what items he may sell or not; whether he may own a firearm or not; whether he should pay for another's birth control or not; what he may wear to school and what not; whether he may fill in a wet spot on his property or not; etc. In the future, the government should have the power to tell the citizen what he may say in public and what not; which churches may hold services and which not; where he may live and where not; how he may earn a living and how not; how many children he may have, if any; what he may earn, and what he must give to others; etc. King Louis XIV is reputed to have said, "The state is me," but Progressives now say, "We are the state and you will obey."

According to Progressive ideology, the checks and balances in the Federal Government are an anachronism. There should be only two branches of government: a political branch and an administrative one. The political branch, such as a governing council of Progressives, should set the direction of government (like the Communist Central Committee did in the now defunct USSR). The administrative branch, under the oversight of the governing council, would create, administer, and enforce the rules and regulations that would control all activities of the citizenry. In short, Progressives believe in the society depicted by George Orwell in *1984* as controlled by a Progressive elite, maybe not in all of Orwell's details, but certainly in general.[193]

Progressives believe in infanticide, abortion, and euthanasia. They steadfastly promote the programs of Agenda 21 that seek to reduce the earth's human population from over seven to under a billion people. For some reason, they believe they, along with the elites of Europe, will be in charge of the new world government, even though, by 2050, Europe will be largely Muslim, and the U.S. probably fragmented into manageable ethnic and religious groups. Most likely, the North American Federation, consisting of Canada, the U.S., and Mexico, will have come into being by 2050, although it may also include some Caribbean and Meso-American states. If so, the power that formerly resided with Protestant Americans will have totally disappeared, submerged under an avalanche of demographic changes.

Under Agenda 21, private property is to disappear, and everything—property and the means of production—will be owned or fully controlled by the dtate. The America of our forefathers, the

America most citizens want their children to inherit, will have left the earth, never to appear again. By 2100, the North American population will probably be less than half of the current American population in all possible scenarios for America's future; reduced not only through the control of birthrates, but also through the purposeful extinction of citizens.

Eventually, the new global man will not have any of the rights currently enjoyed by American citizens, as they will no longer be needed. The government will keep the citizenry subdued through spectacles such as professional and amateur sports, cultural events, non-stop television, pornography, and electronic games and playthings, as well as the legalization of drugs such as marijuana and prescription drugs to maintain a condition of euphoria or, simply, satisfaction. Marijuana is particularly helpful to Progressives as heavy pot-smoking while an adolescent lowers an individual's IQ by an average of eight points.[194] Marijuana smokers have long been characterized as dimwitted and slow, but now that appears to be a result of pot-smoking rather than a characteristic of those who smoke. In any case, the underclass will be leveled at earnings only sufficient to maintain a subsistence lifestyle, but all dwellings will be rented, and, with strict rationing of gasoline, private vehicles will become a luxury.

One of the best Progressive explanations of the social expediency of citizen rights was given by Frank Goodnow in the early days of Progressivism. Goodnow, president of Johns Hopkins University and the first president of the American Political Science Association, literally sneered at the idea that citizens might have rights given by God or nature. He held that Rousseau's emphasis on individuals in his "Social Contract" was absolutely wrong. Goodnow believed in the European concept of citizen rights present in the early twentieth century; namely that an individual was primarily a member of society and only secondarily an individual. "The rights which he possesses are... conferred upon him, not by his Creator, but rather, by the society to which he belongs. What they are is to be determined by the legislative authority in view of the needs of that society. Social expediency, rather than natural right, is thus to determine the sphere of individual freedom of action."[195] Needless to say, Goodnow also foresaw the conversion of the American legal system from common law to civil law.

That Progressives believe in the social expediency of citizen rights from government cannot be overstated, and the recognition of this fact should be a life-altering revelation for all citizens, certainly on par with the Jews in Nazi Germany when they finally recognized that Hitler intended to exterminate European Jewry. Progressive Congresswoman Nancy Pelosi crowed about congress having created a new human right—the right to health care—with Obamacare, although, it actually had done nothing of the sort. But for Pelosi, the "Patient Protection and Affordable Care Act" demonstrated the power of Progressivism and the god-like status of the state.

For the evangelical Christian reader, the emergence of Progressivism as the new all-powerful deity clearly makes Progressivism the anti-Christ, and all of its adherents demons or beasts of the Devil. It is inconceivable that a Christian, Roman Catholic, Mormon, or Protestant, can reconcile Progressivism with Christian teaching, and, quite possibly, none do. They become nominal Christians for political purposes, and any oaths they swear become mere political expediencies of no importance, meaning, or consequence. The atheist secular Jews have no problem with the aspect of rights being social expediencies, to be granted and withdrawn at the government's pleasure, because there is no God to whom they must answer.

The question becomes even larger in scope when one considers those Christian citizens who vote for Progressive Democrat politicians. They are either ignorant of Progressives' true intents, misunderstand Progressive dogma, are willing to throw away their Christian beliefs and morality for government handouts, or are false Christians and should not be allowed to receive Communion. It is simply impossible to be both a Progressive Democrat and a Christian—they are absolutely competing religions. And people who consider themselves conservative Democrats are fooling themselves; the Democrat Party is Progressive and all non-Progressives are destined to become serfs in the new Progressive order regardless of past party affiliation.

Democrat Party leaders such as Hillary Clinton and Barack Obama have repeatedly called for Christian beliefs to give way to Progressivism. Mrs. Clinton said, in April, 2015, that "deep-seated cultural codes, religious beliefs, and structural biases have to be changed" to accommodate women's "reproductive rights."[196]

President Obama stated, in June, 2006, that "Democracy demands that the religiously motivated translate their concerns into universal, rather than religion-specific, values. It requires that their proposals be subject to argument and amenable to reason..."[197] And lest anyone mistake this trend, the Obama Administration is the first since Roosevelt's to have self-described communists and socialists on the White House Staff. Officials like Henry Wallace, Alger Hiss, Harry Dexter White, and Laughlin Curry have given way to the likes of Van Jones, Carol Browner, and Cass Sunstein.

Rights granted by God are immutable and must be recognized by a secular society and its government for that society and nation to be moral and virtuous. The underclass in America is close to losing its right of self-defense, freedom of speech, assembly, and the rest of the individual rights recognized by the Constitution. The media is working every day to mold public opinion in order that those rights might be eliminated through constitutional means. Again, it must be emphasized that Hitler was able to establish his dictatorship in Germany through constitutional means, so simply having a Constitution is hardly a protection against tyranny. Progressives are also extremely adept at using those rights to their own benefit when required, even though they don't believe in them. The case of Lois Lerner, in which she invoked the 5th Amendment after asserting she had done nothing wrong, attests to such Progressive duplicity and their use of the Constitution to help them gain power and move ever closer to a Progressive tyranny.

Senator Harry Reid routinely attacked ordinary citizens in the senate chambers, using his senatorial immunity to destroy the reputations of Americans who were unable to defend themselves. Congresswoman Pelosi attacked the Tea Party as being "Astroturf," meaning the Tea Party organizations were fake grass-roots organizations, and Progressive Senator Blanche Lincoln called them, "un-American." Hillary Clinton, who, with her husband, raised more than three billion dollars for political campaigns, purposely misstated the Hobby-Lobby case ruled on by the Supreme Court to brand the company's owners as being against all contraception for women. Actually Hobby-Lobby objected only to paying for their female employees' use of the "morning-after pill" that induces a de-facto abortion of an unborn human.[198] Ordinary Americans cannot withstand such attacks by powerful Progressive politicians, yet have no recourse when maligned, impoverished, or have their reputations destroyed. Progressives know that and take advantage of helpless Americans every day.

For Progressives, ordinary Americans are getting what they deserve when they challenge Progressivism, for they are standing in the way of progress. It must always be remembered that Progressives hold no truck with constitutional rights unless those rights benefit Progressives in their movement toward a Progressive dictatorship. Not believing in a higher power than themselves (except for a Progressive in a higher position), Progressives are not constrained by morality or any feeling for other human beings. The collective is the only important embodiment of their ideology, and all humans are merely instruments to be used and exploited for the benefit of the collective. The Progressive revolution not only devours its children, but also all citizens under its sway.

For Goodnow and all later Progressives, the Protestant religious and moral influences in the United States produced an extreme and undesirable form of individualism, not the least because it stressed the achievement of personal salvation through Christ. Personal salvation also meant the acceptance of personal responsibility for morality, choices, and actions. Progressives substitute collective responsibility for personal responsibility, and choices and actions are to be directed by the collective.

Goodnow ultimately concluded when addressing students, "[W]e have come to the conclusion that man under modern conditions is primarily a member of society and that only as he recognizes his duties as a member of society can he secure the greatest opportunities as an individual….[G]reater emphasis should be laid on social duties and less on individual rights, [and] it is the duty of the University to call attention to the student to this fact, and it is the duty of the student when he goes out into the world to do what in him lies to bring this truth home to his fellows."[199]

These sentiments, made in 1916, have been echoed across the United States by Progressive educators and politicians to the present day, and they are what has turned the bulk of university students—at least temporarily—into Progressives. Goodnow clearly stated that only by accepting Progressive ideology could an individual reach his greatest potential, a lesson learned well by most American politicians since Goodnow's time. The way to riches and power in the United States soon involved the adoption of Progressivism and the cultivation of Progressive mentors, friends, and contacts.

Woodrow Wilson, one of the greatest or worst American presidents depending on whether one is a Progressive or believer in individual liberty, believed the United States had not kept up in economics or political development as well as other nations, particularly those in Europe.[200] That single fact supposedly forced him to become a Progressive. Never mind that this wonderful European progress in politics and economics brought forth two world wars and untold suffering for mankind; it was superior to what the U.S. had. Wilson was one of the first America bashers, as the grass was always greener in Europe.

The growth in Progressivism was due, in part, to the huge influx of immigrants from Europe during the previous twenty years (1893-1913) who were looking for a land of milk and honey, but found hard work and individual responsibility coupled with opportunity. That distressed Wilson, the quintessential do-gooder, and he hated the status quo. In his opinion, it was an unacceptable situation. Echoing the sentiments of John Dewey, Wilson, the former president of Princeton, stated as a former educator, "I should like to make the young gentlemen of the rising generation as unlike their fathers as possible. Not because their fathers, by reason of their advancing years and their established position in society, had lost touch with the processes of life; they had forgotten what it was to begin; they had forgotten what it was to rise; they had forgotten what it was to be dominated by the circumstances of their life on their way up from the bottom to the top, and therefore, they were out of sympathy with the creative, formative and progressive forces of society."[201]

Presumably, the fifty-seven year-old Wilson was not one of those fathers; he had worked but a single year in private practice as a lawyer, then spent the remainder of his life in academia until becoming governor of New Jersey for a single term. Perhaps no better example exists of a Progressive, totally lacking in the bona fides to make a statement, who, nevertheless, made it. It was also a forerunner of the "I know better than you what is good for you" philosophy that issues daily from Progressive individuals.

Like Goodnow, Wilson was also a president of the American Political Science Association, and known for favoring the British parliamentary system of government over America's. He had little use for the American founding documents and declared the Constitution needed to be Darwinian in structure and practice. He stated, "All that Progressives ask or desire is permission ... to interpret the Constitution according to the Darwinian principle [of evolution to meet changed conditions]."[202] Clearly, that was a lie—and when Wilson went to Versailles and carved up Eastern Europe from a map, not taking into account any of the wishes of the people living in those regions, he established himself as one of the great arbitrary dictators of his day.

Wilson also had help from the Rockefellers, notably one of their foundations, the General Education Board. This foundation was established to guide the direction of education and promote the ideas of collectivism, socialism, and globalism. Education was to be split into two models: education for children of the elite to enable them to rule when adults, and, for all others, a dumbed-down education that lulled its students into apathy and made them docile servants and workers. That this has come to pass by the twenty-first century cannot be doubted; the Ivy League schools (and a few others) annually produce the nation's leaders while all other institutions simply warehouse students for four years and lower their expectations for a life in some meaningless job.

Public universities no longer speak of great goals or achievements in life; they are content to find employment—any employment—for their graduates. High school educations under Common Core are dramatically lowering the educational level of college freshmen coming from public schools and necessitating remedial training. With the advent of high tuition costs and the necessity of assuming intolerable student loan obligations, only children of the Progressive rich and famous can afford the elite universities that truly make a difference in an individual's career. Obviously, this is the way it is supposed to be.

To a very large degree, it is possible to look at the Council for Foreign Relations (CFR), the Trilateral Commission, and the Bilderbergs to see which Americans are included in the ruling Progressive elite.[203] Not surprisingly, practically all of their members state publically that the U.S. economy is not in any danger, and will continue to make such statements until the collapse occurs.

The hyperinflation in Germany in the 1920s impoverished Germany's middle class, paving the way for the two-class system that brought about the rise of fascism. The collapse of the United States' economy should produce the same result, and, this time, Progressives have sworn not to squander their golden opportunity. They have planned it to occur when everything is in readiness for a full Progressive takeover and the fundamental transformation of the United States into a Progressive meritocracy. Do those words sound familiar? They should. "A fundamental transformation of the United States" was what presidential candidate Obama promised in 2008.

Two of the attributes ascribed to Progressives, as well as in all other totalitarian movements, are (1) the inability or unwillingness to compromise and (2) the blaming of anyone but themselves and Progressive doctrine when their ideology proves false. Hitler and Mussolini were, literally, genetically unable to compromise on any issue, and, although they might seem to reach a compromise agreement on some issue at some point, they always came around later to erase the compromise they made. Time after time, men of good faith bargained for a compromise and struck a deal, either formally or informally, only to see the dictators go back on their word or disregard their agreement.

In the summer of 2015, the treaty made with Iran over its nuclear energy program featured negotiators with a similar inability to compromise, this time the Iranians. The president of Iran, Hassan Rouhani, said in effect, 'We got everything we wanted," a statement that should have alerted the Obama Administration that the treaty was a very bad deal for Americans.[204]

The second feature is on abundant display today in the Obama Administration, notably the president's lies with respect to Obamacare. The ideology is never wrong, and any and all failures are due to others opposing the ideology. In a sentence: communism in the Soviet Union didn't fail, it was just implemented incorrectly and not thoroughly enough.

If the full agenda of a Progressive is not approved or interpreted correctly, then any problems are not his fault—his total agenda would have worked. And, almost always, misdirection is used to control the debate. A prime example is that Progressives blame Ronald Reagan for growing government, never mentioning that he was shackled with a Democrat-dominated congress that prevented him from making reductions. On the other hand, Barack Obama blames Republicans in the House for blocking his programs, including those initiated while he enjoyed a Democrat majority in both houses. Even more disconcerting is the Progressive doctrine to always accuse others of doing precisely what Progressives are doing, thereby turning real wrong-doing into "Both sides do it" dismissals.

The citizen must recognize today that almost all information coming out of the Federal Government is untrue or misleading. At best, releases of information by the Obama Administration must be viewed as skewed in favor of the administration, and, at worst, outright lies. Probably most are distortions of the truth, carefully worded to make them sound plausible, and some are even technically correct, but highly misleading. The key is that all government press releases are designed to manipulate the public into believing something the government wants it to believe or to head off unpleasant confrontations or support some program that lacks sufficient merit on its own to garner public approval.

The IRS scandal is a prime example of government misdeeds and manipulation. At the current time, no less than seven personal computers of employees critical to the Lois Lerner investigation have been reported to have crashed and all data lost. All backups associated with the time frame in question have been erased, and, evidently, all computers of all government employees receiving or sending emails to or from Lerner are now unrecoverable for one reason or another. As told with a smile by the IRS Commissioner, supposedly all of this was just a series of unfortunate accidents and there was no intent to destroy information.

Of course, only IRS employees important to the investigation have experienced crashes. All these accidents occurred shortly after the investigation was launched and the contract with the backup agency was cancelled without anyone being informed. Then, somehow, the backup agency subsequently destroyed all backup storage media, even though statutes were in place specifically to ensure that government data could be recovered for up to ten years.

On top of that, the public was informed that NSA neglected to keep copies of the messages it intercepted, so there is no computer in the vast federal communications system that can produce any evidence, including the hundreds that should have copies of Lerner emails. Apparently, it was only necessary for government to say something—anything—and twenty percent of the American citizenry believed there was no wrong-doing. Clearly, Progressives already have a great deal of power over cognitive formulations made by the American people.

Complete control by Progressives over the lives of normal Americans cannot be far away. The availability of ammunition for purchase by the public has fallen off significantly and the 2nd Amendment receives more than its share of criticism from Progressive circles. But most important is the Progressive push on current demographic trends—every day the U.S. citizenry becomes more diverse in every measurable distinction. The American way of life has become supplanted with multiple cultures, all equal in importance, and rather than a unified country, the U.S. is fast becoming a diverse empire.

History has shown that only relatively uniform and cohesive societies can function well under a representative democracy, and even then, local government tends to be more significant to the citizen than regional or national. In the case of a highly diverse population with multiple ethnic groups, only an extremely strong national government can keep the country together. Diversity brings weakness and unrest, along with a substantial increase in daily stress on the citizenry. Progressive leaders know these facts, push diversity in language, culture, religion, and ethnicity on the American public, and thereby render America's current constitutional system dysfunctional.

As a result of its own policies, government fails to respond to citizen needs and Progressives are able to force changes through that bring the country ever closer to an elite dictatorship. Progressives cause the problem, say it is unsolvable under current law, and then change U.S. law to meet their future requirements.

However, history also has shown that strong governments facing diverse populations must call upon large police and military forces to maintain order. Historically, such forces have been recruited with appeals to their political ideology (Communism in the USSR), patriotism (Nazi Germany), or religion (Spain). In general, dictatorships with a "soft ideology," such as Progressivism, have been easily overthrown for the simple reason than most people are not willing to die for an amorphous political theory. For Progressives, the state religion is atheism, making the situation worse. Without a simultaneous cause, such as nationalism, to awaken the citizens, few will be willing to fight for the government. It remains to be seen if "Saving the Earth" is such a cause, but the odds are against it.

One must know Progressives for who they are, what they believe, and what they do—thenforget what they say. Also, they should be known for the fact that they will do anything and everything to protect themselves, yet do nothing for the common citizens whom they perceive are not on their team. Progressives only have one life to live and no Progressive has ever been a martyr. Christians and Muslims may describe Progressives as abject cowards; the label is not inaccurate.

Secular Jews built a Holocaust Center in Washington, DC, *not* because America has ever experienced a Holocaust, but to inculcate Christians with the idea that they must help protect secular Jews from their enemies. Like Britain's intention to fight Hitler to the last Frenchman until May, 1940, secular Jews will fight for Israel and themselves to the last evangelical Christian.

Progressives, however, do not sacrifice themselves for others, and unless subjected to extensive mind control such as what the USSR and China imposed on their citizens, coupled with draconian punishments for not obeying, they make terrible soldiers. They will do anything to survive, exterminating large numbers of non-Progressives if necessary to safeguard themselves. That's why they do what they do, and all of their actions are utterly lacking in virtue and morality.

Progressives sometimes tout the current wisdom in the saying, "Everyone has two lives; the second one begins when you realize you only have one". Yet, they interpret this, not from the Christian viewpoint, but as a calling to commit themselves to maximizing what they get out of every remaining day in their lives and not wasting another minute. The focus is strictly on themselves—hardly a Christian outlook.

Progressives love to blame unbridled ( *laissez-faire*) capitalism for the nation's economic woes, and, within limits, they have a point. But they have to misdirect their criticism at "large corporations" or "Wall Street" because the vast majority of extremely wealthy capitalists are Progressives who have made their wealth through crony capitalism.

Capitalism in the U.S. is no longer free from government interference through regulations, privileges, tariffs, and subsidies, and, therefore, no longer *laissez-faire*. Quite the contrary—most vast fortunes today are made through government connections, government contracts, insider information, and manipulation undertaken in concert with government officials.

In the nineteenth century, the fortunes amassed by Vanderbilt, Rockefeller, and Carnegie were earned honestly and mostly without government involvement. All Americans benefitted. Vanderbilt lowered the cost of mail and water transportation; Rockefeller produced cheap kerosene and gasoline for general consumption; and Carnegie produced steel cheaper than before and turned the U.S. into an industrial powerhouse.

Today, IBM is practically the in-house IT department for the Federal Government, and many other corporations would fail without the government's continued support and contracts from its agencies. Hillary Clinton may rail at Wall Street manipulators, but they regularly contribute vast sums to her campaigns and the Clinton Foundation, and continue to operate unhindered by government. Financial manipulator and speculator, George Soros, is the poster-boy for everything that is held evil in the world of finance by Progressives, yet one would be hard pressed to find a more committed Progressive.

The degree of corruption in this unholy alliance of crony capitalists and the Federal Government is simply staggering. The combination of Bill and Hillary Clinton and their foundation is possibly the most corrupt of all. Although the principals regularly defend their practices as strictly legal, (or that those practices cannot be proven to be illegal), it would be difficult to find another example so morally bankrupt in operating through the use of government connections and prior government service for personal enrichment. The Clintons are perhaps the premier advertisement for instituting the ancient Athenian practice of ostracism for ex-government officials.

Progressives inevitably adopt socialism as their preferred model, and even Woodrow Wilson declared that "[I]n fundamental theory, socialism and democracy are almost, if not quite, one and the same. They both rest at bottom upon the absolute right of the community to determine its own destiny and that of its members."[205]

While Wilson was pontificating on the virtues of Progressivism, he was setting up mechanisms by which the state could put Progressive ideology into practice. Control of the people's individual economic lives could be achieved through the income tax and the establishment of the Federal Reserve System, and Wilson put those strangleholds in place for use against the citizenry at the appropriate time. Since Wilson's presidency Progressives have been successful beyond belief, all through sleight of hand, miss-direction, mendacity, and the control of American education and the media. But when is the time of reckoning?

Many Progressives believe the time to complete the change of the United States to a completely Progressive nation is fast approaching. The "hope" part of "hope and change" is that the Progressive heaven-on-earth will soon become a reality. Ordinary citizens, however, will be relegated to the Progressive hell-on-earth. Progressives are down with that development.

# Chapter 7

## Expectations and Actions by Progressive Government

### The Seven Progressive Beliefs

Until Progressives are vanquished and removed from government, one must always remember seven facts about Progressives. They believe:

(1) **the Constitution is a living document**, subject to being changed at will by the Supreme Court to conform to the opinions of the governing elite;

(2) **individual rights are mere social expediencies**, to be granted or withheld from citizens as seen fit by the governing elites;

(3) **state and local governments have no rights** other than those specifically granted by the national government—states' rights were eliminated by the 14th Amendment which overturned the 10th Amendment;

(4) **mankind must be reduced to two classes**, the ruling Progressive elite and the subservient serfs;

(5) **a new global Progressive man must be forged** from the remnants of mankind after implementing Agenda 21, imposing infanticide and euthanasia as appropriate;

(6) **all religions other than Progressive humanism must be eliminated**; and

(7) **a strong global government of Progressives must be created** for the preservation of the earth and humanity.

All of their actions will be in accordance with these defining Progressive beliefs and objectives, and, while they may repudiate them at times with words to get elected, their actions will remain true to their ideology. The government they are "progressing" toward is a dictatorship of the elite in their ideology, one governing on behalf of the people. They believe that only the intelligent, educated (in Progressivism), and ideologically trustworthy elite Progressives are fit to govern the United States in an increasingly dangerous and complex world, and the common people must be made to believe that giving up their right to having a say in government is necessary for their security and economic well-being. Hitler did precisely that in 1933 and the Progressives are doing so now. Remember at all times: ***Progressive ideology is incompatible with democracy***.

As *Starve The Beast* promotes action on the part of American citizens to rein in a tyrannical and out-of-control Progressive government, like any threatened organism, the government will take action to defend itself. Politicians rarely place the interests of their country or constituents over their own, mostly because they believe they are one and the same. When actions consistent with their ideology have negative results, they cannot admit to making an error because anything bad happening to them is also bad for the country. So they double-down, find someone or something to blame, and negative consequences become disasters.

Fortunately, no government is overly efficient, particularly one growing out of a democratic tradition, and rarely are programs great successes or abject disasters. In this case, where money is expected to become tight, however, bureaucrats will defend their turf and livelihood to the last extremity, and blame will be spread everywhere.

Revenues will fall, but, according to the principle of "normalcy bias," it is difficult for humans to recognize a disastrous change if it has not happened previously. The effects of the Articles of Association have long been forgotten (if ever known), and there has never been a widespread purposeful denial of revenue to government before in the United States.

At first, government bureaucrats will attempt to stimulate economic activity by spending money at the federal and state levels. Of course, that will have no effect, and, as is occurring today (2015), stimulus dollars will remain in banks and financial institutions until given to favored and politically well-connected individuals and corporations. If the American citizenry refuses to buy the products and services of those crony capitalists, those corporations will be unable to meet their government obligations and fail, causing waves of panic to reverberate through the elites. Attempts will be made to increase foreign business, but America has a built-in fatal flaw—its productive capacity has already moved overseas and it will be unable to meet foreign competition.

There are two major ideological campaigns and one political campaign currently underway by the Federal Government, the status of which will materially affect the degree of future government power, and what steps it can take before an armed rebellion occurs. The first in terms of when it was begun—but not the most successful to date—is the war on Christianity and the replacement of Christian morality with secular Progressive humanism. This was discussed earlier, but the more the citizenry looks to God and Christ for their guidance and morality, the less likely Progressive dogma will triumph.

The second is creating the myth of Progressivism's inevitability. It is an outgrowth of the curtailment of the right to private property, and the idea that a Progressive-led socialistic global community is the only solution to the problems of global warming and destruction of the earth's environment by human beings. In order to save the planet, humans must be severely decimated and then controlled by an all-powerful elite. Under the principles of the globalists' prime directive, Agenda 21, democracy, private property, and government by the people must all be eliminated as unsustainable. To forestall the almost certain armed rebellion, it is necessary to propagandize and win over major portions of the populace in the United States to accept Agenda 21 and serfdom as a necessary sacrifice. This campaign is making steady progress, but there is a large segment of the population that has proven recalcitrant and truculent.

The third, and political, campaign is the transformation of the U.S. military into a politically-correct institution under Progressive control. This campaign has made little progress because Progressives are insufficiently disciplined to sacrifice themselves for the good of the cause by going into the military and replacing the patriotic Americans already serving. This campaign may have to wait until the elimination of Christianity and promotion of Agenda 21 are further along.

## Reactions to *Starve The Beast!*

Regardless of the status of the three current Progressive campaigns, the first draconian reaction to Starve the Beast will probably be to make all cash transactions illegal. There is precedence for this move, both in Sweden and Israel. By 2012, only three percent of Swedish bank transactions involved cash, and some banks had stopped handling cash altogether. Their customers are currently forced to use debit cards, as even checks have been eliminated. Public transportation is purchased with prepaid tickets or paid with a cell phone message. Some businesses have gone cashless, accepting only debit or credit cards. Checks, including traveler's checks, money orders, and cash itself have become frowned upon, and an ever-increasing number of stores have become simply unable to make change, therefore requiring the use of debit or credit cards or cell phone payments.

The Israeli government has developed a three-phase plan, which is not yet fully implemented, to eliminate all cash transactions in Israel. Initially, individuals and businesses will be permitted to conduct cash and check transactions only in small amounts, not to exceed $2,150 in any business transaction, or $4,300 in private ones. After a year, these limits will decrease further. Any violation of these transaction limits will be a criminal offense, subject to a large fine. All banks will be required to issue debit cards to all customers desiring to do business in Israel. The goal is to force Israeli citizens to conduct as much business as possible using electronic forms of payment, which are then traceable and verifiable.

The stated reason for this move is that cash is believed to fuel the underground economy and enables people to avoid paying taxes. Although the total elimination of cash and check transactions is supposedly not being contemplated, once most transactions are cashless, it will not be difficult to prohibit banks from handling cash and the citizenry from making any cash transactions at all. This plan has the full backing of Prime Minister Benjamin Netanyahu, as he believes it will increase tax revenue by preventing money laundering and tax evasion. The committee coming up with this plan estimated that Israel's cash-driven black market is more than twenty percent of the country's Gross Domestic Product, and does not pay a dime in taxes. Even worse, the cash is believed to be funding terrorism by Palestinians living in Israel.

The plan would enable the Israeli government to analyze all financial transactions in Israel. The Israeli situation should be watched closely to see its effect on the Israeli economy, and what the Israeli government does to eliminate bartering and exchanges, such as the open-air markets so prevalent in the country. With secular Jews being a large part of the Progressive movement in the U.S., what the Israelis do will probably be a good indication of what will occur in the U.S.

In any case, the United States is not far behind. According to a study by MasterCard released in September, 2013, titled "The Cashless Journey," approximately eighty percent of all consumer transactions in the United States are already cashless.

The trend is also world-wide. A recent report tracked thirty-three major economies, focusing on the value of all consumer payments, and found that of the approximately $63 trillion spent world-wide by consumers, sixty-six percent was done with cashless payments.[206] The report indicated that the most cashless society was Belgium at ninety-three percent, followed by France (ninety-two percent), Canada (ninety percent), the UK (eighty-nine percent), Sweden (eighty-nine percent), Australia (eighty-six percent) and the Netherlands (eighty-five percent). On the other end of the scale came Indonesia (thirty-one percent), Russia (thirty-one percent), Kenya (twenty-seven percent), and Egypt (seven percent). In the middle were Japan (sixty-two percent), Brazil (fifty-seven percent), China (fifty-five percent), Spain (fifty-four percent), Taiwan (forty-three percent), South Africa (forty-three percent), and Poland (forty-one percent).

Obviously, cultural factors were important, and the European Union states were leading the way to more socialization and government control of its citizenry. Peer Stein, a director at the International Finance Corporation, welcomed the trend, claiming that cash "takes time to access, is riskier to carry, and costs a country up to one and a half percent of its GDP.[207] This is the Progressive viewpoint that will be seen more often in the next few years, that having a system whereby the government can know how a citizen spends every dime of his money is supposedly good for the citizen.

At any rate, the attempt to force the American citizen into a cashless society may well trigger a gigantic backlash. How will a congressman pay for the sex services he uses in Washington, for example? How will he get paid for favors when he can no longer accept stuffed envelopes? Obviously, the answer is bartering and swapping, precisely the transactions the IRS is seeking to eliminate. The government will no doubt require all cash, including coin, to be turned in at banks, with owners receiving credits in their accounts. After some date, it will be illegal to accept cash as payment in any transaction.

There is a huge problem if this is attempted in the next few years—dollars are in wide circulation as the world's reserve currency. The vast majority is in bank accounts and can be converted into other currency upon demand, but a global rush to repatriate dollars will end the dollar's reign as the reserve currency. At that point, the American financial system will automatically collapse, pushing the United States into a total economic, governing, and societal wilderness.

No doubt Progressives will call in all precious metals, such as gold and silver, and the private ownership of all such metals will be outlawed. Simply put, this will be a disaster since some medium of exchange will be necessary for people to trade with one another, and the American dollar, as recorded in some bank account, will not be the desired instrument. Perhaps bitcoin or some other instrument will arise to pick up the slack, but, in order to be effective, the medium must gain the confidence of the citizenry. At the very least, bartering will become endemic, and the IRS will be unable to track transactions or collect taxes. If one wants a sure-fire scheme to cause an anti-Progressive revolution, this is it.

As an interesting sidelight to precious metals being desirable to the citizenry, numismatic coins have been popular among collectors since the beginning of the modern age. At the current time, however, many nations are in the process of prohibiting the private collecting of numismatic coins, contending that they are "national treasures" and must be under the control and safekeeping of the country where they were minted or could have been used as coinage.

The importing and exporting of such coins has been outlawed by various countries such as Italy, Turkey, Bulgaria, and Cyprus. As of the date of this writing, Germany has introduced a similar law. The U.S. State Department has been complicit in restricting the importation of such coins, contrary to the wishes of its citizens. Collectors have been demonized in Progressive circles as little more than grave robbers, and, today, hundreds of thousands of such coins are held by universities for study by academics. Although this might sound proper, exactly how many coins of a particular type are needed for study? Cannot some be made available to individuals to bring history alive at the personal level? Once again, the collective wins and the individual citizen loses.

One other trigger for a potential revolution is the seizure of firearms and ammunition throughout the United States. This is seen by Progressives as a necessary pre-condition for establishing a dictatorship of the elite in the United States. As the strategy of Starving The Beast becomes apparent in Washington, gun seizures will probably begin, starting with the reliable socialized states in New England, along with New York, New Jersey, Maryland, Illinois, Iowa, Minnesota, and the "left" coast. Progressives know all too well that their interpretation of the Constitution with regard to the 2nd Amendment is in error, but fact and truth have never yet been allowed to stand in the way of ideology. As long as citizens have guns and can possess gold and silver, they have a chance to overthrow the Progressives and survive the resulting chaos. If their guns have been confiscated and they are at the mercy of a fiat paper dollar, they are goners.

The problem for Progressives is that these two steps have not yet been taken. If Starving The Beast causes sufficient numbers of Americans to wake up and be willing to confront the problem of an out-of-control Federal Government before their guns, gold, and silver have been confiscated, there is a chance the America of our Founding Fathers, one based in individual liberty, Protestant Christian morality, common law, private property, and free-market capitalism, can be resurrected. It is all a matter of timing.

## Choosing Up Sides

There is also the criticalproblem mentioned above: the transformation of the U.S. military into a politically-correct institution under Progressive control. At the highest level, the Progressives are already in control, and the Joint Chiefs of Staff and a number of major commanders in various positions have already been turned into corporate managers who will do anything the Progressive civilian administration orders.

The officer corps has also been softened through politically inspired promotions and by increasing the military's diversity. By 2015, the Navy had promoted eighty-nine females to flag rank, including an African-American to Fleet Admiral (4 stars) who had never been on sea duty. In the Air Force, President Obama appointed a woman to head the Pacific Air Force who had never piloted a military aircraft, and two women to 4-star rank from the twenty-nine female generals in the Air Force. In 2013, nineteen female generals were serving in the Army, one in the Marine Corps, and almost seventeen percent of officers in all services were female. At the same time, the ban on women in most combat duties was lifted (slowly implemented and still in process in 2015), and the U.S. joined Canada, Israel, New Zealand, the Netherlands, Norway, Sri Lanka, Sweden, and Turkey in allowing women to serve in combat units. As of 2015, however, only the U.S. and Israel had actually put females at risk in actual combat. It remains to be seen what impact the rapid rise of females will have on the allegiance of the Armed Forces to the government versus the citizens of the U.S. Disturbingly, there is anecdotal evidence that women on active duty may have aligned themselves more with civilian Progressive leadership than the citizenry from whence they came.

In 2012, the American Armed Forces were comprised of only 1.399 million personnel on active duty (0.437% of the population) plus another million in the Ready Reserve. The ratio of enlisted personnel to officers was 4.8 enlisted to one officer, and the gender/racial composition was 14.6% female, 62.1% Caucasian, 11.3% Hispanic, 16.1% black, 3.6% Asian, and 6.9% multi-racial or other.[208] Military personnel and all veterans still living in the United States numbered slightly more than seven percent of the total population. This was about a third of the number receiving Social Security, half of those receiving food stamps, half the blacks, half the Hispanics, and just slightly greater than homosexuals and lesbians. As a voting bloc, military personnel and veterans have limited significance.

In the twenty-first century, veteran influence in government has become increasingly marginal. In the 2008 senate races, fifty-six of the sixty-six candidates had not served in the military, a percentage of eighty-three and a third.[209] In the presidential race starting in 2015, none of the three Democrat candidates had served, and only two of the seventeen Republicans, both in the Air Force, one as a lawyer and the other as a transport pilot. In Congress, the change from 1971 to 2014 was dramatic; the percentage of veterans in the House declined from seventy-two percent to under nineteen percent in the Senate from seventy-eight percent to sixteen percent.[210] Veterans are an endangered species in government and that marginalization is due in large measure to their patriotic sentiments.

The question is, "How loyal to a Progressive government will the military be?" There is no way of telling, although there is substantial anecdotal evidence that both the enlisted personnel and officers in the army and marines will align themselves to a great extent with the citizens against Progressive overreach, and even the Navy and Air Force will probably refuse to do the government's bidding if those actions entail attacking or killing Americans. The total strength of the National Guard as of 2015 was 460,000 personnel, and they certainly must be considered unreliable by Progressives unless deployed in states other than their own.[211]

Following President Obama's treaty with Iran that practically ensured Iran would have a nuclear weapon within a dozen years, the prospect of a war in the next decade became more real. In 1936, Hitler remilitarized the Rhineland in defiance of the Versailles Treaty and France did nothing to enforce the treaty, claiming that it was unprepared for war if Germany should decide to fight. France's best time to negotiate had been squandered, just as Obama squandered the U.S.'s best time in 2015. In 2025, the U.S. will be in a much weaker position, possibly not even able to respond to Iran at all.

## Scenarios

If the Progressive government fails to respond reasonably to Starve the Beast and, instead, uses force to exert its authority, then the United States will most likely not exist as a single political entity in 2025. Four options are on the table: (1) the U.S. maintains itself as currently organized with fifty states; (2) it joins Canada and Mexico in forming the North American Union (NAU) as will be discussed in

249

Chapter 9; (3) it is broken up into multiple countries based on ethnic and geographical factors as discussed in Chapter 5; or (4) it becomes involved in a ruinous civil war, destroying the very fabric and foundation of the nation for all time.

The first option is totally dependent on the speed by which Progressives proceed with their fundamental transformation of the U.S., but even if still intact in 2025, the nation will be far weaker than at present. The ruling Progressive politicians in the U.S. or NAU if the second option becomes reality, will be unable to halt Iran from becoming a nuclear nation, and a world-wide nuclear war can easily erupt before 2035. In the third option there is no longer a U.S., and the fourth option, in which the U.S. is involved in a civil war, means the U.S. will be a marginal player in the international scene and have little say for hundreds of years.

Most interesting is the third case. In it the question arises as to which of the new nations receive the current military equipment and stores, including nuclear capability. The breakup of the Soviet Union is the only precedent available, and, in its case, the various breakaway states—already in place before the breakup—seized the military equipment within their boundaries. Fortunately for the world, they dissembled all nuclear weapons in their possession (some sixty-five hundred) and returned them to Russia, now the only nuclear nation of the former USSR. However, the new nations formed by the breakup of the United States may not emerge in an orderly fashion. Boundaries of the new countries are sure to be disputed, and the reasons for their formation will include various factors, such as religion, language, race, ethnicity, and the necessity to become economically viable.

Another lesson from the Soviet collapse is that the various Soviet Socialist Republics generally demanded the return of their levies and military formations from the Red Army, Navy, and Air Force. They were to be sent back to their home state when de-mobilized from foreign military installations and those in other SSRs.[212] As bases emptied, military equipment disappeared: some sold to any ready buyer, some seized by the state in which the base was located, and some taken by the troops to wherever they were headed.

After the early riots from 1988 to 1990, the Red Army stood

down and played no part in attempting to uphold the USSR, slow down its disintegration, or even salvage a modicum of its greatness. The Soviet Navy was allowed to rust in its harbors, and the Air force stood idle, waiting for its aircraft to be broken up for scrap.

It is doubtful that the Progressives in Washington will allow the same scenario to unfold in the U.S. Compromise is not their strongpoint and they believe the future of mankind depends on their prevailing at all times. With sixty million gun owners in the U.S. and much of the armed forces (and law enforcement) apparently opposing Progressive rule, it appears that armed conflict will erupt in some locales.

It seems probable that Progressives will fail to secure the military even in the face of a possible revolution. They have assaulted traditional American values, morals, and even very unwisely denigrated military service. Progressives are—and will be—perceived as usurpers by many in military uniform, not the least because Progressives generally have shunned military service. A large number of veterans who have fought for America's freedoms can be expected to choose the patriot side against an inert Washington and its authoritarian, Progressive rule. It has not been the veterans and patriots who have abandoned America and God, it has been the Progressives, and they have brought about a polarization in American politics every bit as unbridgeable as that between North and South in 1860.

Christians want their Christian culture and way of life to continue as it has since the nation's founding, while Progressives want it to end. Yet Christians get blamed for being intransigent? Do Christians have to compromise their beliefs because some politician who has never shoveled a walk or mowed a lawn says a religious answer to an issue isn't sufficient?

At the sixth annual Women in The World Summit, Progressive presidential candidate Hillary Clinton, said that "...religious beliefs...have to be changed." Clearly she was saying that religious beliefs had to conform to Progressive dogma. If Christians do not change their beliefs, they will be blamed for the failures of Progressive politics.[213]

What follows should be considered a worst-case scenario, and it is dependent upon Progressive intransigence and stubbornness.

As individuals begin to Starve The Beast and their actions begin to have effect, Progressive outlets like CBS, NBC, ABC, and the rabidly Progressive cable news networks,CNN and MSNBC, will come at patriots with all guns blazing. They will feature daily sound bites from Progressives Hillary Clinton, President Obama, Senate Minority Leader Harry Reid, and House Minority Leader Nancy Pelosi. That can be expected, but what might not be anticipated is that there will be no support at all from the Republican establishment in Congress. Most conservatives will be silent, and the RINOS will deplore any action on the part of private citizens to force the Federal Government to do its job. Patriots who prize individual liberty will be on their own, supported only by the various Tea Party groups that are headed by individuals not afraid to stand up for their beliefs.

The propaganda will be deafening, but, worst of all, will be what is done in the classroom: teachers will lambast patriots as a Fifth Column, racists, haters, traitors, communists, fascists, criminals, and a whole array of negative characterizations to win the children over to their Progressive position. Patriots will become robber barons, not wanting to pay taxes, seeking to destroy the earth, taking away school lunches and starving children, murdering seniors by ruining Social Security and Medicare—actually, all of the problems the government has not been able to solve for years will become the fault of patriots wanting to Starve The Beast. Conservatives have always been blamed for the ills of the world by Progressives, so none of this will be new. I will, however, increase by several orders of magnitude.

Probably the worst demonizing will occur as contributions to colleges and universities decline. The guns fired at people Starving The Beast by the educational establishment and government will be thunderous; patriots will be ruining America's future, denying minorities their right to a good education, pushing America back into the Dark Ages, pressing an anti-education agenda, destroying freedom of thought and academic inquiry—in short, all those things that Progressives are themselves doing every day to gain authoritarian control over the United States.

In an early counter-move, Progressives probably will impose a tax specifically to aid education, both K-12 and college education, and this will probably be a wealth tax on property, both tangible and intangible. In addition, it can be expected that congress will enact a law making education free through four years of college, and subsequent study will be heavily subsidized. Progressives will trumpet the creation of another "right," and anyone opposing that right will be attacked without mercy.

Except for young people set to receive the benefits of a free college education, such measures will be hugely unpopular. But Progressives don't care about the fast-disappearing middle class or the elderly—their usefulness is limited to paying taxes, and hopefully they will have the good grace to die before they are a burden on the socialistic universal health care system. As in Nazi Germany or Mao's Cultural Revolution, the fascist Progressives assume they will win simply by turning the young against their elders. But to accomplish this, Christianity must be marginalized so young people look to the government (and the earth) as their god and arbiter of morality, not Jesus and Christian teaching. That is one of Progressivism's major vulnerabilities for political action: they have not yet sufficiently marginalized Christianity to the point that its moral hold on America is weak enough for Progressives to ram through their agenda without fear of failure.

As the crisis deepens, most foreign goods will become impossibly expensive for Americans, and trade will come to a standstill, further eroding federal revenues and the ability of the United States government to meet its foreign obligations. Food will disappear off store shelves at an alarming rate, and in the resulting panic, government will ration food. At some point—probably early in the collapse, or as the cause—the dollar will cease being the world's reserve currency, and will face a series of devaluations. Many illegal aliens will be forced to return home to find employment. Gold and silver values will soar, and the elites will impose draconian wage and price controls on American citizens.

Sooner or later, economic analysts will discover that many Americans are not spending money under any circumstances, and that taxes on incomes, sales, and goods will be inadequate to meet current obligations by a wide margin, to say nothing of future ones. Hoarding will be declared illegal, and an extraordinary tax on wealth should follow, mainly on securities and property, but those taxes will fall on the wealthy and people who have maintained extravagant lifestyles , precisely those who make up the governing elite.

Like rats fleeing a sinking ship, elites will depart for foreign countries to escape confiscatory taxes, and revenues will fall still farther below expectations Government will strengthen the law concerning Americans moving to foreign nations by increasing the exit tax to extraordinary proportions and making re-entry extremely difficult.

For the moment, the U.S. is the only country in the Organization for Economic Co-operation and Development that requires citizens living abroad to pay domestic income taxes, even though they receive no services. A penalty for living abroad will no doubt follow the current one that just went into effect.[214] The number of American expatriates living abroad has already ballooned by a factor of one hundred from 1966 to 2015, and the government is attempting to stem that exodus through the Foreign Asset Tax Compliance Act (FATCA). The next two years will determine if that effort is successful or counter-productive.

For the ordinary citizen across the country, the primary problem will be the availability of food. Riots will undoubtedly occur in large cities, particularly in minority areas, and what available food there is will quickly disappear. Even with ration cards, there will be no food to buy. Foreign nations will not ship food to the U.S., as there will be no possibility of receiving payment. NSA will comb through credit card purchases of food on the Internet, and law enforcement will be charged with confiscating those supplies to feed starving people.[215] However, citizens preparing for a collapse are in a tiny minority, probably in the area of one to three percent, and little will be gained by targeting these preppers.[216] Gasoline will be rationed as supplies of crude oil from overseas are suspended, and most people will be trapped in the large cities where they'll face starvation.

Progressives in government will become desperate to do everything in their power to raise revenues and provide food to their backers. Martial law, asset confiscation, impressment, relocation, internment, and all sorts of actions must be expected. As the Progressive government becomes increasingly dictatorial and oppressive, passive citizen resistance will increase. Minority leaders will probably claim that blacks and Hispanics are being singled out for extermination by starvation—they already are being exterminated, through abortion by Planned Parenthood—and rioting will probably become extremely ugly. Massive legal and extralegal civil resistance will most likely take place throughout the nation, and the riots in Cairo in 2012 may be nothing compared to those that might happen in New York.

During World War I, the Progressive Woodrow Wilson arrested nearly a quarter million American citizens for opposing his interventionist policy and taking the country into the war. Anyone who didn't pivot with Wilson, from non-intervention to fighting against the Central Powers, found themselves in trouble with the government and, frequently, in jail. The effects of the Espionage and Sedition Acts of 1917 and 1918 will prove to be tiny warm-ups to what will follow in the looming economic collapse. Instead of a quarter million arrests, the numbers will go into the tens of millions. The FEMA camps will be stuffed to the gills, and Hitler's holocaust will be easily eclipsed.

Once the beast has become fully awakened to its peril, it will devour everyone and anything to stay alive. Progressives will blame everything on hoarders—people not spending their hard-earned funds in order to pay taxes as government expects. Americans will be told to report hoarders, and many citizens will eagerly comply to settle old scores or because they will feel threatened by the potential loss of government goodies coming their way. Banks will be required to report account holders with suspiciously low activity, and the government will seize the databases of credit cards and monitor activity by all individuals. People with low activity on their cards coupled with low bank account activity will be targeted for investigation as hoarders.

As Progressives begin confiscating precious metals, they will probably impose a minimum tax on all Americans. Failure to pay the minimum tax will mean the confiscation of private property from up to three-fourths of the American population. At some point, armed rebellion will probably break out in various areas, particularly when government officials attempt to seize property for non-payment of the minimum tax. That will probably encourage large numbers of local law enforcement to abandon the remote Progressives to their fate and join their neighbors. National Guard units and large segments of the American Armed Forces will probably join the rebellion. Foreign troops will be brought in to subdue American citizens, and American politicians will suddenly discover those troops, particularly the Chinese, expect to receive American property in payment. Government by the people, for the people, and of the people will become a distant memory among those individuals that know it once existed.

If this scenario sounds fanciful, it is possible that the collapse will not be so jarring. But the collection of revenues by the government depends on the citizenry continuing to spend like drunken sailors as if there is no tomorrow. Half of the American population pays no income tax at all, but they pay enormous amounts into local, state and federal coffers with every expenditure in their daily lives. The Progressive government must keep that spending rate high at all costs, and it will do everything in its power to force people to spend. Perhaps bank account balances will be taxed, perhaps bank accounts will be seized as they were in Cyprus, perhaps a minimum tax will be instituted early, perhaps a national sales tax will be instituted to obtain revenues, perhaps a head tax—perhaps, perhaps, perhaps…

Of course, additional taxes on wealth are inevitable, and, although they will raise revenue temporarily, the long term effect will be disastrous. With the exception of certain personal property taxes and real property taxes, Americans are not accustomed to having to pay taxes on wealth so directly. Some states already tax wealth in the form of securities such as stocks and bonds, and eventually the Federal Government will follow suit and with much higher rates. The reaction will not be pretty, especially among people living on wages or benefits coming from the government. Those wages and benefits are currently seen as entitlements, not stipends for their support of government policies, as well as to keep certain politicians in office.

The EPA will probably become the agency of choice to punish resisting Americans in non-urban environments. Following the Supreme Court's decision in *Sackett v. the Environmental Protection Agency*, the EPA has strengthened its administrative procedures and become extremely powerful. The agency can declare an area to be a "wetland" at its sole discretion, then fine the property owner up to $75,000.00 per day for having made improvements to his property. The EPA can schedule an administrative hearing on the matter before an EPA-chosen arbitrator at a time and place chosen by the EPA, and seize the property owner's assets and garnish his wages, all without invoking the court system. The property owner is assumed to be guilty and must file suit against the EPA and prove his innocence in court, all at his own cost. These rules and regulations were put into place by unaccountable EPA bureaucrats through the simple expedient of publishing them in the Federal Register. Pretty slick, huh?

This book will no doubt be confiscated, and simply possessing it may subject an individual to extreme penalties such as the confiscation of all his tangible property. The government most likely will make arbitrary tax assessments and send tax collectors to seize funds, and if sufficient funds are not obtained, seize personal property as well. Since 1788, the people of the United States have not experienced tax collectors with the power to arbitrarily seize property and put people in confinement if tax levies cannot be satisfied, but they probably will if events unfold as discussed. In short, the American government will punish American citizens severely for not maintaining Progressive functionaries in the lifestyle to which they have become accustomed, and all blame will fall on the American people, not the Progressives.

Perversely, it will be the people who have not elected to Starve The Beast on whom the government measures will fall most harshly. They are the ones who will possess the tangible property that Progressives can most easily attach or confiscate, and those with bank accounts that will be most easily stolen. As repressive measures begin, many people will seek to protect or hide their assets, but it will be too late

Government computers will work day and night, emails will be scanned for property data, telephone conversations processed, and the modern surveillance state will reach its logical conclusion. The "metadata" collection program by NSA will be enhanced and extended, and the surveillance of American citizens by the government will reach heights only dreamed about by Stalin. If necessary, the Federal Government will outlaw the ownership of real property, reverting to the medieval system wherein all real property belonged to the king (the government), and people possessed property only by government's indulgence.

On the other hand, it is possible that the Federal Government will be paralyzed by what is, in effect, a strike by the people the government counting on to continue funding its extravagances. If so, the cities in America will turn into one vast Detroit, with their high-end properties being abandoned and allowed to go back to nature. The predictions of up to ninety percent of Americans perishing in the first year of a general economic collapse might come true, and Agenda 21 will be fulfilled insofar as the United States is concerned.

Agenda 21 posits that fossil fuel energy is unsustainable, along with power lines, paved roads, dams, grazing animals, golf courses, cities as we know them, and, essentially, all modern conveniences. The world will be reduced to an agrarian society with a small fraction of today's population allowed to live under full population control by a global government.

The question is, under Agenda 21, who will be allowed to survive? Certainly not Americans, as we have been in the forefront of using up the earth's resources with our modern technology. Europeans believe they will survive because they were the first to recognize the problem of the population bomb, but the Chinese, Indians, Muslims, Latin Americans, and Africans have yet to weigh in. Europe is on track to become predominately Muslim by 2060, and caucasians are on their way out. Possibly a token number of Americans will be retained, no doubt from the Eastern and West Coast elites, but, in between, it will most likely be the readers of this book.

Some will argue that Americans need to stay the course and ride out the troubled times. The same attitude was prevalent in the 1930s in Nazi Germany among the Jewish population, and, for them, it worked out as well then as it will now for Americans.

"Hope" is a slogan, not a strategy. What the American people are not being told by the political class of Progressives is staggering. Every dime ever collected from Americans for Social Security has already been spent, and the Social Security Administration possesses only promises by the Federal Government to meet future Social Security obligations up to a certain amount. That those obligations can only be met by increased borrowing is not told to the American people. And borrowing can go on only for so long.

The wealth (net worth) of the United States and its citizens has been estimated at almost fifty-five trillion dollars in 2009—with twenty-five trillion dollars of America's assets owned by foreign governments and foreign nationals, yet the unfunded liabilities of the federal government at the same time were over a hundred and ninetcen trillion.[217] By 2015, the unfunded liabilities have been variously estimated at over two hundred and thirty trillion, and increasing astronomically every day. Official estimates of unfunded liabilities have been cut in half so as to not panic the people, but, by any number, the United States is bankrupt, and the situation is getting worse every year.

Apparently, Progressives believe there is still time to prepare for the collapse as they continue to put measures into effect to control the American population rather than to address the problems weakening the nation every day. The camps for internment and resettlement already exist, and, in the near future, government will probably send individuals at odds with its actions to those camps for re-education. What failing to adopt the prescribed attitude will bring upon a citizen is anyone's guess. If this sounds like communist dialectical materialism tactics, it's because it is. There is little difference in the tactics of American Progressives and those of Stalin or Mao.

For those individuals who believe that the Homeland Security camps will be relatively benign, they need to think again. For years, Americans have seen leftists and celebrities go to prison and come out stronger, or at least no worse for the experience. That was because they supported Progressivism, and had friends in government and the elite class. The new American patriots are not from the Progressive left, but are populists, demanding individual liberty like our forefathers. Those being taken into custody will not be supporters of the collective, but among those opposing it, and no mercy can be expected.

As in American prisons today, gang affiliation will be a prisoner's salvation, and patriots will be seen by gang members, particularly the blacks, Hispanics, Asians, and Russians, as people attempting to overturn the system of corruption and criminal opportunity they know so well. Therefore, patriots will be treated as enemies. Guards and administrators will also see patriots as a serious threat to their well-being, and can be expected to turn a blind eye toward their fate. All of them, the inmates and their keepers, have a vested interest in seeing the Progressive system of corrections continue as it, and patriots will be the enemies of them all.

Probably ninety percent of incarcerated male patriots will be raped within a week of being released into the general camp or prison population, and female prisoners will be brutalized daily. Families will be separated, and the children subjected to brutal re-education. Those who resist will be abused and suffer fatal accidents on a scale not seen since the Gulag of the Soviet Union or the concentration camps of Nazi Germany. Since patriots are not hardened criminals and experienced survivors in prison environments, the horrors of rape and mutilation will fall heavily on them, many committing suicide as a result.

Many patriots will probably not even survive to reach the camps, as they will be seen by Progressives and those in their employ as enemies of mankind. In a recent conversation among patriots concerning the possibilities of being shot down at will, like what occurred to the wife at Ruby Ridge (she was standing unarmed and holding her baby behind a door, and the shooter was later promoted), a young adult female thought no one would shoot her for expressing her beliefs. An ex-marine sniper said quietly, "They will shoot anyone they are ordered to." The female was shocked that Americans of any persuasion could be so callous and readily take a human life. She had much to learn.

More than likely, the individual ordering the murder will be on the other end of a wireless communication and not even see who is being shot. In 1968, Lieutenant Calley was allegedly ordered by his company commander, Captain Medina, to shoot the Vietnamese civilians in My Lai. He was talking on a radio, and didn't see the civilians lined up or tumble into the ditch. Today, commanders can sit at a computer screen, issue orders, and direct his troops in perfect safety and detachment. Death on the battlefield has become impersonal—like when a bomber pilot drops his bombs, he never sees the carnage that results.

In short, patriots can expect no mercy and would be well advised to fight to the death.

Bill O'Reilly, Sean Hannity, Laura Ingraham, and other Roman Catholic commentators like to say that a citizen might not care for the president as an individual, but the of the president must be respected. This is akin to saluting in the military—a soldier salutes the rank rather than the individual.

Of course, this is hogwash. A president takes an oath to uphold and defend the Constitution. If he actively undermines it and flaunts his disrespect of the Constitution, neither the individual nor the office is deserving of respect. Perhaps it is more appropriate to say a citizen should be loyal to the Constitution. If a president openly acts in opposition to the Constitution, which individual, the citizen or the president, is guilty of treason?

It is important to understand which groups will take the side of the Progressive government to help suppress any attempt to establish fiscal responsibility and restore America to greatness. Of course, there will be individuals who will be exceptions in every group, but the list in Appendix C presents relatively accurate battle lines. The list in is not meant to be exclusive, but is certainly useful as a starting point for consideration.

True Progressives will oppose patriots, but many people in the private sector have been socialized by Progressive schooling to the point that they unreservedly trust the government. They will see individuals who are even remotely taking action to restore individual liberty as seditious, and will brand them as traitors. Coupling these groups with those dependent on government for goodies, possibly fifty to sixty-five percent of Americans will continue to support any Progressive government. Of that number, probably half have been enfeebled through dependent living, and will only do so passively. On the other hand, much of the support for liberty will come from senior citizens who will also be passive in any potential conflict. In any case, it will be a minority revolution, much like the one in 1775.

## Current Trends and Actions

So what are the trends and actions currently being taken by the Progressive government of Barack Obama? How close are we to realizing a fully tyrannical Federal Government? ?

The answer is, "very close."

In 2010, the U.S. Army issued a manual for the internment and resettlement of U.S. citizens within the United States, and established authorities, policies and procedures, and, in 2015, a multi-state exercise was conducted to test the operational methodologies in the manual.[218]

The Department of Homeland Security has been building camps to process and house American citizens in the continental U.S., and the prospect of a Progressive government clamping down on a recalcitrant citizenry is now a reality DHS possesses a great deal of infrastructure to control the citizenry, and this capability would not have been built without the intent to use it. At the same time, Government employees have become a protected class, and the penalties for actions against a federal employee are punished more severely than the same action against a private citizen. Clearly, the government has taken action to protect its handmaidens and loyal subjects. In short, George Orwell's *Animal Farm* has become a reality: all pigs are equal, but some pigs are more equal than others.

Under the Obama Administration government surveillance of private citizens has reached unthinkable proportions. Not only had the capability for the collection and analysis of all cell phone conversations been put into place, but emails are routinely collected from service providers and analyzed for key words of interest. The encoding of communications without providing a decryption key to the Federal Government has become unlawful so individuals cannot communicate with one another without government snoopers being able to know what was said. Organizations supporting the Constitution and those taking a conservative position on political issues have been specifically targeted for harassment, not only by the IRS, but by a host of other federal agencies. American citizens are increasingly in need of protection from their own government rather than from what is happening elsewhere, such as in the Middle East.

Progressive initiatives have continued without letup. A definition for "hate crimes" was promulgated, and such crimes became subject to additional and stiffer penalties. This was making a belief or opinion unlawful, and prosecutors of such crimes have become known as the "thought police." Individuals making politically incorrect statements or ones whereby anyone might take offense became attacked with federal support, many losing their jobs or businesses. Courts have routinely sentenced individuals skeptical of the virtues of Progressivism to "sensitivity training," "anger management sessions," and various other trendy but controversial psychological treatments to bring their thoughts into agreement with approved positions. All this began to approximate communist re-education camps and practices in China, the Soviet Union, and Vietnam, and took place without citizen outcry. To object might cause a person to be forced into such re-education themselves.

Veterans were specifically targeted as potential terrorists, as they were men and women who had fought for liberty once and might do so again. Janet Napolitano, Homeland Security Secretary from 2009 to 2013 and currently president of the University of California system, mentioned veterans, pro-life supporters, "Tea Partiers," and 2nd Amendment supporters as potential (and even possibly actual) domestic terrorists. She stated that undermining respect for Obama's policies was the first step toward violent opposition, and she would "snuff out" trouble before things got out of hand. Obviously, she would eliminate this work and "snuff out" its author if she were still in power. Her policies were echoed by Democrat politicians, and a number of senators specifically asked the IRS to harass "Tea Party" and "Patriot" organizations as much as it could.

Freedom of thought, speech, religion, and assembly, are fast becoming a distant memory.

As significant numbers of citizens begin Starving the Beast, surveillance of the American citizenry by the Federal Government will probably go into overdrive. The NSA, FBI, IRS, and Homeland Security will double in size, then triple. Those states that have not adopted "Real ID" on their driver's licenses will be forced to institute the program regardless of any objections or reliance on the 10th Amendment. By 2013, more than half of the states had already complied, and license images were being sent to the Federal Government to help identify people through the ubiquitous camera surveillance throughout the country by security systems and law enforcement agencies.

For most people, it is already too late to stop driving to avoid having a permanent record made of their likeness in federal archives for population control. Progressives are opposed to requiring a photo ID to vote, however. Minority groups have objected under the correct assumption that Real ID technology will be used to identify and control them, although, at the same time, it would be a huge step toward eliminating election fraud. Since minority groups support Progressive initiatives in perfect lock-step, they are given a pass on Real-ID. Besides, requiring photo IDs for voting would be counter-productive—it would destroy the Progressive election machines and the Democrat Party's ability to control the vote in major cities.

Between bank and credit card records, Progressives will be able to identify hoarders unless citizens take action to lower transactions before working to Starve The Beast. In particular, reciprocal giving involves few, if any, financial transactions, and all transactions can disappear, except for income by direct deposit or check, and expenses such as gasoline, cable, telephone, mortgage payments, rent, and insurance. Make no mistake; Progressives will be able to see that pattern, and, if provoked, will come calling. Everyone must understand that lying to a federal officer is a crime, so the best course of action is to refuse to talk with any law enforcement officer or federal agent unless they furnish a subpoena. Citizens must stand on their ever-diminishing rights, and, if the visitor is within the citizen's curtilage (discussed below), he should be politely, but firmly, told to remove himself from the citizen's curtilage or be subject to arrest for trespassing.

Few citizens are even aware of what curtilage is, but all federal officers know the concept thoroughly even if they play dumb and claim no understanding. Curtilage is an important concept in American common law. It is a person's home and the area surrounding his house or dwelling that the resident looks upon as an extension of his private space. The U.S. Supreme Court noted in *United States v. Dunn, 480 U.S. 294 (1987),* that curtilage is the area immediately surrounding a residence that "harbors the intimate activity associated with the sanctity of a man's home and the privacies of life."[219] Curtilage, like a house, is protected under the 4th Amendment from unreasonable searches and seizures. In effect, law enforcement acting without a legal warrant may be turned away from the areas defined as curtilage rather than the person's actual house or home, thus making detached garages, shops, and lawns protected areas. In some states, the "castle laws" apply to curtilage rather than the interior of a person's home, thereby legalizing the defense of one's family outside the actual house. The reader is encouraged to research how curtilage is treated in his home state.

Determining the boundaries of curtilage is imprecise and subject to judicial determination. There are generally four factors taken into account to classify an area as curtilage: (1) the distance from the home—the closer to the home, the more definite the curtilage; (2) whether or not the home is surrounded by an enclosure—if so, the enclosure will often define the curtilage; (3) the nature of use for the area. In a rural setting, the outbuildings often determine the curtilage, including such things as wood piles, shops, storage sheds, and the area between them (sometimes called a "compound.") The more an area is used for daily or domestic activities, the more likely it will be within the curtilage. And (4) the steps taken by the resident to protect the area from public view. Hedges, trees, board fences, and warning signs will help define an area as curtilage. If a swimming pool is located in the front yard with a fence of shrubs shielding it from the public, a strong case can be made that the pool and its surrounding area are curtilage. One can also put up a sign such as "Begin Curtilage" to strengthen the case for an area being curtilage. In apartment buildings and other urban environments, curtilage becomes confined to one's immediate living space, and, in the case of an apartment, the citizen's rights are further limited.

In his Executive Order on National Defense Resource Preparedness, issued March 16, 2012, President Obama authorized the secretaries of six federal departments to seize, control, and distribute resources throughout the United States as they saw fit: the Secretary of Agriculture with respect to food resources, facilities, farm equipment, and commercial fertilizer; the Secretary of Energy with respect to all forms of energy; the Secretary of Health and Human Services with respect to health resources; the Secretary of Transportation with respect to all forms of civil transportation; the Secretary of Defense with respect to water resources; and the Secretary of Commerce with respect to all other supplies, services, and facilities, including construction materials. The key authority granted to each secretary was to "take actions necessary to ensure the availability of adequate resources." The secretary of each resource department "may use the authority of section 101(a) of the Act, 50 U.S.C. App. 2071(a), to control the general distribution of any material (including applicable services) in the civilian market."[220]

In effect, this executive order gave the Federal Government the authority to seize any hoarded supplies and re-distribute them as it sees fit, and the compensation may be in whatever form and amount it determines. Given this executive order, it is imperative that supplies be hidden from snoopers as thoroughly as possible, or a citizen may find himself the proud owner of a worthless pile of script for his hard-earned and collected survival supplies.

As mentioned earlier, on February 12, 2010, the Army Chief of Staff, General George W. Casey, Jr., under the direction of the

Secretary of the Army, issued Field Manual FM 3-39.40, Internment and Resettlement Operations, that established the Army's role in collecting civilians, interning them as was done to Japanese nationals and ethnic Japanese-Americans during World War II, and resettling them in camps as necessary.[221]

This three hundred and twenty-six page field manual, distributed to the Army, Army National Guard, and Army Reserve, specifically addressed domestic operations. It was issued after most American forces had been withdrawn from Iraq, and the planned withdrawal from Afghanistan had already been announced. Some people have noted that the Federal Emergency Management Agency (FEMA) has set up a number of camps, ostensibly to temporarily house refugees from natural disasters. Sure enough, FM 3-39.40 specifically mentions FEMA and Homeland Security as agencies to be involved in the Army's internment and resettlement program.

In Section 1-40: "Agencies Concerned with Internment and Resettlement," it lists the Department of Homeland Security, U.S. Immigration and Customs Enforcement (ICE), and FEMA as the agencies involved in internment-resettlement (I/R) operations.

Section 2-39: "Civil support is the Department of Defense support to U.S. civil authorities for domestic emergencies, and for designated law enforcement and other activities. Civil support includes operations that address the consequences of natural or man-made accidents, terrorist attacks, and incidents in the U.S."

Section 2-40: "The I/R tasks performed in support of civil support organizations are similar to those during combat operations, but the techniques and procedures are modified based on the special Operational Environments associated with operating within U.S. territory and according to the categories of individuals to be housed in I/R facilities. During long-term I/R operations, state and federal agencies and ...military police commanders must closely coordinate and synchronize their efforts."

Section 3-1 under "National and Theater Reporting Agencies", mentions a headquarters responsible for the issuance of blocks of Internal Serial Numbers (ISNs) for use in the continental U.S. (CONUS). That means all American citizens are going to get ID numbers, and, no doubt, be issued photo IDs using Real ID technology.

Section 3-2: "The Theater Detainee Reporting Center...

functions as the field operations agency for the CONUS( Continental U.S.)-based U.S. Army National Detainee Reporting Center. It is the central agency responsible for maintaining information on detainees and their personal property…in CONUS."

Section 3-56: "The PSYOP [Psychological Operations] team…Develops PSYOP products that are designed to pacify and acclimate detainees or Displaced Civilians to accept U.S. I/R facility authority and regulations, identify malcontents, and political leaders within the facility who may try to organize resistance…[It] Develops and executes indoctrination programs to reduce or remove antagonistic attitudes... [It] Plans and executes a PSYOP program that produces an understanding and appreciation of U.S. policies and actions." This is political re-education, pure and simple.

Section 10-9: "All CONUS-based special operations forces are assigned to the U.S. Special Operations Command. Civil Affairs units are under the combatant command of U.S. Special Operations Command until control is given to one of the geographic combatant commanders."

Section 10-40: "Resettlement operations may be performed as domestic stability operations (due to noncombatant evacuation operations), or due to combat operations." The section continues in discussing the relevancy of Title 18, USC, Posse Comitatus Act, and how authorizations might be needed through presidential authority.

The history of federal control in emergencies goes back to the 1917, but, in 1976, Executive Order 11921 allowed the Federal Emergency Preparedness Agency, an agency most people have never heard of, to develop plans to establish control over the production and distribution of energy, food, wages, transportation facilities, etc., (actually almost everything needed by the public for survival), in any undefined national emergency.

Such planning, the passage of laws to control and snoop on domestic American citizens, and issuance of executive orders to that effect went on steroids under President Obama. In June of 2011, he established the rural councils to help control rural regions; in December 2011, the NDAA (National Defense Authorization Act) authorized the indefinite detention of US citizens; in February of 2012, Obama established a global development council. In March, he issued the National Defense Resource Preparedness Order, giving himself the power to seize practically everything in the U.S. He then signed Bill HR 347 into law on March 8, 2012. It was the so-called "Anti-Protest" bill because it curtailed American freedoms by criminalizing protests in the vicinity of the president. In May, he issued an executive order promoting international regulatory cooperation, and, in June, another executive order tightened federal control over all communication in the U.S.

But the stunner came on June 25, 2012 when Obama issued an executive order giving him an excuse to use his extraordinary powers with impunity. As mentioned in Chapter 3, Barack Obama declared a national emergency in an extension of Executive Order 13159 titled, "Russian Highly Enriched Uranium," stating that, in light of earlier policy EOs (12938, 13085), he found, "that the risk of nuclear proliferation created by the accumulation of a large volume of weapons-usable fission material in the territory of the Russian federation continues to constitute an unusual and extraordinary threat to the national security and foreign policy of the United States, and hereby declare a national emergency to deal with that threat."

The United States was, therefore, put in a "National Emergency," so he could put his powers to use any time he wanted. This power extended through the 2012 election (it ended on December 25, 2012), and caused many citizens to believe that, had Obama been defeated in the election, he would have used his emergency powers to remain as president. In every respect, it was a daunting trial balloon, putting all Americans on notice that martial law is always only an executive order away, and the machinery for a Progressive suspension of citizen rights and the functioning of congress and the judiciary branch is already in place.

With all this power lined up against the American citizen, it appears that Starving The Beast is a long shot. Maybe, but it is the only shot Americans have. The patriots who signed the Declaration of Independence and the Articles of Association probably had less than a ten percent chance of surviving the next five years, but their long shot came in.

Today, the chances of restoring American liberty and preventing a Progressive takeover are still better than the chances in 1775, so there is some room for hope. Unfortunately, time is against the patriots as their children and grandchildren are being indoctrinated in school every day.

In 1775, time was against Great Britain, and the patriots grew stronger every day. Today, patriots are growing weaker with each passing year as the American population becomes steadily more socialized and less Christian.

What Americans forget is that Europeans were astounded when John Adams meekly accepted his defeat and vacated the White House in 1801 for Thomas Jefferson to occupy. The transfer of power was orderly and without incident, if not particularly friendly. In many countries today, that still doesn't happen. Election losers attempt to hold onto their power, and riots and civil wars result. Why hasn't that happened here before now? Partly because of American exceptionalism and its four great pillars, but, most of all, it is because of the country's Christian underpinning—that Americans are virtuous with a strict morality. Not to recognize the winner in an election would be immoral. Nixon had sufficient virtue to not contest the fraud in Texas and Illinois that gave JFK the election in 1960, Gore did not when Bush's margin of victory in Florida was slim in 2000. But Gore was a Progressive, and morality did not count.

Morality has nearly disappeared today, and there is a large number of people in power and positions of influence who aren't Christian and don't recognize any higher power than themselves. These are the moral relativists heard from every day, and they include President Obama. They're the ones who teach the children, stress political correctness, and think homosexuality is just another lifestyle. Unfortunately, history proves that a society without a firm moral base slides into decadence, and then disappears. Only drastic action can save the nation and keep the United States from going the way of all other societies once they became decadent and immoral.

Some believe the American basis in morality is still intact, but consider the following: Christian teaching says that homosexuality is an abomination, yet a Pew Research survey in 2013 found that thirty-five percent of those born prior to 1946 approved of same-sex marriage. Those born from 1946 to 1964 approved by forty-one percent, 1965 to 1980 by fifty-two percent, and those born after 1980 by sixty-six percent.[222] There it is—the destruction of the Christian moral base by public school teaching and government propaganda.

A Progressive government can use troops to maintain control, but it has no power to force people to spend.[223] We must remember that during World War II, when President Roosevelt said on a "Fireside Chat" that some item was not going to be rationed, everyone ran out and bought up that item to the limit of their funds. Why? Because the next day or so, that item was going to be rationed. The government telegraphs its punches by telling lies, and contrarians will have a field day. Although troops could be used to collect supplies and punish hoarders, it is more probable they will be needed to maintain order. Massachusetts National Guardsmen will be used to patrol Texas, and Texas Guardsmen will be sent to Massachusetts. It is a proven tactic to use troops from some remote place to control a population so they will not be sympathetic to the citizens and will fire into crowds as necessary.[224]

During the first two or three months of the collapse, the primary threat will come from a citizen's neighbors—those who have believed the government and made no preparations to protect and feed their families. As in the fable of the grasshopper and the ant, they will be the grasshopper wanting the product of the ant's industry. They will raid suspected hoarders, and, if they survive the confrontation but come away frustrated, they will inform on the suspected hoarders to the authorities. For the great mass of ordinary Americans, survival will depend on the degree of preparedness. Without food, water, and energy to maintain the grasshopper's feckless lifestyle, his situation will rapidly become desperate Government will initially attempt to feed the grasshoppers, but, eventually, troops and authorities will have to look out for themselves first and foremost. That's why so many forecasts of a total economic collapse in the United States feature such low survival rates. The U.S. military and National Guard have been downsized too far to be effective across the nation, and, besides, many of the soldiers, sailors, and airmen are conservative and not likely to support the Progressives against their American brothers.

What will develop over the several years following a collapse is anyone's guess, but it will probably entail a partitioning of the country into more homogenous ethnic blocks, and certainly a substantial regime change. What the new constitutions at the federal and state levels of the successor nations will be like will depend on their degree of socialization and how many Christians have survived.

If any.

# Chapter 8

## Risks and Rewards

### Progressivism's Fatal Flaw

In a conflict of convictions, the question is simple: which side possesses the most courage of its convictions? The one most dedicated to victory will surely win. So who is the most dedicated, Progressives attempting to install a dictatorship of the elite or Christian patriots intent on restoring American individual liberties and rolling back Progressivism?

Starve The Beast must be put into context with modern times, and a little history of the past century is required to understand Progressivism and its appeal to the modern politically apathetic individual.

In the early part of the twentieth century, World War I broke the back of France and Great Britain, and between the wars, pacifist sentiment ran strong, as did communism and appeasement. Germany quickly disposed of an enfeebled France (a condition that has worsened to the present day), and Great Britain was forced to rely on the United States and the Soviet Union to save it. Hitler never seriously intended to invade England, and he believed until 1941 that the British could be induced to see the light and collaborate like France.

Victories for the British were few and far between, and only against inferior or greatly outnumbered opponents. El Alamein was a victory due to overwhelming force and material—the force supplied by the British Commonwealth and the supplies by the United States. In fact, the British General Montgomery was only effective when he possessed huge advantages in men and material, the latter always supplied by the U.S.

France was unable to even put up a good showing in Indo-China in the early 1950s against the Vietnamese. Draftees could not be forced to serve outside of metropolitan France and there were inadequate volunteers. French leaders expected the U.S. to come save them once again, but Eisenhower had had enough of the French.

It took two wars to dampen American enthusiasm for military conflict. First, Korea was sold to the American people as a "police action," and the U.S. barely got out with a stalemate and an armistice, unable to achieve victory due to lack of popular support. Vietnam finally showed the limits of U.S. resolve. Although the U.S. Army fought better in Vietnam than in World War II and Korea (and in worse conditions), the Federal Government was unable to maintain popular support for the war and the troops involved after the spring of 1968. Civilian dedication to winning flagged, opposition to conducting the war increased, and the effort was doomed.

After defeating the Viet Cong and North Vietnamese offensive during Tet in 1968—one of the greatest victories for American arms since the Battle of Nashville—the American media headed by Progressive Walter Cronkite declared it a defeat, and forecast the best the U.S. could do was achieve a stalemate. Anti-war fervor rose to a fever pitch, and, from that point, political defeat was just a matter of time. Although Progressive President Kennedy had been responsible for greatly increasing the war effort and Progressive President Johnson sent in combat troops after the Gulf of Tonkin incidents, the war was seen as a loser to most Progressives. It was a distraction from the Progressive agenda they wished to pursue. Martin Luther King, Jr. was an early opponent of the war, saying, "We are taking black young men who have been crippled by our society, and sending them eight thousand miles away to guarantee liberties in Southeast Asia which they had not found in southwest Georgia and East Harlem." Johnson fell on his sword, and nothing Progressive President Richard Nixon could do would be acceptable to the Progressive Democrats controlling Congress.

The draft was suspended, the armed services were once again made strictly volunteer, and the "tarnished shield" limped along during the latter 1970s. Military veterans were often shunned by American society for two reasons: having "lost" the Vietnam War, and having served in the military at all. Propaganda against military service was extremely effective, and Vietnam was considered a bloody stain on the reputation of the U.S., even to the point of lowering the United States to a position of moral equivalence with the USSR.

When Jimmy Carter attempted to rescue American hostages in Iran in 1980, the effort was a disaster, and many citizens viewed the military as incompetent and useless. It was a dangerous time during which the U.S. survived only because the Soviets became embroiled in Afghanistan and experienced continual problems in adapting to emerging technologies, ones they were stealing wholesale from the U.S.

By the time Carter left office, women were being recruited to help maintain the military at reasonable strength levels. The U.S. became one of only three countries in the world to allow women in combat roles (the Israelis and Dutch were the other two at the time). Fortunately, President Reagan devoted his presidency to defeating and eliminating the "evil empire" of the USSR, and, by the end of 1991, that victory was complete. Reagan's success came as a huge surprise to Progressives, since not only was Reagan opposed by the Republican establishment, but Progressives believed the Soviet Union to be vastly stronger economically and technologically than it actually was. The American armed forces revived under Reagan, but then became the object of incessant cutbacks after the dissolution of the Soviet Union. By 2010, less than one and a half million individuals were serving in the armed forces, or less than one half of one percent of the U.S. population.[225] Military service had become no longer a duty for every able-bodied citizen, but, as President Obama inferred, simply the inevitable and undesirable lot for individuals who did not obtain a college education.

The key element overlooked by most political observers is the influence of religion on an individual's behavior and willingness to risk his life in any conflict, armed or merely one of convictions. Although the old saying is that "there are no atheists in a lifeboat," it is even more accurate to say that no atheists volunteer for low-paying military service unless compelled to do so. But there is an exception to that rule. Communists sometimes have volunteered in communist nations out of a sense of sacrifice to the collective or because they hated the opponent to an extreme, but even in World War II, the Soviet Union found that a more potent reason for fighting was patriotism for "Mother Russia."

In the United States, the elites in the twenty-first century have become overwhelmingly Progressive—and only nominally Christians, if at all—and they have a remarkable penchant for avoiding military service and risk-taking. Nor are Progressives the only elites who avoid military service. The entire lineup of Fox News commentators—Van Susteren, O'Reilly, Kelly, Hannity, Gutfeld, Bolling, the Panamanian-born Juan Williams, and Geraldo Rivera thrown in for good measure—haven't experienced a single day of military service. Notably, all are also Roman Catholic except Scientologist Van Susteren.

Attorney General Holder was correct, at least when speaking of Progressives or liberals, that the United States is a nation of cowards.[226] It was strange talk for someone who failed to serve his country in the armed forces, and although he was speaking specifically on race relations, the comment could be—and was—generalized to wider issues. He was clearly not speaking about Christians and Christian teaching.

Christians sometimes elect to die for the United States because it is seen as God's chosen land and the world's only representative democracy with its primary emphasis on individual liberty. They also are often willing to die for Christ and their beliefs. In either case, they expect to be rewarded in the afterlife for having done God's will, and living for His purpose.

But Progressives cannot look to another life, so they need to avoid all risk of dying before they have done everything they want to do. Progressives, therefore, have to find someone else to take risks and keep them in power to live the good live. They seek power and pleasure while Christians seek salvation, a concept in which death may even be sought and certainly comes before dishonor or being false to one's creed. Up to the present, however, Progressives has been able to manipulate the American public to do what was best for Progressives, even if it was not the best for the vast majority of the citizenry.

For example, the numbers of secular Jews are tiny when compared to the population of the world or even the U.S. Unable to protect themselves through force of arms, they have adopted a unique strategy since World War II: propagandize Christians to fight for them (and Israel) in part out of guilt for the Holocaust, and in part for Biblical reasons. Accordingly, a Holocaust museum was built in

Washington, D.C. and it receives substantial promotion, even though no holocaust ever occurred in the United States.

It is not a foreign nation that will bring down the American Republic, but rather, the Progressives within. But they are not willing to die for anything and cannot defeat a patriot revolution alone—they must find surrogates to do their heavy lifting. That significantly lessens the risk of failure for American patriots if they are willing to die for their country. However, once again, the prospect for success depends on timing—a dedicated minority of patriots must have reached the point where they are willing to die for the sake of their country and their children, and that minority must have reached the threshold where their numbers can repel foreign mercenaries and the zombie-like Progressive support from thoroughly propagandized Americans.

## Home Schooling & Education

The risk in Starving The Beast is that such action will merely speed up the economic collapse of the United States and bring about the Progressive's dream of an elitist authoritarian state before that threshold is reached. But, as pointed out in Chapter 6, Common Core and the educational establishment are churning out fully-committed socialists from the nation's public schools in great numbers, changing the demographics in political belief at a rapid rate. The only thing slowing down this progression is the incompetence of teachers and administrators. Parents are having little impact in delaying the imposition of Common Core, and Agenda 21 is being taught from kindergarten onward. The only option available to a parent to fight for his child's education and belief system is to home school, and, faced with the necessity to earn a living, many parents are unable to use that alternative.

Progressive Deweyism is universal, and there is no chance of reforming the educational establishment since it is firmly wedded to Progressive ideology, just as schoolteachers in Germany in 1939 were wedded to Nazism. The school system must be destroyed in order to be rebuilt. Many Americans still believe that higher education is the pathway to success, but it is merely an illusion due to "creeping credentialism." Many positions currently require a college degree, but only because both the high school and college degrees have become so cheapened. "No Child Left Behind" really meant "no child is required to learn anything to advance." College degrees have been cheapened to the point that degrees in many disciplines are meaningless. Even PhDs can be easily obtained if the student understands that he is slave labor to his advisor. All he has to do is work like a slave on his advisor's (or some other department member's) research project, gain permission to use a part of it for his dissertation, and thereby earn his union card to a lifetime of ease and guaranteed employment (and pension) as a college professor.

The educational establishment jealously guards the entry portals to those selected institutions that will determine an individual's success or failure in an increasingly bureaucratically controlled government and crony capitalist private sector. Ivy League schools clearly dominate government, and admission is carefully controlled to ensure their graduates will have the "right stuff," much like the schools that have dominated the British government for the last one hundred and thirty years.

A strict hierarchy is used to fill their freshman slots. First are athletic scholarships that build winning teams to attract positive publicity and alumni contributions (if the school has an athletic program). Second are children of international, national, and regional personalities, again to keep the school represented in high places and ensure its influence. Children of foreign governmental officials and foreigners of great wealth fall into this category and are as high on the list as American VIPs. Third are the admissions necessary to fulfill racial and diversity goals, including foreign students. Unfortunately, this then often lowers average entry test scores. Fourth are applicants from families who have made significant contributions to the college, often in the millions of dollars. This is the vehicle that keeps Asian enrollment high, as families will often begin donating to their school of choice at the birth of a child, and eighteen years later, their contributions ensure that child will be accepted for enrollment. Fifth are legacies—children of alumni. The selection here is often made again on the level of contributions made by the alumni. Sixth and last are applicants from the great unwashed, and often there are no slots for these applicants at all.

If there are admission slots still open when the sixth tier applicants are considered, the process will be weighted heavily in favor of children of recent immigrants, (if they were missed in filling racial and ethnic quotas) who can be easily propagandized with Progressivism, and can become important in dealing with their parents' country for the United States. Next to be considered are qualifications, indicated by letters of recommendation, test scores, and high school performance, but the most important of these factors are the written essay and subsequent interview by an assigned alumnus. Here is where a determination is made as to the applicant's probability of success in life, and whether or not the individual will be a credit to the college, become a committed Progressive, and eventually remit substantial contributions. Although religious questions will not be asked, a determination will be made as to the applicant's religion and the degree of importance of that religion in his life. Secular Jews and atheists are preferred, and if the applicant is Christian, nominal membership is preferred over being devout. Evangelical Christians need not apply.

Personal appearance is also important.The individual should be tall, athletic, and handsome or beautiful. "Type A" personalities are sought, along with the applicant possessing confidence and expressing goals with the intention of their attainment. Those goals should be in a national or international career, probably the best being in international foundations, a national government, or international banking, economics, or statesmanship. Desiring to gain a good education and then work in a family business is seen as being more appropriate to a run-of-the-mill state university. Last, but not least, conservatives of all stripes are shunned, and political questions are sometimes used to ferret out an applicant's attitude toward Progressivism. If he believes in fiscal responsibility or the Constitution, the interviewee will be headed to a no-name college or university.

Although the above is categorically denied by admissions personnel at top-rated universities, the selections and compositions of freshman classes prove otherwise. For example, in 1998, a seventeen -ear-old male applied for admission to Yale, Harvard, Princeton, and Stanford. His mother was a Stanford graduate, and she took him to visit a number of faculty members on campus. He had received maximum scores on the SAT and ACT exams, been co-valedictorian at a large suburban Midwestern high school, lettered in golf, was a National Science Foundation Scholar, and Eagle Scout.

Unfortunately, in his essay he failed to mention international and national employment interests, was a Christian, conservative, and helped meet no diversity goal. The result was a two-line rejection from Harvard, Yale, and Princeton, all on the same day, and a one paragraph rejection from Stanford on the next. He did, however, receive a nomination from his congressman to the Naval Academy. Several university personnel familiar with the admissions procedures in Ivy League schools opined that the boy's application was never even considered at Yale, Harvard, and Princeton.

In the 2015 college acceptance season, a number of applicants to Ivy League schools received multiple acceptance letters, and were able to take their pick of schools. The common characteristic was that they belonged to a minority group and were the children of immigrants.[227] Wags quickly noted the trend, and opined that Americans who could claim American ancestry from before 1896 were no longer wanted at America's top universities. It does not take a rocket scientist to understand what that policy means for the future of our republic. Leaders are no longer being taken from Americans who might cherish American common law, exceptionalism, and traditional institutions.

Since Starving the Beast includes the termination of contributions to higher education until academics accept citizen control, not only will tuition and fees increase, but the institutions' dependence on government grants will rise significantly. The government will be forced to greatly increase subsidies to universities, pushing government ever more deeply in crisis, and driving many colleges into insolvency.

The risks in not supporting the teacher's unions in K-12 education and ending contributions to higher education may look enormous, but, in actuality, they are not. In K-12 education, the situation simply cannot become worse than it is today even if teachers strike and close down all public schools. There are still enough teachers and parents with knowledge and experience to teach American children, although they will undoubtedly have to use homes, churches, and other makeshift facilities. The school buildings of today are little more than fancy monuments to school administrators and politicians, and often add little or nothing to a student's education. There are other benefits to teachers striking:

alternative education will only be provided to American children, a situation that will drive illegal aliens back to their homelands, and education costs will decrease dramatically. The only risk is that not all state legislatures will have the morality of the one in Wisconsin, and not all governors will have the courage of a Scott Walker to hold the line and think first of the children, rather than building political strength catering to a teachers' union.

In colleges and universities, the situation is somewhat different. If public schools were truly educating students through twelfth grade—which they are not—the vast majority of high school graduates would be ready to take their place in the adult world and earn a respectable living. Probably not more than a third of college graduates today gain an educational level above what they should have attained in high school, and those students are swelling college numbers beyond all reason, thereby degrading the educational process. At one time it could be assumed that an individual had obtained certain reading, writing, and mathematical skills from a high school education. Now, that cannot even be assumed for many college degrees, particularly those in education, general studies, women's studies, black studies, and the various trendy programs constructed simply to increase enrollments. One survey even found that less than fifty percent of college courses required a student to read more than two hundred pages of a textbook or other reading material in a semester.

As a result, closing most of America's colleges and universities will probably have little effect on the overall education of the citizenry so long as K-12 schooling is strengthened. Progressivism will lose its most fervent adherents—the college professors who currently do little except suck the lifeblood out of the citizenry in the form of high salaries and wonderful benefits while telling everyone else how to live their lives.

Every time the Scholastic Aptitude Tests are modified, they are made easier; every time standards are changed for education, they are lowered. The United States has become a nation where mediocrity is rated as being superior, average has become the new minimum, and no one is below that. It is not unusual for college classes in Education to give ninety percent of their students "A" grades, a single "C," and the remainder "B"s. No one fails, and often attending class with only one or two absences automatically earns a student an "A". Unfortunately, these are the people who become teachers in local schools. They have little knowledge of the subjects they teach, but have Dewey's atheistic/Progressive philosophy down pat, and have been taught how to propagandize their charges and manipulate the parents. These teachers need to be fired and put out on the streets.

In any case, the federal education standard "Common Core" further reduces K-12 standards and turns high schools into day care centers. To learn how to read, write, and make change, a student must attend a community college, another institution maintained by tax dollars. Few high school graduates can calculate the amount of sales tax on a retail purchase without a computer, and fewer still can compose a sentence longer than a few words without grammatical errors. Electronic devices that read books to people are now widely purchased, lessening the incentive to read and further putting the common citizen at a disadvantage. Comprehension is not increased by using those same devices, and the result is a large number of high school graduates who believe "Me and him had done went to WalMart while her sleeps" is fully acceptable and correct English.

At the same time, ratings of schools and school districts have risen dramatically. Unfortunately, this is all smoke and mirrors. Standards have been lowered and ratings include such factors as test performance, teacher qualifications, administrative efficiency, school policies, student retention, discipline, graduation rate, leveling of performance between students of high income and low income families, etc. Teachers teach the achievement tests to promote themselves and their schools, to no benefit for the students. Grades are inflated to move students along and lesson criticism of teachers. In middle America, a graduating class from a highly rated high school often contains no students who plan to attend an out-of-state college or university, and, sometimes, even the state university.

All in all, the closing of schools provides citizens the opportunity to establish effective standards and take back the educational process from Progressive "professionals" intent on reducing the U.S. to a two-class society. There is no better indicator for the coming serfdom than Common Core, and literally no risk at all in getting the government out of education. Abolishing the Department of Education would do wonders.

## Surviving Collapse, Tyranny, and Insurrection

Much of the risk inherent from government action against citizens Starving the Beast can be anticipated by studying past government actions when congressional failures to raise the debt ceiling supposedly could lead to government shutdowns. On one occasion, President Obama immediately threatened the elderly by saying that Social Security checks might not be sent out. For many years, SSA has run a deficit (fifty-five billion dollars in 2012 out of a total budget of 3.6 trillion), collecting less money than it was paying out and cashing in "trust fund" bonds from the Federal Government to make up its deficit while increasing the government's overall deficit. In 2013 when Obama made his threat, monthly revenues were covering nearly all of SSA's payments, and other expenditures could have been delayed to cover the shortfall on a temporary basis.

Nevertheless, the government's action plan was to eliminate those services the citizens of the U.S. either depended on, such as Social Security, or most directly affected them. There was no thought given to reducing bureaucratic overhead, but, instead, to penalize the common people directly by eliminating policemen and firefighters. Similarly, the government closed national parks, veterans' memorials, and other services to punish the citizenry as much as possible. Obama could have furloughed the EPA for a month, but that would not have punished the people. Government by the people, of the people, and for the people was shown to be long gone.

This type of action can be anticipated as the shortfall of revenues versus costs grows, particularly when enough people begin Starving The Beast. In the meantime, the IRS will continue to persecute churches, the EPA will continue to promulgate new restrictive regulations, NASA will continue to promote self-esteem among Muslims in accordance with Obama's directive, the Energy Department will continue to shut down coal-fired power plants, Agriculture will continue to make payments to gentleman farmers, various agencies will continue to fund grants to universities for ridiculous research projects, Education will continue meddling in local school systems, and the attorney general will continue to sell arms to drug smugglers.

Government will take punitive measures against the citizenry as it has in the past to mobilize support for its Progressive policies and keep the citizenry dependent on government. But every time the debt limit has been raised, the people's patience with the Federal Government has receded, and its approval rate has fallen. At some point, such actions will be seen for exactly what they are—anti-citizen measures designed to punish the citizenry for not going along with the Progressive agenda. Citizens will take possession of their national parks by force or break down the barriers to national cemeteries (as an example), and the fat will be in the fire.

The biggest question is whether or not the U.S. Army, Marines, or National Guard will fire on American citizens protesting unconstitutional actions by the Progressive government or side with the protestors. At Kent State in 1971, the Ohio National Guard opened fire on students (and non-student agitators) and there was considerable popular support for both sides, but in particular the student side. The most chilling recent action by military personnel was in 2005 during the Katrina hurricane in New Orleans when they confiscated weapons from law-abiding citizens without justification, pretext, or later remuneration. The National Guardsmen on the scene left honest citizens defenseless while enabling criminals. One can expect this scenario to be replicated many times over throughout the country if the government is smart and ships in National Guard units from out of state.

On the other hand, National Guard units as well as Army units can be expected to resist penalizing frustrated citizens at least for a few more years and be sympathetic with patriot goals and actions. The government, of course, will use its expert manipulators to attempt to frame the debate, with government standing on the high ground to represent law and order even though the government brought on the disorder by first breaking the law.

The Obama government has been particularly lawless, enforcing laws it favored, disregarding those it didn't, and making up new laws through executive and secretarial orders as it has seen fit to meet various situations. The Supreme Court has been complicit in these actions as well and become lawless itself, clearly making law from the bench and ruling extra-constitutionally.[228] Changing the written words in the Patient Protection and Affordable Care Act to fit the Court's agenda was clearly unconstitutional, but necessary to leave

Obama's signature initiative in place. That the Court acted in place of the congress was seen by Progressives to be a minor technical point of no account. But the frightening point was made: the Obama administration, pursuing its Progressive agenda, seems quite comfortable in enraging the citizenry and breaking the law, so future confrontations are probably more likely than not.

At the current time, the U.S. military is not trusted by Progressives. Betraying an almost pathological fear of the American military on U.S. soil, Donald J. Atwood, Deputy Secretary of Defense under Progressive President George H.W. Bush, signed Department of Defense Directive 5210.56 into effect in February 1992. The directive stated that it was DoD Policy to "limit and control the carrying of firearms by DoD military and civilian personnel." However, "DoD personnel regularly engaged in law enforcement or security duties shall be armed." Army Regulation 190-14, a policy promulgated in 1993 under President Clinton implemented, "applicable portions of Department of Defense Directive 5210.56," and removed weapons from military personnel on federal property, military posts, and recruiting offices, turning service men and women into uniformed soft targets for terrorists. President Obama could have reversed that policy with a stroke of his pen, but that would have been a setback for his agenda. Instead, DoD Directive 5210.56 was reissued in April 2011 by Deputy Secretary of Defense, William J. Lynn, III. Apparently Obama preferred that military personnel die under jihadi bullets such as at Fort Hood or in Chattanooga than lose any Progressive momentum.[229]

It will be imperative to defuse confrontations with law enforcement and military personnel until the distribution of goods and services breaks down completely and everyone can readily see the effects of the Progressive government's stupidity. If military units are charged with confiscating citizen supplies for redistribution to government supporters, it will be necessary to have alternate locations already in place so supplies and equipment can be moved from place to place and even back to their original location to avoid confiscation (e.g., keep meals on wheels.) The same will be true for firearms and ammunition, and patriots are advised that the present time is not too early for such planning. Having supplies in a static location and believing that federal troops, assisted by neighbors, will not be able to locate a substantial stash, will be self-defeating. A good plan will be to have no large stash at all, but a number of small stashes that can be readily concealed not only on the property to be searched, but adjoining and even remote properties. The citizen should remember that Progressives will not compensate citizens for what troops take—indeed, the owner of the supplies, if they are in substantial quantity, will be lucky to escape arrest for hoarding.

As the collapse deepens and people begin dying in relatively large numbers, desperation will become common and people will begin killing each other for water, food, and shelter. Gangs will appear and take control in police "no-go" zones (already present in some cities), and people attempting to ride out the crisis with only their families will find themselves out-gunned and easy prey (soft targets.) It will probably take a minimum of sixteen to twenty adult people organized in a group, armed and willing to do whatever is necessary for their families, to have a good chance to survive. Travel will become extremely hazardous, and for the first year at least, citizens should not count on acquiring supplies from more than a couple blocks away in an urban environment, nor two to four miles away in a rural setting. Gasoline will be one of the first items to be unattainable, and here the government will have a huge advantage as it will always be able to move its troops for substantial distances, even by air if necessary.

In his book *Surviving the Economic Collapse*, Argentinian author Fernando Aguirre gives an unvarnished look at what a citizen can expect when a government can no longer maintain order. He writes about the Argentinian economic collapse in 2001, and what actions were needed to survive the year-long crisis and lack of effective law enforcement. Large zones were written off by law enforcement and left to the rule of gangs. Americans saw this same phenomenon in the sixties during various inner-city riots, in Washington D.C., Cleveland, Ohio, and Los Angeles, California. The police pulled out from riot areas like Hough and Watts, allowing rioters to run free, as it was too dangerous for them to attempt to intervene. The same thing occurred again in Baltimore in 2015. The riots were allowed to run their course while citizens suffered from a lack of law enforcement and medical services.

Aguirre wrote that the head of a family has essentially two

choices when a gang arrives at his house: (1), attempt to reason with the gang and die under torture after watching his family die in unspeakable ways (the gang then takes what it wants and burns the rest), or (2), shoot the gang leader and anyone else who doesn't immediately flee.

Under the second option, the police should be called after the incident is over, but they will not respond as the situation is too dangerous for them to become involved. The dead should be photographed, buried, and the incident written up. Much later (possibly a year), the police will show up and arrest the household head for murder, but the evidence, photos, and reports should cause the charges to be dismissed. It is for the reader to decide which scenario is to be favored.[230]

The reader should note that the second option is only available if the head of household is armed and willing to kill to protect himself and his family. If the gang is large, multiple weapons will be needed to drive off the looters and killers. To prepare for such an eventuality, all family members old enough to handle weapons should shoot regularly and learn how to handle firearms effectively. For the moment, the 2nd Amendment is still in effect, and, hopefully, the collapse will take place before the Progressives eliminate a citizen's right to defend himself. Every head of household should define his curtilage, and steel himself to defending it if he wishes to protect his family from the atrocities that will occur.

In the event that authorities or military units show up to strip the family of its food supplies and other survival items, the citizen must expect to lose everything that is not well hidden. This will include firearms and ammunition, so they need to be hidden close for emergency use, but not where they will be found in a moderately thorough search. In this situation, it will be imperative that some early warning system be present; either by a neighbor with a walkie-talkie or CB, or a locked gate or other hindrance to slow down the arrival of the unwanted guests.

One should remember 1775 and how the patriots of Lexington and Concord were warned of the British approach, and the extreme efforts citizens in Georgia and the Carolinas made to avoid losing their supplies and belongings to Sherman's and Wheeler's foragers. A Neighborhood Watch association should be organized, and an effective system of warning worked out. In no case, however, should authorities or military units be fired upon unless they commit outrages and give a citizen no choice but to take action to save his own life or the lives of his family. Unless the confrontation is with a rogue group, the authorities will be in communication with higher authorities and their location known exactly by a continually-monitored GPS unit. The failure of a detachment to return will cause additional and stronger forces to be sent out. The troops will be essentially fighting a war (against recalcitrant citizens) on behalf of the elite, and if a detachment is eliminated through citizen resistance, the resisters' only option for survival is to flee the area of the fight.

Perhaps the greatest advantage elites will have is the ability to monitor citizen activity through satellites and drones at all times, even during nighttime. The government already possesses the authority to kill American citizens on foreign soil through a drone attack, and it is only a very small step to do the same within the continental U.S. This will be the riskless murder of American citizens; young people will sit at control consoles in a secure environment and direct unmanned drones against civilian targets. It will be much like playing a video game, except that the citizens they kill will really be dead. Since the targeting will be accomplished through thermal sighting, citizens will have to provide themselves with thermal barriers. Techniques for accomplishing this are not yet common knowledge, so casualties can be expected to be high.

At some point in time, government will attempt to use its ability to identify friend from foe through thermal signatures to round up or kill all American citizens on land designated under Agenda 21 to go back to nature. Surviving citizens will be moved into government housing in highly concentrated urban centers and stripped of all rights. At this point, even the most rabid believers in the goodness of Progressivism will probably see the light, and can be expected to rebel. Progressives will have to call in foreign troops because the American military will become unreliable, and when that occurs, most probably that part of the remaining Americans troops possessing consciences will join the rebellion. If satellite and drone control becomes available to patriots through military defections, that development could well prove decisive.

However, if patriot forces remain fragmented and lightly armed, elimination of the enemy control centers will become crucial. If patriots are able to infiltrate and destroy drone and satellite control, they may have a good chance of winning. In fact, the main patriot effort when hostilities break out must be to secure major portions of the armed forces, in particular Air Force bases and those installations controlling satellite communication and drone operations. Given that there will be no initial rebel organization for patriots—all uprisings will be "ad hoc" —it will take extremely dedicated personnel who are willing to sacrifice themselves for the cause to level the playing field.

If current forecasts for deaths in the economic collapse of the United States are accurate, the surviving American population will fall to somewhere between thirty and sixty million people in twelve months. If serious civil warfare breaks out, that number can be expected to be as much as halved, depending on how rapidly the armed forces go over to the patriots. From the beginning, patriots will be much better armed than Progressives as individuals, and the key will be which way military units go as the conflict deepens.

There will also be a geographical separation. New England can be expected to remain under Progressive control throughout, as will the populated areas of California, but many military bases and the NSA installation in Utah are in red states. Progressive forces will also probably be concentrated in cities, but that is also where most of the fighting over food will take place. In the resulting chaos, attacks by Progressive forces on patriots in rural areas will not be a top priority.

U.S. troops probably will be deployed initially to quell disturbances in large cities as backup to police and National Guard formations. They will concentrate on guarding government stockpiles, seizing private stockpiles and distribution storage facilities owned by private corporations, and escorting truck convoys transporting food and supplies to critical areas. Air Force bases probably will be effectively quarantined and Naval bases closed to all non-DoD civilians. Fighting ships will be sent to sea on maneuvers for security reasons, and combat planes in the Air Force grounded until released by presidential order. The main use of Air Force units will be in drone operations for surveillance and transports to support ground troops. Appendix D lists the current Army bases in the continental U.S., and also prioritized actions by patriots in a full-fledged economic collapse.

Many preppers are fearful of authorities coming to confiscate their stocks, but such actions are problematic while troops are fully engaged in attempting to save lives and maintain some semblance of order. Gun confiscations won't be high on the list for uniformed troops either, first, because records will quickly be found useless for determining the present locations of most civilian weapons, and, secondly, the weapons being used by looters and gangs will pose a far greater threat to troop safety.

Military installations themselves will probably come under attack by criminal gangs and even foreign drug cartels, beginning with bases near urban centers, then followed by small National Guard depots to seize heavy weaponry and explosives while troops are maintaining order elsewhere. Patriots might consider assisting the military at this juncture in return for becoming deputized or assigned as auxiliaries to obtain fuel and supplies. Such action will have to be carefully negotiated, however, as most, if not all, federal commanders probably will be under orders to confiscate all civilian weapons and ammunition stocks wherever they find them.

Eventually, as cities become burned out, troops will be assigned to protect and feed refugees. Shelter will have to be found in suburban and rural areas, along with food supplies. Help from other countries will be minimal as they will be facing many of the same problems as their supply systems fail to deliver food to their own population centers. With farmers unable to plant or harvest their crops due to shortages of fuel, military units will be assigned to assist in maintaining supplies. Gasoline will be strictly rationed, even to the point that it is available only for official use. From that time onward, government will prove to be incompetent to protect, feed, or shelter people, and many military personnel will desert to their home areas to take care of their own families, taking their arms, ammunition, and military supplies and vehicles with them. With every desertion, the Progressive government will become less able to maintain order, and a peaceful, orderly United States will have passed into history. Only after two seasons of negligible crop yields and a great dying off of the common people will the situation begin to stabilize.

Not to be overlooked is that by taking actions to Starve The Beast, citizens put themselves in a much better position to survive the inevitable collapse. At some point, all banks will be closed, credit and debit cards useless, and there will be no mail delivery. All those poor souls who had depended on government checks for their survival will find they have no way to access those funds or pay for anything. Money in a checking account will be useless, for there will be no way for a recipient to cash the check. Nor will companies be able to collect on accounts for their services or be able to sell items to those on welfare or Social Security. Medical care will become spotty, and even if doctors and nurses are available, medical stocks will be quickly used up and no replacements forthcoming. The Starve The Beast family will be already operating mainly on a non-monetary basis, and should survive easily if authorities don't seize or destroy their shelter, garden, and supply stocks. This will require keeping a low profile and having a good plan.

The family plan must take not only defense into consideration, but include measures to drop out of sight. Mail boxes, address signs, and even street and road signs should be removed to make it more difficult for an outsider to find a citizen's location. Mail should be discontinued or sent to a post office box that will probably not be accessible anyway. As mentioned before, much guidance is available for such planning in various disaster preparedness manuals and books. There are many on the market, and it is recommended that the reader purchase three or four at a minimum.

During all this, the entire world will experience a depression, the depth of which has never been seen before, and governments everywhere will be faced with the huge problem of feeding their people. The breakdown in trade and restrictions on the use of fossil fuels will bring economies to a standstill, and it will be found that, without using great amounts of energy, the world's large population is unsustainable. There will be a great die-off through starvation, disturbances, and warfare, and the population of the world can be expected to decline by upwards of ninety-three percent. Only the remotest and most agrarian of societies will remain untouched, and in most nations, authoritarian governments will arise to bring an end to the hopes of democracy. Heavily theocratic governments and dictatorships with strong religious backing will become the norm, and it is questionable if the U.S. will be able to retain its republican structure.

Probably the only way for the U.S. to survive at all is to erect an impenetrable barrier to not only foreign forces, but also to immigration from all countries except possibly Canada. Draconian laws must be put into effect and rigidly enforced to eliminate all immigration. The same principles of survival for compounds of patriots will apply to the nation as a whole, and all American debts must be cancelled.

At this juncture, it is difficult to determine if the above denouement should be expected from the U.S. economic collapse without a large portion of its citizenry Starving The Beast, or if it is the most likely outcome in any case. Certainly, the case can be made that it is already too late to prevent the U.S.'s economic collapse and subsequent world-wide collapse, but Starving The Beast is the only chance the American citizenry has to head off the catastrophe. The Progressive government must be denied the means to pursue its folly of unbridled spending, at the latest by the end of 2016. Even then, President Obama may invoke his extraordinary powers to delay a new president from taking office, effectively making himself a dictator. If he is successful in becoming the first U.S. president to not relinquish power according to the Constitution, civil war may erupt immediately and the collapse could quickly reach catastrophic proportions. It is only by Starving The Beast that a collapse can be averted, and the sooner the Beast is Starved, the more likely it is that the collapse will not take place. The risks of not Starving The Beast are enormous, as then there will be no opportunity to save the United States or one's family. The risks in Starving The Beast are also high, as a third of the patriots actively engaged in bringing a Progressive government to its senses will probably die in the resulting convulsions.

But the risk of doing nothing is higher, as so many will perish in the ensuing strife and starvation if the Beast itself is not Starved Government will always seek to maintain its power over its citizenry and will take from the citizenry whatever it needs for its own benefit and waste. It cannot reform itself—no government in history has ever reformed itself without a regime change—and will not allow itself to be reformed by the people or other non-governmental interests. The Obama administration exemplifies the worsening of the trend in the Federal Government to avoid all responsibility for its actions while, at the same time, murdering American citizens through its incompetence, malfeasance, and self-absorption.

Hundreds of veterans have died due to the Veteran Administration's drive to make itself look good at the expense of the veterans it is supposed to treat. Hundreds of thousands of veterans have seen the records on their waiting times destroyed, yet no one is held accountable. IRS agents target and harass specific individuals because of their political beliefs, and no one is held accountable. Illegal aliens who have been convicted of murder and rape are let loose in the United States rather than being deported by Homeland Security, and no one is held accountable. Americans in Benghazi, Libya, are killed while State Department officials watch. No one is sent to help, yet no one in either the State Department or the Department of Defense is held accountable. A 4-star general explains the reason he didn't send help to the embattled Americans by saying, "No one asked me to." What happened to "marching toward the sound of the guns?"

The answer is the Progressive Federal Government is no longer responsive to the American citizenry, and no one in the government feels a smidgen of responsibility to the people.

Thomas Jefferson, James Madison, and many of the Founders believed the American republic under the Constitution would work because of the natural alignment of self-interest with national policies and the government's performance. But they forgot to put in term limits to prevent the development of a government class, one that has now become alienated and distinct from the remainder of the population. There is probably no one in a high position in the Progressive Federal Government who would sacrifice himself for the good of the nation, certainly no one who already has taken an oath to preserve and protect the Constitution. But every day, ordinary citizens are asked to sacrifice themselves for the nation and they live up to that duty. The citizens have become vastly more virtuous than their government, and deserve better.

There is an inherent right of revolution in the Declaration of Independence to be exercised when government behaves in a tyrannical fashion or exploits the people to the aggrandizement of itself rather than behaving responsibly towards its citizens. The crimes of the Progressive Federal Government are literally overwhelming, and every year they become more egregious. Progressives must be denied the ability to commit further crimes, and brought to heel and made subject to the will of the people.

The reward, if successful, is the continuation of the greatest nation the earth has ever seen.

# Chapter 9

## Doing Nothing

In spite of all the evidence that the Federal Government is taking extraordinary steps to deny American citizens their God-given rights and reduce the vast majority of the population to serfdom, most Americans continue to work, play, spend, and behave as if their lifestyle will go on forever. Somehow, technology will save them from bad effects of their fecklessness, and political races between Progressive Democrats and moderate Republicans take place with a regularity that is stunning considering the abject avoidance of critical issues. The crises have been engineered by Progressives, and are exactly what they want—the looming collapse and pressures from terrorists allow them to enact extraordinary measures to save the people, save the planet, and "make America safe."

For over a hundred years they have prepared for the day when Christianity could be eliminated. The old Soviet slogans are more applicable in the United States than ever before: "The Battle against Religion is the Battle for Socialism," "Religion is the Enemy of Industrialization," and "Religion is Poison, Protect Your Children."[231]

## Dumbing Down, Debt, Democide, & Destruction

With the implementation of Common Core in the public schools, the great mass of public school students will be "dumbed down" as one New Hampshire teacher said, to help eliminate "white privilege" by reducing white kids to the levels of black kids. The idea was to make all kids equal coming out of high school on the lowest possible standard.[232]

Since one might think that black kids should be challenged and motivated to do as well as white kids under conditions where teaching is strict and standards the highest possible, there is more to Common Core than just the idea of leveling students. It is the idea to level the great unwashed at serf or slave level, making the elites' task of controlling the citizenry much easier. Essentially, Common Core is a major step in eliminating the middle class, or the bourgeoisie the Communists were so intent on eradicating. Private schools, with hefty tuition, have become the pathway for elites to educate their children and join the nomenklatura—the ruling class of functionaries that emerged in the communist society of the Soviet Union. In fact, all communist societies have experienced the emergence of a privileged, ruling class, dictating through authoritarian rule to the great mass of downtrodden citizens.

This was, of course, precisely one of the main complaints in the American Declaration of Independence and what Jefferson attacked when he wrote that "all men are created equal." The two class system of nobility and commoner was firmly rejected, yet now Progressives are re-instituting it with different names: the ruling elites and the common serf. The serfs will have but a single mission in life—to obey the rules and regulations promulgated by the elites. Welcome to the People's Republic of the United States.

Many Americans hide their heads in the sand, contending that such a catastrophe cannot happen in the United States. Many of the same people, President Obama among them, think the institution that has caused the greatest number of deaths in the history of the world is the Roman Catholic Church, and they cite the Crusades as their evidence. But the Church hardly rates an honorable mention on the list of culprits. By far the greatest killers of humankind were three twentieth century governments, featuring one of two variations of socialism—fascism and communism. Not only were they inhuman to an extreme, but they all produced an astronomical level of state-sanctioned murder. According to R. J. Rummel, the top countries in democide (the murder of people by a government including genocide, mass murder, and reckless and depraved disregard for life, (excluding abortions and war deaths) from 1900 through 1987 were: the communist Soviet Union (1917-1987), 61,911,000 people murdered; Communist China (1949-1987), 35,236,000; and Nazi Germany

293

(1933-1945), 20,946,000. The remainder of the top ten nations in democide were all either fascist or communist: Nationalist China (1928-1949), 10,214,000; Imperial Japan (1936-1945), 5,964,000; China (Mao's Soviets, 1923-1949), 3,466,000; Khmer Rouge Cambodia (1975-1979), 2,035,000; Turkey (Young Turks, 1909-1918), 1,883,000; Vietnam (Viet Minh & Viet Cong, 1945-1987), 1,670,000; and North Korea (1948-1987), 1,663,000.[233]

Clearly, to live in a socialist authoritarian state, either fascist or communist, is to live at risk of being murdered by one's own government. There is no reason to assume that the situation will be any different once the United States becomes authoritarian under its Progressive elites,. If Barack Obama becomes dictator, he might very well make Josef Stalin look benign.

With each passing month, the educational establishment further propagandizes their charges to become good little serfs on the government's plantation. With each passing month, the national debt becomes more unmanageable. Government sources routinely point to the debt not in absolute dollar numbers, but as a percentage of Gross National Product (GNP). That's a great idea because the money (sixty-five billion dollars per month as of May, 2014) the Federal Reserve prints and sends out to stimulate the economy (called "quantitative easing" to increase the money supply), is counted as part of the GNP. The Federal Reserve could triple the number of dollars it prints, and the GNP would look even better. It might as well: it's all smoke and mirrors anyway.

Meanwhile, one-third to one-fourth of American workers are either unemployed, underemployed, employed part-time, or working in the underground economy. The debt recognized by the Federal Government has topped eighteen trillion dollars, more than nine times the government's annual revenue, not counting the revenue borrowed from Social Security. And the nation's "unfunded" obligations, (money it must spend in the future by contract, commonly called long-term debt) lies somewhere between $119 and $230 trillion.

It is instructive to understand how the Federal Government determines debt. If an individual takes out a mortgage on his home for $100,000, with a yearly payment of $5,000 in principle and interest, he would say he has $100,000 of debt. If he is unable to pay the $5,000 and borrows it from a friend, he would say he has $105,000 of debt.

The Federal Government sees the situation differently. It would say the man has only $5,000 of debt in the same classification as the government's $18 trillion, and $100,000 in unfunded liabilities. In truth, the government doesn't have either the $18 trillion *or* the $230 trillion—it is all just smoke and mirrors. While our hypothetical man has $100,000 in assets (his home), the entire U.S. government and its citizens have only $55 trillion, so just where is the government going to get the $248,000,000,000,000 it needs to retire its debt? The answer is blowing in the wind of political hot air.

One fact is indisputable: the U.S. economy cannot survive the removal of the American dollar as the world's reserve currency. Yet that is already under way. A consortium of nations, Brazil, Russia, India, and China (the BRIC nations) are already taking steps to replace the dollar with a basket of currency, and have entered into a number of agreements with various countries to settle international financial transactions bilaterally rather than using the dollar.

In short, doing nothing means the U.S. will suffer a financial and economic collapse in the near future, and doing nothing is exactly what the Federal Government is doing about it. If there has ever been a more feckless and incompetent Federal Government in the nation's history, one would be hard pressed to find it. Yet the minions in government are and will be protected—it is the citizens working in the private sector who will suffer. So the collapse is certain, only the date is in doubt. Also certain is that Progressives will use the crisis for their own purposes. They will strip away any remaining vestiges of individual liberty and produce a regime change to an authoritarian structure because it will have been proven that the people cannot govern themselves.

In fact, that is the Progressive mantra—the people lack the ability to govern themselves, and Progressives must govern on their behalf. In part, they have a good case, such as using Minnesota as an example. The people elected former professional wrestler Jesse Ventura as governor and nasty comedian Al Franken to the Senate. Clearly, Minnesotans have proven they can't elect reasonable representatives to govern themselves. Other states are even worse—California, Massachusetts, and Illinois for example.

The people do not have to take this planned catastrophe laying down, however. They can Starve The Beast in an attempt to expose the sheer fecklessness of the Federal Government and spur their representatives to action. They can support the growth of Christian churches that stress salvation, individual liberty under God, and Christian morality, and they can prepare their families for the coming collapse, regime change, and the massive disturbances and civil uprisings that will occur. Cable television currently pokes fun at extreme preppers, people preparing for the collapse, but any reasonable prepper would never allow others to know he's a prepper if at all possible.

The age-old question, "What is government for?" is now answered. In the United States, it is for the good of the people employed by the government. That leads to another question for the citizenry, "What should the citizen work for?" The answer parallels the question for the government—the citizen should work for his and his family's well-being. And that means the citizen has to retain a maximum amount of his earned wealth for his family instead of sending it to a government that may or may not send any back to that citizen or use it on the citizen's behalf. In any case, a huge slice is taken out in corruption and inefficiency.

The prepper simply seeks to hold his wealth available to his family in times of want. And those times are coming. As the American economist, Herbert Stein, once remarked, "If something cannot go on forever, it will stop."[234] The prepper recognizes this homily as intrinsically true, and, therefore, acts to protect his family from the actions of government, in particular, his Progressive government. Regardless of his political motivation, the prepper's actions are virtuous according to Christian morality, as government is a human construct, and rarely beneficial to the individual and his family.

Even if an individual feels that to Starve The Beast is excessively radical or borderline seditious, he would be well advised to become a prepper to give his family a fighting chance of survival in the years ahead. The welfare state began over a century ago, then caught fire under FDR, and has dominated the life of every American since the 1960s. Its days are numbered, if for no other reason that the U.S. is running out of resources, ideas, entrepreneurial spirit, Christian morality, the ability to innovate, and certainly money. It is at the cusp of transforming itself into a dictatorship of the elite, and its descent into authoritarianism is imminent. Many political commentators thought the imposition of the Foreign Asset Tax

Compliance Act (FATCA) on July 1, 2014, would be the trigger for an economic collapse, but the Obama administration illegally delayed the start date for various features, including the imposition of withholding for potential tax liabilities, giving the country a breathing space of a year and a half. Nonetheless, the U.S. is on very thin ice economically, and the Progressive government is dancing.

The alternative of doing nothing allows the Federal Government to become more powerful politically and the United States weaker economically. In 1950, less than a tenth of American professions were licensed by the government; by 2010 that number had risen to nearly half. In all government intrusions into American life, there seems to be no limit to the bureaucratic hunger for controlling the citizenry, and the imposition of Obamacare, in which everyone (except certain privileged people and groups who are exempt) must purchase a product or pay a fine, clearly takes government into an entirely new dimension. Perhaps next, the citizen will have to vote or pay a fine, or work a certain number of hours in community service or pay a fine. The possibilities are endless.

In addition to emasculating Christianity, Progressives have put a solid majority of minorities and other voting blocs into place that pull the levers like robots for Progressive political candidates. They have constructed a critical mass of fully socialized young people through Progressive education, but all these gains are still not enough. There is the little matter of gun, gold, and silver confiscation that Progressives must implement prior to an economic collapse in order to insure their success in fundamentally transforming the United States into a dictatorship of the elite.

As of this writing, none of the three confiscation initiatives are very far advanced, but with conservatives focused on the side issues of abortion, Obamacare, marriage between homosexuals, and legalizing marijuana, Progressive legislators and judges are elected or appointed with little opposition from conservatives. Patriots need to forget about the side issues. Obamacare has now been declared constitutional by breathtaking tortuous contortions of the Supreme Court, banning marriage between homosexuals has been declared unconstitutional, abortion has been forced on the states, and legalizing marijuana is nearing national approval. Next are the confiscation of gold, silver, and guns, though not necessarily in that order.

## Goodbye Guns & Private Property

The 2nd Amendment has already been put in great danger. Connecticut passed a gun control law on April 4, 2013 that required gun owners of "assault weapons" (a definition based on how scary the weapons look) to register their weapons before the end of the year. Most gun owners in the state immediately assumed that registration would later lead to confiscation. An estimated three hundred thousand Connecticut owners of AR-15s, a popular semi-automatic rifle identified by the legislation as an "assault weapon," did not comply with the law. This was massive civil disobedience by eighty-five percent of gun owners subject to the law. Although possession of an unregistered assault rifle was made a felony, potentially meaning prison time, just fifty thousand of the estimated three hundred and seventy-two thousand so-called "assault weapons" in the state were registered by the deadline—less than fifteen percent. That was still far better than the thirty-eight thousand "high capacity" magazines that were reported to authorities, out of two million estimated to be in the state and requiring registration.[235] Apparently, most gun owners in Connecticut were willing to take the risk of being arrested for an unregistered magazine or rifle, and Progressive politicians in Connecticut began wringing their hands over how to resolve the impasse.

The fifty thousand gun owners who did register their weapons were told unregistered arms would probably be confiscated, but then it was found that at least sixty-eight percent of police officers had failed to register their weapons. Showing both zero courage and zero sense, the Progressive Connecticut governor and state legislators first considered firing all officers who had failed to comply to the new law (the text of which had been furnished by the Obama administration and had not been read by anyone in the legislature before voting), then decided to treat the whole thing as if it had never happened. This could be an indication as to what amount of citizen support the Progressive government will receive as it hits more trip wires in its march to enslave the American people. Connecticut is considered to be a bastion of Progressivism, and the Connecticut River's watershed had been made a federal Blueway and subjected to federal land and water management regulations, over almost no citizen opposition.

The requirement for gun owners in Connecticut to register their firearms put them in the same category as sex offenders who must register with government so they can be tracked for the rest of their lives. Just like sex offenders, a failure to register his firearm made a gun owner someone who had committed a criminal act, and likely to be treated accordingly. Yet the gun owners were merely patriotic Americans who were exercising their constitutional right to keep and bear a firearm. The stage is now set for more massive civil disobedience if prosecutors and law enforcement officers attempt to uphold this type of legislation pushed through by gun-control activists in other states. Are police going to take on tens of millions of patriotic, freedom-loving Americans?

With respect to gold and silver, the government is remaining silent, even though it appears there is a critical shortage of gold owned by the government and the Federal Reserve. FDR confiscated gold early in his first administration, believing (wrongly) that banning gold ownership would cause spending and the loosening of credit, especially to farmers. The only thing that occurred was that Americans could not participate in the gold market for the next forty years. Like a little child, FDR laughed all the way to the bank, setting daily gold redemption price with numbers used by the mafia for payoffs in their numbers rackets and others that he saw under various circumstances. Meanwhile, American citizens suffered. Of course, FDR was a true Progressive.

Sooner or later, the government will probably confiscate bullion gold, most likely through an executive order from the president (that was what FDR initially did), making bullion gold possession illegal and requiring all citizens possessing it to turn it in to the government. If the government runs true to form, shortly before the executive order is released, the administration will deny that any thought is being given to calling in privately-owned gold. That will collapse the price of gold, making it cheaper for the Federal Government to redeem.

Silver bullion may also be called in at the government's pleasure although there is a distinct chance it will not. It has a number of industrial uses, and with its low price, is hardly an economic factor. Nonetheless, government restricts ownership on a number of metals and other items (like uranium), and following its penchant for control, it may include silver as well as others, such as platinum, on the restricted list. One less freedom, more or less; what does it matter?

There are other bellwethers to look for as well: for example, the potential movement of private IRA accounts and 401K holdings into a government annuity. The government will whittle away freedoms one at a time until few, if any, are left. The denial of individual liberties is progressing like death from a thousand cuts.

As the economic crisis becomes more intractable, censorship will probably be introduced to control the media and its message. The Internet will come under government control, and bloggers posting critical articles will be blocked and punished for the "good of the people." It is only necessary to remember some of the communist propaganda put out in the Stalin era to be able to put into context what Jay Carney, Josh Earnest, Marie Harf, and other government mouthpieces spout. The government always waits for all the data or information to come in before it takes any action (and then there usually is a cover-up) unless it serves the president's purpose to shoot from the hip. All actions must be "comprehensive"—that way, the opposition, which cannot stomach some element of the action, is put in the wrong and blamed for the defeat of some bill the administration never wanted in the first place. For example, the southern border of the United States remains as open as the Strait of Gibraltar, while action is waiting on finding a "comprehensive" solution to the illegal immigration problem. Actually, there never is a comprehensive solution to any problem in a democratic, compromise-dominated environment, and insisting on one is only a semantic ploy.

The IRS has yet to launch a full scale jihad against bartering and trading, but that also is just a matter of time. Swap-meets will have to be advertised on local media to be legal, require sales tax IDs and registration, and be subject to monitoring by local law enforcement. No doubt farmers' markets, garage sales, yard sales, and other places where cash sales might take place without proper records being maintained will come under increased scrutiny, or be banned altogether because of their potential use to avoid taxes.

Meanwhile, the Department of Justice has been clamping down on business sectors and occupations it doesn't like. The DOJ identified some thirty types of businesses with Operation Choke Point and encouraged banks and third party payment processors to drop such "high-risk" clients beginning in March, 2013. Included as "high-risk" businesses were those selling ammunition, firearms, fireworks, mailing lists, payday loans, pharmaceuticals, surveillance equipment, and tobacco, as well as coin dealers, dating services, pyramid-type sales distributors, telemarketing companies, and travel clubs.[236]

One of the compliant payment processors that refused to service a number of businesses on the DOJ's list was PayPal. It rejected any business selling ammunition, firearms, certain firearm parts or accessories, knives, and other weapons regulated under applicable law. The DOJ has used various tactics to strong-arm the banks and payment processors into compliance, such as flooding them with subpoenas, civil investigations, and other burdensome and costly legal demands. It is only a matter of time before this DOJ jihad forces most businesses out of selling items the government dislikes.

Many citizens believe nothing can be done about the Federal Government: it is too powerful and there in no way to change things. So they simply ignore the government, apparently hoping it will just go away. But it won't.

The United States has been operating on the good will (if there is such a thing) of Asian nations for the last three presidential administrations. Led by China, Asia has been a huge buyer of U.S. Treasury bonds, not the least because they needed somewhere to park their dollars.

In the eleven years that ended with 2012, forty-three percent of all U.S. Treasury security issues were bought by foreigners, and most of those purchases were made by foreign governments. As of 2012, the Chinese government's holdings probably totaled more than $2 trillion.[237]

These purchases have been the primary reason the Federal Reserve has been able to keep interest rates low, and without the Chinese and other Asian governments buying U.S. bonds, interest rates might have soared to over twenty percent and exceeded even those of the Carter years. They have also encouraged and allowed Americans to spend as if there was no tomorrow, and effectively eliminated any major saving by American consumers.

Various writers such as Alan Tonelson of the United States Business and Industry Council have noted that the Chinese government is the functional equivalent of a drug pusher feeding the insatiable American habit for "stuff." Starve the Beast would curb that habit, and eventually end China's purchase of American property and hard assets. But as long as the American public does nothing, foreigners will continue to buy up American assets while selling items of limited durability. China has already found a lucrative stash hole in financing reverse mortgages, totally unbeknownst to the American citizen. The day that most of America's hard assets will be owned by foreign governments is not far off.

Of course, there may soon be nothing for the Chinese and other foreign governments to buy. The Federal Government has been madly pursuing Agenda 21, in particular through programs designed to eliminate property rights and eventually relocate rural American families to high-rise cities where they can be more easily controlled. Mostly through the Department of the Interior and the EPA, the government has been attempting to seize outright control of millions and millions of acres, all in addition to the many millions it already controls. One of President Obama's programs to seize large tracts was the National Blueway program, under which the Secretary of the Interior would designate entire watersheds of various rivers as National Blueways subject to federal control.

In January of 2013, the Secretary of the Interior announced the creation of the White River National Blueway covering almost eighteen million acres of the White River's watershed in Missouri and Arkansas. In announcing the Blueway, Secretary Salazar overreached by not calling for a single public hearing, and totally ignoring the property owners in the Blueway area. The White River Blueway was eventually defeated by massive citizen protests that went unreported by the national media.

President Obama had announced the National Blueway initiative in 2012, and the White was the second river to be so designated. The entire White River watershed was designated as being subject to a federal land management and water use plan, effectively stripping all residents in the watershed of their rights to use their property as they saw fit. A controlling committee was set up involving the Department of Interior, the EPA, the Department of Agriculture, and the Corps of Engineers, along with a number of national and international conservation organizations. Landowners were not included.

A few privileged politicians were informed of the designation, and one, a senator from Arkansas named Mark Pryor, spoke favorably of the designation, saying the federal control would open up new lands and be great for hunting, fishing, and other tourist activities. One hundred-foot wide buffer zones would be created around all bodies of water in the watershed, including rivers, creeks, lakes, and ponds, and cattle and other livestock would be fenced off from water to control pollution. New regulations on land use would ensure that the area would retain a great deal of wildlife and forest land for subsequent generations.

Since the public had not been involved in the process of creating the Blueway, opposition built slowly at first as the Blueway was kept under wraps. But, by April, citizen meetings were being held all over the watershed, and the opposition became very vocal. Campaigns of writing letters to Congress and calling representatives slowly began to take effect, and, in June, a congressional delegation from Missouri and Arkansas demanded an accounting from the Interior Secretary as to why no public hearings had been held. In their letter, they pointed out that the initiative was unconstitutional as the waters mentioned were under control of the two states, and the whole program was a usurpation of state sovereignty. In July, the Secretary withdrew the designation, and the Blueway was defeated.

Afterward, when a Republican candidate for governor of Arkansas was asked why he didn't get involved in the fight against the Blueway, he stated that he was only a private citizen at the time, but, had he been governor, he would have fought the Blueway tooth and nail. Somehow he ignored the fact that the Blueway had been defeated mainly by private citizens. He didn't even win the Republican nomination.

The White River Blueway defeat, coupled with strong opposition from the Congressional Western Caucus to the designation of the Yellowstone as a National Blueway, caused a cancellation of the whole national program. But it was only a momentary setback for Obama's Progressive administration. In the spring of 2014, the EPA put forth a new definition of "Waters of the United States" to replace the former definition that limited such waters to those that were coastal or navigable. The new definition expanded the definition so that the EPA could control essentially all water in the United States, limiting and regulating its use. At the time of this writing, the proposed change was still making its way through the approval process. If approved, the simple change of a few words in a bureaucrat's regulation will have an extremely profound and adverse effect on property owners throughout the United States. Defeated with its Blueway program, the EPA had found another way to skin the cat.

The Department of the Interior continued at flank speed to rob citizens of the use of their lands through critical habitat designations. In the 216-page Draft Environmental Assessment for the utterly obscure and not-so-important Neosho Mucket and Rabbitsfoot Mussels prepared by the Department of Interior / U.S. Fish and Wildlife Service in 2014, one notes the following on page 4, "The environmental issues identified by the Service during resource analysis include: conservation of the Neosho mucket and rabbitsfoot, water resource management, energy development and production, socioeconomic conditions and environmental justice." "Environmental justice" is a code term for including everyone who could be possibly be interested in environmental issues in the decision-making process. To this end, the term "stakeholder" was coined to include all individuals and organizations who were not property owners but might possibly be affected in any way, be it ever so farfetched, by some environmental issue. Stakeholders are written into federal regulations, thus insuring that national and international environmental and conservation organizations, such as the Audubon Society, the Nature Conservancy, and many others have more say concerning a property's use than the property owner himself.

All this is being accomplished with an eye to fulfilling the mission of Agenda 21, which has as one of its primary goals the elimination of private property. Another major objective of Agenda 21 is to integrate national and international social, economic, and environmental policies to result in social equity, reduced consumption, and preserving and restoring biodiversity.

Proponents of Agenda 21, or as it is more commonly known, Sustainable Development,) demand that all decisions affecting land use should take into consideration global environmental impact, population control, and the reduction of man's footprint. Current Western civilization is incompatible and unsustainable with the earth's resources, and the list of unsustainable activities and elements of American lifestyles is simply mind-boggling: all grazing animals, fossil fuels, appliances, single family homes, dams, power lines, air-conditioning, asphalt and concrete roads, private property, golf courses, fences, deep plowing, etc.[238] The middle class must be eliminated world-wide, and Progressives in the United States are in the lead in that elimination. Under Agenda 21, land cannot be treated as an ordinary asset and available for private ownership at a value subject to economics and its actual or potential use. Private land ownership is a principal instrument of accumulation and concentration of wealth; therefore, it contributes to social injustice and is unsustainable.[239]

The effect of the Federal Government's actions in pursuing Agenda 21 is to give the United Nations control over Americans' choices regarding food, water, housing, and private property ownership. In regard to global warming, aka "climate change," various Progressive politicians continued to tell the public in 2014 that "the science is settled," in particular, using the 3rd U.S. National Climate Assessment, released on May 6, 2014. It was purported to be the most authoritative and comprehensive source of scientific information to that date about climate change impacts across all U.S. regions and on critical sectors of the economy.

This was a political document, married to President Obama's series of executive actions to reduce carbon pollution, prepare the U.S. for the impacts of climate change, and lead international efforts to address global climate change. It was also total fiction, produced by a coterie of individuals participating in the U.S. Global Change Research Program and dedicated to proving that man-made global climate change was occurring. It failed to determine through objective research if (1) global climate change was occurring; and (2) if man had anything to do with it.

Global climate change is occurring—that is without doubt—but it has occurred throughout the history of the earth and will continue to do so until the sun burns out. The earth has experienced a large number of climate changes during its existence, from an extremely hot planet to one totally covered with ice. There are many factors at work producing changes in the earth's climate, and man has about as much to do with it as the Rabbitsfoot mussel. In the last one hundred and fifty years, the earth has experienced a period of substantial volcanic activity from its fifteen hundred active volcanoes, from Krakatoa to Mount St. Helens to Mount Pinatubo. Each of these eruptions put more pollutants and particulate matter into the earth's atmosphere than man has done during all of recorded history. In 2013, over fifty volcanoes erupted, spewing steam, ash, toxic gases, and lava, including Italy's Mount Etna, Alaska's Mount Pavlof, Indonesia's Mount Sinabung, Argentina's Volcán Copahue, and one even forming a new island off the coast of Japan.

Rejection of the Progressive dogma that man is causing climate change demolishes the entire ideological foundation of Agenda 21 and Progressivism. Progressives use man-made climate change as the ultimate proof that the common man cannot govern himself. In their Nazi-like lock-step adherence to their self-serving ideology, they are unable to allow any contrary facts to upset their carefully crafted belief that common man, uncontrolled by Progressive elites, is destroying the planet earth. This simple contention drives the Obama administration and, indeed, all recent Progressive administrations, to subvert the Constitution and govern lawlessly in violations of their public oaths.

The evidence against man-made global warming is overwhelming, but that leaves Progressive politicians pursuing Agenda 21 totally unfazed. For example, the "hockey stick" graph produced by Michael Mann of the University of Massachusetts that purported to show definitively that mankind, or, more accurately, the industrial revolution, was producing global warming, has been totally debunked. Stephen McIntyre and Ross McKitrick showed that Mann's methodology was so flawed the model would produce the "hockey stick" shape even with vastly different and random inputs.[240]

Following that jarring revelation, the United Nations was further embarrassed when their British researchers were found to be altering data to pursue the Progressive agenda rather than performing objective research on global warming.

Facts turned out to be meaningless in the Progressive campaign to convince the people of the dangers of man-made global warming. Progressives are shackled to a cart without a horse, and are fully committed to Agenda 21 and the need for "global governance" — they are afraid of saying "a global government" because of the feared reaction of the people, so they continue to beat the drum. Using an organization called the International Council for Local Environmental Initiatives (ICLEI) (an oxymoron in itself), American cities, counties, and states have been signing up for sustainable development programs with the rapidity of a drunken sailor spending money. Sustainable development is the code term for Agenda 21, and hiding behind this term, Progressives often deny that Agenda 21 is being made into law in the United States. But it is. For example, President Clinton required that every federal department include Agenda 21 goals in their initiatives, and President Obama has increased government efforts to put Agenda 21 initiatives into practice tenfold.

The assault on private property ownership through Agenda 21 initiatives is hardly limited to "blue" states. An example is the city of Fort Smith, Arkansas, a red city in a red state. In June of 2014, it passed a resolution supporting the "Sustainable Arkansas Program," an Agenda 21 initiative put together by the Applied Sustainability Center at the University of Arkansas, modeled after the "Sustainable [New] Jersey Program." Supposedly, the increased regulation of private property by outsiders would lead to greater economic prosperity, since corporations would favor Ft. Smith as a location because they are looking for locations that help them meet their sustainability goals "that are often mandated by their customers."[241] Obviously, the contention that a company must meet Agenda 21 goals because they are mandated by a corporation's customers is complete hogwash. But even worse is the resolution, written by outsiders promoting Agenda 21. It states unequivocally that "Formal recognition of sustainable development policies and practices is essential to promoting progressive economic development in all Arkansas cities." There can be no doubt that Progressives are pushing Agenda 21 to the maximum, even touting it as "essential" to economic development. The facts point to the precise opposite; sustainable development / Agenda 21 seeks to eliminate economic development rather than promoting it, and this resolution would move Fort Smith in that direction.

The more the American public becomes socialized and accepts Agenda 21's programs, the less they will care about traditional freedoms. It is all just a matter of time, unless the Muslims take over Europe in time to derail the smug European elites who are promoting Agenda 21. Petroleum, the use of which is to be eliminated under Agenda 21, is Islam's great economic advantage at present, and the West may well see itself committing economic and demographic suicide as it pursues Agenda 21.

## Death by a Thousand Cuts

Concurrent with the drive to Agenda 21 and the Progressivization of America is the budding requirement that everyone become "highly educated." In practice, this means spending many years in school, even if students are learning nothing useful. For the last sixty years, Progressive educators have sneered at education designed to teach students skills helpful to achieve success in life, opting instead for a "liberal education" designed to broaden an individual's general knowledge and interests. By the twenty-first century, less than a dozen members of Congress could build a working outhouse, and few could accomplish home repairs more complicated than changing a light bulb.

Since World War II, universities have taught Progressive ideology in all non-technical subjects, and the Ivy League has become renown for turning out functionaries in the sense used in communist countries. These are individuals qualified to fill any bureaucratic position in a party or government, even though they possess no skills at all. The last four presidents of the United States were excellent examples of this genre as none of them had created anything or accomplished anything of note by themselves. Only the two Bushes had become anything but a functionary—they had both become accomplished pilots. The elder Bush became the head of the CIA without ever being a case officer or creating and running an intelligence operation, and Obama's career as an attorney was undistinguished, never rising above being a minor attorney on teams representing slum landlords in Chicago. He was appointed as an adjunct professor (a non-faculty position) at the University of Chicago Law School at the insistence of Board Member Valerie Jarrett, continuing his extraordinary career of being handed honors and positions without having to earn them. Even when involved in drugs as a youth, Obama never became a significant player, reputedly because he lacked the ability and toughness to run a drug operation.

To a large degree, Progressive education is responsible for government functioning so poorly. With individuals unable to understand technical details and effectively process information regardless of their putative decision-making and intellectual capabilities, management by committee takes over, and the results usually fall far below expectations. Responsibility and accountability are supposedly shared, but, in reality, neither are present, and few functionaries ever suffer any penalties for their poor performances or bad decisions.

Even more damning is the evidence that Progressive education often means no education at all. Studies since 1979 have consistently shown that university upper-classmen have retained little general knowledge at that point in their education, and in multi-discipline examinations designed to test an individual's general knowledge, average scores were below forty percent, and few scored higher than seventy.[242] The most common complaint by students with low scores was that the test covered high school knowledge, and all that had been forgotten when they went to college. Yet, at the high school level, performance was even lower. By 2010, few high school graduates could perform elementary math operations, and English language proficiency was abysmal. Community colleges were forced to offer remedial math starting at the second grade level as prerequisites to lower-level college math courses. And this was even before Common Core was initiated to further "dumb down" American students.

Before the great grade inflation period of the 1960s when Progressive educators moved the bar downward to keep students in school rather than lose them to the Army and Vietnam, many college and universities had high standards. Engineering schools required a hundred and forty-five to a hundred and eighty semester hours of credit for an undergraduate degree, and the majority of grading was rigorous rather than being "on the curve." "C" was often a good grade when the scale was 94-100 for an "A", 86 to 93.9 a "B", 78 to 85.9 a "C", and 70 to 77.9 a "D".[243]

By the end of the 1960s, grade averages had increased by half a grade, and they continued upward in the 1970s. By 1980, the earlier standards in instruction and grading had almost vanished; 60 became a passing score, 90 was an "A," and grades were often curved upward when few students had scored sufficiently high on a numeric scale. Faculty members bribed students with good grades for good student evaluations. Course loads were lightened, and schools that formerly required a hundred and forty-eight semester hours for graduation moved down to only a hundred and twenty. One school, with a minimum of eighteen semester hours for a full-time student, lowered the full-time load to only twelve. From nine courses in a semester, a full-time load became only four. The result of all this relaxation in requirements was evident: Americans had built the Hoover Dam from 1931 to 1936, but the bridge by-passing the dam was built by Japanese from 2005 - 2010. The push to excellence in the United States had shattered on the shoals of unionized teachers and professors seeking an easy life for themselves.

Universities had truly become "laboratories in liberalism" by the twenty-first century, and rather poor ones at that, at least in non-technical areas. Revolutions may eat their children, but university students in liberal arts eat their parents. The best of the students in the U.S. during the twenty-first century have gone into engineering and other technical areas, and they have remained at least marginally competent in spite of lowered requirements and falling standards in their coursework. But the others, particularly those ending up in law schools, have absorbed the propaganda by their Progressive professors, believe they know everything they need to know, and arrogantly assume they inherited a calling to join the American elite. In truth, they know very little, and as the nation lurches closer to collapse, it can be expected that universities will become leading indicators of discord as students take to the streets in classic leftist revolution demonstrations.

Bill Ayres and others of his ilk led the abortive revolutions of the 1960s, and Barack Obama learned from his friend Ayres that opposing the law was not as good a strategy as using it. Obama could have learned the same thing from Hitler, but history was never his strong point. Accordingly, he said he would "fundamentally transform" the United States in 2008, and, in 2009, he began to do just that.

Unnoticed by Progressives was a fatal flaw in their program for a non-violent revolution: all successful revolutions in the twentieth century came about after the army was either destroyed (the Soviet Union, Cuba, China) or absorbed (Nazi Germany, Argentina, Spain). The American military was—and is still in large measure—conservative, and the current conservative campaign to honor and respect serving troops and veterans, has allowed the military to maintain a close relationship with their civilian counterparts. The military today enjoys a highly respected position in red states..

Unless Progressives are able to replace the current citizen volunteers in the military with more Progressively-minded individuals or easily-manipulated civilian contractors, they have a severe problem. Forecasts that Obama or his Progressive successor will use NATO or other foreign troops against American citizens might well have to become actuality.

In many respects, citizen involvement in the political process and action against egregious overreaches by government may only delay the inevitable. Doing nothing, however, allows Progressives in government to blindly plow full steam ahead to a totalitarian state without any citizen input or objections. But the question is, "When do the totalitarian Progressives forces in the U.S. government want the economic collapse to occur?" Obviously, they are delaying it until they are ready, possibly waiting for a more "true blue" Progressive like Hillary Clinton to be at the helm instead of an inattentive and ineffectual Barack Obama.

Starving The Beast may bring about the collapse of the Progressive Federal Government earlier than Progressives expect, otherwise it will occur on whatever schedule Progressives have devised. STB also protects one's family, and makes the Progressive plan to preside over an orderly change to a dictatorship infinitely more problematic. The planned Progressive transformation process could easily change into a nightmare when their tactics are exposed and a viable opposition emerges. Burdened with the need to keep order in a chaotic nation, Progressives may have to delay the implementation of Agenda 21. If the collapse occurs before the Progressives are ready, the ensuing unrest might give patriots a chance to take control, demolish the welfare state, and reform the government along small government lines. In essence, this is the only chance for America that does not entail a revolution.

In addition to all these dire predictions and unfavorable trends, yet another development, this time from outside America's boundaries, threatens American tranquility and its survival: the emergence of an Islamic Caliphate. Conservative media personality Glenn Beck predicted in 2009 that the emergence of an Islamic Caliphate was the objective of the Obama-supported Muslim Brotherhood and warned the U.S. citizenry about this development. He was roundly ridiculed by the leftist commentators at CNN,

MSNBC, and the New York Times as "looney toons" and spouting lunatic nonsense, but, in 2014, even the left-wing, Progressive New York Times editorialized that Beck was being vindicated by current events. Even more telling is the common belief in 2015 among American military personnel that Obama *is* a member of the Muslim Brotherhood.

Under Sharia law as espoused for the Caliphate, Christians would become *dhimmis*, as they currently are in Islamic nations under Sharia, which is a third-class citizen status with many restrictions and fewer rights than Muslims, effectively, a class just above "slave."

Progressives carefully and universally avoid mentioning *dhimmis* or *dimmitude* when they praise Islam, as if there is no problem with civil rights in Islamic nations. Nonetheless, if the Middle East establishes a strong Caliphate and is able to subsume Europe into its sphere of influence, it could rival China as the world's most powerful economic and political entity, and also take first place in the world with respect to having the most powerful religious force.

The Islamic threat can hardly be overestimated since the U.S. is growing less able to meet this threat every day. The Caliphate would control most of the world's oil, and at least two of its nations will possess nuclear weapons. Europe is clearly doomed to G. K. Chesterton's stages of empire: "Victory over barbarians. Employment of barbarians. Alliance with barbarians. Conquest by barbarians."[244]

In Europe, Islamic immigrants and their children have resisted assimilation into Western culture to a very great degree. Their religion and culture are considered incompatible with Christianity, and they have insisted on living according to Sharia law. Even worse is the focus by Muslim women on producing babies, rather than equal rights or women's issues. European women might have attained a high level of equality between the sexes, but without progeny, their achievement will soon be meaningless. Even today, forecasts of Europe succumbing to Muslim control before the end of the century are commonplace, some even by mid-century. And if there is any doubt about the goals of Islam's leaders, maps of Islam frequently include all of Europe west of Poland and Ukraine as being in the Caliphate. Cities such as Cologne, Germany, are forecast to have Muslim majorities by 2035, and Belgium's capital city Brussels already features major Islamic neighborhoods and sectors. In short,

America can expect to receive no assistance from an enfeebled and increasingly irrelevant Europe.

Under President Obama, Muslim immigration into the U.S. has mushroomed to the point that it may already have overtaken the Jewish population. Since the immigrants' home states are awash in oil money, it can be expected that elections will increasingly be won by politicians favorable to Muslims and the Middle East. One might expect Jewish-Americans to ally themselves with evangelical Christians to turn back the Muslim tide, but they are busy entrenching themselves behind the same Progressivism that is enabling Muslims numbers to grow so rapidly domestically. Where one would expect a growing awareness of an American Islamic threat, there is only what appears to be willful blindness.

In 1990, one forecaster stated: "The question is not when the U.S. elects its first black as president, but when it will elect the last white." Today, the nearing advent of the North American Union with Mexico and Canada might alter the question, but major demographic changes will be forthcoming in the near future, assuming that the United States survives at all.

The alternative of doing nothing, therefore, means the end of American and Western civilization within the next decade or two, if not the end of the United States itself. President Franklin Roosevelt stated there was nothing more critical than saving Western civilization, but all the while, he furthered Progressivism, an ideology incompatible with American and Western ideas. Sooner or later, Progressivism will bring Western civilization to a crisis: either go forward to the brave new world of an elite dictatorship, or return to the democratic principles that made America great. Those dual possibilities presume Western civilization survives the threat of the Caliphate, of course—an increasingly unlikely prospect after the Iran Nuclear Treaty of July, 2015.

Many conservatives believe the country can still be saved by the Republican Party and electing Republicans to office. While this strategy might put a few speed bumps in the way of the Progressive juggernaut, it will not alter the inevitable outcome. Today, the Democrats are the Progressive/Socialist Party, and Republicans little more than Democrats Lite. The demographic composition of the United States has been allowed to change toward a welfare state, and one must promise to bring home a certain amount of bacon to get elected from either party.

Ronald Reagan was able to win the Cold War in spite of nearly universal opposition from American elites, but neither President Reagan nor Prime Minister Margaret Thatcher were able to arrest the growth of their governments, primarily because Progressivism was too far advanced in both the U.S. and Great Britain. Thatcher was able stop the socialist rot in England temporarily and restore her country to a modicum of financial health, but Reagan focused on the great mission of winning the Cold War to the exclusion of halting Progressivism. Thatcher was able to give Great Britain the opportunity to find its way back to greatness, but, unfortunately, the people were too enfeebled to rouse themselves for any crusade. Reagan gave America a shining example of what could still be done with a firmness of purpose and absolute dedication, but, until the present time, American citizens have floundered ineffectually, not knowing what to do.

Within the next decade, the Federal Government can be expected to grasp at straws to maintain liquidity while politicians promise to restore America's greatness. Such promises are nonsense and worse than misleading. The North American Union, as backed and organized by the Council for Foreign Relations, will come under close scrutiny as a mechanism to shed some of the crushing debt, but it is difficult to see how it would offer an escape from the nation's problems. The key is to find a way to immediately have Mexicans and Canadians augment the tax rolls without increasing entitlements, but the inverse is more likely.

The replacement of the dollar as the world's reserve currency is imminent, and that event will trigger a devaluation of the dollar and possibly run-away inflation. Calls for expelling all aliens will be made in order to lower entitlement payments, but the Democrat Party will fight such a move to the last man and call such proposals "un-American." IRA accounts and 401K investments will have to be seized and replaced by a guaranteed investment program in government bonds, but it will be impossible to sell the assets to raise cash in the short run. Such a sell-off, by itself, could cause the market to crash, assuming it hadn't already when the confiscation program is announced. The North American Union might then look more attractive and allow the U.S. government to simply default on foreign obligations and spread their cost with Mexico and Canada. Only time will tell.

Some patriots have read the handwriting on the wall, and after the failure of the Tea Party movement to revitalize the Republican Party with true conservatives, now see their only option as preparing for the worst with a "bunker mentality" and attempt to ride out the storm. Once upon a time such a strategy would have worked in the United States as it was entirely possible to form enclaves, usually religious in orientation, that the government would leave alone as long as the community paid its taxes. Such toleration is no longer a feature of the Progressive Federal Government. Progressives see such conservative and Christian movements as existential threats to Progressive principles, and they will face eradication one way or another. The destruction of the Branch Davidians at Waco will be used as the model for action against conservative, patriot, and Christian groups, including those that would consider themselves mainstream.

Like runaway slaves, patriots will be hunted down by government operatives or foreign troops. If they are lucky, they will be given the option to recant and change their ways, otherwise they will be exterminated. The new Progressive dictatorship of the elite will have striking resemblances to Stalin's Soviet Union, Mao's China, Hitler's Germany, and Pol Pot's Cambodia. Only this time, it will be the United States Federal Government making war on its citizens and stamping out all dissident behavior. Doing nothing is the worst of all possible strategies, for it means dying without dignity. Stalin's record of murdering sixty-two million people may well be eclipsed.

# Chapter 10

## The Call To Action

Compare King George III to President Obama. The British thought they had given the colonists everything and the king was only asking that they help defray the Crown's costs through taxes. Obama said, "You didn't do that; somebody else made that happen," in essence, the government gave you your business or your livelihood, so you are to pay the Progressive Federal Government like the colonists were to pay England.

Obamacare provides for a tax/fine if a citizen doesn't purchase something—even worse, your property can be attached in the case of non-payment and then seized by the government. All private property in the United States is taxed, and if the owners become delinquent in their tax payments, the property is sold at auction, often to a friend or relative of government officials involved in the seizure of the property. This is as if the king owns all the property, and private property exists only at the pleasure of the government. Perhaps, more correctly, the citizen owner has only a right to use his property as allowed by the interested government agencies. Zoning restrictions and regulations by government entities at the federal, state and local levels may even prohibit an owner from using the property at all, but, nonetheless, the taxes must be paid. Such situations are already present on the Left Coast, in particular the People's Republic of California.

All this has not been particularly onerous during the first hundred and eighty years of our country's existence, but with the rise of arbitrary bureaucratic governance under successive Progressive administrations, the people's rights to liberty have been trampled into the dirt. Criticism of government has been muted out of fear of

316

retaliation, and what ordinary citizen can withstand the long reach of government with its millions of employees and its trillions of dollars it seems willing to spend for everything but the people's *general* welfare? More often, the money is spent on persecuting and prosecuting the citizenry through faceless government agencies such as the EPA, IRS, Homeland Security, and Department of Energy.

" *We know what is best for you, and you will obey!*" seems to be the twenty-first century motto of government. It is clear that the American system of government only works when government represents the people, shares their Christian values, and is virtuous and moral. Unfortunately, that no longer seems to be the case.

During the Revolutionary War, the coffers of the British crown became emptier every year the war dragged on, and, with the continued lack of trade, the English people could see little benefit arising from the war. Indeed, King George was forced to hire German mercenaries, and only recruiting troops among Catholics in the highlands of Scotland, as well as in Wales and the Midlands, was successful to any degree in Great Britain.

The citizens of London were soundly against the war, and even raised money for the alleviation of suffering among the prisoners— the American prisoners. Elsewhere, such as among the Puritan communities in East Angelica and the eastern and southern areas of England, sentiment ran in favor of the Americans. In Parliament, the majority Tory Party supported the king and the war, but the Whigs generally did not. Today in the United States, the Democrats almost unequivocally support Obama's dictatorial style and the progression to a dictatorial elite; the Republicans sometimes do not.

American law is based on the Judeo-Christian Ten Commandments, and its development can be easily traced through German Salian Law, the Magna Carta, Sir Edward Coke's writings, especially on citizenship and the rights and responsibilities of the English citizen, and the speeches and writings of James Otis, Samuel Adams, and the Founding Fathers. The Protestant Reformation and the English Bill of Rights of 1689 tied the English government to Protestant morality and enabled a republic to emerge in which ordinary citizens could determine who would represent them in government.

The Magna Carta contained two provisions establishing the very core idea of American individual liberties, if no longer the British.

The first stated, "No free man shall be taken or imprisoned or deprived or outlawed or exiled or in any way ruined, nor will we go or send against him, except by the lawful judgment of his peers or by the law of the land.[245] Yes, but who makes the law? In the United States, the law initially came from the Christian God, was developed by the customs and actions of the people, and then written and enforced by the people's representatives.

By 2014, the law of the land in the United States more often than not had originated within groups of special interests, become a body of statutes unknown to the people and unrepresentative of their values, and written to enrich or favor those special interests that originated the law. The Constitution had been hammered completely out of shape through egregious Supreme Court rulings and the usurpation of power by the executive branch, the courts, and unelected bureaucrats. The law of the land had become whatever a few individuals said it was, and the citizenry had become completely disenfranchised.

The second great principle established by the Magna Carta was, "To no one will we sell, to no one will we deny or delay right or justice."[246] This was a great principle indeed, and although the United States was able to finally throw off the yoke of slavery, today, rights and justice are for sale or denial as never before. Congress votes itself special rights and exemptions from its own laws, and the IRS and the executive branch selectively prosecute citizens and organizations under various laws as they see fit. The principle under Progressivism has become, "To no one will we sell unless the price is right, and we will deny or delay rights and justice to anyone when it serves our purposes."

## Serfdom or Liberty?

The Federal Government has become a giant hall of smoke and mirrors, no one doing what they promised, and everyone gaming the system. John F. Kennedy was one of the United States' less adept presidents and brought the world to the brink of extinction in order to not suffer a further loss of manhood, but he delivered some of the most memorable speeches in American history. The words of his inaugural address in 1961 were inspiring: "Let every nation know... that we shall pay any price, bear any burden, meet any hardship, support any friend, or oppose any foe, in order to assure the survival and success of liberty." Even more importantly, he stated: "...ask not what your country can do for you, ask what you can do for your country."[247]

Yet American politicians during the decade of the 1960s, and the Democrat Party in particular, failed to hear Kennedy's words, and, under Johnson, the "entitlement age" was ushered in. The Federal Government became the dispenser of a cornucopia of goodies to be handed out for favors or demanded as a new "right," and no one asked what they could do for their country. The healthy paid for others with unhealthy life styles, patriots served on the front lines of the cold and hot wars, while Progressives enjoyed a secure, good life of luxury, and "the American" vanished under a sea of hyphenated Americans, all with special needs that enabled them to extract special benefits from those still paying in to an increasingly dysfunctional system.

Kennedy also ushered in the age of the corporate president. Speechwriters were employed to craft the president's speeches, and although Eisenhower had used assistants and various officials to help produce statements and speeches, Kennedy took the process to a new level. His main writer was Ted Sorenson, who also ghost-wrote Kennedy's *Profiles in Courage*.

By the time of President Obama, not only were all of Obama's speeches written for him, but the use of teleprompters eliminated ad-libbing, and made Obama's speeches little more than staged and artificial events. In modern times, only President Reagan either wrote his own speeches or so heavily edited drafts from others that he could call them his own.

By the time of Obama, presidents had become figureheads for shadow interests, and certainly not representative of the American citizenry. This had occurred earlier from time to time, but the difference now was that the puppet masters were hidden behind the curtain, and generally unknown to the citizenry.

Perhaps the most shocking change was exhibited during the Syrian revolution in 2012. President Obama answered a question concerning possible American military action in Syria in a press conference on August 20 by saying that the use of chemical weapons by Syrian President Bashar Assad would cross a "red line for us."[248] After he left the conference, he was brutally assailed by his handler Valerie Jarrett for straying from the script.[249] She shrieked at him as if he were a wayward child, telling him he wasn't elected to be a war president, but to fix things here at home. By that, she meant he was to advance the Progressive agenda rather than get the U.S. involved in a diverting war. It is simply impossible to imagine such an incident occurring to President Eisenhower or JFK—although Carter supposedly was subjected to tirades from his wife Rosalynn. Bill Clinton had to endure screaming from Hillary, and Obama suffers under interference and, some say, control from Michelle. In the age of the corporate president, his handlers are perhaps more important than the president, especially when he is as inept as Obama.

Mendacity has become so commonplace that one must have a PhD to separate the lies from the truth—if the truth can be found at all. In an interview with *The Huffington Post*, August 4, 2014, ex-Congressman Barney Frank, former chairman of the House Financial Services Committee and self-described Progressive atheist homosexual of Jewish heritage, criticized President Obama for lying when promoting Obamacare. He stated that Obama "should never have said… that, if you like your current health care plan, you can keep it. That wasn't true. And you shouldn't lie to people. And they just lied to people. He should have said, 'Look, in some cases, the health care plans that you've got are really inadequate, and in your own interests, we're going to change them.'"[250]

The most astounding thing about these statements was that Frank. himself, had lied when he told the American people that Fannie Mae and Freddie Mac "are not facing any kind of financial crisis" when he blocked tightened oversight by his committee in 2008. The financial meltdown followed only a few months later and was caused, to a large degree, by those two institutions assuming housing loans to risky borrowers.

Another classic Progressive feature was also evident in Frank's criticism. Frank thought Obama should have followed standard Progressive paternalistic ideology to force upon the American people something that would cost them more but supposedly was in their best interest. Once again, Progressives always knew better than the citizen where the citizen should spend money and even how much. Well, Starve The Beast is an attempt to put those decisions back in the hands of the citizen.

Secular Jews such as Barney Frank generally only nominally support democratic institutions regardless of any self-serving statements to the contrary. Criticisms of Jewish politicians, however, are generally muted for fear of being charged with anti-Semitism, much like the criticism of blacks is countered by labeling the critic racist. Anti-Semitism was firmly and forever discredited in the West by Nazi Germany, although it survives on steroids in Islamic states. But the governing model of a dictatorial elite has been relentlessly pushed by secular Jews since the time of Karl Marx, himself a secular Jew. A majority of Lenin's Central Committee of the Soviet Communist Party was made up of secular Jews, and one-third of the German communist party leadership following World War I was comprised of secular Jews. Even more astounding, a very large number, perhaps a majority, of the known spies for the USSR unmasked by the Venona Project in the U.S. following World War II were secular Jews, yet to point out any of these inconvenient truths is to be labeled anti-Semitic, risk arrest for a hate crime, and endure universal condemnation in the U.S. from the Progressive media.

Jewish author, Norman Podhoretz, studied the question, "Why Are Jews Liberal?" in his book of the same title, ultimately coming to the conclusion that they are liberal because they always have been liberal since the advent of the nation-states in Europe during the late nineteenth century.[251]

Podhoretz missed the obvious—that Jews, often an oppressed minority, sought to gain power in those states through the political process, including revolutions, to protect themselves from the Christian majorities. He failed to differentiate between the atheist secular Jews who gravitated to communism or Progressivism to gain power, and the bulk of the Jewish population that is merely liberal and that sought acceptance as good Americans.

Nonetheless, the Jewish leadership in the Progressive U.S. government, with few exceptions in 2015, is resolutely secular in orientation and pushing hard for the destruction of the United States as a Christian nation.

Of thirty-four Jewish members of Congress in 2013, only one was a Republican (Eric Cantor, who resigned in 2015), indicating an adherence to the Democrat Party that rivals the forty-four black legislators, of which only one was Republican.

By comparison, the other substantial minority group, Hispanics, featured a count of thirty-one, of which seven were Republican.

Compared to their respective populations, Jews were over-represented by two hundred and fifty percent, blacks under-represented by over fifty percent, and Hispanics under-represented by seventy percent. The majority of Jews in Congress are secular Jews and rabidly Progressive, reflecting a position of wealth and privilege not attained in any country outside of Israel since Stalin's purges of Jewish communists in the 1930s.

Although there are good Americans professing many religions other that Christianity, religion is one of the key elements in restoring America to the land of the free. It is simply a matter of culture; latitudinarianism can reign, but Protestant Christianity established the basic flavor of American culture and way of life, and no other religion can be allowed to become dominant, or even contend against Christianity for the hearts and minds of the American citizenry. To do otherwise is to destroy America and its exceptionalism.

Religions other than Protestantism can be tolerated, respected, and even honored, but they cannot be favored, accommodated by changing American common law practices, or allowed to reduce Christianity to just another religion in the mix. Nor can marginalizing attacks on Christianity be allowed—an attack on Protestant Christianity is an attack on the very cultural fiber that holds the United States together. It is one of the four factors that define American exceptionalism, and if it is replaced by Catholicism or Islam, the character of the United States will change dramatically.

The citizenry, even if not Protestant, must understand that fact, and decide whether the Protestant based United States is worth saving or not. Secular Progressivism is actually a competing religion to Christianity, and that is why Progressives are so intent on destroying all evangelical Christians. Progressives must deny that the United States is a Christian country in order to reduce the dominant culture to just another lifestyle.

Christianity is the primary obstacle to Progressive social justice because it champions the common man (held in contempt by Progressives) and individual liberty (which Progressives say must be eradicated.) Under Protestant Christianity, law comes from God to every individual, whereas under Progressivism, law is made by the Progressive elite, acting as if they were God, and the common man is to simply obey.

To take the Progressive dogma of social justice to its logical conclusion, women desiring to have children will be required to put in an application with the Progressive government, and they will be issued sperm from approved males (all Progressives, of course) so the population will be not only genetically improved, but made more alike and, therefore, more easily controlled. Defective females will be sterilized, along with males determined to have undesirable characteristics. Infanticide and euthanasia have always been championed by Progressives, and they believe decisions on such matters must rest with government rather than with parents, family members, or relatives.

In the short run, Americans can expect to see Progressives championing inter-faith and inter-racial marriages, both in order to reduce the element that can claim to be carrying the banner of their Founding Father ancestors, and to make the population easier to control. The elite will remain separate, as always befits an aristocracy, but if the common people all become brown with a common history of emerging from underclass status, their rule by an aristocracy becomes much easier.

Sexual experimentation is important and should be taught in schools, so not only is the nuclear family abolished and children become wards of the state, but if a woman has children by more than one man, the state's position is greatly strengthened. The Christian teaching of sexual abstinence before marriage and marriage as sacred between a man and a woman is counter-productive to the Progressive agenda.

Every day television hammers home the Progressive message, and it is so ubiquitous that people no longer even notice it. For example, in the popular television drama, *The Good Wife*, the main character and heroine is atheist Alicia Florrick. When she is troubled by the loss of an extra-marital partner, her daughter offers comfort by saying that the man is now in heaven with God. Alicia will have none of it, correcting and lecturing her daughter. She states there is no heaven, and tells her daughter the fact that there is no God is not better, "just truer." A better Progressive could not have been showcased, and the show clearly proselytizes atheism as at least the moral equivalent of Christianity, if not superior, and, actually, the correct belief. In 2015, the show was in its seventh season and had won numerous awards and critical acclaim from Progressives.

In a nutshell, any potentially successful defense against a

323

Progressive Federal Government first requires that Protestant Christianity be strengthened.

Roman Catholicism is not excluded from this program, but Protestantism is better fitted for a democratic republic under common law as it does not require intermediaries such as priests and the pope to facilitate an individual's dialog with Christ or God. Christians must boycott advertisers who pay for Progressive propaganda shows such as *Law and Order, The Good Wife, The View*, and the daily fare on Progressive networks such as MSNBC and CNN. Christian pastors **must** drop their emphasis on social justice and start preaching salvation, morality, and God-given liberties as preachers did in 1774 through 1783. Every minister should have a copy of John Wingate Thornton's 1923 work *The Pulpit of the American Revolution, or the Political Sermons of the Period of 1776, with a Historical Introduction, Notes, and Illustrations*, and use it, along with the Bible, to guide his flock out of the Progressive morass in which his congregation is floundering.

Second are the primary individual rights reserved to the people through the Constitution's Bill of Rights—they must be clarified and strengthened. Most important are the rights to assemble, the protection of religion from government rather than government from religion, freedom of speech, and to keep and bear arms. These rights are the key to maintaining a free society, and must be protected at all costs. They protect the citizenry from government, pure and simple, and it is precisely these rights that are attacked daily in Congress and the executive branch in order to increase government power. As of this writing, some forty-one Democrat members of the Senate are moving forward with Senate Resolution 19, to re-write the 1st Amendment of the Constitution to restrict political speech except by certain media outlets that will be authorized by the government.[252]

Needless to say, what government grants, government can also take away. Any move to change any of the first ten amendments to fit Progressive ideology must be fought with every ounce of energy a citizen possesses. Citizens must always remember that Progressives view the Constitution as outdated, and most favor creating an entirely new constitution along the lines of Rexford Tugwell's (known as "Rex the Red" for his promotion of communism during FDR's New Deal) *The Emerging Constitution*, the output in 1974 of a ten-year project by the Ford Foundation, absolutely dedicated to creating a

Progressive constitution to guide a socialist United States into a Progressive/elite dictatorship.[253] Note also that the Ford Foundation was, and is, a tax-free (501c3) organization, yet promotes a socialist political agenda. Take that, you Tea Partiers!

The 2nd Amendment is under attack daily not only in the Progressive Federal Government but by the media across America. Although gun-related deaths other than suicides have steadily declined in the United States, phony statistics continue to surface to support gun registration and confiscation. Most gun owners in Connecticut opted to ignore the registration law following the Sandy Hook school shooting in 2012, and dodged a bullet. A regional newspaper published the names and addresses of citizens who registered their guns, and privacy issues were raised without effect. Demonization of gun owners was obviously the intent, and the Federal Government did nothing about the civil rights of gun owners that were being trampled.

As Chairman of the U.S. Civil Rights Commission, Mary Berry, once said, "Civil rights laws were not passed to protect the rights of white men and do not apply to them."[254] Perhaps counterintuitive to Progressives, deaths involving firearms are highest where the laws are the most restrictive, and, in Australia, where firearms were confiscated, crime has skyrocketed. But all this misses the point of the Amendment—the possession of guns by the civilian population was to put a curb on *government* power—the same power today that is seeking to outlaw private gun ownership.

Third, any and all attempts to implement the principles and practices of Agenda 21, many of which are already in place, must be resisted with courage born of desperation. Inherent in these initiatives is the destruction of the right to own property and to use that property as the owner sees fit. Almost daily, new laws come out of Congress along with orders and regulations from of the executive branch that infringe on the rights of property owners. Originally, property taxes were placed only on productive property, and, to a large degree, they were taxes on the means of production and gain. To satisfy government's insatiable thirst for money, property taxes were re-worked and placed on wealth, as if wealth was an evil to be taxed out of existence.

Patriots need to campaign for the restoration of taxes only on the means of production, not on private homes and other items of wealth that earn no income for their owners. A good rule would be that if a homeowner's exemption is in place, the property should not be taxed at all. If the rich must be taxed for their luxurious lifestyles, then government could tax very high-priced properties (such as those appraised at over one million dollars) with an exclusion of some basic amount (such as a half million dollars).

Fourth, all Progressives must be voted out of office at the federal, state and local levels, regardless of party, although the majority are members of the Democrat Party. Every vote for a Progressive speeds the destruction of America, and every citizen must register his protest. No doubt many Progressives will be elected and re-elected, but there is no excuse for not making every effort short of assassination to rid the country of the agents for its own destruction. A good rule for the voter would be to always vote for a Republican and always against the incumbent in the primary. Increasing the turnover in public office lessens the penchant for corruption, as it takes several years for politicians to learn how to be corrupt on a truly damaging scale. In addition, the rule to apply to every politician is: *a politician who passes laws, but does not believe the laws apply to him in the same manner as the ordinary citizen, does not deserve to have the power to pass laws.*

But patriots cannot hold the barricades much longer in the face of Progressive dominance. Sooner or later the right to keep and bear arms will be abolished, and, with it, the rights to assemble and freedom of speech. Already a law is in place limiting freedom of assembly and freedom of speech in the presence, near or expected, of the president. Taxes on property go up every year, and, in some jurisdictions, the budget of the locality is made first, and taxes adjusted to raise the required income. Taxes have reached the point where a large portion of the citizenry is in bondage as serfs: citizens who cannot afford to put money aside for their own pension or retirement are required to pay for the pensions and retirement of government employees.

Serfdom and slavery are already upon us, and the United States is rapidly breaking apart into a two class society, Progressive elite and serf. This phenomenon has been well documented by social scientists such as Robert D. Putnam in his bestseller, *Bowling Alone*.[255] Progressives are choosing to live in enclaves, sometimes gated and guarded, for their own well-being and protection from the masses. Sociologist Charles Murray found that Progressive elites self-segregated themselves into elite bubbles easily seen in socio-economic data by zip code across the U.S.

The elite zips, called "superzips," tended to cluster around certain locations, and the privileged could go weeks or months without contact with common people except as domestics. The top clusters of superzips were (in declining order of size) New York, Washington, D.C., Chicago, Boston, San Francisco, Silicon Valley, Los Angeles, Philadelphia, Dallas, Houston, and Atlanta. Thirteen states had no elite clusters at all, and eleven states had only a single cluster of five thousand adults or less.[256] According to that data, literally half of the states could be written off as politically meaningless. Wealth, education, and importance in the United States had become highly concentrated into eighteen specific areas, and people living outside those power centers today possess little or no influence concerning the future of America. They are only to consume, pay taxes, and obey.

When Islamic terrorists flew into the twin towers of the World Trade Center in 2001, President Bush counseled the American citizenry to continue their normal habits and consume. Supposedly, if Americans continued to purchase new cars and went on with their lives as always, it would be a signal to terrorists that America couldn't be defeated. What he didn't say was that the government needed Americans to continue consuming so tax money would continue to roll in. Nonetheless, the proper comparison was made: after Pearl Harbor the nation's military recruiting offices were jammed with volunteers; after 9-11, there was no surge at all except in people seeing their counselors and psychiatrists to deal with their anger. Americans had lost their willingness to defend themselves and had turned into disturbed, bleating sheep.

**Time to Take Action**

The Progressive government of the U.S. is well on its way to realizing the fundamental transformation of the United States into a dictatorship of elites on the fascist government model first promulgated by Benito Mussolini. The American citizen is in a race for the life of the United States. On the Progressive side, the politicians are eliminating individual liberties, propagandizing American children, and changing the demographics of the country to construct a manageable (or easily manipulated) majority dependent on government to the point they will support it even at the cost of their personal liberties.

One must always remember that Adolf Hitler came to power through normal constitutional processes, then was voted extraordinary powers by the Reichstag in a supposedly emergency situation. President Obama possessed such extraordinary powers from June to December, 2012 (during the 2012 presidential election). He can re-assume those powers at any time today by declaring a national emergency. The citizens of the U.S. have already given their head of state the power to rule as a dictator.

Quite possibly Obama is waiting for the proper time to use those powers, and it may not be long in coming. It is easy to forecast how this will all happen, Progressives are hell-bent on marginalizing Christianity, eliminating the citizen's right to keep and bear arms, restrict freedom of speech, and destroy the citizen's property rights. All four of these goals are within reach, and, as they get nearer, Progressives grow stronger. When the time is right, Progressives will collapse the economy, the president will declare a national emergency, and the nation will stride into the Progressive brave new world of Agenda 21 with a country run by a dictatorship of Progressive elites. If it doesn't happen under Obama, it will surely happen under Hillary Clinton if she is elected president.

But now comes Starve The Beast! This is the only way the individual citizen can save the United States.Government must be forced to cut its size and give up power to the people while the people still have freedom of speech, remain armed, and look to Christianity and the Christian God for guidance. With the decline in revenue that Starve the Beast could bring about, Progressives could become unable to fund the payments they need to make to control the dependents they have created, and using the Federal Reserve to prop up government almost certainly will bring on runaway inflation. The resulting discontent with Progressives could cause either a massive political re-evaluation and rejection of Progressivism, or a revolution, either peaceful or violent. Hopefully, any revolution would be short and relatively peaceful, but, in any case, at least the reader will have taken steps to protect himself and his family.

Take the first step and lower consumption and expenditures as much as possible. Start putting money aside into items that will hold their value in an inflationary spiral such as trade goods and precious metals. Instead of going to a professional football game, buy a water filter so drinking water will be always available. Instead of a new dress, buy dehydrated foods so you will have something to eat when grocery stores are closed or gutted. Jettison all expenditures that are not absolutely necessary. Become the ant, and give up being the grasshopper. Learn from Michelle Obama as she spends your hard-earned money jet-setting around the world with her two girls. She only has that money to spend because you are continuing to spend.

Second, clean house. Sell all the "stuff" that isn't necessary or that you bought because you thought at one time it might be nice to own. Pare down to the necessities, and at the same time, convert what you own from "stuff" to assets. Assets are prepper items such as gold, silver, food, toilet paper, tissues, antibiotics, medical supplies, ammo, ammo cans, diesel fuel, gasoline (be sure to use a stabilizer for long term storage), shoes, clothing, soap, and many other items found on prepper web sites. A good rule is to store up everything rationed during World War II, and everything likely to be rationed in the future. Get rid of luxury items like second homes, cars, trucks, boats, collectibles—in fact, everything that is not essential for day-to-day living. Collectible markets collapse in hard times—people only collect when they have an excess of cash. Things such as collections of Nike shoes, Barbie dolls, Beanie Babies and the like, should be sold at auction as soon as possible. And pets—make sure they can't reproduce, and pare them back until they cost no more than a total of twenty-five dollars per month, including veterinarian bills. Any pet that becomes badly injured or sick and will cost more than $100 in medical services should be put to sleep.

Third, make like a mole and disappear. Government is currently monitoring emails and recording domestic phone calls supposedly to fight terrorism, but are actually conducting surveillance throughout the United States like all heavy-handed dictatorships needing to closely control the citizenry to maintain their grip on power. Loosen that grip. Start using thepost office again—it's a lot harder to open letters, copy the contents, and reseal, than to intercept an electronic transmission and record it electronically. Use land lines for phone calls—cell phone calls are easier to intercept. Cut down on the number of bank accounts, and eliminate the use of credit cards in favor of cash.

Swap or gift goods and services as discussed earlier, and do not purchase anything important on the Internet where the government can obtain full details of your transaction and build a history of your commercial life. If you purchase items on the web, use a series of email accounts, migrating from one account to another on a regular basis and terminating the previous account to eliminate unwanted messages after you decide not to purchase further from that supplier. Limit your web purchases to normal items and never use the web to purchase preparedness supplies, ammunition, and other items that will be sure to draw the government's attention. At all times remember, the American surveillance state is already an actuality, and all those employees in Homeland Security have to be doing something. DHS has also purchased billions and billions of rounds of ammunition, so they can also be expected to shoot someone.

Fourth, reduce your obligations and debts. Move to cheaper digs or refinance your home on a fifteen year fixed mortgage. The economy won't last fifteen years, and when the collapse comes, you'll be able to pay off your mortgage with very cheap dollars. Variable-rate credit card debt will be a killer, and you should either pay the debt off, or convert it to a fixed rate through a bank loan such as a second mortgage. Under no circumstances should you take out a demand loan that is subject to being called in at the bank's pleasure.

Fifth, plan for the collapse: don't be stuck with a pricy house in Detroit that no one wants. Go back to school and learn practical skills that will be important in a collapse. Knowing how to preserve food through canning or dehydrate it, build a smokehouse or root cellar, garden with heirloom seeds, communicate with a ham radio, defend yourself and your family with the appropriate firearms, and many other skills may mean the difference between life and death at some point. Put aside one or two years of food for your entire family, and read a few of the many preparedness books on the market. Two highly recommended works are Fernando Aguirre's *Surviving the Economic Collapse* and James Wesley Rawles's *How to Survive the End of the World as We Know it*.

Sixth, communicate with like-minded citizens for mutual benefit, both in swapping and in mutual defense. Attend a church with a knowledgeable pastor, one who stresses salvation and community, but scorns the teaching of social justice and Progressivism. Ask him where the bible says it is proper for the citizen to be taxed so the government can give the taxpayer's money to another person to "spread the wealth." Times will get hard, but at least you'll be somewhat prepared rather than having everything suddenly cave in and leave you with nothing. Remember, whatever government says it won't do is probably exactly what it will do. Also, whatever government says you shouldn't do is probably something you should do. Progressive politicians lie; that is their stock in trade and they see no sin in lying—that is, *their* telling of lies. You, however, are not allowed to tell lies. You already know they lie, so believing anything they say is now on you, not on them.

There are various opinions as to the minimum size a community needs to be for survival when faced by looters, gangs, and raiders of all sorts, but generally it appears to be sixteen to twenty adults, armed and outfitted, and capable of conducting a military defense. Solitary couples in isolated locations will have little chance of surviving, and to be unarmed will probably and automatically mean abuse, sexual attack, torture, and, ultimately, death in unspeakable circumstances for all members of your family.

Today, the Federal Government is optimistically taking in roughly $3.18 trillion per year in revenue (including Social Security contributions which shouldn't count) and spending $3.76 trillion (spending eighteen percent over revenues). That doesn't seem to bother any of our politicians, but perhaps spending $3.8 trillion and only receiving $1.9 trillion (spending a hundred percent over revenue) might. It will also have another impact, particularly if many of the Chinese goods coming into the U.S. go unsold. The balance of payments between China and the U.S. should reverse, ending China's economic hegemony over the U.S.

From that point on, it is difficult to foresee an exact sequence of events. Whenever the dollar is removed as the world's reserve currency, and that is a certainty, economic collapse will begin—only the speed of the collapse will be in debate. At that point, government will be totally impotent to stop the collapse. Progressivism will have been shown to be the height of stupidity, but Progressives will blame their own incompetence on people who decided to Starve The Beast rather than looking in the mirror.

At any rate, the Progressive nanny state will be unable to become dictatorial as people turn to God and the Christian Church, and prepare to defend their families with arms if necessary. This depression will be the first one the government will have caused by spending beyond its means, and the citizenry must demand a cessation of all non-essential government activities. The government may go for the gold instead, and attempt to establish a Progressive regime following fascist lines. A domestic jihad may result, the character of which will be unlike anything ever seen before in the U.S. If so, one can confidently forecast a second civil war.

At that point, the list of installations in Appendix D will be of great importance, as military actions will probably determine the success or failure of the revolution. Today, the military is still generally sympathetic to the patriot cause, particularly with the Obama administration failing miserably to provide the obligated services to veterans and Obama's own published attitudes. However, that may change in the near future as Obama curries favor with the military, eliminates conservatives and Christians from the armed forces, and increases the percentage of minorities on active duty. It is difficult to forecast what military units will do toward the end of 2016—the most likely time for Obama to collapse the economy—but patriots need to stay close to the military and the men and women they know on active duty.

Few Progressives serve in the military as officers, and the writer wife of one who did recounted an incident in which she was approached by another wife. The lady said the writer was the first Democrat among the military wives she had ever met.[257]

The military is changing, but still has a long way to go before it is safe for the Progressives. The former director of the Harvard ROTC in 2004 noted that the Harvard Law School held the military in disdain, and even after 9/11, uniformed Harvard ROTC students were abused as "Fascists."[258] The services today are still largely conservative, Republican, patriotic, and generally view Washington accurately as a sink hole of rats and parasites. The Progressives have made a huge mistake in alienating the military, a mistake some are currently attempting to rectify by appearing to support programs honoring veterans and service members, even if their pious pronouncements ring hollow.

As of November 23, 2013, five-eighths of active duty military personnel was still white, and, with the exception of the marine corps, over fifty percent were married, including officers of which over seventy percent were married. The military was also well-educated, in spite of Obama's deprecating comments. Over ninety-two percent had at least a high school diploma or GED, and eighty-nine percent of officers had a BA or BS degree from college. The average age was thirty years old, and over fourteen percent were female.[259] With continual replacement of military personnel by civilian contractors in non-combat duties, the armed forces have shrunk to under 1.4 million personnel, not counting the National Guard. That trend will undoubtedly continue since contractors are more responsive to money and more easily controlled by civilians. It is quite possible that less than ten percent of these men and women will follow Progressives over the cliff to a dictatorship, and the military may well back a coup to eliminate Progressive madness. Only time will tell, but time is running out for Progressives to win over the military. If enough citizens Starve The Beast, the Progressives can surely be defeated.

Unfortunately, with every passing month, Progressives grow in strength and the future for American liberties grows dimmer. The number of atheists increases, as do the number of government-managed minorities and political groups increasingly dependent on Progressivism for their economic health and well-being. The middle class grows weaker, and the gap in income between the top five percent and the bottom sixty-five percent grows wider. With every day the nation becomes more sharply divided into two classes: the Progressive elites, rich and powerful, and the common citizen, becoming increasingly poorer. The eventual lot of the common citizen is that of serf, unable to practice Christianity, without private property, without the American dream, without individual liberty, and without hope.

The choice is yours: misery and ignominy, or rising up and announcing to all that the freedom-loving American is alive and well, and that you will settle for nothing less than the right to live as you see fit within the framework of God's law and the common law of your ancestors. You will determine what your children are to be taught, you will police your community, you will defend your nation from foreign aggression, you will support a government that honors and respects its citizens and promotes individual liberty, and you will dispense charity to your fellow man in need. In the words of Abraham Lincoln, you will see to it "that this nation, under God, shall have a new birth of freedom—and that government of the people, by the people, and for the people, shall not perish from the earth."

Following the words of John F. Kennedy, you will not ask what government can do for you, but what you can do for the government. A good government first and foremost grows out of good citizens, and you will be one of the virtuous upon whom the government can depend for protecting and saving individual liberty and the American way of life. The various Tea Parties have already shown us the way—without leaders or money they rose to challenge the corrupt and evil and told the apathetic that remaining uninvolved meant eventual serfdom. You must become the government, and right the sinking ship of state.

Beware the politician who says he's a champion of the common man. Did he start working as a teenager? Did he serve in the armed forces? Did he work as an adult to pay the mortgage on his home, provide for his family, and take responsibility for all of his setbacks? Or did he simply game the system, attend an Ivy League school, take advantage of government programs, and blame others for his failures?

Beware the individual who has never delivered a newspaper, shoveled snow off a walk, mowed a lawn, fired a gun, repaired a plumbing leak, fixed a leaky gutter, changed a tire, pumped his own gas, taken care of animals, built anything with a hammer and nails, or chopped firewood. Worst of all is someone who hasn't driven a car in the last twenty tears (like Hillary Clinton.) It is not enough—and perhaps even irrelevant—to attend your child's ball game—you must teach your child right from wrong and infuse in him a love of God. Your Progressive government will teach him all the wrong things, concentrating only on how to be a good servant of the ruling elite. You must relieve government of this burden—it is one done poorly by government minions, and always accomplished against your best interests.

So that's it: is the United States and the American to become footnotes in history as failed experiments and concepts, discarded by enfeebled citizens grown indolent from television, professional sports, love of celebrities, and noninvolvement? Or is it possible, maybe even just possible, that there are enough Americans remaining who have not succumbed to Progressivism and its "political correctness" to reinvigorate American society and its political body?

As one person said after reading the above, "I don't know the answers to the above questions, but if the United States becomes a dictatorship of the Progressive elite, then count me out. Not down for the count, but totally out, for I will no longer be in existence."

So mote it be.

# Appendix A

## Proposed Constitutional Amendments

### 1—Term Limits & Rotation in Government Service

No Congressman shall serve more than four consecutive terms, nor senators two consecutive terms. Judges are limited to twelve years consecutive service. No individual shall serve in government, all positions combined, without private sector experience for eight years for more than ten years, after which he must work again in the private sector before becoming eligible again for government service. After working in the private sector for eight years, the individual is eligible for twelve years of continuous government employment, after twelve years in the private sector, sixteen years, after sixteen years in the private sector, twenty years in government. This rule applies to all government employees, including civil service, elected officials, and teachers. (For example, a person could work ten years in the private sector, then twelve years in government, then six years in the private sector, then up to another twenty years in government.)

The purpose of this amendment is to eliminate the professional politicians and bureaucrats who become detached from the people and the reality of life in the private sector. Service in government is not a career or a job; it is a privilege and with it comes heavy responsibility.

### 2—Government Service Remuneration and Limitations

Congress shall make no law that exempts Congress or its staff personnel or any other civilian employee or elected official of the federal government from its provisions. Nor shall Congress pass any law that treats any federal civilian employee or elected official, differently from any ordinary citizen.

335

Neither the Congress nor any state legislature shall pass any law that requires public monies to be used to fund, wholly or in part, any pension or retirement plan for any civilian employee or elected official of the federal government, state, and local governments, or any institution or organization funded wholly or in part with public monies. Labor and employee unions and organizations shall be limited in their powers and activities in federal, state, and local government organizations and those institutions funded primarily with public money. Activities that are prohibited are strikes, work stoppages, and collective bargaining for wages, pensions, retirement plans, and benefits.

All federal, state, and local government civilian personnel shall be included in the national old-age entitlement systems of Social Security and Medicare without exception, and shall be responsible for both contributions in the amount legislated as "self-employment" tax. All money already held for such employees by other retirement and health systems shall be transferred to the Social Security and Medicare systems.

Any individual who has been in a decision-making position in the federal government at the level of GS-12 or higher, or receives retirement pay for military service as an officer, shall not be employed by any corporation or organization that received five million dollars or more from the federal government in fulfillment of any contract or contracts during the five years prior to the individual's departure from federal employment. This restriction shall be in effect for five years after said individual's employment by the federal government was terminated.

This amendment also applies to executive orders, secretarial orders, and administrative rules and regulations of all types. The Congress shall have power to enforce, by appropriate legislation, the provisions of this article.

The purpose of this amendment is to ensure that government employees do not become a special class of citizens, an aristocracy, with special rights and privileges, particularly since they did not pay for those privileges themselves. All citizens should be equal under the law.

## 3—Citizenship

Citizenship in the United States is divided into four classes: Citizen, Denizen, Friendly Alien, and Enemy Alien.

Citizen: An individual in the United States automatically is a full citizen if both natural parents were United States citizens at the time of his birth. If an individual was born in the United States and the citizenship of one or both of his natural parents is unproved, said individual shall be considered a Denizen, but may gain citizenship through naturalization. Individuals born in the United States with one natural parent being a United States citizen and the other claiming citizenship from another nation is a United Citizen until the end of his eighteenth year, during which he may elect to take the citizenship of one or the other parent. Failure in his eighteenth year to declare United States citizenship as his sole citizenship shall change the individual's class to Denizen.

Denizen: A Denizen is an individual allowed to reside in the United States without restriction, but who may not vote in any election for government offices or be eligible for any government office at any level. Certain rights and benefits, such as to a free education, may be withheld from a Denizen according to Congressional and state legislation. This class is subject to the same obligations of a full citizen, including service in the armed forces and subject to the laws of the United States and its states. United States citizenship may be attained by anyone in the class of Denizen excepting those with criminal records containing a class "D" felony and according to the rules and regulations of naturalization as established by Congress.

Friendly Alien: A Friendly Alien is an individual maintaining citizenship from a foreign nation that is considered "Friendly" by the U.S. State Department, and who is allowed to reside in the United States according to Congressional legislation. He may apply for the class of Denizen or Citizen according to Congressional legislation, but must have arrived in the United States after having been processed for the appropriate visa by the competent authority. Congress may exempt individuals as it sees fit from certain neighboring countries from the visa process for specified lengths of time and specified reasons. In the event an individual in this class over-stays his visa, commits a felony, or otherwise becomes an undesirable resident according to Congressional or state legislation, his status automatically is changed to Unfriendly Alien and subject to the laws promulgated for that class. Friendly Aliens are subject to U.S. income taxes and all federal, state and local laws, and, in certain cases, may be allowed to work in the U.S. according to law. The ability to receive government benefits would be subject to applicable federal and state law.

Unfriendly Alien: An Unfriendly Alien is an individual who is a citizen of a nation that has been considered "Unfriendly" by the U.S. State Department. In times of war or other national emergency, Unfriendly Aliens may be interned or expelled according to Congressional legislation, and are subject to stricter laws, rules, and regulations, and have limited standing for benefits as determined by law.

Current Citizens who gained citizenship by being born in the United States and are already eighteen years old will retain their citizenship under this article, but only if they renounce citizenship to other countries to which they were previously entitled. Individuals under eighteen years who were born in the U.S. will be subject to the above rules concerning the citizenship of their natural parents.

This amendment would eliminate the problems of anchor babies and many of the problems with the current immigration system. It would eliminate special rules that allow certain foreign nationals to remain in the United States while maintaining dual citizenship. Dual citizenship would be abolished, and the amendment would allow for regulations to ensure that only citizens in good standing would be able to vote.

## 4—Education

All matters dealing with education at all levels are strictly the province and competency of the states, local school districts, and the people. The only exceptions are the military service academies and other training and education limited to serving members of the armed forces and, in the case of dependents temporarily resident with serving members in foreign countries, dependent education through high school.

No public or private educational institution, other than the education facilities for armed forces members and their dependents, including any institution or foundation connected to or with such institution shall receive from the federal government in any fiscal year more than $100 for each student enrolled full time in an accredited graduate or undergraduate program on March 15th of the year in question for any reason of program, whether it be research, tuition, operating costs, or any other.

This amendment would eliminate the failed federal Department of Education and return education to the states and local communities. It would remove federal funds from influencing education and local schools, allowing them to operate in a much less bureaucratic mode. Universities would be thrown back on their own methods of raising funds, resulting in more effective use of resources, and force faculty to teach instead of enjoying a life of high-paid leisure. It would also uncouple universities from their dependence on taxpayer funds while, at the same time, refusing to submit to taxpayer control.

## 5—Modification of the 14th Amendment

The 14th Amendment of the Constitution of the United States is hereby repealed, and all laws made by the United States Congress in support of the 14th Amendment are hereby declared unconstitutional and unenforceable.

All persons born of two citizens of the United States or naturalized in the United States, and subject to the jurisdiction thereof, are citizens of the United States and of the state wherein they reside. No state shall make or enforce any law which shall abridge the privileges or immunities of citizens of the United States as defined in the United States Constitution; nor shall any state deny to any person within its jurisdiction the equal protection of its state's laws.

Representatives shall be apportioned among the several states according to their respective numbers, counting the citizens and denizens in each state.

Congress shall make no law affecting private property or commerce except where such property or commerce can be demonstrated conclusively to be beyond a single state's jurisdiction or when negotiations between the several states to arrive at a satisfactory solution have failed after a substantial effort. Such laws by Congress shall then only affect those states involved in the case or cases at hand and no other. No executive orders shall be issued affecting private property or commerce. No state shall make or enforce any law which shall abridge the civil rights of citizens of the United States, nor shall any state deprive any citizen of the United States of life, liberty or property, or the use thereof as the citizen owner sees fit, without due process of law. Neither the Congress, the president, nor any state shall enact or enforce any law that treats one citizen differently from another except for mental incapacity or commission of a felony. Specifically, no law can invoke different penalties for a crime depending on whom the victim is or to what

339

group, without reservation, the victim belongs. Congress shall also make no law that exempts Congress or any federal employee from any valid law made by Congress or a state. In the case that an individual is found "not guilty" of a crime involving a specific set of circumstances, those circumstances shall not be used for further prosecution by any appropriate jurisdiction.

The Congress shall have power to enforce, by appropriate legislation, the provisions of this article.

This amendment is intended to eliminate the overreach possible with the current Supreme Court by using the current 14th Amendment as a club to force compliance by all states to the justices' opinions. It would streamline due process in the justice system, and re-establish the proper relationship between the state and federal government with respect to judicial matter.

## 6—The Federal Judiciary

Federal judges at all levels may be terminated from federal employment by a majority vote of the registered voters or by a vote of "no confidence" by a majority of the state legislatures in their jurisdictions or districts. Judges removed by this mechanism are barred from any further government employment at any level, as well as the forfeiture of all federal government pay, pensions, and benefits accrued by that judge during his government employment.

The federal judiciary shall be restricted from assuming oversight power on the compliance of its rulings; such power shall pass to the executive branch. The failure of the appropriate federal department to properly enforce a valid court decision within a reasonable length of time, but not less than six months, shall automatically trigger a contempt citation by the affected court against the delinquent department, and against key personnel involved in the department's failure to enforce, severely and personally. This contempt citation would automatically prohibit and invalidate any further rulings or actions by that department and its cited employees, including drawing funds, pay, or benefits, until any such named individuals are terminated with cause from the department involved.

This amendment is intended to make the Supreme Court and other judges responsible for their actions and eliminate the last vestige of Alexander Hamilton's aristocracy in the government. It also gives the Court a mechanism by which it could enforce its rulings on the other branches of government without being at the mercy of a president who might disagree with its findings.

## 7—Freedom of Religion

The 1st Amendment's clause on religion "Congress shall make no law respecting an establishment of religion, or prohibiting the free exercise thereof" is deleted and replaced with: "Neither the Congress, the president, nor the judiciary shall in any law, order, ruling, regulation or proclamation, or in any other manner, shall restrict the free exercise of any religion, so long as such exercise does not cause harm to individuals or restrict others' free exercise of religion. Christian interdenominational practice and prayer and other voluntary Christian religious observations without cost to the government are specifically allowed on public property and during public events."

This amendment is to enable the rolling back of anti-Christian and anti-religion rulings made by the Supreme Court over the last century. The 1st Amendment has been egregiously interpreted to protect government from religion rather that following the original intent of protecting religion from government, and that is reversed by this amendment.

## 8—2nd Amendment

The 2nd Amendment is hereby deleted and replaced with: "As an armed citizenry proficient in the use of its arms, is necessary to the security of a free state, the right of all citizens of the United States to keep and bear arms shall not be infringed upon or restricted in any fashion. Such right is forfeit through conviction of a felony involving the use of such arms, loss of citizenship, or mental incapacity."

This amendment strengthens the previous 2nd Amendment and eliminates all doubt as to the intent of the previous amendment with respect to the role of the militia.

## 9—Treaties and International Agreements

Treaties and international agreements shall be clearly subordinate to the Constitution and ratified by two-thirds of the Senate in order to take effect. The use of executive orders, secretarial orders, administrative rulings, and court judgments to implement the substance of any international agreement, except as exempted by Congress, shall be prohibited. The substance of all treaties and international agreements shall be fully disclosed to Congress within seven days of signing to be eligible for ratification or to take effect.

This amendment strengthens the Senate's position, requiring its ratification of all international treaties, agreements, and covenants before becoming law in the United States. Without the Senate's approval, international agreements have no force or effect on American citizens or in the United States.

## 10 - Removal of Elected Officials

The sentence: "The Senate shall have the sole power to try all impeachments" in Article 1, Section 3, is deleted.

An Impeachment tribunal shall be constituted for the impeachment trial of a president after impeachment charges have been brought by the House of Representatives. The tribunal shall be composed of one individual from each state, and elected or appointed by the several states according to state law. It shall be the sole power to determine the proper judgment.

Any and all senators and congressmen may be removed from office by a vote of "no confidence" by their respective state legislatures or by a referendum by the citizens of said state in accordance with said state's laws for citizen referendums. Upon a vote for removal according to state law, all federal government pay, pensions, and benefits accrued by the individual removed shall be forfeited.

Termination of all civil service employees are subject to an administrative hearing if requested by the party terminated. Termination with cause as differentiated from a termination due to a reduction in force, or the elimination of an employee's job for a valid or technological reason, shall eliminate the rights of such terminated employee to all federal government pay, pensions, and benefits accrued during the individual's government service.

This amendment enables the swift termination of government employees and the levying of penalties for misconduct while in office or government employment.

## 11—Welfare Rights

The clause: "provide for the common defense and general welfare of the United States" in Article 1, Section 8, (Enumerated Powers of Congress) is hereby replaced with: "provide for the common defense and those services and assets that promote the general prosperity of all citizens such as the building and maintenance of waterways, ports, interstate transportation, the nation's security, scientific research, old age assistance, disaster relief and other general activities that otherwise would require consortiums of multiple states to implement."

This amendment re-defines the scope of the government's involvement and responsibilities in providing welfare funds to American citizens, and places the primary emphasis on those items and policies that improve the living standard and general welfare of all citizens rather than individuals.

## 12—Powers of the President

The president of the United States shall exercise those powers enumerated by this Constitution and all such powers granted to him by Congress to conduct activities as defined and funded by Congress. The president specifically shall not implement initiatives without first seeking congressional approval except as in the conduct of his duties enumerated by this Constitution and having received funding from Congress.

This amendment places additional restrictions on the powers of the President and directs him to faithfully carry out the will of Congress

# Appendix B

## Changing the Debate

The following organizations, terms, and individuals should be made subject to the listed modifiers or adjectives in order to eliminate the Progressive advantage in using politically correct (to Progressives) language. Call things for what they are, and stop ceding the high moral ground to Progressive propagandists!

ACORN—corrupting organization

ACLU—former communist front organization

Al Sharpton—former police informer

Anyone from the federal government—Death star emissary

Authoritarian—Fascist

Banker—Bankster

Bar Association—The Communist Party in the U.S.

Barack Obama—homosexual, Muslim president of uncertain parentage

Bible—Holy Bible

Bill Clinton—sexual predator

BP—British Petroleum

California—where the young people go to die

Celebrities—America's royals

Charlie Rangel—corrupt politician

Chinese goods—cheaply-made

Christmas—Christmas, not "holidays"

CIA—technology dependent

Citizen—ignored, disregarded, excessively taxed, persecuted, taken for granted

Common Citizen—trying to make ends meet, doing his best

Communism—failed system

Communist—misguided, delusional

Debbie Wasserman Schultz—rabidly anti-Christian, anti-military, anti-constitution
Democrat—misguided, left-wing, leftist, socialist fellow-traveler
Department of Education—useless, white elephant
Department of Energy—failed
Department of the Interior—out-of-control, Agenda 21-driven
Entrepreneurs—life blood of the economy
EPA—Agenda 21-driven, anti-people, extremely misguided
Eric Holder—anti-white, anti-Christian
European Union—greatly troubled and failing European Union
Evangelical Christians—Believers in Christ
FDR—2nd rate intellect who made socialism America's state religion
Federal Government —the problem, not the solution
Federal Program—always use the adjective "failed" or "disappointing"
Federal Reserve System—private, unaccountable, secretive
FEMA—most incompetent organization in Washington
Florida—where old people go to die
Forceful Progressive—dictatorial, anti-liberty
Foreign-owned Companies—always lead with the Nation (e.g. British Hollday Inn)
Gays and lesbians—homosexuals
George Soros—anti-American, anti-British, SNAZI financier
Global Warming—bogus, phony
Government Contracts—crony capitalism
Government Employee—One of the privileged
Government Grants to Universities—academic welfare
Government Information or Explanation—propaganda
Government Spokesperson—spindoctor
Great Britain—socialist Great Britain
Harry Reid—union goon
Hillary Clinton—evil radical politician
Hollywood—narcissist heaven
IRS—politician-serving, unaccountable
Ivy League Graduate—One of the anointed
Jan Schakowsky—Communist-wannabee
Japan—the closed marketplace of Japan (to American goods)
Jesse Jackson—pseudo-extortionist

Justice Department—hack, arbitrary, anti-conservative
Koran—Holy Koran (only if "Bible" is "Holy Bible")
Lawyer—Functionary, privileged
Members of the Teachers' Union—destroyers of American values and patriotism
Middle-class—disappearing, taxed out of existence, strawman
Mitsubishi—builder of the Japanese Zero
Movie & Television Stars—behavioral liars
Nancy Pelosi—fabulously wealthy machine politician
Native Americans—NASAM, for North American Stone Age Man
NLRB—union-favoring
NSA—super-snooping
Politician—dissembling, out-of-touch, self-important, manipulating, lying
Politicians in Office for more than 12 Years—probably corrupt
Professional Athletes—self-absorbed, narcissist
Progressive Christians—soulless, adrift, sad-faced
Progressives—SNAZIs, misguided believers in the lies they were taught, delusional
Rahm Emanuel—grimmer-faced Mayor Dailey
Ramadan—Muslim religious month of Ramadan
Russia—resurgent, aggressive
Shell—Royal Dutch Shell
Small Business—embattled, persecuted
Socialism—failed system of socialism
Socialist—misguided socialist
Supreme Court—unrepresentative, liberal, arbitrary
Taxes—confiscatory, excessively high
Television Personalities—narcissistic and arrogant
Terrorists—when true, use "Islamic terrorists"
Transvestites—Cross-dressers
United Nations—anti-American, useless, ineffective, incompetent
Universities—troubled, controversial, expensive, unproductive
University Professors—free-riding credentialed leeches
Veteran—respected, honored
Wall Street Financier—Money manipulator
War on Poverty—immediately lost
Welfare—bloated, family-destroying, spirit-crushing

# Appendix C

## Patriots vs. Progressives

| Tend to be Progressives | Tend to be Patriots |
|---|---|
| AARP Members | Anglers |
| ACLU Members & Supporters | Constitutionalists |
| Actors | Construction Workers |
| Animal Rights Activists | Engineers |
| Atheists | Entrepreneurs |
| Bankers | Evangelical Christians |
| Bicyclists | Farmers |
| Buddhists | Homeowners in red states |
| CFR & Bilderberg Members | Hunters |
| Chambers of Commerce | Law Enforcement Personnel |
| Civilian Government Employees | Libertarians |
| Communists | Mechanics |
| Criminals | Medical Doctors |
| Defense Industry Executives | Military Personnel |
| Crony Capitalist Executives | Motorcycle Riders |
| Gun Control Supporters | People who worked before the age of 17 |
| Homosexuals & Transgender individuals | Ranchers |
| Illegal Immigrants | Rural Inhabitants |
| People with Assets over $10,000,000 | 2nd Amendment Supporters |
| People with Incomes over $1,000,000 | Small Businessmen & Businesswomen |
| People living in Gated Communities | Tea Party Members & Supporters |
| Insurance Salesmen and Executives | Truck Drivers |
| Ivy League Graduates | Veterans |
| Japanese-Americans | Women adept at canning food or sewing |
| Jews | Working People without pensions |
| Lawyers | |
| Low information voters | |
| Muslims | |
| Non-Profit Corporation Employees | |

DAVE DOUGHERTY

Politicians
Public School and University Employees
Public School Teachers
Socialists
Union Members
University Students
University Faculty
Welfare Recipients
Women in interracial marriages

# Appendix D

## Military and Critical Infrastructure Locations

As law and order breaks down in the anticipated economic collapse, as has happened in literally all other instances of full economic collapse in history, the critical infrastructure that has been maintained by the government and public service corporations is almost certain to come under attack. Food supplies are widely dispersed, but other necessities are not. First and foremost is the electric power grid, a woefully vulnerable network of power plants and distribution facilities that are tied together at a number of critical connection points. The equipment is unique at a number of points, and replacement times are in months and, in some cases, as long as a year. Not only is this grid open to terrorist attack with explosives, it is also vulnerable to cyber attacks that could possibly plunge major portions of the U.S. into darkness at any time.

Since it is impossible for ordinary patriots to defend the grid, the only option is to plan for the time when it will be inoperable. For openers, each person should know where the power supplied to his home comes from. Some power companies do not generate power themselves, and are dependent on others as power sources. Such firms will probably be the first to experience outages as power goes into short supply. Secondly, everyone should know how their power is generated: by coal, oil, natural gas, nuclear materials, wind, solar, hydroelectric, and so forth. President Obama and the Progressives are committed to eliminating all coal-fired power plants in the U.S. at the earliest possible date, and if your energy source is coal, you are in an extremely vulnerable position. In your checklist for survival, you should locate those power plants that could be used to provide power in an emergency to your area so you can assist whatever government bodies remain to keep power flowing.

Second to the power grid comes the transportation network. With seven million Muslims, some percentage of which can be expected to attack the U.S. from within, highway and rail bridges and infrastructure cannot be expected to remain open without protection. Every citizen should make a map of his local area, identify those structures that are likely to be destroyed, and determine how he and his family can survive without them. Bridges over the Mississippi, for example, are likely to be destroyed, and the nation cut into two distinct parts. Can you live without traffic crossing the Mississippi, or any of the other choke points in our geography. Families should make lists of such points, and either stand ready to defend them or to live without them functioning.

Third comes the military and its bases. The U.S. military is located throughout the world, but as the collapse deepens, most troops can be expected to return to the continental U.S. (CONUS), particularly from Germany, Italy, Japan, Kuwait, South Korea, and Afghanistan (if still there.) Probably all the units currently in Europe will be withdrawn—a long overdue move since the collapse of the Soviet Union in 1991—and only an eye on North Korea and China will be maintained in the Far East. There are also a number of supply facilities with "War Reserve Stock," mostly in NATO countries, but a few are in "Major Non-NATO Allies."

In CONUS, the closure of bases since 1970 has lowered the number of important installations to a reasonably small number, even including logistics and storage facilities. For example, by state, the list includes:

Anniston Army Depot (Alabama), Depot & Chemical Weapons
Fort Rucker (Alabama), Army Aviation
Redstone Arsenal (Alabama) Missile Command
Fort Greeley (Alaska), Anti-ballistic Missiles
Fort Wainwright (Alaska), 1st Brigade, 25th Inf. Div.
Elmendorf-Richardson (Alaska), 673rd Air Base Wing
Fort Huachuca (Arizona), US Army Intelligence Center
Marine Corps Air Station Yuma (Arizona), Aircraft Gp. 13
Pine Bluff Arsenal (Arkansas), Chemical Weapon Storage
Beale AFB (California), 9th Recon Wing
March ARB (California), 452nd Air Mobility Wing

Marine Corps Air Ground Combat Ctr 29 Palms (California), 7th & 11th Marines
Marine Corps Air Station Miramar (California), 3rd Marine Aircraft Wing
Marine Corps Base Camp Pendleton (California), 1st Marine Exp. Force
Marine Corps Logistics Base Barstow (California), Logistics Maintenance
Marine Corps Recruit Depot San Diego (California), Basic Training
Naval Base Point Loma (California), 3rd Fleet
Presidio of Monterey (California), Defense Language Institute
Sierra Army Depot (California), Ammunition Storage
Vandenberg AFB (California), 30th Space Wing
Fort Carson (Colorado), 4th Infantry Div. & 10th SF Gp
Fort Leslie J. McNair (DC), Mil. Dist. Of Washington
Fort Benning (Georgia), Infantry School, Airborne School, Armor School
Fort Gordon (Georgia), Signal Corps
Fort Stewart (Georgia), 3rd Infantry Div.
Marine Corps Logistics Base Albany (Georgia), Logistics Maintenance
Fort Shafter (Hawaii), US Army Pacific
Marine Corps Base Hawaii (Hawaii), 3rd Marines
Schofield Barracks (Hawaii), 25th Infantry Div.
Charles M. Price Support Center (Illinois)
Rock Island Arsenal (Illinois), Joint Munitions Command
Iowa Army Ammunition Plant (Iowa), Ammunition Production
Fort Leavenworth (Kansas), Command & General Staff College
Fort Riley (Kansas), 1st Infantry Div.
Blue Grass Army Depot (Kentucky), Munitions Storage
Fort Campbell (Kentucky), 101st Airborne Div.
Fort Knox (Kentucky), Army Human Resources
Fort Polk (Louisiana), Training Center
Fort Detrick (Maryland), Medical
Fort George G. Meade (Maryland), NSA
Natick Army Labs (Massachusetts), Soldier Research
Detroit Arsenal (Michigan), Tank Research
Fort Leonard Wood (Missouri), Engineers
Hawthorne Army Depot (Nevada), Munition Storage

McGuire-Dix-Lakehurst (New Jersey), 87nd Air Base Wing
Picatinny Arsenal (New Jersey), Weapon Research
White Sands Missile Range (New Mexico), Rocket Testing
Fort Drum (New York), 10th Mountain Div.
Fort Bragg (North Carolina), 82nd Airborne Div, Special Forces
Marine Corps Air Station Cherry Point (North Carolina), 2nd Marine Aircraft Wing
Marine Corps Air Station New River (North Carolina), Marine Aircraft Gps. 26 & 29
Marine Corps Base Camp Lejeune (North Carolina), 2nd Marine Exp. Force
Fort Sill (Oklahoma), Artillery School
McAlester Army Ammunition Plant (Oklahoma), Ammunition
Carlisle Barracks (Pennsylvania), War College
Letterkenny Army Depot (Pennsylvania), Missile Systems
New Cumberland (Pennsylvania), Eastern Distribution Center
Tobyhanna Army Depot (Pennsylvania), Electronic Systems
Fort Jackson (South Carolina), Soldier Support Institute
Marine Corps Air Station Beaufort (South Carolina), Marine Aircraft Gp. 31
Marine Corps Recruit Depot Parris Island (South Carolina), Basic Training
Holston Army Ammunition Plant (Tennessee), Joint Munitions Command
Milan Army Ammunition Plant (Tennessee), Joint Munitions Command
Corpus Christi Army Depot (Texas), Rotary Wing Aircraft
Fort Bliss (Texas), 1st Armored Div., Anti-Aircraft
Fort Hood (Texas), 1st Cavalry Div.
Fort Sam Houston (Texas), HQ US Army North & South
Red River Army Depot (Texas), Wheeled Vehicle Repair
Tooele Army Depot (Utah), Munitions Storage
Fort Belvoir (Virginia), Defense Logistics Agency
Fort Eustis (Virginia), Army Transportation Corps
Fort Lee (Virginia), Army Quartermaster Corps
Marine Corps Base Quantico (Virginia), Marine Corps
National Ground Intelligence Center (Virginia), Intelligence
Radford Army Ammunition Plant (Virginia), Munitions Works
Lewis-McChord Joint Base (Washington), I Corps, 62nd Airlift Wing

There are sixty CONUS navy bases and sixty-eight air force bases in addition to the above, many of which are located near urban centers. Most states have national guard facilities that provide training and depot services. New Hampshire is the only state without a U.S. armed forces facility.

All of these facilities may come under attack at one time or another. At the outbreak of the Civil War, U.S. military bases, supplies, and equipment were seized by the rebellious states and used to arm the Confederate forces. What will happen this time around is anyone's guess, but these installations need to be secured by whatever forces are available locally to forestall criminal elements, drug gangs, renegade groups, and radical groups seizing the opportunity to gain power through arms, munitions, and military equipment. Many have minimal security and depend on local law enforcement to protect the servicemen assigned to those facilities. If drug gangs manage to seize heavy equipment such as tanks and artillery, lawlessness will rise to a new level, one never seen before in the U.S.

Next come the civilian businesses that will become important. Every family should make a map of their local area, noting gas stations, pharmacies, food stores, hardware stores, clothing stores, feed stores, and all stores that normally sell items that would be good to have in an economic collapse. Record the distances to all stores, phone numbers and hours, although many cannot be expected to remain open for long in a collapse. As stores close, mark them off on your map, so you won't waste time and precious fuel going somewhere needlessly. Forget restaurants and banks, they will close immediately and stay closed for the duration.

Be prepared to work with law enforcement and even the military to help maintain order. Law enforcement is barely holding its own today—in a collapse they will become unable to maintain control of most areas at some distance from their stations. Fire departments and emergency services will also be unable to answer many calls for assistance, and as the transportation network breaks down, hospitals and clinics will be increasingly unable to handle patients.

Think of your family in a lifeboat. You only have what you took with you, and you don't know how long it will be before you're rescued. That's a collapse—only no one is looking to provide you with aid. The only ones roaming around are those looking to take things from you.

# Notes:

[1] T. H. Breen, *American Insurgents American Patriots* (New York: Hill and Wang, 2010), 69

[2] Charles Murray, *American Exceptionalism An Experiment in History* (Washington, D.C.: AEI Press, 2013), 31

[3] Mark Steyn, *America Alone* (Washington, D.C.: Regnery Publishing, 2006); Godfrey Hodgson, *The Myth of American Exceptionalism* (New Haven, CT: Yale University Press, 2009); Seymour Martin Lipset, *American Exceptionalism A Double-Edged Sword* (New York: W. W. Norton, 1996, (this reference also summarizes the literature on why the United States failed to follow Europe's fall into socialism or Marxist predictions)

[4] Barack Obama News Conference, April 4, 2009, http://www.presidency.ucsb.edu/ws/index.php?pid=85959&st=american+exception alism&st1=#axzz1Tn2f9R8i

[5] Larry Schweikart and Dave Dougherty, *A Patriot's History of the Modern World, Volume 1 Its Exceptional Ascent to the Atomic Bomb, 1898-1945* (New York: Sentinel, 2012), 4-8

[6] David B. Barrett, George T. Kurian, and Todd M. Johnson, *World Christian Encyclopedia* 2nd Ed (New York: Oxford University Press, 2001), 3-5

[7] Murray, *American Exceptionalism*, 36

[8] Larry Schweikart, Dave Dougherty and Michael Allen, *The Patriot's History Reader Essential Documents for Every American* (New York: Sentinel, 2011), 308-309

[9] Schweikart, Dougherty, and Allen, *Reader*, 339-342

[10] Schweikart & Dougherty, *Modern World*, Vol 1, 6-7

[11] University of Maryland College of Education, "Education Through a Social Justice Lens," *Endeavors*, Vol. 19, Issue 28, Winter 2014, 5-9

[12] Alan Colmes, *Thank the Liberals For Saving America (And Why You Should)* (Carlsbad, CA: Hay House, 2012)

[13] Frank Goodnow, *The American Conception of Liberty* (Providence, RI: Standard Printing Co., 1916), 9-13

[14] Rexford G. Tugwell, *The Emerging Constitution* (New York: Harper's Magazine Press, 1974)

[15] Goodnow, *American Conception,* 29-31

[16] The White House, "Remarks by President Obama at Strasbourg Town Hall," April 3, 2009, retrieved 3/13/2014 from http://www.whitehouse.gov/the_press_office/Remarks-by-President-Obama-at-Strasbourg-Town-Hall/

[17] See Robert D. Putnam, *Bowling Alone* (New York: Simon & Schuster, 2000); and Charles Murray, *Coming Apart The State of White America, 1960-2010* (New York: Crown Forum, 2013) for a definition of superzips and how America is splitting into elite enclaves that rule the U.S. (superzips) and how the rest of us, the great unwashed body of serfs, live in zips that do not produce America's leaders.

[18] Eric Metaxas, *Bonhoeffer* (Nashville, TN: Thomas Nelson, 2010), 332

[19] Ibid., 85, 101-107

[20] For Roman Catholics who would dispute this, see the documentation in Saul Friedlaender, *Pius XII And The Third Reich A Documentation* (New York: Alfred A. Knopf, 1966); Daniel Jonah Goldhagen, *A Moral Reckoning The Role of the Catholic Church in the Holocaust and Its Unfulfilled Duty of Repair* (New York, Alfred A. Knopf, 2002), and also John Cornwell, *Hitler's Pope The Secret History of Pius XII* ((New York: Viking, 1999), Susan Zuccotti, *Under His Very Windows The Vatican and the Holocaust in Italy* (New Haven, CT: Yale University Press, 2002), and Pinchas E. Lapide, *Three Popes and The Jews* (New York: Hawthorn Books, 1967)

[21] Alexander Hamilton, John Jay, and James Madison, *The Federalist* (New York: Willey Book Co, 1902), 289-293; and Larry Schweikart, *7 Events That Made America America* (New York: Sentinel, 2010), 8-9

[22] Schweikart, *7 Events*, 9

[23] Nate Silver, "As Swing Districts Decline, Can A Divided House Stand?" *New York Times*, 12/27/12, retrieved 3/15/2015 from http://fivethirtyeight.blogs.nytimes.com/2012/12/27/as-swing-districts-dwindle-can-a-divided-house-stand/?_r=0)

[24] *Swann v. Charlotte-Mecklenburg Board of Education,* 402 U.S. 1 (1970)

[25] 576 U.S.___ (2015) Opinion of the Court (written by J. Kennedy), Supreme Court of the United States, Obergefell v. Hodges, (June 26, 2015, 1-32)

[26] 576 U.S. ___ (2015) J. Thomas dissenting, Supreme Court of the United States, Obergefell v. Hodges, (June 26, 2015, 1-18)

[27] http://www.census.gov/compendia/statab/cats/federal_govt_finances_employment/federal_civilian_employment Retrieved 3/15/2015, also United States Department of Labor, Bureau of Labor Statistics. Note: Government employment numbers are understated, as date of statistics vary from 2007 to 2013

[28] Span of Control refers to the number of subordinates a manager or supervisor can effectively manage. It is affected by homogeneity, structure, dispersion, technology, competence, and cohesion in an organization. An American president's span of control is far too large for effective management, the optimum being that he should have from five to nine subordinates. Without effective use of the vice president and multiple heads of department and agency groups, at best, the president is a reactive executive attempting to manage crises.

[29] Schweikart, Dougherty & Allen, *Reader*, 82

[30] See William A. Niskanen, Jr., *Bureaucracy & Representative Government* (New Brunswick, NJ: Aldine Transaction, 2007); *Bureaucracy and Public Economics* (Brookfield, VT: Edward Elgar, 1994); *Reflections of a Political Economist* (Washington, DC: The Cato Institute, 2008)

[31] See David Halberstam, *The Powers That Be* (New York: Alfred A. Knopf, 1979)

[32] Ibid., 8

[33] Ibid., 9

[34] Benjamin Sumner Welles held the position of Under Secretary of State, but was a major influence on FDR's foreign policy. He was more influential and powerful that the Secretary of State, Cordell Hull. The other primary advisor on foreign policy was Harry Hopkins, later unmasked as a Soviet spy working for Joseph Stalin. See Herbert Romerstein and Eric Breindel, *The Venona Secrets* (Washington, DC: Regnery Publishing, 2000), 473

[35] Address to the New York City High School Teachers Association, January 9, 1909, Published in Woodrow Wilson and Arthur S. Link, *Papers of Woodrow Wilson*, Vol. 18 1908-1909 (Princeton, NJ: Princeton University Press, 1975), 593-606

[36] United States Department of Labor, Bureau of Labor Statistics. Government dependency numbers are understated, as date of statistics vary from 2007 to 2013

[37] Arkansas awards elected offices in counties two years pension credit for each year of service for up to ten years.

[38] A good example is in Liam Riordan, *Many Identities, One* Nation (Philadelphia: University of Pennsylvania Press, 2007), a study of three towns in the Delaware River Valley in which the author, a self-styled "Irish-American" touts the "remarkable and vital cultural diversity" relentlessly in support of the modern progressive mantra that diversity is America's strength. However, in his over three-hundred-page book produced from his doctoral dissertation in history, the author, although he comments on extra-legal "patriot committees," fails even once to mention the Articles of Association or the Association. In the three towns studied, the apparently all-important diversity was that four ethnic groups were present: Blacks, English, Scotch-Irish, and German, and four Protestant denominations, Quakers, Presbyterians, Lutherans, and Anglicans. The reader should consider how much "diversity" in the modern sense was truly present.

[39] Yale Law School, Lillian Goldman Law Library, Avalon Project, "The Articles of Association" retrieved 3/15/2013 from http://avalon.law.yale.edu/18th_century/contcong_10-20-74.asp

[40] Ibid.

[41] Patrick Griffin, *The People With No Name* (Princeton, NJ: Princeton University Press, 2001); see also David Hackett Fischer, *Albion's Seed Four British Folkways in America* (New York: Oxford University Press, 1989), 609-619; James G. Leyburn, *The Scotch-Irish A Social History* (Chapel Hill, NC: North Carolina University Press, 1962); John C. Lineham, *The Irish Scots and the "Scotch-Irish"* (Concord, NH: American-Irish Historical Society, 1902); Thomas D'Arcy McGee, *A History of the Irish Settlers in North America* (Baltimore, MD: Genealogical Publishing Co, 1974 (facsimile of 1852 edition); Larry J. Hoefling, *Chasing The Frontier Scots-Irish in Early America* (New York: iUniverse, Inc., 2005); Michael

J. O'Brien, *A Hidden Phase of American History Ireland's Part in America's Struggle for Liberty* (Baltimore, MD: Genealogical Publishing Co, 1973 reprint of 1919 edition)

[42] Yale Law School, Lillian Goldman Law Library, Avalon Project, "Declaration and Resolves of the First Continental Congress" retrieved 3/15/2013 from http://avalon.law.yale.edu/18th_century/resolves.asp

[43] Ben Baack, "The Economics of the American Revolutionary War." EH.net Encyclopedia. Economic History Services, 13 Nov 2001 retrieved Mar 7, 2013 http://eh.net/encyclopedia/article/baack.war.revolutionary.us

[44] Edward C. Burnett, ed., *Letters of Members of the Continental Congress*, Vol I (Washington, DC: HardPress Publishing, 2012 reprint of 1921 ed.), 18-36

[45] Peter Force, Ed., *American Archives: Consisting of a Collection of Authentick Records, State Papers, Debates, and Letters and Other Notices of Publick Affairs...*, 4th Series, vol. 3 (Washington, DC: 1837-1853), 99-100, contained in Hermann Wellenreuther, Ed., *The Revolution of the People Thoughts and Documents on the Revolutionary Process in North America* 1774-1776 (Goettingen, Niedersachsen, Germany: Universitaetsverlag Goettingen, 2006), 186-187

[46] Robert A. Gross, *The Minutemen and Their World* (New York: Hill and Wang, 1976), 36

[47] Wellenreuther, *Revolution of the People*, 159-160

[48] Ibid., 160-161

[49] Ibid., 161

[50] Ibid., 161-162

[51] Ibid., 184-185

[52] Ibid., 147-148

[53] Ibid., 148-149

[54] Christopher Hibbert, *First Blood The American Revolution Through British Eyes* (New York: Avon Books, 1990), 22

[55] Ibid.

[56] John Shy, *A People Numerous and Armed: Reflections on the Military Struggle for American Independence*, Revised Ed. (Ann Arbor, MI: University of Michigan Press, 1990), 166

[57] Ibid.

[58] Edwin G. Burrows, *Forgotten Patriots The Untold Story of American Prisoners During the Revolutionary War* (New York: Basic Books, 2008), 193-204

[59] Peter H. Lindert and Jeffrey G. Williamson, "America's Revolution: Economic Disaster, Development, and Equality", 15 July 2011, retrieved 12/20/2013 from http://www.voxeu.org/article/america-s-revolution-economic-disaster-development-and-equality

[60] James F. Shepherd and Gary M. Walton, *Shipping Maritime Trade and the Economic Development of Colonial North America* (New York: Cambridge University Press, 2011), 204-236

[61] Wilfred B. Kerr, *Bermuda and the American Revolution, 1760-1783* (Princeton, NJ: Princeton University Press, 1936), 5

[62] Ibid., 53-54

[63] Jack P. Greene, *Pursuits of Happiness: The Social Development of Early Modern British Colonies and the Formation of American Culture* (Chapel Hill, NC: University of North Carolina Press, 1998), 182

[64] Gordon S. Wood, *The Radicalism of the American Revolution* (New York: Vintage Books, 1991), 140-142

[65] Bruce E. Burgoyne, *Enemy Views The American Revolutionary War as Recorded by the Hessian Participants* (Bowie, MD: Heritage Books, 1996), 53

[66] Hermann Wellenreuther, Opening Address at the symposium on "The Impact of Halle Pictism on Continental North America and the Young United States", Wittenberg, October 4-6, 2002, contained in Wellenreuther, *Revolution of the People,* 91-124

[67] Burgoyne, *Enemy Views*, 241

[68] William Starnes, *A Sermon Preached in Marlborough, May 11, 1775* (Watertown, MA: Benjamin Edes, 1775), 13-14

[69] Wellenruether, *Revolution of the People*, 104-105

[70] Ibid., 122-124

[71] James Otis, "Against Writs of Assistance," a Speech before the Supreme Court of Massachusetts, February, 1761, and James Otis, "The Rights of the British Colonies, Asserted and Proved," contained in *The Annals of America*, Vol. 2 1755-1783 (Chicago, IL: Encyclopedia Britannica, 1986), 74-77, 103-115

[72] James Otis, Rights of the British Colonies, contained in *The Annals of America*, Vol. 2, 111

[73] Godfrey Hodgson, *The Myth of American Exceptionalism* (New Haven, CT: Yale University Press, 2009); Seymour Martin Lipset, *American Exceptionalism A Double-Edged Sword* (New York: W. W. Norton, 1996); Barry Alan Shain, *The Myth of American Individualism The Protestant Origins of American Political Thought* (Princeton, NJ: Princeton University Press, 1994)

[74] Retrieved 6/14/2015 from http://www.wsj.com/articles/why-u-s-manufacturing-is-poised-for-a-comeback-maybe-1401475962

[75] Defense Manpower Center, "Total Military Personnel and Dependent End Strength by Service, Regional Area, and Country", March 31, 2014.

[76] *Reichtshauptsicherheitamt* (Empire's Head Security Office) and *Schutzstaffel* (Security Staff)

[77] July 2, 2008 speech by Barack Obama in Colorado Springs, Colorado

[78] Retrieved July 9, 2015 from http://www.armytimes.com/story/military/pentagon/2015/07/07/army-plans-to-cut-40000-troops/29832955/

[79] Vladimir Lenin, "The Proletarian Revolution and the Renegade Kautsky" in Vladimir Lenin, *Lenin's Collected Works*, Vol 28 (Moscow: Progress Publishers, 1974), as cited in Erich Wollenberg, *The Red Army* (Scottsdale, AZ: Prism Key Press, 2010), 8

[80] Willem Frederik Zuurdeeg, *A Research for the Consequences of the Vienna Circle: Philosophy for Ethics* (Utrecht: Kemink en Zoon N. V., 1946), 162

[81] The Fairness Doctrine was a policy of the United States Federal Communications Commission (FCC), introduced in 1949, that required the holders of broadcast licenses to discuss political issues in a balanced manner by presenting both sides.

The doctrine was eliminated in 1987, but with the explosion of conservative talk radio, Progressives have sought its re-instatement to reign in criticism of Progressivism.

[82] Retrieved 4/12/2015 from http://www.rpc.senate.gov/policy-papers/obamacare-on-mothers-day-higher-costs-fewer-doctors-less-care-for-women

[83] For example see *National Federation of Independent Business v. Sebelius*, and *United States v. Windsor*.

[84] For example see https://www.whitehouse.gov/issues/immigration/immigration-action

[85] V. H. Heywood, Ed., *The Global Biodiversity Assessment - United Nations Environment Programme* (Cambridge: Cambridge University Press, 1995)

[86] Retrieved 7/21/2015 from http://www.marketwatch.com/story/pope-francis-leading-the-new-american-socialist-revolution-2015-07-20?siteid=yhoof2

[87] J. V. Langmead Casserley, *The Retreat from Christianity in the Modern World* (London: Longmans, Green and Co., 1953), 99-104

[88] Ibid, 106

[89] Soenke Neitzel and Harald Welzer, *Soldaten* (New York: Alfred A Knopf, 2012), 29-34

[90] Ibid, 24-25

[91] Alexis De Tocqueville, *Memoir, Letters, and Remains of Alexis de Tocqueville* Vol. I (Unknown City: White Press, 2014), 360

[92] Casserley, *Retreat*, 99

[93] Ibid., 30-31

[94] Ibid., 40

[95] R. J. Rummel, *Death By Government* (New Brunswick, NJ: Transaction Publishers, 1994); and R. J. Rummel, *Statistics of Democide* (New Brunswick, NJ: Transaction Publishers, 1997)

[96] Schweikart & Dougherty, *Patriot's History of the Modern World*, Vol. II, xvi, xvii

[97] "Affiliated" means actual church members, in 2000, affiliated Christians in Independent churches (nominally or a variation of Protestant) were 28.2%, affiliated Protestants 23.2%, and Roman Catholic 20.8%. David B. Barrett, George T. Kurian, Todd M. Johnson, *World Christian Encyclopedia*, 2nd Ed (New York: Oxford University Press, 2001), 772-773

[98] Ibid.

[99] All other "surpluses" were constructs, such as the one in the Clinton Administration which counted funds coming in from the Social Security Trust Fund as "income."

[100] Retrieved 10/20/2012 from http://fas.org/irp/offdocs/eo/eo-13617.htm

[101] Daniel F. Rice, *Reinhold Niebuhr Revisited Engagements with an American Original* (Grand Rapids, MI: William B. Eerdmans Publishing, 2009), xxii

[102] Casserly, *Retreat*, 65-6)

[103] Michael Burleigh, *Sacred Causes The Clash of Religion and Politics, from the Great War to the War on Terror*, (New York: HarperCollins, 2007), 42

[104] Daniel Peris, *Storming the Heavens The Soviet League of the Militant Godless* (Ithaca, NY: Cornell University Press, 1998)

[105] A third of the leadership of the German Communist Party was Jewish at the end of World War I.

[106] See Goldhagen, *Moral Reckoning*

[107] Ibid., 443

[108] Ibid., 436

[109] Retrieved 10/17/2014 from http://dailycaller.com/2014/08/28/doj-to-give-money-from-bank-of-america-settlement-to-liberal-activist-groups/#ixzz3C1TQt46W

[110] Metaxas, *Bonhoeffer*, 333

[111] Ibid.

[112] Rice, *Niebuhr*, xviii

[113] Israel is a contemporary exception, but it exists only because of the continued support of the U.S.

[114] David Hume, a Scottish philosopher, see his works: *A Treatise of Human Nature* (1740), *An Enquiry Concerning Human Understanding* (1748), and *The Natural History of Religion* (1757)

[115] Dr. Hugh J. Schonfield, *The Passover Plot* (New York: Bernard Geis Associates, 1965)

[116] Eric Zuesse, *Christ's Ventriloquists* (New York: Hyacinth Editions, 2012)

[117] Retrieved 5/25/2015 from new.exchristian.net/p/disclaimer.html

[118] Zuesse, *Christ's Ventriloquists*, 42

[119] Retrieved 6/2/2014 from http://www.foxnews.com/politics/2010/07/05/nasa-chief-frontier-better-relations-muslims/

[120] Retrieved on 12/23/2014 from http://www.cnsnews.com/mrctv-blog/barbara-boland/obama-thanks-muslims-building-very-fabric-our-nation

[121] Azmat Khan, "America and Muslims by the Numbers" Retrieved 7/23/2013 from http://www.pbs.org/wgbh/pages/frontline/religion/man-behind-mosque/america-and-muslims-by-the-numbers/

[122] Text from "Call to Renewal" Keynote Address, Obama.senate.gov. Washington, D.C., 28 June 2006. The delivered speech is given in http://www.cbn.com/cbnnews/204016.aspx

[123] Retrieved 4/16/2014 from http://cnsnews.com/news/article/obama-if-catholics-have-their-schools-and-buildings-and-protestants-have-theirs

[124] Larry Schweikart and Michael Allen, *A Patriot's History of the United States* (New York: Penguin, 2004), 221

[125] *The Holy Bible, King James' Version, Holman Edition The New Testament* (Philadelphia, PA: A. J. Holman, 1940), 101

[126] Robert Creamer, *Listen to Your Mother Stand Up Straight! How Progressives Can Win* (Santa Ana, CA: Seven Locks Press, 2007), 362

[127] Pew Forum, retrieved 4/2/2014 from http://www.pewforum.org/2011/01/05/faith-on-the-hill-the-religious-composition-of-the-112th-congress/

[128] Creamer, *Stand Up*, 362, 363

[129] Ibid., 362

[130] Ibid., 532

[131] Herbert Croly, *The Promise of American Life*, (Princeton, NJ: Princeton University Press, 2014 (reprint of 1909 edition)), 340

[132] Retrieved 6/11/2014 from http://www.nowtheendbegins.com/blog/?p=15200>

[133] Ibid.

[134] Dave Dougherty, Radio Program "Through The Looking Glass," KJMT, Mountain Talk Radio, July 14, 2013

[135] Saul Alinsky, *Rules for Radicals* (New York: Random House, 1971; and Richard Cloward and Frances Fox Piven, "The Weight of the Poor: A Strategy to End Poverty", *The Nation*, May 2, 1966

[136] Retrieved 6/16/2014 from http://chronicle.com/article/2013-14-AAUP-Faculty-Salary/145679?cid=megamenu#id=table

[137] Retrieved 6/16/2014 from http://www1.salary.com/Chief-Executive-Officer-Salary.html

[138] Retrieved 6/16/2014 from http://go.bloomberg.com/multimedia/ceo-pay-ratio/

[139] Retrieved 6/17/2014 from http://www.forbes.com/sites/susanadams/2014/06/16/the-highest-paid-ceos-are-the-worst-performers-new-study-says/

[140] Retrieved 6/17/2014 from http://www.business.utah.edu/article/mike-coopers-new-research-suggests-paying-ceos-big-bucks-doesnt-pay-companies

[141] Retrieved 6/16/2014 from http://www.celebritynetworth.com/dl/bill-hillary-clinton-net-worth/

[142] Chelsea Victoria Clinton (2014), The Biography.com website, retrieved Jun 17, 2014, from http://www.biography.com/people/chelsea-clinton-547578

[143] The Koch brothers are Charles G. and David H. Koch, heirs to the Koch fortune and operators of Koch Industries started by their father Fred C. Koch, who invented a catalytic cracking method for the refining of crude oil into gasoline.

[144] Sebastian De Grazia, *The Political Community* (Chicago: Chicago University Press, 1948), 187

[145] Norman Stone, *The Atlantic and its Enemies* (London: Basic Books, 2010), 564

[146] C. G. Jung, *Modern Man in Search of a Soul* (New York: Harcourt, 1955), 204

[147] Retrieved 6/2/2013 from http://www.snopes.com/politics/obama/obamafuture.asp#43EzE4pBXSQrY5om.99

[148] "President Obama Campaign Rally in Roanoke" *Road to the White House.* C-SPAN, July 13, 2012 Retrieved 8/13/2012 from http://www.c-span.org/video/?307056-2/president-obama-campaign-rally-roanoke

[149] Retrieved 3/3/2014 from http://azconservative.org/2010/01/02/

[150] Barack Obama, Executive Order -- National Defense Resources Preparedness, Office of the Press Secretary, The White House, March 16, 2012

[151] Offer of Noah's Pantry Foods by SurviveUSA.biz, 3/1/2014

[152] Alex Deacon, Backyardliberty.com, accessed 4/2/2014

[153] *Science Daily*, June 31, 2007

[154] Actual tax bills for 2013 in author's possession

[155] Research America, retrieved 4/2/2013 from http://www.researchamerica.org/uploads/ObesityUpdated.pdf

[156] See www.earthworkshealth.com/ for more information on this wonderful substance

[157] Retrieved 6/1/2014 from http://www.bls.gov/opub/ted/2013/ted_20130529.htm

[158] Internal Revenue Service, Instructions for Form 709, United States Gift (and Generation-Skipping Transfer) Tax Return, Retrieved 6/1/2015 from http://www.irs.gov/pub/irs-pdf/i709.pdf; also see IRS Tax Tip 2012-62, Retrieved 6.1.2015 from http://www.irs.gov/uac/Eight-Tips-to-Determine-if-Your-Gift-is-Taxable

[159] Investment Company Institute, 2013 Investment Company Fact Book, retrieved 5/6/2014 from www.icifactbook.org/fb_ch7.html

[160] William L. Timmons, The Gold Trial of Ercell and Paul Slone (El Paso, TX: Timmons Publications, 1971), 2-27

[161] Retrieved 6/1/2013 from http://www.globalresearch.ca/u-s-dollar-collapse-where-is-germanys-gold/5321894

[162] Retrieved 2/27/2015 from www2.epa.gov/residential-wood-heaters

[163] Jackson's negative feelings towards the Cherokees for taking the British side in the Revolutionary War apparently played themselves out ultimately in the "Trail of Tears."

[164] John Gilmary Shea, *Life and Times of the Most Rev. John Carroll, Bishop and First Archbishop of Baltimore: Embracing the History of the Catholic Church in the United States. 1763-1815* (New York: Edward U. Jenkins' Sons, 1888), 326-368

[165] This excludes the persecution of white slaves and indentured servants prior to the Revolutionary War, the continued Negro slavery until 1865, and the suppression of Negro rights in the South during the Jim Crow era.

[166] Retrieved on 7/1/2014 from http://washington.cbslocal.com/2014/01/14/obama-on-executive-actions-ive-got-a-pen-and-ive-got-a-phone/

[167] General staff training was adopted and modified from German Wehrmacht programs in the 1950s.

[168] Civil War Diary of William H. Harding, 5th Ohio Volunteer Cavalry, Unpublished papers in possession of the author.

[169] George Washington, "Letter to Alexander Hamilton, May 2, 1783, On Creating a Peacetime Military Establishment," *The Writings of George Washington from Original Manuscript Sources, 1745-1799*, ed. John C. Fitzpatrick (Washington, D.C.: Government Printing Office, 1938, 26: 374-391, cited in Larry Schweikart, Dave Dougherty and Michael Allen, *The Patriot's History Reader Essential Documents for Every American* (New York: Sentinel, 2011), 35-43

[170] George Mason, "Final Draft of the Virginia Declaration of Rights," Robert A. Rutland, Ed., The Papers of George Mason 1725-1792, Vol. I (Chapel Hill, NC: University of North Carolina Press, 1970), 288

[171] Retrieved 5/12/2015 from http://www.weeklystandard.com/blogs/general-benghazi-we-never-received-request-support-state-department_700403.html

[172] Thomas E. Ricks, *The Generals American Military Command from World War II to Today* (New York: Penguin Press, 2012), 447-482

[173] Ibid., 440

[174] See the case of Lt. Col. Paul Yingling who wrote "A Failure in Generalship," *Armed Forces Journal* (April 27, 2007)

[175] Headquarters, Department of the Army, *FM 3.39.40 Internment and Resettlement Operations* (Washington DC: US Government Printing Office, 2010)

[176] Retrieved 9/21/2013 from http://www.infowars.com/nobel-peace-prize-nominee-obama-asks-military-leaders-if-they-will-fire-on-us-citizens/

[177] Harry F. Atwood, *Back to the Republic* (Chicago, IL: Laird & Lee, 1918), 13

[178] Ibid., 30-49

[179] Tony Horwitz, *Confederates in the Attic: Dispatches from the Unfinished Civil War* (New York: Vintage, 1999)

[180] James M. McPherson, *For Cause and Comrades: Why Men Fought In The Civil War* (New York: Oxford University Press, 1998)

[181] *Jewish World Review* 9/23/2002 Retrieved from http://www.jewishworldreview.com/cols/will092302.asp

[182] Francis Cardinal George, "The Cardinal's Column," *Catholic New World*, September 7, 2014, retrieved 9/12/2014 from http://www.catholicnewworld.com/cnwonline/2014/0907/cardinal.aspx?

[183] G. Edward Griffin, *The Creature from Jekyll Island 5th Ed* (Westlake Village, CA: American Media, 2010), 5

[184] Schweikart and Allen, *Patriot's History*, 550-554

[185] Lee Rainwater and Walter Yancy, *The Moyniham Report and the Politics of Controversy* (Cambridge: MIT Press, 1967)

[186] Obama drew the teeth from the Welfare Reform under the Contract With American (1996) in 2012.

[187] Walter Lippmann, "War and the Elections," *Newsweek*, December 5, 1966

[188] Retrieved from http://www.snopes.com/politics/business/waters.asp#3h4IZMLbOVUEYqmC.99 9/1/2014

[189] Hillsdale College Politics Faculty, *The U.S. Constitution A Reader* (Hillsdale, MI: Hillsdale College Press, 2012), 629

[190] Mark Tooley, *Taking Back the United Methodist Church* (Anderson, IN: Bristol House, 2010), 18

[191] Lawrence Soloman, *The Deniers* (Minneapolis, MN: Richard Vigilante Books, 2008), 12-15, Chapter "The Case of the Disappearing Hockey Stick" written by Dr. Edward Wegman; Stephen McIntyre and Ross McKitrick, "Hockey sticks, principal components, and spurious significance", Retrieved 6/2/2015 from https://climateaudit.files.wordpress.com/2005/09/mcintyre.grl.2005.pdf

[192] Such as the People's Republic of China (Communist China), Democratic People's Republic of Korea (Communist North Korea), German Democratic Republic (Communist East Germany), and Republic of Cuba (Castro's Cuba).

[193] Frank Goodnow, *The American Conception of Liberty* (Providence, RI: Standard Printing Company, 1916); Herbert Croly, *Progressive Democracy* (New York: The Macmillan Company, 1914); Ronald Reagan, "A Time for Choosing," (1964 speech) in Alfred A Boltzer et al, eds, *A Time for Choosing The Speeches of Ronald Reagan, 1961—1982* (Chicago: Regnery Publishing, 1983), 41-57

[194] Retrieved 6/1/2015 from http://www.forbes.com/sites/travisbradberry/2015/02/10/new-study-shows-smoking-pot-permanently-lowers-iq/

[195] Goodnow, *American Conception of Liberty*, 9-13; as cited by Hillsdale College Politics Faculty, *Constitution Reader* , 630-631

196 Retrieved 5/2/2015 from http://nation.foxnews.com/2015/04/24/hillary-religious-beliefs-must-change-sake-abortion
197 Retrieved from http://www.nytimes.com/2006/06/28/us/politics/2006obamaspeech.html?pagewanted=all&_r=0
198 Retrieved 7/2/2014 from http://www.washingtonpost.com/blogs/fact-checker/wp/2014/07/03/hillary-clintons-claim-that-hobby-lobby-wanted-to-stop-covering-all-contraception-procedures/
199 Goodnow, *American Conception of Liberty*, 29-31
200 Woodrow Wilson, "What is Progress?" *The New Freedom* (New York: Doubleday, Page, and Company, 1913), 33-54
201 Ibid.
202 Ibid.
203 See Robert Gaylon Ross, Sr., *Who's Who of the Elite V9* (Spicewood, TX: RIE, 2011)
204 Retrieved 7/16/2015 from http://www.breitbart.com/video/2015/07/15/cruz-iran-deal-jihadist-stimulus-bill-will-make-us-leading-financier-of-terrorism-against-america/
205 Woodrow Wilson, "Socialism and Democracy, August 22, 1887, in Arthur S. Link, ed., *The Papers of Woodrow Wilson, Vol. 5* (Princeton, NJ: Princeton University Press, 1966-1993), 561
206 Retrieved 5/21/2014 from http://newsroom.mastercard.com/press-releases/mastercard-study-reveals-the-rapidly-growing-cashless-economies/
207 Ibid.
208 Retrieved 7/2/2015 http://download.militaryonesource.mil/12038/MOS/Reports/2012_Demographics_Report.pdf
209 Retrieved 7/15/2015 from http://www.electoral-vote.com/evp2009/Info/senate-military.html
210 Retrieved 7/15/2015 from http://www.pbs.org/newshour/rundown/by-the-numbers-veterans-in-congress/
211http://www.nationalguard.mil/portals/31/Documents/PostureStatements/2015%20National%20Guard%20Bureau%20Posture%20Statement.pdf Retrieved 7/2/2015
212 William E. Odom, *The Collapse of the Soviet Military* (New Haven, CT: Yale University Press, 1998), 261-304
213 Retrieved 7/1/2015 from http://dailycaller.com/2015/04/23/hillary-on-abortion-deep-seated-cultural-codes-religious-beliefs-and-structural-biases-have-to-be-changed/#ixzz3g6jBqTcX
214 FATCA, the Foreign Asset Tax Compliance Act
215 This is why preppers should never buy food or prepper supplies on the Internet with credit cards
216 Author's estimate based on surveys in Missouri, Utah, and Oklahoma as representing states favorable to prepping
217 Federal Reserve System, "Federal Reserve Funds Flow", Retrieved 2012 from http://www.federalreserve.gov/ releases/z1/Current/annuals/a2005-2009.pdf
218 Jade-Helm was the exercise, and FM 3-39.40 the manual

[219] United States Supreme Court, "United States, Petitioner v. Ronald Dale Dunn," Cornell Law School, Retrieved 6/14/2105 from https://www.law.cornell.edu/supremecourt/text/480/294

[220] Retrieved 4/15/2014 from https://www.whitehouse.gov/the-press-office/2012/03/16/executive-order-national-defense-resources-preparedness

[221] Department of the Army, FM 3-39.40, Internment and Resettlement Operations, Retrieved 3/21/2013 from https://info.publicintelligence.net/USArmy-InternmentResettlement.pdf

[222] Retrieved 8/30/2014 from http://www.pewforum.org/2015/07/29/graphics-slideshow-changing-attitudes-on-gay-marriage/

[223] Except as the Supreme Court ruled in Obamacare. The government could tax people for not purchasing health insurance. This opened Pandora's box.

[224] Policy in the Soviet Red Army prohibited the sending of SSR troops to duty in their home republics.

[225] US Department of Defense, reported in http://www.census.gov/compendia/statab/2012/tables/12s0511.pdf retrieved 8/20/2013

[226] Retrieved 11/29/2013 from http://www.cnn.com/2009/POLITICS/02/18/holder.race.relations/

[227] Retrieved 5/1/2015 from http://www.businessinsider.com/students-accepted-to-all-8-ivy-league-schools-have-one-specific-thing-in-common-2015-4

[228] See *Obergefell v. Hodges* (June 26, 2015) on the "right" to marry, and *King v. Burwell* (June 25, 2015)

[229] Retrieved 7/15/2015 from http://www.theblaze.com/stories/2013/09/17/this-is-why-most-military-personnel-are-disarmed-on-military-bases-and-its-not-clintons-fault/

[230] Fernando Aguirre, *Surviving the Economic Collapse*, (Buenos Aires: Fernando Aguirre, 2009)

[231] Peris, *Storming the Heavens*, 113-117

[232] Retrieved 5/28/2014 from http://www.youtube.com/watch?v=LQ8Nr3_2724

[233] Rummel, *Death by Government & Statistics of Democide*

[234] John Micklethwait and Adrian Wooldridge, *The Fourth Revolution* (New York: Penguin, 2014), 13

[235] Retrieved 5/22/2015 from http://townhall.com/tipsheet/townhallmagazine/2014/04/12/the-assault-weapon-rebellion-n1822409

[236] Federal Deposit Insurance Corporation, "Managing Risks in Third-Party Payment Processor Relationships", 2011

[237] John B. Benedetto, "Who Financed Recent U.S. Trade Deficits?" Journal of International Commerce and Economics (May, 2014) retrieved from http://www.usitc.gov/journals/Volume_VI_U%20S%20_Trade_Deficit.pdf

[238] United Nations, "Biodiversity Assessment Report", 1993

[239] United Nations, "Report of the 1976 United Nations' Habitat I Conference"

[240] Solomon, *Deniers*, 15

[241] Sustainable Arkansas, "Where the Natural State meets the Land of Opportunity", report retrieved from

http://arkansas.securetherepublic.com/home/2014/06/03/emergency-alert-tonight-6314-sustainable-development-agenda-21-resolution-presented-ft-smith-surrounding-areas/

[242] Dave Dougherty, "Liberal Education Exam, 1979-2000, a Study of Seniors at Three Universities", privately published 2001

[243] Grading scale for the Colorado School of Mines, 1950-1960

[244] G. K. Chesterton, *The Flying Inn* (New York: Dover Publications, 2001), 312

[245] Translation given by Danny Danziger and John Gillingham, *1215 The Year of the Magna Carta* (London: Coronet Books, 2004), 5

[246] Ibid.

[247] Schweikart & Dougherty, *Patriot's History Reader*, 340, 342

[248] Retrieved 8/10/2014 from http://www.factcheck.org/2013/09/obamas-blurry-red-line/

[249] Edward Klein, *Blood Feud* (Washington D.C.: Regnery, 2014), 241-242

[250] Retrieved 8/10/2014 from http://www.huffingtonpost.com/2014/08/01/barney-frank-obama-lie_n_5642132.html

[251] Norman Podhoretz, *Why Are Jews Liberal?* (New York: Doubleday, 2009)

[252] Greg Campbell, "What They're Not Telling You: Democrats Pushing Constitutional Amendment To Change Bill Of Rights", retrieved 6/4/2014 from http://www.tpnn.com/2014/06/04/what-theyre-not-telling-you-democrats-pushing-constitutional-amendment-to-change-bill-of-rights/

[253] Rexford G. Tugwell, *The Emerging Constitution* (New York: Harper's Magazine Press, 1974)

[254] Patrick Buchanan, *The Death of the West* (New York: St. Martin's Griffin, 2002), 205

[255] Robert D. Putnam, *Bowling Alone* (New York: Simon and Schuster, 2000)

[256] Charles Murray, *Coming Apart The Story of White America, 1960—2010* (New York: Crown Forum, 2012)

[257] Kathy Roth-Douquet and Frank Schaeffer, *AWOL The Unexcused Absence of America's Upper Classes from Military Service—and How It Hurts Our Country* (New York: HarperCollins, 2006), 151

[258] Brian L Baker, "A Perspective From the Professor of Military Science", retrieved 11/29/2014 from www.AdvocatesforROTC.org, November 30, 2004

[259] Retrieved 6/6/2014 from http://www.statisticbrain.com/demographics-of-active-duty-u-s-military/

Manufactured by Amazon.ca
Bolton, ON

29426992R00205